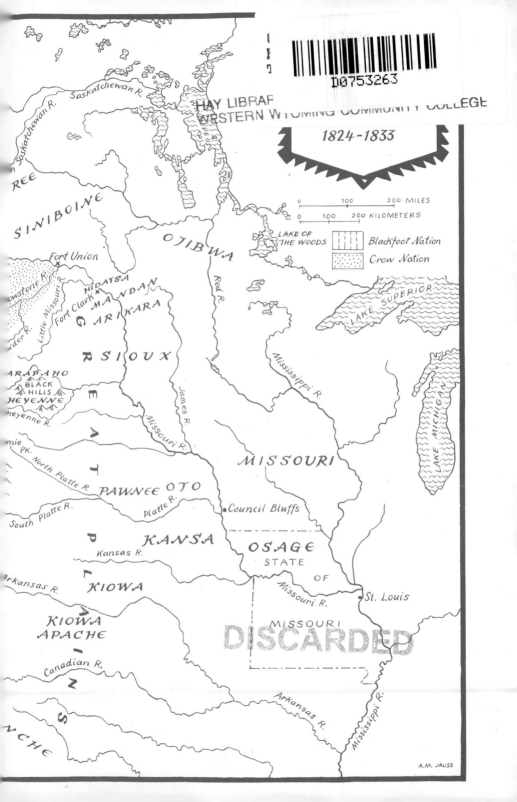

1824-1833

0   100   200 MILES

0   100   200 KILOMETERS

LAKE OF THE WOODS

Blackfoot Nation

Crow Nation

Saskatchewan R.

N. Saskatchewan R.

CREE

SINIBOINE

OJIBWA

Fort Union

Yellowstone R.

HIDATSA

Fort Clark

MANDAN

ARIKARA

Little Missouri R.

Powder R.

Red R.

LAKE SUPERIOR

G   R   E   A   T

SIOUX

ARAPAHO

BLACK HILLS

CHEYENNE

Cheyenne R.

James R.

Missouri R.

Mississippi R.

LAKE MICHIGAN

mie PK.

North Platte R.

PAWNEE

OTO

MISSOURI

South Platte R.

Platte R.

P   L   A   I   N   S

KANSA

Council Bluffs

Kansas R.

OSAGE

STATE

KIOWA

Arkansas R.

KIOWA APACHE

OF

Missouri R.

St. Louis

Canadian R.

MISSOURI

Arkansas R.

Mississippi R.

COMANCHE

A.M. JAUSS

THE
MEDICINE
CALF

W · W · NORTON & COMPANY · NEW YORK · LONDON

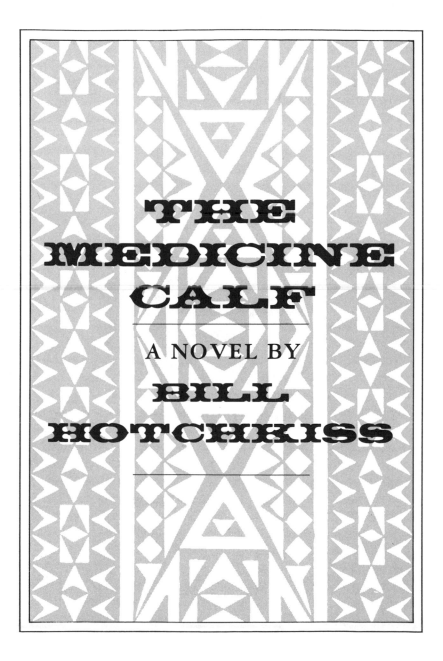

THE MEDICINE CALF

A NOVEL BY

BILL HOTCHKISS

First Edition

Book and binding design by Antonina Krass
Typefaces used are V.I.P. Garamond and Thunderbird
Manufactured by Vail-Ballou Press, Inc.

Frontispiece Photograph courtesy of the Nevada
Historical Society, Reno, Nevada.

Library of Congress Cataloging in Publication Data
Hotchkiss, Bill.
The Medicine Calf.
1. Beckwourth, James Pierson, 1798–1866—
Fiction. I. Title.
PZ4.H83Me   [PS3558.078]   813'.54   80–15019
ISBN 0–393–01389–8

W. W. Norton & Company, Inc. 500 Fifth Avenue, New York, NY 10110
W. W. Norton & Company Ltd. 25 New Street Square, London EC4A NT

1 2 3 4 5 6 7 8 9 0

For Judith Shears, My Wife

CONTENTS

CONTENTS

FOREWORD AND
ACKNOWLEDGMENTS

Several years ago, just at sundown, my wife and I pulled our car to the side of the road atop Beckwourth Pass at the north end of the California Sierra Nevada. As the sky blazed red and gold to the west, Judith and I climbed upslope from the highway, heard a gray owl cry, heard the wail of a coyote. Perhaps it was the ambience of the moment, of the place, but we could feel the presence of Jim Beckwourth amidst the sagebrush and the junipers and the gathering darkness, could feel his presence as something almost tangible. And at that moment I knew, in the manner of creative intuition, that the next few years of my life would be spent working with the figure of the old mountain man.

James P. Beckwourth is an historical figure, and the events depicted in *The Medicine Calf* are largely based on fact—historical fact that has been dramatized in accordance with a novelist's needs for continuity of action and characterization and in keeping with a sense of the aesthetic. Old Jim was a highly intelligent man, one with an analytical mind and a gift for languages. He was a titan in a world of titans, contemporary of such figures as William Ashley, Jim Bridger, Black Harris, Jim Clyman, Bill Sublette, Caleb Greenwood, Jed Smith, Louis Vasquez, Kit Carson, and the great Crow chiefs, Rotten Belly and Long Hair. Jim's capacity for astounding acts of bravery was unquestioned by those who genuinely knew him. And Jim was a tale-teller, one who delighted in regaling greenhorns with all manner of stories, some of them true, some of them classic fabrications. Indeed, the capacity to produce a well-wrought lie was seen as a valued area of accomplishment among the buckskin men who explored and opened the great American West.

Ultimately Jim entered into a contract with T. D. Bonner for the book entitled *The Life and Adventures of James P. Beckwourth.* Bonner ghosted the volume into a strangely discordant species of Victorian English and saw it through to publication in 1856, from Harper & Brothers. *The Life and Adventures,* still in print through various editions after all these years, was immediately the subject of great controversy, and many saw it as little more than a rambling novel, largely a fiction. Jim was seen as a "gaudy liar," one who was much given to self-aggrandizement. As the years have passed, however, more and more of Beckwourth's account has been found to be essentially accurate. In particular, I would direct the interested reader to Delmont R. Oswald's edition of *The Life and Adventures* (Nebraska: 1972), Nolie Mumey's *James Pierson Beckwourth, 1856–1866* (Denver: 1957), and to Elinor Wilson's systematic and thorough biography, *Jim Beckwourth: Black Mountain Man and War Chief of the Crows* (Oklahoma: 1972). Two highly readable treatments of the mountain man phenomenon are Don Berry's *A Majority of Scoundrels* (Ballantine: 1971) and Winfred Blevins' *Give Your Heart to the Hawks* (Avon: 1976). I would also direct the reader to Robert H. Lowie's *The Crow Indians* (Rinehart: 1956). There are hundreds of other significant sources, of course, historical, anthropological, and fictional, from *The Lewis and Clark Journals* to LeRoy R. Hafen's multivolume *The Mountain Men and The Fur Trade of the Far West.*

What became clear to me as my own studies progressed was that Beckwourth had in large measure become the victim of his own book—and that beneath the Victorian rhetoric of Bonner's treatment lived the spirit of an archetypal American hero. Of all the mountain men, Jim Beckwourth had most become one with the idea of wildness. Though historians have often rebelled at the excesses of Jim's book, they are nonetheless forced to rely upon it as a primary source. Even DeVoto, in introducing his edition of *The Life and Ad-*

ventures (Knopf: 1931), though he is sometimes outraged by what he supposes to be Jim's fabrications, still feels obligated to comment:

> If the book lacks the careful and sympathetic study of Indian ways that may be found in many later books written by those who have lived among reservation Indians, it is nevertheless the most valuable account we have of a plains tribe in the days of its greatness. Here are the Crows at the height of their power, while they are still uncorrupted by whisky and syphilis, and their spirit is yet unbroken by the terrible attrition of the sixties. They have not sunk to the loathsome parasitism of the reservation: they exist in the splendid vigor of savagery. Descriptions of the plains Indians by men who saw them in their strength compose a numerous literature. I am aware of its importance, but I do not hesitate to call Beckwourth's autobiography the best of it. Here one may find the American savage unretouched.

In closing, I would like to express acknowledgment to a number of people who have provided suggestions, proofreading, critical commentary, discussion, and the loan of books. My debt to these individuals is a very real one, and my thanks is profound: Judith Shears (proofreading the whole over and over again), William Everson, James B. Hall, Stan Hager, John Berutti, Marlea Berutti, Dick Hotchkiss, Don Jordan (K'os Naahaabii), David Carpenter, Gary Elder of Holmgangers Press, Dick Berger and Edith Snow and the other members of the Blue Oak Writers' Group, Kathleen Anderson and Starling Lawrence of W. W. Norton, and Russ Galen (who worries about *los osos*).

—Bill Hotchkiss

Spring Equinox, 1980
Woodpecker Ravine
Nevada County, California

What really happened to these men? All America lies at the end of the wilderness road, and our past is not a dead past but still lives in us; thus the question is momentous. But it has not been answered. Our forebears had civilization inside themselves, the wild outside. We live in the civilization they created, but within us the wilderness still lingers. What they dreamed, we live, and what they lived, we dream.

—T. K. Whipple

THE
MEDICINE
CALF

UP THE PLATTE

Nearly everywhere throughout these vast plains—throughout the grasslands and the badlands and in banks near the broad, shallow rivers that sweep eastward from the Rocky Mountains, one is able to see a fossil record so jumbled and strewn about that the patterns are nearly gone, and what remains stuns the observer, a tremendous sense of the passing of indeterminate spans of time—buffalo skulls and the bones of elk and antelope, myriads of shells and petrifactions, ancient bones mixed in with those more recent, dinosaur and mastodon and extinct reptiles and birds: in places there are great deposits of bones in every stage of preservation and decay. And the land stretches outward, huge and inhuman—drylands, grasslands, sandhills, plateaus, sometimes not so much as a single tree in sight as far as one can see, and over all the immensity of sky.

Jim Beckwourth drew his horse to a stop, studied what seemed to be a trace of smoke rising a mile or so on up the Platte, and whistled softly.

"It's them, all right. Good news for the General."

He turned his horse and started back the way he had come, rode through a big, empty world that seemed to wither visibly before the force of a freezing north wind. The cold weather had come early, but nothing unusual in that, Beckwourth reflected. Anyhow, they had made good time coming up country, and they would reach the upper camp nearly a week sooner than General Ashley had figured. Game had been scarce for the past several hundred miles, and the little party of seven had ridden onward almost non-stop, hoping that the trappers at the encampment had enjoyed better luck with their Hawken rifles.

"A coon heads up country," Beckwourth thought, "and there's two things he can be sure of—he's going to be hungry half the time, and he's going to be cold the other half."

Well, at least there'd be company by nightfall, and something to eat, too, if the other members of Ashley's Brigade, as the General called them, had been able to take in a supply of meat before the cold wind had come drifting down out of Canada. Then it was on to the Ammahabas, the Rocky Mountains, and over to a winter encampment on the Seedskeedee.

They were quite a bunch, Beckwourth mused, and he was one of them—and not the least experienced, either. He was a skilled hunter. His father had put a rifle into his hands as soon as he was old enough to handle it, and his boyhood had been a long series of hunting ventures. "I'm a tolerable madman," Jennings Beckwith had said once, "and I figure you're going to be just like your Pa, Jimmy my boy."

This was his third venture up country, but it would be the first time he had reached the mountains themselves, the great ranges of peaks that rose like dreams in the back of his mind.

Beckwourth ignored the hunger-knot in his stomach and whistled into his horse's ear, sweet-talked the animal into moving a bit faster.

Ashley's group reached the upper camp just at sundown, and the General was greeted by his captain, Jed Smith, the Bible-toter who had opened South Pass, spent a winter with Long Hair and his River Crows, and been nearly mauled to death by old Ephraim, the grizzly. Others there to greet the General were the indomitable Black Harris, Red Beard Miller, the big Kentuckian, and the skilled trapper, Robert Le Pointe. Ashley's group included Tom Fitzpatrick and Jim Clyman, both of whom had managed, afoot, to find their way down from the mountains and across the plains to Fort Atkinson during the preceding summer, the two of them within ten days of each other, both half starved, utterly exhausted. Clyman had turned to a

Pawnee village for help at one point, and the Indians had taken his Hawken, shot, and powder in exchange for some parched corn—had set him off onto the plains again, doomed to apparent starvation. Fitzpatrick's journey had been no less desperate, but both men had made it.

Also with the new arrivals were Robert Campbell, one of Ashley's party leaders, Pierre Le Blueux, a trapper of such skill that even Robert Le Pointe readily admitted his superiority, Le Blueux's mountain apprentice, Baptiste La Jeunesse, and big Jim Beckwourth, the son of a Virginia aristocrat and a Negro slave girl—or so the story went.

Bill Sublette, Davy Jackson, and Jim Bridger and their men would already be up near the headwaters of the *Roche Jaune* and on their way over the mountains, if the Arikara or the Blackfeet had caused no trouble. Ashley had given some thought to bringing everyone in together the following summer, of unifying their fur shipments back down the Missouri.

The trappers greeted each other warmly, for most were old friends. But even the arrival of the new party did little to revive spirits at the encampment, for rations were extremely low, and cold air from the north had flooded down over the plains, early it was, early this cold. Great fringes of ice formed along the Platte, and the driving, bitter wind first froze and then shredded away the remaining leaves on the cottonwoods. Game had seemingly vanished several days before the General's arrival, and now there were seven more mouths to feed. Ashley's own provisions were low, and the ground underfoot was frozen hard.

Hungry times now.

The temperature rose as the sky clouded over, and directly a wind-whipped snowstorm was upon them. The band of men, thirty-six in all, huddled around four separate fires but slept little during the night. Shortly before sunrise the storm abated, and the deadening cold returned.

In the morning, Ashley addressed the group.

"We'll move up river. Break camp in an hour. We'll find game. There's varmints somewhere, be sure of that. But until we bring down some meat, here's the situation—we're going onto hungry times rations. Don't have much more than that, anyway. Each man is to be allowed half a pint of flour a day. You ugly bastards all like gruel, don't you? Well, that's the situation. If anyone pops a duck or a goose, we share it as fairly as possible. We've all been in worse straits than this. We'll make out, don't doubt it. And gentlemen, keep those rifles loaded. I don't need to tell you that. Now let's get things together and head out!"

They moved on through the terrible cold for three more days, and then more snow began to fall. The entire band, horses and men, took on the appearance of ghostly white forms moving through a grayness that reached out in all directions. At nightfall they found scanty cover among a stand of young willows, and with some exertion they were able to kindle their fires. The north wind howled around them, the snow swirling down through the leafless willows, and the men ate silently.

About midnight the snow ceased, and once more the cold settled in. Hunger tore at their bellies, and some cursed their luck that none of the horses had come up crippled so that it could be shot and eaten. In another day or two, crippled or not, the horses would begin to go. Food then—food to last them until the weather turned better, until they found game, until they could begin to fend for themselves.

In the morning, General Ashley called for a day of rest.

"I want four hunters," he said. "Le Blueux, Miller, and a couple of the younger men—you, Beckwourth, and Baptiste La Jeunesse. Take your rifles and fan out on foot. And you, Baptiste, I know you're a good shot, but take a clear look at your fellow hunters. We're not about to resort to eating each other yet. First the horses go, and after that we'll see."

"Me, I know the deer from the men," Baptiste said, not certain whether to take offense or to laugh.

"Damn well see that you do, then. Now you men, you get anything, you bring it back. And don't go running after any Pawnee squaws out there."

The four moved out away from camp, into the frozen wind that was beginning to fill with falling snow.

Jim Beckwourth walked southward. Like all the others, he had by now grown accustomed to the sensation of hunger. He felt it but accepted it. Not accepted. Expected. And the terrific cold. The wind-driven snow. Lightheadedness alternating with moments of complete control, complete clarity of thought. Even the strength and endurance of his twenty-four-year-old body threatened to desert him at any moment.

"Goddamn that man," he said, wiping the snow out of his face. "That stupid ass! Why *not* shoot a couple of the horses? Wagh! Maybe we ought to stick him on a spit and roast him."

But he knew better. Maybe the weather would break, and maybe it wouldn't. No way of knowing. *You don't sacrifice horses until there's no choice.* Well, this was the alternative. Find game. Shoot it. Bring it back to camp. Get things going again. The weather *had* to break.

Where had the animals gone? A mystery.

Beckwourth moved on through the white and swirling world. He sighted a low rise ahead. Walked toward that.

Below him was a small stream, partly frozen, with exotic lace-works of ice that had formed where the water spilled down through the rocks below a little pond. He stared fixedly. A movement.

Ducks. Two of them, near the center of the pond where the water was not yet glazed over with ice.

"Damn me, this coon's found him a pair of fat teals. Now if I can just get a little closer without them flying off into the snow, I'll have one of them anyhow."

He moved slowly down the slope, came around behind a dead, weather-blasted cottonwood, the main trunk broken off just about shoulder height. He leveled the rifle, drew aim, then hesitated. Would the report frighten off anything larger that might be near? One duck wasn't going to go very far among thirty-six hungry trappers.

"Worry about that if I get him."

The shot was accurate. One duck flapped helplessly up onto the ice, the impact of the ball knocking it out of the water, as the wings of the other whirred off into the thin, driving snow.

Jim scrambled around to the edge of the ice, broke off a dry willow branch, and managed to slide the bird over to him. He lifted the duck by the neck, let the warmth of its body penetrate his numb fingers, felt the hot slipperiness of the blood dribble down his wrist.

"Wouldn't even go very far among us four hunters," he reflected. "But it's enough to give me a good meal, give me strength again, fill my belly and keep me going until I find something big."

He continued to stare at the teal. His mind was telling him one thing, his conscience was saying something else. Ashley's words: ". . . *you get anything, you bring it back.*"

At length he stuffed the duck under his coat and resumed walking, up the draw, the wind in his face, then over the next low rise and out onto a high prairie. The snow was beginning to drift, and the sage bushes were partially covered, some of them in fact making small white mounds on the interminable surface of the plain.

He walked on for what he judged to be another hour and then took brief cover behind a single large cottonwood, slapped his gloved hands against the trunk, looked back in the direction from which he had come. For a moment he wondered if he might have lost his sense of direction—that would be it, an ending. He'd heard stories about even skilled trackers losing their bearings in a storm, freezing to death, or wandering in circles until they collapsed from exhaustion and cold.

He brushed the snow out of his face once more and nodded.

"Okay, Big Jim, okay. Just think a moment. Hell, follow your own tracks back, at least as far as they're visible in this snow and all. Let's see. Yeah, it's all right. Wet powder 'n no fire to dry it. I'm no *iggerant dunghead.* I'll make it, damn sure."

The snow swirled around him. He was dizzy with hunger.

"Well, damn now. For sure this coon's not going to starve to death while he's got a Goddamn duck in his coat. Have summat in his belly, maybe he'll get his wits together."

His own voice was oddly foreign to him. He sounded, now, as much like a mountain man as any of them, the words coming naturally, calmly, no need to use the lingo self-consciously. Mountain man—starving to death with a damn duck inside his coat, starving to death and lost in a snowstorm. Hell, he hadn't even seen the mountains yet. The Rockies. The great wall of the mountains, in his imagination the real boundary of the wild country, still to the west, still days ahead of them if the weather ever broke.

He thought of the vast, empty plains behind him to the east, and of the little city of St. Louis, nearby where he had grown up.

His father's voice: "When you're out in the woods, Son, you do what you have to."

A child. Himself. His own voice: "Poppa, I can't split this log, it's too thick."

"Use the wedge, Son. Pound it in until the log splits."

Then the image of Eliza.

Half-breed Indian. Dark eyes, full lips, the soft, warm body he had known first on a summer afternoon, beneath the big oak trees near the river, the sunlight above a reticulation of small white points through the nettings of branches. Eliza. He had promised to marry her when he came back from the mountains. He'd have money by then, and they'd move north, maybe up into Illinois or Wisconsin country. They'd have children.

"Nigger Jim and his half-breed wife," he said aloud, then laughed bitterly. "Well, right now Nigger Jim's going to build him a little fire and dine on roast duck. Just like back home. Roast duck and white wine and candlelight in the big house."

He tore down a dead branch and broke it up into segments, placing the smallest twigs into a mound. He poured out some gunpowder and struck steel against flint, blowing on the sparks, managed to get a small flame started. Nursed it. Fed it. Finally the flames grew, took to the larger chunks of wood, and Jim smiled and bit at his lower lip, whistled. Quickly now he defeathered and cleaned the teal, spitted it, and held it over the flames.

After a few minutes he tore off a leg and began to eat. Half-cooked, perhaps, but seldom had anything tasted so good. Maybe even his own sense of guilt at the thought of his hungry companions made the flesh of the bird taste better.

His strength returned, and his head cleared. But he had to fight off an urge to sleep.

Men who fell asleep in snowstorms didn't wake up.

He moved on, taking what he assumed to be a northwesterly direction, angling back across the plain. Thought of finding the little stream once more, of following it upward.

Then, unexpectedly, he saw the water below him—and something else as well. *Deer tracks.* Fresh in the snow. Now his senses were fully alive. He moved carefully, quietly, his heart speeding up with the excitement of knowing that game was near.

He stopped abruptly.

Near the stream, between clumps of rushes, only the center of the body visible—deer. The points of the rack, a slight movement. The head was up, the buck was aware of his presence, aware of something at least. The wind was right—he was downwind. But the buck *knew.* Were there more than one? Perhaps several?

How quickly could he reload?

Best concentrate on the one.

He leveled the Hawken, squeezed the trigger. The explosion of the shot, and the brown form in the rushes crumpled. He'd had to estimate the position of the head, the position of the neck. A belly shot would have been no good—a gut shot deer could still run, might still escape to die where it could not be found by the hunter. He'd taken a chance, firing at an obscured target, but the shot had been true.

Beckwourth reloaded quickly, scanning the rushes and the brush for the fleeing movements of other deer, but there were none. He walked down to the deer, found it still alive, and killed it by drawing his knife across its throat. Working quickly, he partially dressed out the buck and hefted him into the branches of a scrub oak.

The excitement of the kill now drove him on up the stream. He had only walked a few yards when there, in the snow before him, stood a large white wolf, evidently attracted by the scent of the slaughtered deer. The animal stood its ground.

"Friend, I guess you're hungry too. Game's scarce, scarce as hens' teeth. I figure you've come to the wrong place this time. . . ."

The rifle snapped, and the wolf twisted about and lay dead.

"Maybe you wanted my deer, old fellow, but it looks like you're going to get eaten instead. Times like these, even wolf meat will do. Don't you go away now. I'll be back directly."

Blind luck was with him, and within an hour Beckwourth succeeded in killing three good-sized elk. Wherever the game animals had been hiding before, now they were suddenly all about, but the afternoon was drawing to a close.

"Three elk, one deer, and one wolf," Jim thought. "Enough to save the horses for awhile. Le Blueux, he's probably brought down a few varmints himself. Old Pierre finds antelope sitting in trees and geese in prairie dog holes. Me, I've just had a little of Pierre's luck. Guess we'll make it to the Rockies now—at least we'll have summat in our meat bags. And look at that! That's blue sky over there. Sunlight at the end of a snowstorm."

He realized that he was actually beginning to sweat as he gutted out the last of the elk.

"Damn big animals," he said aloud. "Beautiful animals. What a rack this fellow's got."

The glazed eye of the elk stared back at him. He contemplated the stare. The animal, gutted as it was, still looked strangely alive.

Beckwourth was surprised by the sound of his own voice:

"I will use you well, my brother. You have died to save me, you have opened yourself to me so that I might shoot you and kill you and eat of your flesh. May your spirit find its way into the other world."

Where had he heard these words before? Was it Le Blueux or his old friend Black Harris?

No.

A year earlier, another starving time, when he and Harris had found refuge with the Pawnees down on the Kansas, the Pawnees who had taken them in and fed them and nursed them back to health—they were the words of Two Axe, powerful chief counselor of the Pawnee Loup band, the same Indian who had been sent to Washington to make a treaty with Monroe, the Great Father—the same Indian who had listened to the Whiteman's words and who had seen through them and who had declared that he would make no treaty that would cause his own breast or those of his people to sorrow. Two Axe had abruptly broken up the council and had returned to his tribe.

Beckwourth tried to envision the face of Two Axe. Now he could hear the chief's voice. *Thank the animal you have shot. Chant. I will use you well, my brother. May your spirit find its way into the other world.*

Beckwourth started back to camp. He would return with some of the other men, and they would cut up the meat and carry it in. There would be laughter and tale-telling around the fires this night. When he came to the scrub oak where he had left the deer, he severed the hind quarters and slung it around his neck, then moved off briskly toward the camp. Not too much light left. They would have to return quickly.

"Thank God for that little duck," he thought as he approached the encampment. "Best I don't mention it, though."

For a moment he stopped, looked back. Nodded his head.

But the bad weather persisted.

The iron lock of ice was broken. A warm south wind thawed the earth, but for two days the wind not only continued but increased greatly in force, bringing with it yet more gray skies. Then rain— driving sheets of rain slanted in as the winds gained velocity, until finally the rain was being driven almost horizontally. Late afternoon of the third day a monstrous burst of rushing air tore out two of the three great cottonwoods near the camp. As darkness came on, the wind rose to a continuous, mournful, howling intensity, and rain stung the men's faces as they attempted to cook their evening meals. The fires streamed long trails of sparks through the night until the flames were doused or blown out. The men ate half-cooked meat, took what shelter they could, and slept fitfully under their wet buffalo robes.

By morning the Platte was rising rapidly, and what had been a wide, shallow river the day before was up out of its banks, a mile across, running brown and angry beneath an avalanche of rain and wind.

"Move 'er out!" Ashley shouted into the storm, gesturing wildly. But his voice was drowned in the screaming wind and downpour.

In another hour or so the camp area would be under several feet of swirling, muddy water. The men, their clothing soaked through, grimly loaded the horses, and the little band was in motion, moving toward the low rise to the south.

"*Mon Dieu!*" Pierre Le Blueux shouted. "*Incroyable!* This rain, it will drown all of us! Ten years ago I ride up the *Poudre* with Baptiste's father, just such a storm as this. *Vent et pluie.* Now I ride with his son. Twenty years in the *désert,* and still I get wet. You, Jim, is it that you enjoy this?"

Beckwourth drew his horse alongside Le Blueux and shouted back at him.

"Forty days and forty nights, Pierre! We must build a big boat! I think the world is ending!"

"*Alors, c'est ça!* In any case, is a hell of a storm! We must keep going, I think!"

"You were with Lewis and Clark, then?" Beckwourth yelled.

"*Non.* La Jeunesse the father, he was boatman for Clark. *Moi,* I am always the stupid trapper. I stink of *le castor.* Baptiste's father and I, we trapped one season together."

"Hooraw, coons, keep it moving!" Black Harris shouted. "A nigger drowns if he just stands still!"

"Can't hear you," Beckwourth shouted back. "It's starting to rain!"

"Keep them horses goin', you bastards!" Red Beard Miller yelled. "This ain't no time for fun 'n games!"

"Miller, your skin's the wrong color—you ain't fit for a little weather!" Harris said.

"Not mine, it ain't. Keep moving!"

"Ugly offspring of coyote and dog, red-beard dog," Le Blueux laughed, "where is *la bouteille?* Me, I need *la bouteille!*"

"Just drink the damn rain and keep moving, Frenchman! This ain't New Orleans."

"Dieu ne plaise! Jim, what's this place he speaks of? Some Blackfoot village, *non?*"

The march in the wind, as they later called it, lasted through the day and the night and into the following day. Even Black Harris and Le Blueux, the most experienced of the lot, were no longer sure of their directions. But by mid-morning the rain and wind abated. Finally the clouds seemed to shatter, and the blue sky poured through. Sunlight—and a strange, almost unearthly calm fell upon them. The wind had been with them for so long that the silence was now unreal.

"It's either past or building up for a new one," Ashley announced. "Whatever it is, let's get some fires going and see how much of our gear we can get dried out. And some food. I don't know about you gentlemen, but I think maybe we should roast some of that meat we've been hauling around through the hurricane."

The men whistled and shouted, then set to work.

The last of the clouds vanished as the afternoon wore on, and the respite was more than welcome. Despite the soggy earth underfoot, and despite the fact that they all knew the high plains winter had arrived, the sunlight seemed a blessing—even if it didn't last long.

They hewed down a dead tree and cut away the rain-soaked outer wood to get at the drier wood inside—and soon the fires were blazing. The rich odor of cooking meat floated in the pleasant air.

"Is this what you call *shinin'* times?" Beckwourth asked as he wiped down his rifle and applied deer fat to the barrel and firing mechanism.

"Naw," said Harris. "This is what you call eatin' times."

"Sacré Dieu!" Le Blueux laughed. "Does not any man among us have *la bouteille?* My thirst, it is raging. *Alors,* it is bad, very bad."

The group moved westward, past the forks of the Platte, and once more game became scarce. The great river had again diminished, and the empty nights came cold, bitter cold. The ground was everywhere frozen, and six of the horses had been lost. Three others had to be slaughtered. When this meat gave out, the trappers were without provisions. Well within buffalo country, but where were the great, shaggy animals? The men had seen no sign.

Seven Pawnee Loups rode into camp, offering friendship and assistance. Thomas Fitzpatrick, one of the most able of Ashley's men, knew the language of the Pawnee well and acted as interpreter.

"Their village is just four or five miles off," Fitzpatrick said, "and they invite us to share their lodges. Say they'll supply us with everything we need."

"That's fine," Ashley responded. "First we need horses. Tell them we'll trade for foofuraw. Maybe even whiskey if they behave themselves."

"Arwerdenty?" the leader of the Indians said, his eyes opening wide.

"He knows some English," Fitzpatrick nodded, "you got to be careful what you let them hear."

"All right, Mr. Fitzpatrick. I don't need to be told twice. See what you can do about the horses. We've got more pelts right now than our animals can handle. Let's take care of that first."

Fitzpatrick rode off with the Pawnees, and by the time the group reached the village, the Indians had gathered about, the women and children behind the men, laughing and joking and ready to trade.

Antoine Behele, a half-breed Spaniard who had become one of the chiefs of the band, and the great chief Two Axe rode forward to meet the group of Whitemen as they approached the village.

"Blue Jesus," Miller said. "Look at the body on that female Injun over there, the one with the yeller fringes on her dress. Goin' to get me a piece of that one if I can."

Beckwourth looked too, fixed his eyes on her. She returned his stare, openly, directly.

The girl was tall, slim-waisted, voluptuous. Perhaps sixteen years old, she stood out dramatically among the other Indian women. She was poised, her features sharp, her eyes glinting.

After a moment, Jim turned his eyes away and pretended not to notice her further.

"Ain't she something, now," Red Beard Miller chuckled. "What you think, Nigger boy?" he said, glancing sideways at Beckwourth. "These squaws will do things no decent Whitewoman would ever think of." He paused, then said with effect: "You ever had you a Whitewoman, Jimmy? You get you a good squaw, you won't ever want to."

Beckwourth's face felt hot, and he clenched the reins of his horse.

"You, Red Beard," Le Blueux said in an even voice. "You got words all wrong. *Mon frère,* is because there are no Niggers in the Rocky Mountains. We are all Niggers out here, you should remember. We are all Niggers, and so we come here to be free men. We are all free men in the Rocky Mountains."

Miller smiled widely. "Frenchy," he said, "we ain't in the mountains yet—ain't that right, Jim?"

Beckwourth also smiled.

"I think I may have to kill you," he responded.

"Jesus, boy, don't get all riled. Keep your mind on what one of them squaws is going to do to your young body."

Ashley's voice, sharp and precise:

"Get out the baubles, men. It's time for us to do some horse trading."

The trappers dismounted, and the Pawnees moved forward to greet them.

To one side Beckwourth could see Fitzpatrick and Two Axe. Their faces were serious. They were talking. Perhaps they were attempting to come to agreement on the rates of exchange. Jim now glanced back to where the tall girl had been standing.

She was no longer there.

Beckwourth had pitched his elk-hide tent near the edge of the camp, on the side away from the Pawnee lodges. From where he sat by his own small fire beneath an old and deformed pine, he could watch the milling throng of trappers and Indians. The arwerdenty—the whiskey—had of course ultimately been brought out, specially laced with water and tobacco and licorice for the consumption of the Noble Savage. The Indian women were keenly interested in trading for glass beads, scarlet cloth, and vermilion, but the braves wanted whiskey, whiskey perhaps even more than powder and lead and steel-bladed skinning knives.

"I guess there's just two ways to solve the Injun problem," Jim thought, "and I suppose it will come to one or the other or both. One way's to kill all the buffalo. The other's to give the Injuns plenty of whiskey—they lose interest in doing anything but drinking. Maybe whiskey alone would do it . . . they'd starve to death because they'd be too busy drinking to hunt."

Jim watched the goings on. He saw Le Blueux and a squaw slip off together, away from the cooking fires, into the darkness.

Aw buffler shit, let's go join 'em. What yuh setting around here for, like a damn dunghead?

Jim shook his head, drew a spit of elk meat from the fire, and ate. But he felt himself drawn, unaccountably drawn to the Indians, the way they lived, a different world, maybe a better one. They pulled at him, drew him to the fierce wildness they represented. Le Blueux had told him how much things had changed already, in just the past few years. The Whiteman was slowly taking over from the inside. He drove the Indians before him, pushed them ever westward, bestowed the worst of his civilization upon them, gave them whiskey. And guns. It was illegal, of course. But what was law out here? A man's law was his knife, his Hawken rifle, his capacity to endure hardship, and the keenness of his wits. If he were to survive, he would learn from the Indians or from those who, like Pierre Le Blueux, had already learned.

"The guns," Pierre had said. "Soon the Indians they all have guns. We sell them guns to kill us with. And then we move into their lands so they will have to kill us. *Alors,* it is a bad thing this. The settlers—me, I think the settlers will come even here. They will find a way to cross the plains and the mountains and the desert places beyond. *Enfant de garce!* Why do you think Clark and Lewis were sent to look at the Pacific Ocean? *Mon frère,* it will come."

Beckwourth looked across at the drunken gathering. He listened to the shouts and the laughter. He felt the winter night on his face. He stared down into his fire.

Two Axe.

Two Axe was standing before him.

"He could have killed me," Jim thought. "Where did he come from?"

The Indian chief spoke softly:

"Do you want a woman tonight?" he asked.

For a moment Beckwourth could think of no appropriate answer.

Two Axe spoke again:

"My sister wishes to sleep with the dark-skinned Whiteman. I will show you to my lodge if you wish to do this."

"Your sister?"

"She is not truly my sister. I captured her from the Shoshones a year past. She has not yet married. Now she has told me that she wishes to sleep with you. She is too proud to approach you herself. She is still young. She has many suitors. I said that I would ask you because you have stayed away from the others."

Beckwourth stood up to face Two Axe, a man shorter than he but powerfully muscled, a man known by the Whites to be a great warrior, the man who had walked away from the White Father. Whoever the girl was, Jim instinctively realized that a rare honor was being bestowed upon him. It would not be right to decline.

"I wish to make love to your sister," he said.

Two Axe led him to the lodge and then was gone.

A small fire was burning inside, and Beckwourth entered. On the ground were two woven baskets with food in them. From one of the poles hung a string of perhaps a dozen scalps, some of them evidently the scalps of Whitemen.

Seated, cross-legged before the fire, was the girl with the yellow-fringed dress.

34

"I am Jim Beckwourth. Two Axe has honored me."

Suddenly he realized it was unlikely the girl knew any English. She did not look up.

"Beckwourth," he repeated, not certain what to do next.

Her voice was soft, almost a whisper: "Beck-wourth," she said slowly, and then repeated the word once again.

"Do you know my language?" he asked, uncertain whether to remain standing or to sit down beside her.

"Know little English," she said. "Shoshone."

She offered him one of the baskets. He took a piece of cooked meat and ate from it. The flesh was not that of deer or antelope or elk. Buffalo meat. He savored the taste.

She looked at him then. The same fierce, almost defiant eyes, accentuated now in the firelight, the slightly smoky firelight inside the lodge.

"Darkskin Whiteman," she said. "I nurse you and then you sleep with me."

"Nurse?" he repeated, supposing she had used a wrong word.

"Nurse," she said, reaching her hands up to touch his loins. "Nurse you as child nurses mother. Suck. You like this?"

She kneeled before him, her eyes closed, her mouth opened to receive him.

Ashley conveyed to Two Axe that he and his trappers wished to leave. Fitzpatrick explained to the chief, but Two Axe said they must wait until after the buffalo hunt was completed.

"Tell the White chief that he and his men would frighten the buffalo away."

Fitzpatrick started to translate the message, but Two Axe did not wait. Instead he spoke in English, clearly and firmly.

"You must not leave until we have killed the buffalo. You frighten them."

Ashley nodded in agreement.

"We will wait," he said.

35

The trappers watched. Many more of the Pawnees had arrived during the morning. Two Axe spoke with several of the other chiefs, and then they moved—perhaps as many as a thousand hunters in all, some with their wives—to a low-lying area three or four miles from the village. Here the buffalo grazed, pawing at the hard earth, cropping the dry grass of winter.

In a very short time the surround was formed, some of the hunters on horseback, some afoot. As yet the buffalo seemed undisturbed, though one or two of the older bulls had ceased grazing and had begun to move their great, shaggy, horned heads slowly back and forth.

The Pawnees closed in from all sides, and then, at a command from Two Axe, a number of hunters rushed to the center, and the killing began. The buffalo began to mill confusedly about, their attempts to escape blocked at all points. Arrows sang through the air, punctuated by the occasional crack of a rifle, and the great animals continued to mill about, stumbling over those buffalo already fallen, but apparently without any sense of direction or resistance.

The killing continued for a long while, with some of the hunters taking wild chances in the face of onrushing and turning buffalo.

Beckwourth watched the spectacle with a kind of grim fascination. The bravery and skill of some of the hunters astounded him. Incredible. The bellowings of the bulls, the snorting and thrashing of the wounded animals. The wild delight of the hunters, whose efforts appeared to redouble as the slaughter proceeded.

Finally a large cow lurched purposively toward one edge of the surround. Instantly what remained of the herd seemed galvanized into frantic motion.

The stampede to escape had begun.

"Got them a slaughterhouse full of meat, didn't they Jimmy boy? You never seen a buffalo hunt before, did you? Well, they'll be two weeks at flaying and dressing and preserving the meat. Keep them busy enough. And whoever's killed the most buffalo, you know what happens to him?"

Beckwourth stared at Red Beard Miller, but said nothing.

36

"Well now, I'll tell you. Tonight a whole bunch of them squaws will fuck him half to death. That's their way."

"Miller . . . ," Jim began.

"It's true, I'm telling you. And I heard about someone else got fucked to death last night. Just a story I heard this morning. You and that tall squaw, ehh?"

Beckwourth started to respond, but Miller continued.

"That ain't right, you know. I seen her first, Jimmy. But I guess an Injun will fuck any color hide."

Red Beard pulled his horse quickly about and rode off laughing.

SEEDSKEEDEE

Once the American buffalo ranged from Alaska to Mexico, from the Appalachians to California, and nobody knows how many there were. They owned the beautiful continent, oblivious to bears or mountain lions or wolves or the hunters of the Blackfeet, the Crows, the Arapahos, the Cheyennes. Single herds were sometimes miles across, great shaggy brown cattle, with the cows in control, a grand matriarchy, though the bulls might paw and bellow and in rutting season infiltrate the female groupings. But where the cows chose to lead, the bulls followed or were left behind, lonely and morose. A disturbance might set the herds into stampede, an explosion of hooves and snorting flesh bursting suddenly forth, tens of thousands of the great animals in flight, bunching, flooding into motion, and the herds ran, streams of them, miles long, dust and roarings and hissings of breath—they might change the very landscape in their fury of passing.

"*Sacré Dieu!*" Le Blueux laughed. "These Indians, their names are all mixed up. Jim, you and Baptiste, you listen to Pierre."

"*Oui,*" La Jeunesse groaned.

"*Attendez!*" Le Blueux insisted. "It is all very simple, *tres facile*. First, the *Nez Percé* do not have pierced noses, but the Flat Heads do."

"Do the Nez Perce have flattened heads?" Beckwourth asked, his face a mask of seriousness.

"*C'est vrai,* it is true. We have confused these people, but now they call themselves Pierced Noses and Flat Heads, because that is what we call them. What they call themselves is usually just *the people*. Each tribe is *the people,* and all others are different."

"Like the Whites are *the people,* and all others are different kinds of varmints?" Beckwourth asked.

La Jeunesse laughed uneasily but nodded.

"Enfant de garce, it is so," Le Blueux continued. "Now these Pawnees with Two Axe, they are the Pawnee *Loups.* Also in the Pawnee Nation are the Republican Band, those who live along the Republican River, the Tattooed Pawnees, and the Black Pawnees."

"Do the Tatooed Pawnees have tattoos?"

"Some of them, *mon frère.* And so do some of those in the other bands. It is as I say, *tres facile.* And yet a man must know these things, he must remember these details. La Jeunesse and Beckwourth, they will learn. It is very important. *Un homme* must know these things to survive, be able to recognize the prints of the moccasins in the dust, for some are laced one way, some another. *Aussi,* there are differences in the arrows, differences in the designs of the lodges, differences in the ways the warriors paint their faces. We laugh now because we are in the good mood, and yet a man must notice every detail if he wishes to keep his hair, *c'est vrai."*

"Are there different groups of Crows?" Beckwourth asked.

"Oui, Jim. The Hidatsa, on the Big River, they are Crows, and yet we do not call them that. Then there are the River Crows and also the Mountain Crows who are two groups, the Kicked-in-their-Bellies and the Many Lodges. We call them Crows, but they call themselves Absarokas, the Sparrow Hawks."

"They do not kill the Whitemen?" La Jeunesse asked.

"Non, but the mind of the Indian, it is subject to change. If we survive in the Shining Mountains, it is because we learn to think like the Indian. We anticipate what he will do, *prévenir.* Also along the Big River are the villages of the Mandans, the peaceful people, and the Arikaras—none may trust these people. We call them the Rees and the Rikaras. Sometimes they are friendly, and sometimes they kill on sight. They are not good Indians, *je pense que oui."*

"How many bands of Blackfeet are there?" Beckwourth asked.

"Plusieurs, several. Some call the Mountain *Gros Ventres,* the Grovans, Blackfeet, or *Pieds Noirs.* Alors, these Big Bellies are the

cousins of the *Pieds Noirs*. Those who are cousins to the *Pieds Noirs*, we think of as *Pieds Noirs*, even though they are separate. *Mais*, the *Gros Ventres* of the prairies, the Hairy Noses, this is a complete different tribe."

"*Tres facile*," Beckwourth nodded.

"Now the *Pieds Noirs* Nation," Le Blueux continued, "they are composed of the Bloods and the Piegans and also the Siksikas who are larger than the other two tribes. And sometimes we call all the *Pieds Noirs* by the name of Siksikas, all except the Big Bellies."

"Even a child could keep these things straight, Pierre."

"*Oui*. There are the Assiniboines *aussi*, and these are allies with the *Pieds Noirs*. The Assiniboines live north of the Muddy River, and they are not to be trusted."

"What about the Shoshones and the Utes?" La Jeunesse asked. "We are going into their lands, *non?*"

"*C'est vrai, mon fils*. The Shoshones, they are the Snakes, and that is why we call the big river of the West the Snake River, though some call it the Columbia. But that is not right, for it only runs into the Columbia. The Snake is the Accursed Mad River. . . ."

"What about the chiefs?" Beckwourth asked. "I thought Two Axe was head of the Pawnee *Loups*, and it sure seemed that way a year ago, when I spent some time with them. But now Antoine Behele seems to have just as much authority, and sometimes Two Axe defers to him. This child doesn't understand."

"*Enfant de garce!* There are many chiefs among the Indian peoples. When a warrior leads a war party, he becomes a chief, and there are a number of leaders in each tribe or band. Two Axe, he is the head chief, and he is war chief and peace chief *aussi*. Sometimes the medicine men are very powerful, and many of the old warriors have also been leaders. Now Behele, he is a war chief—he is one that came to live with the Pawnees and was adopted. He has become counselor to Two Axe, and he is a great leader in battle. Each band also has a village chief, one who selects the encampments. The women tell such a man when to move, for the women are in charge of the villages."

"Each of the Pawnee bands, it has a head chief?" La Jeunesse asked.

"*Oui, c'est vrai.* If the head chief is old, then the strongest of the warriors may be the one who is the actual leader. Leg-in-the-Water, for instance, a man no older than you, Jim, he is the great warrior of the Cheyennes, though he is not a head chief. Friend of me, among the Snakes is a medicine man and prophet named Woman's Dress, and he is not head chief, though the people follow him. Among the Siksikas, the head chief is named Heavy Shield, and he is great warrior *aussi.* Even the Bloods and the Piegans will follow this man. The Crows have two great chiefs, Long Hair who leads the River People, and Rotten Belly who leads the Mountain People. These men are said to be very close friends, and sometimes they lead all of their people together. And Bad Arm leads the Flat Heads. Where we are going now, it is possible that we will meet with Woman's Dress and Bad Arm, who can say?"

"We have much to learn," La Jeunesse nodded, "*mais,* Pierre, he will tell us all that we need to know."

"*Non. Un homme,* he must learn from everyone and from everything that he sees. *Sacré Dieu,* one must see everything and remember it all."

Ashley's band of trappers continued to journey westward until the high, white wall of the Rockies rose precipitously before them. As the men approached, the great mountains loomed ever larger, rising from the rolling plains like the forms of recumbent giants.

Baptiste La Jeunesse pulled up his horse alongside Beckwourth's.

"*Alors,* that's *some* now," he said. "Me, I never see mountains like these before. *C'est incroyable.* But you have seen them before, *oui?*"

"No, Baptiste my friend. First time I've been this far west."

The men trapped as they went, and the beaver was good.

As the group entered the mountains, the snow became deeper, and at one point they were forced to forego further journeying for nearly two weeks. It was during this interval that some twenty of their horses disappeared during the night. No one had heard any-thing, not a noise, but the horses were gone.

"The work of them damned Crows, if my name's Black Harris. They're the worst horse thieves in the mountains. They writ the book on thieving horses, that's sure. The Absarokees."

Ashley ordered the journey resumed, despite the snow that still lay heavy on the ground. Food was in short supply, and the hunting forays produced scant results. The General's plan consisted of mak-ing friendly contact with the Indians—the Utes—trading for provi-sions, and then devoting the remainder of the season to continuous trapping.

Finally they were able to cross through the mountains and come down into what the mountain men called North Park.

Red Beard Miller shot two elk and left them where they fell. He returned to the encampment and directed La Jeunesse to get some-one to help him dress out and cut up the meat and haul it in.

"The one who kills . . . ," Baptiste started to say, but Miller turned quickly and with a blow of the forearm sent the youth sprawling, his nose and mouth bloodied.

"Ain't no boy tells a man how things is done," he said and then laughed. "Now you get your young ass up and get you some help and get out and fetch in what a man's done killed."

Jim Beckwourth stood close by, watching the incident. His ear-lier dislike for the big Kentuckian had subsided somewhat, for Miller had played a key role in getting them across the mountains. He was both a skilled hunter and tracker, and when the mood took him, he could outwork nearly any man in the company. But this was something else, for Baptiste was a friend, and clearly no match for the burly Red Beard.

Beckwourth drove his hand axe into a pine and walked slowly toward Miller.

"Leave the boy alone," he said simply.

But Miller's blood was up, and he was suddenly in no mood to be chastised by a man younger and less experienced than himself.

"That right, Nigger Jim? You goin' to get the General to help you protect him, are you? I think mebbe you and him best get the hell out there and tote in them elk. Goddamn greenhorns!"

He spat into the snow and started to turn away, supposing the matter was settled.

Beckwourth took him by surprise, grabbed his shoulder, and spun him about.

"Keep your hands off my friend, Red Beard."

Miller looked at Beckwourth in astonishment, then burst out laughing.

A number of the other men had now gathered about, curious to see what would happen.

"Don't think I heard you right, *Nigger boy.*"

A quick fury flashed through Jim, and he drove his fist full into Miller's face. Red Beard staggered backward and laughed. Then he came at Beckwourth.

The older man was a veteran of many such brawls, but when he charged Beckwourth, another blow caught him flush on the jaw, and he spun sideways and fell into the snow.

Jim stood calmly and observed the man who was now pulling himself to his feet. The other trappers closed in a ring and howled with glee, shouting encouragement now to one, now to the other.

Miller wiped away the blood from his mouth and spat. Then, staring at Beckwourth, he drew his knife.

"I want your scalp," he said.

Jim's knife was suddenly in his hand, and the two men circled each other cautiously.

The other trappers grew quiet now. The stakes had gone up.

Miller's knife cut an easy circle through the air, a testing motion, designed to discover how Jim would react, whether he had ever fought with a knife before. It was a mistake. Beckwourth brought the back of his blade down across Miller's arm and then drove into him with his shoulder, deftly flipping Red Beard onto his back. Then he was on top of his man, knife poised at the throat.

Miller's eyes were wide, not knowing what to expect.

43

"Miller, I'll say it once more. Keep your hands off Baptiste, or I'm going to kill you."

With that, Beckwourth rose, sheathed his knife, and walked back to the campfire, the gang of trappers making way for his passage. Red Beard reached for his own knife, and from a crouching position, sent it end over end through the air. The knife struck the trunk of a spruce and vibrated in place.

"Beckwourth!" Miller snarled. "We ain't done yet."

Jim stared back at the man.

"You just keep calling me by my last name, and we'll be fine," he said.

General Ashley was worried. Red Beard Miller had disappeared from camp and had been gone for several days. Ashley thought it likely that his big Kentuckian had decided to go it on his own. Traps, pack-horses—all were gone. Tension was growing within the camp. The Miller-Beckwourth fight had polarized the entire group, and the danger remained that a number of the men might elect to follow Miller's lead. Clearly, something would have to be done.

He directed the Irishman, Eddie Sullivan, to track Miller down and persuade him to return. Trap with him for awhile and then come back when the whole matter had blown over. A little band of Whitemen a thousand miles into the wilderness could not afford the petty luxury of squabbling.

"A fucking schoolyard fight!" Ashley said. "Sully, you go find our man, and you two pick up whatever plew you can in the next couple of weeks. Then head west, over to Seedskeedee country. We'll meet you down at the Green River Suck. . . ."

The season was turning.

As the troupe moved toward Green River, they came upon fresh buffalo droppings. A small group of wanderers, from the sign.

Le Blueux, La Jeunesse, and Beckwourth rode in the direction the big animals had traveled, for the meat supply, though not critical, could stand to be replenished.

Two hours to the south they came upon a couple of stragglers—an old bull and a single cow. They dismounted on a crest above the swale where the animals grazed and proceeded on foot, slowly.

The cow looked up, stared in their direction.

"They're going to run, *à Dieu ne plaise!*" Baptiste said softly.

"*Non,*" said Le Blueux. "The buffalo, they do not see well. Also they are very stupid animals. They do not run. They stand and wait for us to shoot them, ehh? You remember how the Pawnees killed so many."

They continued to walk slowly toward the buffalo.

"We're downwind," Jim said. "We've got that much riding for us."

"*Oui,*" Pierre whispered. "Do not talk loud now. If they could smell us, they might run. Baptiste, you and me we both shoot the cow. That one we want bad. The old bull, he's tough—but we get him too. Jim, you shoot the bull, I tell you how to shoot the bull. The wiping stick—use it for a rest. You aim at the brisket, this far."

He gestured with his hand.

"Take good aim, *vrai*. We get them both."

The three shots were nearly simultaneous. The cow dropped to its knees as though it had grown suddenly and inexplicably sleepy, and its head sagged over. The bull stood a moment, as if trying to decide what to do, and then it too fell forward, its great strength vanished.

Pierre loaded again immediately, shot pouch and powderhorn, pulling the stopper with his teeth, deftly, and tipped the horn up. Then rammed down the load.

His two students followed suit.

The knives were drawn across the throats of the slain animals, and the task of skinning and slaughtering was begun.

"A good thing we brought the extra horses," Jim said. "Pierre, look at that."

Half a dozen coyotes sat on the rimrock, not fifty yards away. They waited, quite patiently, for the men to finish.

Cahuna Smith was held by some to be the finest fist fighter in the mountains. He was a quiet, even taciturn fellow, somewhat solitary but nevertheless well-dispositioned. It was said that as a young man

45

in Boston he had fought professionally and had been hugely success-
ful. Black Harris, on the other hand, claimed that Smith was not
from Boston at all but from Michigan country and that he had
learned box-fighting as a natural consequence of having worked in
the woods as a timberman.

No one asked Smith, who had responded to numerous personal
questions with a simple "Don't want to talk about 'er," spoken in
such a way as to put a permanent end to the conversation.

Whatever their persuasion as to who was at fault in the matter of
Beckwourth and Miller, the simple ease with which Jim had han-
dled Red Beard could not fail to have impressed itself upon their
minds.

"Be good to *know*, though, wouldn't it now?" Harris said. "Jim's
a big, strong fella, but a coon can get lucky sometimes. You know,
things just kind of go right for him. Now if Jim and Cahuna was to
have a fist fight, we could have a little betting game and satisfy our
curiosity together. What you think, Mr. Fitz? Who'd you pick?"

Tom Fitzpatrick chewed absently on a pine twig.

"Well," he said, "I've *seen* Cahuna knock a couple of drunken
Injuns cold with just one punch, and I heard about the time three
years back when Smith stretched out that big French Canadian—
what was his name? Anyway, it's supposed to have happened at the
whorehouse in St. Louis. You've heard the story."

"Me, I was there," said Le Blueux. "It was my countryman, Mar-
cel Rostand. A good fight, but Cahuna, he won, just like you say. Is
so, *mon frère.*"

"Well, who'd you bet on then? Cahuna or Jim?"

"*Mon Dieu,* who can say? My friend Beckwourth, he is very strong
and very fast. Also, he is bigger than Smith."

"Maybe we should persuade these two that they want to have a
box-fight," Harris said, chuckling to himself.

By the end of the following week, the contest was arranged, al-
though neither of the participants was much interested when first
approached. Eventually, though, both gave in to pressure, and they

shook hands and agreed that it was all in fun. It's possible that their
motives for acceding were somewhat different. Smith, aware of the
talk of the other trappers, may well have felt his reputation was
under scrutiny. For Beckwourth, perhaps there was an urge to try
his as yet generally untested powers.

Ashley was not pleased, but he gritted his teeth and agreed to let
his men conduct the match. He didn't think Beckwourth would be
able to handle Smith in any case, and a little come-down might go a
long way toward teaching the man some humility.

Ashley placed a five dollar bet on Cahuna. Harris insisted on
odds—five dollars to his three—but he took the bet. In point of
fact, he took several bets, and so stood to lose fifteen dollars if
Cahuna Smith won.

"You're betting on Jim?" Baptiste asked. "Is because you think
he will win, *non?*"

"Let's just say this old Nigger's got a strong hunch, Little
Frenchy. A man's got to bet if he thinks he sees the stick floatin' the
right way."

Jim and Cahuna stripped to the waist, and the men formed a ring
around them. Fitzpatrick explained the rules: "Whoever knocks the
other man down a third time wins the match and is declared the
winner."

"Let 'em go until one whips!" someone shouted.

Fitzpatrick turned to the group and said, "Naw, this is the way
it's going to be. The General don't want anybody busted up too bad.
We still got our plews to take. A man's down the third time, and
it's over."

"That ain't the way it's supposed to be done!"

"That's the way it is. Anyone don't like it and he's made a bet,
the bet's off right now if he says so. Anyone here want to cancel
out?"

There were no voices.

"Okay then, I declare the fight to begin!"

Smith and Beckwourth circled each other with some caution,
their fists up, Beckwourth looking far the more awkward of the

two. Then Smith drove in, and Beckwourth nailed him with two straight punches. Smith backed off a step or two, squinted at Beckwourth as though he were utterly unimpressed, then moved forward once more, looping a roundhouse right. Jim slipped the punch, moved to one side, and drove home his own right hand, clean to the jaw, grunting as he did so.

The effect was electric.

Cahuna Smith doubled backward at the knees and fell heavily to the ground.

"End of round one," Fitz intoned.

"Round one hell! Jim's knocked him cold. Smith ain't going to get up."

"Maybe his neck's bust."

"Give him a chance."

But Smith lay still. He did not move for several minutes.

"Somebody get a pot full of water. We can't let it end this way."

"Get the water," Fitzpatrick said. "But the fight's over. Old Jim here is the winner."

A round of cheering went up.

"What about the bets? Who wins the bets?"

"It's clear about the bets," Black Harris said. "I wins the bets— that man's knocked cold."

"Nobody was down three times—so there's no winner. The bets are off."

"You bastards got no sense of what's *fair*," Black Harris howled. "Any fool can see who won."

Finally Jim himself went to get the water, returned, and splashed it over the recumbent Smith. Cahuna shook his head, looked around, and got up.

"Let's continue the fight!" someone yelled.

"Fight's over," Fitz said with determination.

Cahuna Smith pulled at his moustache and then shook Beckwourth's hand. "You whipped me fair," he said, then turned and walked slowly back toward his campfire.

48

General Bill Ashley was feeling more than just a little out of sorts. It appeared that he had lost not just one but two of his best men, for neither Sully nor Miller had returned. True, he had told Sullivan to meet him at Green River, on the Seedskeedee—but still, he had an intuition. Beyond this, he had paid off his bet with Black Harris, being one of the few who had. It was a damned annoyance. This Beckwourth, this mongrel offspring of an insane Virginia aristocrat and the slave girl he had married (if the rumor could be believed) had become virtually the camp hero. No respect for seniority. No respect for any damned thing. He would no doubt prove, in the long run, to be a valuable man—if he lived that long—but for now, so the General felt, Mr. Beckwourth needed to be put, subtly, into his place.

Black Harris was another matter. Harris had proven himself by virtue of his years in the mountains. If a man survived the hardship, the cold, the heat, Old Ephraim the grizzly, rattlesnakes, the Arikara, and the Blackfeet, he emerged as one of the genuine few—a mountain man, a graduate of Rocky Mountain College. And Harris was as good as a Whiteman, he'd proved that. A legend for endurance, a man who could walk two hundred miles, if need be, through bears and hostile Injuns and winter storms—and survive.

But insolent. Especially now that there were two of them.

The group had stopped to take their noon meal. Ashley saw Beckwourth joking with La Jeunesse. Ashley's horse had thrown a shoe, and someone would have to fix it.

"Beckwourth, you know how to shoe a horse don't you?"

"Sure, Mr. Ashley. Pretty good at it, too."

"Mine's thrown a shoe. The others are bad. I want you to fit him up."

Jim was still working when the other men began to move on. Ashley's annoyance grew. Consciously, he knew there hadn't been enough time for the job, but he spat out the words: "Come on, let's hurry that damned job up—they'll be ten miles ahead of us by the time you're finished."

49

Jim had fit three of the shoes and was nearly finished with the fourth. At Ashley's words, he turned and stared up at the General.

"Don't do it right, your horse will turn up lame, Mr. Ashley. I'm almost done."

"All right, get on with it then."

At this point the horse, becoming restless, withdrew his foot. Furthermore, Ashley's whole tone of voice was biting. Why didn't he shoe his own horse? And why was he, Beckwourth, picked to do the job? Suddenly his temper flared, and he gave the General's horse several thumps to the belly with his hammer—a not unusual mode of communication between blacksmith and horse.

But Ashley flew into a rage, heaping a whole string of curses upon the head of his trapper.

Jim stood up.

"Mr. Ashley, I have one more nail to drive. You can drive it yourself or let it go undriven. I'll see you dead before I lift a finger to help you again."

Beckwourth walked over to his own horse, mounted, and rode off in the direction the other trappers had taken.

Ashley was both astonished and exasperated. He stood there, shaking his head as he watched Beckwourth ride off.

"You fucking runaway slave," he muttered and then reached for the hammer. "Come here, horse," he said. "Now I'm the black-smith's helper. Come here, you son of a bitch."

At camp that evening, Ashley chose to berate Beckwourth in the presence of the others. Jim listened quietly as the General raged on. When the General had run out of breath, Jim said simply, "Mr. Ashley, you're a pig-headed ass."

Dead silence hung in the air.

"You God-cursed scoundrel, I'll put a ball in you!" He reached for his rifle, cocked it, and turned it at Beckwourth. But when he turned, he was facing Beckwourth's own rifle, also cocked and ready to be fired.

Tom Fitzpatrick stepped between them.

"Put them damned guns down—Beckwourth! General! Let's get calmed down and get a handle on this thing."

"You'll suffer for this," Ashley sputtered.

"Not under you, I won't. You can take your horse and equipment and do what you please with them. If I have to walk back to St. Louis, that's where I'm heading."

Ashley burst out laughing.

"You'll play hell getting back to St. Louis!" he said. "Harris himself couldn't walk that far. . . ."

In the morning Beckwourth delivered all of his company equipment to Fitzpatrick. Fitz just looked at him, uncertain what to say. But at this moment Robert Le Pointe presented himself.

"*Enfant de garce!*" he said. "You go, some of us, we go too. Mr. Fitz, you tell the General what I am saying."

"*Et Moi,*" said Le Blueux, stepping forward. "Harris, him too. And Baptiste and Cahuna, they will also go. We steal equipment from the *Pieds Noirs, peut-être,* and set up our own fur company, *non?*"

"Jesus!" Fitzpatrick said. "Look, Jim, why don't you come with me and talk to Ashley? I think maybe you both need to get cooled down. We came out here to take beaver, we gotta remember that. No profit the other way."

Baptiste pushed forward.

"I talk to General. He talk to me because we are friends. He says good things about you now, Jim. I tell him if you go, then I go too. He says, go talk to Jim. Tell Jim I want him to stay. Tell Jim to come talk with me. He makes apology. You stay with us, then if he curses you any more, we will all go. We will each take a horse and our blankets and some *viande* and some *poudre*—then we live. If we go now and take nothing, then we will die, *c'est ça.*"

"*Mais non,* we could steal horses from the Crows," Le Blueux insisted. "Then we come back and steal traps and guns from *le General. . . .*"

51

"Pierre, he makes the joke," Baptiste said. "In any case, you go talk to the General."

Beckwourth looked at each of the men in turn and then nodded his head.

With tempers cooled, the party moved on toward the Green River Suck. Provisions were once again low, and another few of their horses were liberated by a wandering band of Crows, who left their mark.

"Them Absarokees are the damnedest thieves on earth," Fitzpatrick said. "They'd harvest every horse in the mountains, if they had their way. Only good thing about it is they don't kill Whitemen. You lose your horses but not your ha'r."

Then Ashley fell sick and had to be carried on a litter. As the party crossed Green River, just above where it descends into its canyon, the General's bullboat, caught by the rolling current of the river, capsized, and Ashley and his companions were thrown into the water.

"Jim!" Cahuna shouted. "He's sick—and besides, he don't swim!"

The two men plunged in, swam beneath the surface as far as possible to avail themselves of the current, and emerged near where the General was clinging to some rocks. Between them they managed to drag him to the far bank, where Fitzpatrick and Le Pointe had waded out to give assistance.

Once ashore, Ashley was seized with a violent spasm of coughing. He lay on his side, hacking, gasping for breath. His men stood around him, looking down at their stricken leader. The General's face was pinched, his eyes red. Finally he sat up, blinking, then started to laugh, doubled over with coughing, then laughed again.

"Pulled me out like a big fish," he said, controlling his voice. "Where were my *mangeurs de lard, voyageurs,* my Frenchmen? My men of the river? Instead the two fist-fighters save my life—my Pa never taught me how to swim when I was a lad. Jim Beckwourth,

I'd have figured you to let me drown. Thanks, Smith. Thanks to both of you. . . ."

Tom Fitzpatrick said solemnly, "I guess even generals cain't breathe Green River mud, even if they think they can."

Everyone laughed.

"Boss man," Harris said, "we all figured they weren't no danger with you out there in the river. Even if you cain't swim, yuh could always just walk on the water. We was just waitin' to see yuh do her."

"Miserable sons of bitches!" Ashley sputtered and then started coughing once more.

Seedskeedee.

Flaming Gorge. Green River Suck.

Great fractured slabs of orange-red stone, a world of stone, treeless rims, ancient rock, forms twisted and sculpted by wind and blowing sand and the torrential but infrequent rains.

Beneath the silently growing explosion of crimson sunrise, Jim Beckwourth stared across a land that might once, he supposed, actually have been beneath the surface of some timelessly distant sea. Mesas, canyons, dry tablelands seemingly endless in extent. Holes in the rock, holes big enough for a man to walk through, a world of grotesque shapes, wind-blown sand and rain and frost and ice, chipping away through a passing of time that he could not even begin to comprehend, the elements smoothing the stone, polishing.

Old Man Coyote having a hell of a lot of fun.

Half an inch of snow, the whiteness clinging to anything remotely level, the snow glittering in the gaining light of the new day.

Three vultures perched in a twisted juniper. Now they extended their wings, moved them easily, an awkward fanning motion, in preparation for the day's first flight. Ungainly birds, their appearance curiously earthbound. Could these be the same creatures that

53

glided and hovered during the long blue days, that played the wind currents over canyon and mountain?

Now one took to the air, effortless motion, suddenly a different creature, a being of another order as it spiraled upward, out of the shadows, found the sunlight high up, and blazed almost white in the air. Its two fellows continued their fanning motions in the top of the juniper. Then they, too, were transformed and drank the air.

"Good luck to you, brothers, and good eating!" Jim laughed.

The sun was a flaming globe which seemed to melt its way up out of the stony headlands to the east. The snow became fields of glittering diamonds, dazzling, and the entire world took on the semblance of some dream vision, something unreal, something totally beautiful and without flaw.

Within an hour, Jim knew, the snow would all be gone, and the warm sunlight would leave the great heaps of stone and the level expanses of sagebrush damp and steaming. Even now little clutches of snow were beginning to fall from the graygreen boughs of the juniper.

Slowly the sky turned to a light golden hue, and the shadowed areas began their retreat back into the piles of stone which caused them and harbored them by daylight. Below, down over the rim, Beckwourth could see the figures of his fellow trappers as they moved back and forth about the fires. The odors of coffee and cooking meat drifted up to him. He breathed in deeply and laughed for no reason at all, picked up a small gray stone, and hurled it far out, away from the encampment.

BIDDLE'S BEAR

One day Cirape the coyote ran across the prairie, looking for food, and he sang as he ran. But then a voice said, "I do not like your singing and dancing!" Cirape was not very impressed, and so he continued. Then the Buffalo Skull pursued and caught him, and ate him. In fact, the Skull ate most of the inhabitants of the Indian village. Only one girl escaped. She fled from the village, but the Skull chased after her, jerking along behind. The girl could not run any faster. Finally, she threw herself down in front of a little hut and cried out for protection. The White Bear inside the lodge heard her screams, and out he came, just as the Skull caught up with the girl, waved its horns and was about to devour her. "Leave her alone," said the White Bear. "I'll eat you too," said the Buffalo Skull. But the White Bear fired a little blue bead from his mouth, and the Skull fell to the ground and was silent. Then the old White Bear turned to the girl and spoke to her: "You must never disturb these Buffalo Skulls," he said, "for they have great powers, and they do not wish to be touched."

Shortly before Ashley was ready to leave for St. Louis to get financial backing and to purchase supplies for the first summer rendezvous, both Sullivan and Miller showed up, their horses heavily laden with beaver plew. They'd been northward, and the trapping had been extremely good.

For a day or two, Beckwourth avoided Red Beard as best he could, but finally Miller came up to him and offered to shake hands.

"We got to work together, so we got to get along," he said. "But we'll have us a rematch some time or other. Long as we're out here, I'll work with ye."

"You and Sully brought back a pile of beaver," Beckwourth said. "Good looking furs."

Ashley came to Beckwourth before leaving.

"James, I want to talk to you before I go. Life in the mountains is full of danger, and when a man parts with someone, he knows he may never see that person again. I've already apologized for the thing back on the trail, so there's no need to mention that again. And I've already thanked you for saving my life. . . ."

"It wasn't just me, General Ashley. Cahuna and I just happened to be closest. If we hadn't jumped in, someone else would have. We're all grateful to have had you as a leader."

"No. It was you and Smith, not the others. But look. I want to offer you the leadership of one of the parties. You've learned a great deal on this trip over the mountains, and I know you'd do a good job."

"Thank you, sir, but I'd rather stay with Le Blueux's party. Maybe in another year I'll know enough to be able to handle a party of my own, if you still want me to. If there's a party to give, give it to Cahuna. He's been with you longer than I—and he's been in the mountains a lot longer than that."

Ashley reflected for a moment. Then he said, "All right, Jim Beckwourth, best of luck to you. If the bears and the Injuns are willing, I'll see you the first week of July. We're going to have us a little Rocky Mountain party."

The logic was simple. Summer was not a good time for trapping—the beaver plew were poor. It took cold weather to produce the finest hides, prime fur. But summer was easily the best time to bring a pack train across the mountains, through the big slot at South Pass, for though the Indians and the bears remained a problem, the weather was good for travel.

By the Fourth of July, General Ashley was back from St. Louis with a wagontrain full of goods. Ashley's men and numerous other trappers came in to the Rendezvous on the Henry's Fork of the Green. The word had spread, and the pack train brought in a wide variety of necessary goods, trade goods for the Indians, and no small supply of arwerdenty, Ashley's Special, Mountain Medicine. There were contests and fist fights and knife fights, and a band of Snake Indians brought their women with them, women who were notoriously willing, willing to do anything for a few trinkets or for some scarlet cloth, or maybe just for the fun of it.

A band of Arapahos also came in and seemed quite friendly, but when they left, Charley Le Brache was found with a tomahawk driven into his skull. Baptiste and Beckwourth discovered the body, crumpled where he had been standing watch. And the Frenchman's rifle was gone.

Ashley was now partners with Jed Smith, the Bible-toting little man who had wintered with the Crows three years earlier and who knew the mountains as well as any man alive. Prayin' 'Diah Smith, he was called, the man who had discovered South Pass.

At the conclusion of the Mountain Saturnalia, Ashley was ready to return once more to St. Louis. When he asked Beckwourth if he wished to make the journey, Jim quickly assented—for the goings-on of the Rendezvous had done anything but appeal to him, and as a result he had kept fairly much to himself. Suddenly Jim was growing weary of the mountains. No, not of the mountains. Of something else, then. Or perhaps it was Eliza. Perhaps it was time to take his woman and head up into Illinois or Michigan, buy some land, and live the life of a civilized person. He would have some money now, maybe even enough to get a start with. The trapping had gone well.

Or perhaps it was simply that he needed a woman. Perhaps he should have done as the others had. Wrestling in the willows. . . .

He had found friends here, men loyal to him, men to whom he was also loyal. At times the world of civilization seemed very far away indeed—another lifetime, a dream he barely recalled. At other times his present existence seemed more like a bad dream. Eating half-cooked meat, fighting through blizzards, burying Le Brache. . . .

He would go to St. Louis. He would take Eliza with him, and they would head north.

What kind of a life would they find? What kind of work would be available to one whose blood was not completely White? His father was a Virginian, an aristocrat—but how little difference that made. He contemplated the fact that Le Pointe was a quarter Iroquois, though no one thought of him as anything other than a Frenchman. Jim Beckwourth, on the other hand, was one-eighth Negro, and yet Miller and the others persisted in calling him "Nigger Jim."

Did he regret his parentage?

No.

He thought of his father, Jennings Beckwith. Jim Beckwith. Jim Beckwourth. He had changed the last name so that he might forge his own identity. *Or was it so that he might not prove an embarrassment to his father?* Certainly, that was not the reason. His father had fallen in love with a slave girl. Determined to marry her, whatever the consequences, he had moved first to Kentucky and then, disgusted with the prejudices and hatreds of his fellow men, had moved to the frontier, to the tract of land near St. Louis, only to discover that St. Louis, too, was destined to become civilized. His father, from whom his present life in the wilderness was no doubt derived, had, during Jim's boyhood, ventured again and again into what he called the Far West, sometimes taking Jim with him, sometimes taking the entire family for a month or two at a time. Jennings, Jim reflected, was a *black sheep* in every sense of the word. Someone had once told him that no man ever understands his father. But Jim understood Jennings. At least, he thought he did.

"He's probably out on some Missouri creek, fishing, right now," Jim thought. "And I am his son."

His mother was dead. Jim remembered the strange emptiness in the house, his father drinking steadily for two weeks. The burial on the wooded knoll behind the big house, the knoll where, his father had told him, he and Winey had stood together when the family had first come to Missouri, dreaming together, mentally laying out the house and grounds.

Winey.

In the long run, Jim reflected, a man with parents like these was a man most thoroughly blessed. His brother and sisters. His father. The old home place. As his contemplations continued, Jim managed to work himself into a state of extreme homesickness. It was almost tangible.

And Eliza.

"What are you thinking about tonight, Eliza? Patiently waiting for your crazy man to return?"

The night previous to their departure, Beckwourth and La Jeunesse were awakened by the sentinel, Caleb Greenwood.

"Injuns out there, Jimmy, where they ain't supposed to be. Get yourselves ready, quick like. I've got to alert the General."

Jim and Baptiste raised themselves immediately and moved through the brush toward where the horses were kept. In the shadows they could see the dark forms of the Indians—in the act of moving the horses. They aimed, fired. Several men ran. Two fell, one shot through the arm and body, the other through the head.

"Siksika?" Baptiste said.

"Just hope they weren't those horse-thieving Crows. No way of telling in the middle of the night."

With the sound of the guns, the others arrived in a matter of moments. Greenwood had a torch.

"Them's Crows all right. Damnation."

"At night," Le Blueux said, "someone steals horses, you shoot them, n'est-ce-pas?"

Beckwourth and La Jeunesse took hair, a first-time experience for both men. Cutting the circle was easy enough, but Jim was surprised at how hard he had to pull to tear the scalp off.

Ashley's troupe started out with an escort of fifty men. They followed the Wind River down to the Yellowstone, the *Roche Jaune,* and set to building bullboats to descend the river. It was the sixth day after leaving camp, and the men were stowing packs of plew in readiness for an early start the following morning.

"Injuns!"

A large number of mounted warriors, perhaps as many as a thousand, moving directly down to their landing. The trappers grabbed for their rifles. Took cover.

"No one fires until I do!" Ashley shouted.

Le Blueux flopped down behind a stack of beaver packs, beside Beckwourth.

"The living tornado, it is here," Pierre grunted.

Greenwood shouted, "They're Crows! Don't shoot!"

Ashley hesitated, then stood up, holding his weapon at an angle to the ground. Almost immediately the camp was filled with Indians, the warriors of the Crow Nation.

A large, gaunt, dignified Crow rode forward, drew reins to his mount.

"I am Ap-sar-oka Bet-set-sa," he said, "Chief of the Sparrow Hawks."

"I'm General Ashley. These are my men."

Caleb Greenwood was by the General's side within moments. He knew the Crow language and could act as interpreter.

The chief made a number of inquiries about the success of the hunting, what animals seen, which taken. Then he asked, "Where have you come from?"

"Seedskeedee," Greenwood replied.

Le Blueux moved over to where Beckwourth was standing.

"Jim, you know who this chief is?"

Beckwourth stared at the Indian, at the long loops of hair festooned down his back. There could be only one answer.

"Long Hair?"

"*Alors,* it is him. What have you done with the scalps? Baptiste, where is he?"

"I don't know. The scalp's on my belt."

"Bury him, quickly. *Sacré Dieu,* quickly. . . ."

Now the chief spoke again:

"Ash-ley," he said, "we heard that you killed two Siksika on the Seedskeedee. If this is so, we wish to have their scalps so that we may dance."

"Our men did not take the scalps," Greenwood said slowly. "The Blackfeet came into our camp at night and tried to steal our horses. The trappers left the bodies for the wolves."

"That is strange," the chief said. "One should always take the scalps of the Siksika."

Ap-sar-oka Bet-set-sa turned his war-horse about, rode back to his advisors, and talked briefly. Then he returned to Ashley and Greenwood.

"You will come with us, to our camp," he said. "Long Hair has spoken."

The Crow encampment was close by, and the trappers rode along surrounded by the Crow warriors. In the village, a woman emerged from one of the lodges and approached Long Hair.

"These men killed my son when he went to Seedskeedee. Are these the men? You must avenge my son's death!"

The woman was covered with dried blood. Knife wounds, three of them, made irregular marks down one cheek. Two fingers on her left hand were missing, having recently been hacked off. These were the signs of grief for her son. She stood there, almost naked. Smaller wounds had been self-inflicted all over her body.

Long Hair turned to Ashley and Greenwood and said, "The two men you killed were not of the Blackfeet. They were my own warriors, good horse-thieves and very brave men. One was this woman's son. You must give her gifts to ease her mourning and make her cease her cries, for it angers me to see such grief."

Ashley made the woman a present of those things he had close at hand, some trade goods from his saddlebag.

"Now," Long Hair said to the woman, "go back into your lodge and cease your crying. Your son was a brave man, and now he is dead."

Among the horses of the Crows were a number that the trappers recognized as their own, stolen months earlier at the time of the General's sickness, prior to reaching the Green River Suck. The horses were in a group, tethered prominently. This information was conveyed to Ashley.

"Chief Long Hair, some of your horses appear to be horses that were stolen from us some time ago."

"Yes, we stole them from you."

"Why did you steal our horses?"

"We were tired of walking. I had led a party to fight with the Blackfeet." He then turned to Greenwood and continued: "We would have stopped at the camp, and you would have given us tobacco, but we could not ride the tobacco home. When we stole the horses, they were very skinny, but now they are fat. Now we have plenty of horses. You may take back all that belonged to you. If you need more, we will trade for them. We have many to choose from. We also have many beaver and otter skins, and we would like to trade."

A free trapper named Jourdan was carrying a portion of buffalo meat on his horse. He stopped to drink from a small stream near the trail. As he stooped over the water, a grizzly attacked him, biting, mauling, and tearing him to such an extent that he might have died immediately. But Le Blueux saw the dismounted horse, stopped, and found the man unconscious where the bear had left him. His head was almost completely flayed. Pierre draped the man over the saddle of his horse, tied him in place, and brought him back to the camp.

"Ephraim," he said simply. "Jim, you help me. *Enfant de garce,* he is chewed up. Maybe we can save him."

Several others gathered around as Pierre Le Blueux's practiced hands began the task of binding up the man's wounds.

"He will live, this one," Le Blueux snorted.

Just as the bandaging was completed, they heard the sound of horses approaching. Looking up, the trappers saw a party of men driving another bear—or was it the same?—a bear of enormous size. Instantly nearly everyone scattered and took to the trees.

"Jim," Le Blueux said. "We both shoot. *Le coeur!* In the heart of the bear!"

Confused, the magnificent grizzly reared to its hind legs and roared, prepared now to make a stand against all odds. The riders wheeled past the animal and discharged their pistols, the shots doing little more than to infuriate the beast. Le Blueux and Beckwourth took careful aim with their Hawkens and fired. The grizzly roared as it fell, turned on its side, and lay with one hind leg kicking spasmodically.

"Jesus, Pierre," Jim said. "That's the biggest damned animal I've ever seen. Christ what a monster!"

"He is not so big as the buffalo," Pierre laughed, already reloading the Hawken. "But the white bear, he is very dangerous animal."

The men proceeded down the *Roche Jaune* to its junction with the Big River. Where the currents came together, the trappers attempted a landing, but the river sank one of the bullboats, and thirty packs of beaver plew were left floating and were caught by the main drift of the river. With much shouting, those who could swim plunged into the water, and within minutes all thirty of the packs had been retrieved.

The noise drew the attention of a body of United States troops who had been camped just down the river. Soon officers, sergeants, privates, and even musicians lined the shore. The men were under the command of General Atkinson, an old friend of Ashley's, then attempting to negotiate a treaty with the Indians of that region. When the furs were set out to dry and all the equipment was in place, the trappers and soldiers greeted each other. In short order a quantity of rum was produced from within Ashley's stores, and the festivities began.

"Hurrah for the Mountains!" the voices shouted.

Le Blueux, Beckwourth, La Jeunesse, Harris, and Cahuna Smith sat around their fire, drank from *la bouteille,* and smoked their pipes. They were still thinking about the confrontation with Long Hair, the great Crow chief.

"That old rascal's a damned diplomat," Harris said. "Not only did he have us outfucked and outflanked, he had us complete under his power. He knew we'd put under two of his warriors, and he damned well knew that we knew he did. That squaw was a set-up, and you kin lay to it."

Le Blueux pulled at the bottle.

"No accident that we saw the stolen horses, *c'est vrai.*"

"Hell no," Harris said. "That was set up too. Long Hair planned it all. If he didn't want us seein' our horses, he'd of hid 'em. Old bastard even pointed out what good condition they was in, how fat they was."

"Wanted to see if we'd have the guts to want 'em back," Beckwourth nodded.

"*Oui,*" Le Blueux said. "If we hadn't noticed, *mon frère,* he'd have known we were fools."

"An' if we didn't ask for 'em back," Harris laughed, "he'd of figgered we was cowards."

"*Alors,* it is true," Pierre chuckled.

"So we ended up buying more horses," Beckwourth said.

"*Incroyable!*" Baptiste nodded. "We had to buy *les animals* to get back our own. And Long Hair gets presents for the squaw. . . ."

"Hell, that gal probably warn't the mother of them we shot," Harris said. "She was mourning all right and pretty well hacked up, but Long Hair's chief of the River Crows. Probably it was Mountain Crows who was tryin' to steal our horses."

"*Moi,* I think the squaw was mourning one of her dogs," Baptiste said, leaning forward to put wood on the fire.

"Le Blueux," Harris said, "if that nigger was a Whiteman, he'd probably be president of the United States."

"I kin tell you boys a story about Long Hair," Cahuna Smith said. "A good one too. They was tryin' to draw up a treaty with the Crows, over to Fort Clark. Them Crows had been fightin' with the Blackfeet, as usual, and they'd took prisoner a half-breed woman and her kid. Blackfeet had captured her over on the Snake, from what I heard. Anyhow, old Atkinson told the Crows to give up the woman an' her kid, and they just wouldn't. The general insisted, and they said they'd fight, right then and there. Atkinson told 'em to come back the next day if they wanted to fight. Well, they come in with a bunch of warriors, and a chief rode in to talk with Major O'Fallon. Rose, he was the interpreter. The major told the chief to give up the captives or fight, and the chief told O'Fallon his troops wasn't no match for the Crows."

"Probably right at that," Harris laughed.

"You never know," Cahuna nodded. "But O'Fallon got hot and drew his pistol, but it misfired. Wagh! Of a sudden the stick warn't floatin' so good. Then he let the old chief have it with the butt of his pistol. Word got back to Long Hair, and in he come."

"These blue coats," Le Blueux snorted, "they have the dumb asses. . . ."

"Anyhow," Cahuna continued, "a good thing Rose was there—he knew how to talk with the Absarokees. And while they was talkin', a couple of Injuns stuffed the guns with grass and wood spikes, since they didn't figger the soldier boys knew how to shoot 'em anyway. Then Long Hair said his braves had never shed White blood, but now they'd have to fight. Atkinson thought for a minute, and then he said something about Clark, the Red-Haired Chief. How he was a friend to the Sparrow Hawks. Then Long Hair said for Atkinson to go home and tell the Red-Haired Chief the Crows had decided not to kill the soldiers. Clark must of given Long Hair a red feather or somethin', years ago. Then the Crows pulled back, but sent in the woman and her kid. So old Atkinson made the Crows a present of a bunch of guns and ammunition."

Le Blueux laughed.

"So, *Monsieur Long Hair,* he got the guns, and the general got the squaw, *non?*"

"That's how the stick floats when you go tradin' with Crows," Harris said.

Beckwourth whistled.

"When all along what Long Hair had in mind was probably to trade the half-breed and her kid for guns, if he could manage it?"

"Baptiste, let me have *la bouteille.* My thirst, it is very bad," Le Blueux said. "I am old man. I need the drink."

Black Harris re-lit his pipe, squinted at Cahuna Smith.

"I don't think this nigger's ever heard Cahuna talk so much since I've knowed him. Hell, if we could just get him wound up, mebbe he'd tell us stories every night."

Smith was nonplussed, looked away, then said, "I guess I done talked too much. . . ."

"Cahuna is the true mountain man," Le Blueux said. "He does not speak when there is nothing to say. But he tells the good story, *peut-être*. Then we listen."

"You know," Beckwourth said, "in dealing with Long Hair— maybe what we've got on our hands is a superior intelligence. But it's a different *kind* of intelligence, one that we don't understand very well."

"That's when you know the mountains have got hold of yuh," Black Harris said. "When you start thinkin' like an Injun, I mean."

"It is true, *enfant de garce*," Pierre agreed. "In the mountains, it is the only good way to think. We become Indians, and we have our own tribe."

"I guess that's true," Beckwourth said. "But right now, maybe we should all go down and investigate the celebration. *La bouteille* is empty—Pierre's drunk it all. And I think they've got a tub full of the stuff down there. Isn't that Le Pointe dancing with one of the soldier boys?"

"This nigger thinks there's goin' to be a lot of red eyes in the morning," Black Harris said.

The friends got to their feet and moved slowly in the direction of the great fire and the sound of the fife. Le Pointe had a yellow sash around his middle, and the soldiers were vying to dance with him. Overhead the summer stars burned in a pure black sky, and a soft wind was blowing in across the Big River.

Far off they could hear the howling of a solitary wolf.

Most of the trappers departed from Ashley and headed up river, back to the mountains. The General and his small escort, including Beckwourth, put down river and began the long voyage to St. Louis.

Beckwourth had known it would not be easy to part with Baptiste, Cahuna, Black Harris, and old Pierre. The parting was even more difficult because he could not bring himself to tell his friends he had no intention of returning to the mountains. He felt this chapter of his life was at an end. He had experienced the wildness, experienced it more fully in these two years, perhaps, than his father ever had. These were his wild oats, and they had been strange oats indeed. His life now lay ahead of him, while his four friends would almost certainly die in the Rocky Mountains, whether soon or late.

He would never forget the mountains, he knew that. In particular, he knew he would never forget the barrel-chested Frenchman who had, in effect, adopted him—Pierre Le Blueux.

"Pierre," he said, embracing his mentor, "you're the best damned man in the mountains."

"*Mon fils,* you will be back. Me, I think you do not know this right now, *peute-être*. But you will be back, it is so. You have begun to think like the Indian. And when that happens, *alors*. The mountains, they get into a man's blood, and then he is no good for anything else. He swallows the wildness with the flesh of the buffalo. Pierre, his beard is gray and he grows bald, *la calvitie*. The Indians will not want his scalp, so he will be here, *ancien homme des frontières*."

"Goodbye, Pierre. Baptiste. Moses Harris. Cahuna Smith. Sing to the Great Coyote."

"*Baptiste et moi,* we will sing."

Cahuna Smith nodded, said nothing.

"This nigger'll be thinkin' on ye," Black Harris said. "Hang onto your ha'r, and I'll do 'er too."

Ashley and his small group stopped at Fort Kiowa, the American Fur Company post, where Joshua Pilcher, the man in charge, made the General the recipient of an unusual present—a large grizzly bear, which was tied fast to the cargo box on deck, by an iron chain. From Fort Kiowa onward, the bear ruled his portion of the deck, and none challenged his territorial rights, though Beckwourth spent a good deal of time talking to the animal, from a respectful distance, concluding in short order that the bear was probably the best conversationalist on board. Jim talked, and the bear seemed to study him, snorting from time to time or emitting a low, almost contented growl.

On down the river they went, the little group of trappers regaling the soldiers with tales of adventure which, in a few details, differed from the events which had inspired them and which, in some instances, bore no resemblance to anything that had ever happened or ever could happen. But the soldiers listened with rapt attention and undisguised astonishment, and in turn they supplied one or two tales of their own. . . .

Jim kept on talking to the bear.

"Ephraim," he said, "we're both leaving the wilderness. Maybe we're both going to get put into cages. I know you are, old friend. Me, I've got a chance to stay loose. But lots of men don't. I've seen enough of the world to know that. I've got an idea, Bruin. I'll cut your chain, and we'll both slip overboard and hightail it back up river. Think you'd like that?"

Aw shit, Beckwourth, you're goin' to do that anyhow. I cain't figger why you decided to come down river in the first place. Mebbe you've got buffalo dung for brains.

"I've got a young lady waiting for me, big fella."

Ain't seen 'er for a while, though, have ye?

"She'll be there, you can count on it. Her name's Eliza. A real pretty gal—you'll see. She'll be there when we get to St. Louis. I tell you, when Jim Beckwourth fucks 'em, they stay fucked. Besides all that, Eliza's in love with me. Can a bear understand that? About love?"

The grizzly chewed at the fur on the back of his paw, snorted, sighed.

The boat arrived at Council Bluffs. Here the soldiers remained while the trappers continued down the big, muddy river, the boat riding easily on the powerful current which bore them ever closer to their destination.

They landed at St. Charles, about twenty miles above St. Louis,

68

and Ashley dispatched a courier to his partners, Warndorf and Tracy, to advise them of the successful completion of the venture and to tell them that he and his cargo would arrive the next day about noon.

The landing at St. Louis was marked by salutes of artillery, and the boat was greeted by a good-sized crowd—relatives, the curious, well-wishers. The courier had spread word of their arrival, and a festival atmosphere prevailed.

Bill Ashley pondered the problem of the grizzly bear.

"Well, Jim, what do you think? How do we get that animal off the boat? I thought about getting him drunk, but he's too heavy to carry."

Beckwourth had had a few drinks himself and, feeling pleased with the General's amiable tone, volunteered to get the bear ashore. He got a sharp stick and walked straight up to the grizzly and spoke to him in his most authoritative voice—something he'd been in the habit of doing throughout the voyage down river—and resolutely unlocked the chain. The bear gave a low whine, dropped his eyes, and allowed himself to be led off the boat along a staging that had been prepared.

The crowd fell back, giving the grizzly and his keeper a wide berth.

"Think you can get him to Biddle's place, about a quarter mile up the way?"

"Got Ephraim under my power, General," Jim laughed. "Lead onward."

The crowd, astonished and amused, followed at a distance—and the bear, somewhat confused by the goings-on, cooperated fairly well. Jim and the grizzly made it to Major Biddle's home, and Beckwourth tied the chain to an apple tree in the front yard. Just as Jim fastened the chain, the bear, perhaps realizing that he was once again locked up, made a furious leap toward his erstwhile leader.

Beckwourth leaped backward and rolled out of reach, the chain fortunately being a strong one and holding fast.

The crowd applauded.

RETURN TO
THE MOUNTAINS

Darts of winged blue, they settle in an aspen. For a moment the jays make no noise. Then one cries. Another, several all at once. One flies to a different tree, watches. In the small mountain valley below, in the tall amber and green of summer grasses, a buck mule deer raises his head, some of the velvet still clinging to his antlers, not yet stripped off. The wide ears tremble in the morning sunlight. He listens, watches, lowers his head to nibble the grasses once more, then looks up again. Without words he wonders why the jays are shrieking. He sees nothing, smells nothing. But suddenly he bolts away, the graceful body almost in flight as he bounds across the meadow and disappears into a cover of spruces. In the aspens above, the jays are laughing.

"James!"

The voice was his father's. The two men embraced, the one dressed in the clothing of a gentleman, the other bearded, in buckskins and moccasins, a wide-bladed knife dangling from a rawhide strip about his middle. The men shook hands and then embraced once more.

"Almost didn't recognize you, Son. Here I thought you were trapping up river, and all the time you were training bears. How are you, Jim?"

"I'm fine, Pa. Where's the rest of the clan?"

"Come on, Son, you can get your things off the boat later. I moved into St. Louis while you were gone—we're just at the edge of town.''

"How'd that happen, Pa? Ain't anyone out at the old place now?"

"Had to sell the property. I'll tell you about it later."

Jim placed his hands on his father's shoulders and looked at him. The man had aged this past year. That much was certain. Something was different, perhaps many things.

"Where's Eliza? I was sure that she'd be in the crowd or I'd never have played the damn fool with that bear."

"Eliza's married, Son, about four months ago. A wool merchant from Louisville. It all happened quickly, but she came to talk to me first. I told her you'd be back, but I guess her mind was made up. I'm sorry, James."

"A wool merchant? I'll be damned. . . ."

He could feel the knot forming in his stomach.

The next day, in the company La Roche and Pellow, trappers who had worked the area near the Mandan villages the preceding year, Beckwourth went to the store of Messrs. Warndorf and Tracy, where their accounts with Ashley were paid in full. With money in hand, the three of them proceeded to a tavern and then, after numerous rounds of drinks, to the Le Barras Hotel, where Jim spent the entire night in the company of a lady of the profession, a thin little blonde girl who was somewhat nearsighted and who, when provoked, had an exceedingly sharp tongue.

Jim tormented himself with thoughts of Eliza and, oddly enough, of a tall Shoshone girl. The vision of the girl in the yellow-fringed dress, the smoky light of a Pawnee lodge and the woven baskets full of cooked buffalo meat, the vision of the Indian girl who did not know enough English for him to converse with her and who would not tell him her name. These fragments of memory faded gradually to images of great white mountains, of clear-running rivers, of the tall, gaunt figure of Long Hair, of the knife fight with Red Beard, of good, wise, barrel-strong Pierre Le Blueux and the shooting of the two buffalo, the shooting of the bear, the shooting of the teal duck, the tomahawk buried in Le Brache's head, the fierce dignity in the eyes of Two Axe, the voices of the song dogs across the canyon rim on the Seedskeedee, the great muddy Platte River, the water rising, of his friends La Jeunesse and Harris and Cahuna Smith.

He did not want to talk. He wanted to drink. He wanted to fuck this little blonde whore. He wanted to drink. He wanted. . . .

Some time after midnight the candle-lit room with the yellowed lace curtains began to spin about, and he was unable to force the spinning to cease. And then he was unconscious.

Jennings Beckwith stared at his son and smiled. The younger man sat there, slouched, his head in his hands, hung over and miserable. Young men took these affairs of the heart so seriously—put a woman into their heads, and they would give up anything and everything just to have her. Was his own life not a testament to this absolute truth of the male condition? The first love: a compelling force, an experience certain to founder on the boulders hidden beneath the murky, shallow waters. What was it that Napoleon was supposed to have said? *A man seldom remembers but never forgets his first love.* Well, Eliza was a good little gal, but Jennings didn't figure his son was ready to take to a settled existence anyway. Not with a whole world out there to the west, and him in his twenties.

"Pull 'er together, Son. That girl was destined to be the wife of a wool merchant. I'm going to tell you something, James, and it's true. If you'd really wanted her, you'd not have gone up river with old Ashley these past two years. A young, hot-blooded woman's not going to sit around waiting while her man's out God-knows-where, shooting deer, wandering the mountains, and diddling with Indian women. It's just not in the cards. I know it hurts. Damn me, I know that. But mostly it's your pride, the old male pride. You know what I'm saying's true. You cottoned to the idea that she was waiting for you. I tell you, Son, there be lots of women. If there's a right one, you won't be running off from her. But if ye had to, she'd wait for sure. And when push came to shove, you'd give up everything you've got to have her. I tell you, most men finally decide it's not worth it, and when they marry, they marry with their heads, not their hearts. Can't say that I know which way is right. Just know what I did, and I've never regretted it. Any case, I figure you'd have gone back up river again. 'Just one more year, Eliza, and I'll be ready to settle down—you going to wait for me, aren't you?' Right now it's just that you've been rejected. Come on, Jimmy, let's get some breakfast into ye, and you'll feel a lot better. We'll ride on up to Snake Creek this afternoon and catch that big old catfish that's down under the logs. He's still there, anyhow."

Jim Beckwourth rubbed his eyes and looked up at his father. Then grinned.

"Pa, you've been worrying about that catfish for five years. He'll die of old age if we don't do something about it."

"We all going to die of old age if something don't catch us first. In the meanwhile, there's wind in the forest and sunlight in the water. I don't know what that means, but I know there's no point worrying about it. I'll fix us some bacon and eggs and tomato juice. Nothing finer for taking care of a hangover. Believe me, Son, I speak from dreadful experience."

"Don't know if my stomach'll handle it, but I'll give 'er a try."

"It's going to be all right. You just listen to your old Pa. Go get washed up, James. You'll feel a hell of a lot better. Your brother and sisters should be here in a little while. Afterwards we'll go catch us that big catfish."

"I don't think there's any catfish out there. Just your imagination."

"You've seen him, Jimmy. You remember that time about three years ago—when there he was, just lying there so easy in the water, just movin' his fins a little, damned near as big as a grown man, with whiskers the size of lead pencils."

"It was your own reflection in the water, Pa. Wasn't no catfish."

"It was, I tell you! How can you doubt such a thing? We'll get that old sucker today."

73

Jim stood up, stretched, shook his head, and winced. Jennings laughed. Clapped his son on the back.

"See what happens when you go doubting The Catfish? That devil is in our blood, Son. Likely it'll be the death of both of us."

With a new six-shot British-issue pepperbox handgun fastened to his belt by rawhide thongs, the weapon a farewell gift from his father, Beckwourth rejoined La Roche and Pellow, and the three men prepared to set out for the Ammahabas. Ashley furnished his mountaineers with two good saddle horses apiece, sufficient supplies to get them to the high country, three dozen new steel traps, and a pair of mules to carry the hardware.

The little party left St. Louis and proceeded up the Big River, passed through the last of the settlements, and then moved on into the wilderness. They traveled with great caution, stopping before dark to build a fire and eat their meal, and then continued their ride until they found a camping site that was safe. Here they lit no fires, to avoid alerting the Indians as to their whereabouts.

At the forks of the Platte, the three men held council and discussed the best way to proceed, concluding at length to follow the North Platte to its source, through Cheyenne country, and then to cross over to Seedskeedee at a point further upstream than they had ever been before. They were forced to make one wide detour around a large Indian encampment and then moved on up the North Platte to its juncture with the Sweetwater. From the head of this stream, they crossed over South Pass, then Sandy Creek, and finally Green River. From there they traversed the Wyoming Range and the Salt River Range and came down to the Bear River at the point where it makes its great turn southward. They rode upstream on the Bear and thence to Cache Valley, where they found a party belonging to Ashley's company, the larger group under the command of Bill Sublette.

Winter was drawing down from the mountains by this time, with freezing winds that whistled over the ranges. A first light snow began to fall.

Sublette himself, who had been trapping to the north, up on the

Snake River in the land of the Blackfeet, now arrived. All of the various parties were coming in, and Sublette's was among the last of them. When all were accounted for, Sublette gave orders to move on to the Great Salt Lake, and so the winter encampment was established at the mouth of Weaver's Fork. The community, in its entirety, numbered above six hundred, with as many as two hundred and fifty Indian women and half-breed children among them.

La Jeunesse, Le Blueux, and Cahuna Smith were there, and so Beckwourth was reunited with his old friends. They had come in as the last of the parties.

The men embraced.

"Well," said Cahuna, "Bugs' Boys didn't get my hair, and no white bears chewed on me neither!"

After that he sat quietly by while the others talked, recounting their various adventures.

Pierre Le Blueux moved quietly along the edge of the stream, the thin, hard snow crunching softly beneath his moccasins. There were fresh cuttings along the streambank, and directly he came to a low mud and stick dam with its glassy-smooth pond behind it. He surveyed the pond carefully, but saw no beaver. Nevertheless, he knew they were present. He lay down his string of traps and rifle, cut a long, dry stick with his knife, and then picked up a trap and his rifle again.

He stepped through the fringe of ice beside the pond and then into the shallow water itself, bone-cold water that burned the skin and made the ankles ache. He was used to it.

A pair of ducks flew from the dry reeds upstream, the muffled sound of their wings coming to him. He did not look up. He set the trap, a hand's breadth beneath the surface of the water, slipped the ring of the trap chain over the sharpened end of the stick, and then used his hand axe to drive the stick down to firm mud. He reached above his head and drew down a willow branch, cut a green twig, and doctored the end of it with beaver medicine from a small flask he carried on his belt. Carefully he slipped the opposite end of the stick into the mud between the trap's jaws.

With a critical eye he surveyed the placement of the trap and concluded that it was set well.

"Mon frère Castor," he said softly, "come to Old Pierre's trap, and he will give you a present. He will send you to London."

Le Blueux returned to the bank of the pond, shouldered his string of traps, and moved on upstream. The early light was just breaking through the pines along the canyon rim, dropping down over the frozen snow, glittering.

The Pun-naks (Bannocks) slipped into camp on the night of a windy rainstorm and stole eighty horses. Sublette's men did not realize the horses were gone until the following day. A party of about forty men, Jim Beckwourth among them, was formed to track the Pun-naks back to their villages, where the trappers observed their own horses among a number of others.

Sublette divided the group into three, himself to lead one band of men, Tom Fitzpatrick the second, and Jim Bridger the third. Sublette's men were to provide a cover of rifle fire, Fitzpatrick's were to charge the Pun-naks, and Bridger's were to stampede the horses.

Beckwourth knew Bridger. They had both grown up in St. Louis, and both had been apprenticed to blacksmiths. Beckwourth was the older by about four years, but Bridger had been in the mountains for a longer time. Bridger's parents had died, leaving the fourteen-year-old boy to support his younger sister. He had operated a ferry across the river, and, after his apprenticeship, had gone up river with the Henry-Ashley party. A year later, when Beckwourth began to think about what lay up river, the fact that young Jim Bridger had gone provided yet one more reason for Jim Beckwourth to follow suit.

Jim knew that Bridger was supposed to have ridden a bullboat down the Bear River and to have discovered the Great Salt Lake, reporting back that he had come to the Pacific Ocean. And Beckwourth had heard a number of times the story of how Fitzgerald and Bridger had left behind the maimed Hugh Glass, torn and broken by a grizzly and apparently dying—and how Glass had miraculously crawled his way two hundred and fifty miles back to Fort Kiowa, recovered, and set out to take revenge upon Fitzgerald and Bridger. Finally Glass's need for revenge had simmered down, though he had trailed and confronted both men. Bridger was a greenhorn then. Le Blueux had been there when Glass caught up with Bridger.

Now Beckwourth wanted to see how Bridger would react under pressure, and so he went along with Bridger's group.

The attack began. The Pun-naks, unsuspecting, were thrown momentarily into confusion, and during the hullabaloo, Bridger's brigade drove off nearly three hundred horses.

Six Pun-naks were killed and scalped. None of the trappers were killed or even wounded. But the first night, after the trappers returned from the marauding party, the Pun-naks stole back about half the horses they had lost. And one trapper took an arrow in the shoulder.

In the morning, as Beckwourth was cinching his saddle, Jim Bridger came up to him.

"You're Beckwourth? I guess you don't remember me—I shoed your Pa's horse a couple of times down in St. Louis. But older kids never remember the younger ones. I'm Jim Bridger."

"I remember you," Beckwourth said. "You lived over by Six Mile Prairie."

"They say you knife-fought Miller," Bridger said. "Don't know as I'd want to tangle with that red-bearded son of a bitch."

The two men shook hands, sized each other up.

"Two kids from St. Louis," Beckwourth smiled. "Some call you Gabe?"

"Yep. Some do, all right. How's your dad, Jim? Always liked him—a damned fine hunter. Guess that's where you get it. It's in the blood."

Beckwourth thought about the unexplored land to the west, thought about the stories he had heard of California and Oregon. The Buenaventura River? Was this the same river which flowed out into the Pacific through the great bay north of Monterey, at San Francisco? Certainly that river came from somewhere in the interior.

Jed Smith had circled the Great Salt Lake and had found no outlet, so the inland sea was not the source of the Buenaventura. If such a river flowed westward into California, it would have to rise out in the desert somewhere.

Whatever the case, Beckwourth knew that Jedediah Strong Smith intended to go to California directly from Rendezvous, intended to travel south along the canyon-rims and then to cross overland to Pueblo de Los Angeles. Smith was a strange duck, a man who often read his Bible at night and who broke out into prayers at the damnedest times. Still, the mountain men swore by him and would follow him almost anywhere—the man had an infallible sense of the terrain.

"Maybe I'll take a little ride on over to California myself one of these years," Beckwourth mused.

Even the prospects of new beaver country were not so important as simply finding out about the land that lay to the west, and Smith had an itch for seeing new places. Furthermore, it seemed quite likely that the United States Government would be interested. It only made sense that the United States should extend completely across the continent, and the mere presence of a band of Rocky Mountain trappers in California might well change the entire course of history.

If it were someone else leading the expedition, Sublette for instance, Beckwourth figured that he, himself, just might have volunteered to ride along.

There was no question that winter had set in, for the creeks were already beginning to freeze. Davy Jackson had set up camp down in Cache Valley. Word was that Davy had probably set some kind of world record for the number of beaver he had taken. The man didn't talk much, Beckwourth observed, except when it mattered, but he knew how to lay a trap—even Le Blueux was impressed. Sublette's group had also done well, and feelings were running high when the two partners joined up.

Beckwourth and Black Harris rode in with Sublette and shared the hospitality of Jackson's lodge for an evening. The men embraced, ate hump rib, and drank a bit of rum.

"I'm thinkin' of the '27 Rendezvous," Bill Sublette said as he lit his pipe.

"A good thing to think upon," Jackson replied.

"Now what I'm thinkin'," Sublette continued, "is that we don't actually know whether Ashley's going to get those supply trains up here at all. Maybe the man's lost interest in the mountains. Guess I'd just feel a hell of a lot better if we actually *knew* the supplies would get here. What if trappers and Injuns come in from all over the damned place, and we ain't got no goods to sell 'em?"

"This child's thinking that wouldn't be too good. Why don't you mosey over to St. Louis and fetch him back? Take Beckwourth or Harris here with ye?"

"Why that's a capital idea, Davy. Just kinda *mosey* over to St. Louis, is that what you're sayin'?"

"Why not? Streams is going to be froze pretty soon anyhow. Won't be gettin' many plew until spring weather hits."

Sublette got a drink and sat down. He lit his pipe once more and pondered the matter for a few minutes.

"This nigger's not too pleased with the idea," Harris snorted.

"Well, a man's got to have summat to do," Jackson said.

Sublette puffed on his pipe and then winked at Beckwourth before he spoke:

"Davy, m'partner, since Harris is up for the idea, and since he's never caught a beaver in his life anyhow, I believe I'll just do that little thing."

"Wagh!" Harris groaned.

"Yep, it's you and me, Black. We'll hit the trail as soon as I get a few things shaped up back at camp. . . ."

Barchk-Parchk. Medicine. Prophet or dreamer.

The winter encampment was now much enlarged, enlarged several times over. Snake Indians, six hundred lodges of them, had surrounded the trappers with their own encampment. Perhaps two thousand warriors. Friendly Indians.

As the winter wore on, the trappers were even invited into the medicine lodge, presided over by the old prophet, O-mo-gua—Woman's Dress, in English. One evening the magician delivered a prophecy for the trappers, and Beckwourth in particular listened with great attention.

"I can see Whitemen on the Big Shell," O-mo-gua intoned. "I see them boring a hole in a red bucket. I see them drawing out arwerdenty. I see them fighting each other. Sublette has gone down on the other side of the river, he does not see them. He has gone to the White lodges."

"That's true, at least part true," Greenwood said. "Sublette and Black Harris have gone down to St. Louis. They'll be back."

"Yes, it is true," O-mo-gua said. "And you, where will you trap now?"

"We're going to trap on Bear Head in the country of the *Pieds Noirs.*"

"No," said O-mo-gua. "You will go to Sheep Mountain. There you will find the snow so deep that you cannot pass. You will then go down Portneuf to Snake River. If you are fortunate, you will see the *Pieds Noirs* before they see you, and you will beat them. If they see you first, they will kill all of the Whites. They will take the scalps of the Long Knives and they will make their lodges dark with them. Bad Hand—Fitzpatrick—I tell you there is blood in your path this grass. If you defeat the *Pieds Noirs,* you will retrace your steps and go to Bear River, whose water you will follow until you come to Sage River. There you will meet two Whitemen who will give you news."

Later that night Beckwourth, Le Blueux, La Jeunesse, Le Pointe and Cahuna Smith sat around the fire, talking and roasting strips of buffalo meat. The fire flickered in the cold light, and the smoke drifted straight upward.

"I think old O-mo-gua's a fake, a pure fake," Jim said. "Hell, he must have been told where Sublette and Harris went."

"Me, I do not know," Pierre answered. "This Woman's Dress has predicted many things before, *c'est vrai!*"

"Like what for instance?"

"*Mon frère,* this man has very strong medicine. Soon you will come to believe in *la puissance* of the medicine. You will find your own medicine. It is well to listen to what this Woman's Dress says."

Baptiste broke in: "My father, he told me to listen when such a man speaks. He told me not to believe, but to listen. To listen and then to wait and remember what was said."

"*Oui,*" said Pierre. "That is how to do it. Listen and remember and wait."

"And keep your damned rifle loaded," Cahuna Smith added.

Le Pointe smoked his pipe and nodded, seemed to drowse.

"Even *la fumée,*" Pierre said, "some men, they even read signs in the smoke. Regard the pipe of our *frère,* Le Pointe, as he falls into *sommeil.*"

"Is because you think like Indian," Beckwourth laughed, mimicking Le Blueux. "Me, I am a Whiteman."

After a moment of silence, they all laughed. Le Pointe was startled back awake, and he also laughed, even without being quite certain why. Their laughter drifted up with the smoke from their fire and through the overlaced boughs of the trees.

The trappers moved on to Sheep Mountain but had to change directions when they found the snows still too heavy for them to proceed. And just as O-mo-gua had said, they followed the Portneuf down to its confluence with the Snake. No other trappers had preceded them into this country, and they had excellent success all the way to the junction, a journey of some three weeks.

But now there were signal smokes all around them.

"Me, I think maybe we have troubles," Le Blueux said. "The *Pieds Noirs.*"

A few of the Blackfeet, making signs of friendship, came into the camp, but Fitzpatrick and Bridger were well aware that such signs were not to be trusted. The Indians had no doubt been sent in to discover exactly how well armed the trappers were and otherwise to do whatever mischief they could. The guards were doubled, and every man kept his rifle close at hand and loaded. A number of the trappers could speak fairly well in the language of the Blackfeet, and the Indians continued to pretend friendliness.

At daylight on the third day, the Blackfeet were caught stealing horses, and the Hawkens began to explode. Six Blackfeet went down, and a seventh crawled to the river and fell in. The scalps of the others were taken.

The signal fires continued.

The trappers packed up immediately and began a forced march to the south, pushing on relentlessly throughout the day.

"They can drop thousands down on us if they want to," Bridger said. "Hell, we're right in the heart of their country."

Fitzpatrick agreed.

"But I guess we knew that when we decided to come up here. Strange what a man will do for the hides of some big wet rats, ain't it?"

Yet the Blackfeet did not seem inclined to follow them. Beckwourth and La Jeunesse, having fallen back to act as scouts, caught up with the main party at nightfall and reported no Blackfeet anywhere.

"It is mysterious, this," Baptiste said. "They have all vanish."

A few days later, however, twelve trappers under the charge of Ezekiel Logan left the company to try their fortune in the area immediately to the east and were never heard from again. Several parties were sent out to find the missing men, but nothing was ever learned.

Cahuna Smith summed it up: "Them Blackfeet is the evilest Injuns that God ever created. A man can trust a grizzly a lot farther."

"It's true," Beckwourth agreed. "And I don't think we're done with them yet."

"Siksika," grunted Le Blueux. "They are not friendly, these *Pieds Noirs.*"

5

SIKSIKA

Selecting a proper encampment is no small matter, though to the inexperienced it might seem little more than no matter at all. One must have wood, water, and grass for the horses. But the place itself, its relationships to all that is about it, is of the utmost importance, whether journeying upon the plains or among the mountains. During the night the party is most vulnerable, whether to stealing of the horses or to attack by hostile Indians. Fire and storm are other matters, and it is the duty of the leader to select the one place which will prove most secure, should something out of the ordinary occur. The larger the party, strangely enough, the more vulnerable the entire encampment becomes. Mounted pickets should be sent out to occupy those nearby points which afford the best views of all possible approaches to the camp. While on guard, a man must never allow himself to fall asleep, for in doing so, he endangers all.

Fitzpatrick's party continued trapping up the Portneuf until they came to Sheep Mountain. The snows had by this time disappeared, and so they passed on over the mountain without difficulty and descended to Bear River, continuing their trapping as far as Sage River, where, to Beckwourth's astonishment, they met two "Whitemen," just as O-mo-gua had said.

Black Harris and Porty Portuleuse greeted them warmly.

"From St. Louis," Harris said. "The long ride."

"Ashley and Sublette, they's just a little piece behind us," Portuleuse added. "Them old coons, they don't ride so fast."

The party took up their traps and moved on to Great Salt Lake, forming an encampment to await the arrival of Ashley and Sublette.

Then a group of Flat Heads rode in to say that a party of thirty Whitemen and women and children were camped on a creek a few miles distant. They had guns, the Flat Heads said, but they were without ammunition.

Etienne Provost, Jacob Jarvey, and Beckwourth gathered together some powder and shot. They mounted and rode.

It was Robert Campbell's party. Though they had run out of ammunition, they had had extremely good luck on their expedition and had lost none of their men. The three riders camped with them that night and then escorted them back to the main camp the next day.

They were joined by a group of perhaps five hundred mounted Indians, coming up directly behind them with a good deal of singing and shouting.

"Flat Heads," Provost said. "Come on, Beckwourth, let's ride back and meet them. They're good Injuns."

As the two approached within a short distance, however, they were struck with horror.

Pieds Noirs.

Provost and Beckwourth wheeled about on their mounts and rode to give the alarm. The group coalesced immediately, and with the women and children in the forefront, rode madly toward the only cover visible, a patch of willows several miles across the prairie. The women made good time, despite the poor condition of their animals, and the men brought up the rear, occasionally turning in their saddles to fire at the Blackfeet, who seemed to be in no particular hurry to pursue them.

"Them damned Siksikas figure they've got us dead to rights!" Provost shouted. "A whole passel of White scalps."

They made it to the willows and took such cover as they might. The Blackfeet approached at their leisure, considering their prey as good as taken. But when they began charging the little band of Whites, they did so with some degree of caution, not wishing to take unnecessary casualties in the face of the trappers' rifle fire. They knew well enough that the Whites would be forced at length to emerge into the open country if they were to make an attempt at escape, and at that point they could be taken with a minimum of risk.

During the ride to the willows, one man had been taken by an arrow. It was old François Bolliere, a trapper of many seasons in the mountains. Beckwourth turned his horse about and grabbed hold of Bolliere before he fell from his mount.

"They fotched me, boy. This coon's a dead man. You save your skin!"

Jim grasped the shaft of the arrow and ripped it out of Bolliere's back, then gave the horse several lashes to quicken his pace. But Bolliere pitched backward and fell. Beckwourth hesitated, then spurred his own horse away, firing back over his arm as he did so.

The Blackfeet were upon Bolliere in a moment and tore off his scalp.

Jarvey and Beckwourth were momentarily surrounded by the howling Indians.

"This way!" Beckwourth shouted. The two men rode furiously toward an open slough, which their mounts were forced to leap across. One Blackfoot attempted to follow in like fashion, but Jarvey fired back at him and the ball struck home. The Blackfoot pitched from his horse.

They rode on around the slough in order to join the others, but the Blackfeet had outflanked them. A rank of Indians blocked their escape route.

"Ride low, Jimmy!" Jarvey shouted, and together they charged the waiting Blackfeet.

A hail of arrows. Bullets sang in the air.

The ranks of the Blackfeet opened, and the two trappers passed through unharmed.

But they were cut off. Again they charged, firing their rifles as they did so, and again the ranks broke.

They gained the willows.

Not much ammunition.

The Blackfeet, who never grant or receive quarter.

Outnumbered by more than ten to one.

Isaac Eroquey spoke: "Let us put our trust in God and make one charge—for the sake of the women and children! If we die, let us die protecting those who cannot defend themselves. We must die with honor!"

"Use your head!" Campbell shouted. "Keep calm or we don't have the chance of a snowball in hell."

"We got to break out of here," Provost said. "We got to get through to Fitzpatrick or we ain't got no chance at all. We need six men—six men to try and ride through them bloodthirsty bastards. Who'll go?"

Beckwourth and Jarvey nodded. Then Eroquey. Three more.

They charged, firing with deadly accuracy, and broke through two ranks of the Blackfeet. But they were turned back. Beckwourth's horse was shot, and Jim was thrown off, hitting the dirt on his back but with his rifle still in hand. He rose to one knee and fired directly into the face of a Blackfoot who careened toward him, war axe drawn back.

Jarvey swung about and reached out. Beckwourth grabbed his hand and vaulted onto the horse, and in a moment they were within the cover of the willows.

An arrow had creased Beckwourth's scalp. Only now did he become aware of it, the blood dripping down the side of his face.

"You got to stay mounted, coon," Jarvey said. "That's rule number one."

"That just about did for me, all right. Thanks."

The Blackfeet still did not charge the willows except for individual forays. They were content to wait. To wait for the inevitable.

"I want to try it again," Jim said. "By myself. They won't be expecting it. Over to the far side."

"That's insane," Campbell said, shaking his head.

"Crazier than hell," Provost said. "But it might work. We don't have too many choices."

Danny Calhoun said, "I'll go too. That doubles our chances."

Campbell nodded.

Provost suggested that the two strip down, Indian style, and put handkerchiefs around their heads. Look as much like Indians as possible. Jarvey agreed.

They rode through the Blackfoot ranks almost too quickly for the Indians to realize what was happening. Then, belatedly, a hail of arrows and gunshot. A group of four Blackfeet took to their horses in pursuit, but Beckwourth and Calhoun soon opened a wide lead, and the Indians turned back.

They rode. Their horses moving smoothly, easily, at a full run, eating up the miles that lay between the embattled group in the willows and the assistance of the main party.

"Calhoun! You all right?"

"Slick as a whistle. How about you?"

"Nary a scratch—we took them completely by surprise."

About five miles from the camp, they saw men on horseback, riding slowly toward them. Jim pulled up his horse and signaled with his blanket. The signal was understood, and one rider turned about and set off at a gallop for the main camp. The rest of the men came on, sixteen of them, including Le Blueux, Le Pointe, and La Jeunesse. Calhoun and Beckwourth now turned about and rode toward the battle site.

When word reached the camp, the result was immediate—complete mobilization. Men checked their rifles and leaped to horseback. And the full body of trappers and their Flat Head allies set out on a fast ride.

As Calhoun, Beckwourth, and the others approached close to the rear guard of the Blackfeet, they urged their galloping horses to a full run. Surprise was once more the element, for the Blackfeet had no reason to suppose so small a group would be attempting to ride their way precisely back into the trap. As a result, no one was wounded, though Baptiste's horse took an arrow in the side of its left rear leg just as the animal and its rider reached the cover of the willows. The horse spun about, spilling Baptiste into the arms of his fellow trappers.

The Blackfeet, now enraged, began to make their charges in a more serious fashion, but the trappers' rifles plucked first one, then another from his horse.

One assault came on foot, with four Indians leaping through the willows into the midst of the trappers. Le Blueux fired almost point blank into the chest of one, and then, as the Indian lay groaning, cut off his scalp.

Abner Johnson took a tomahawk to the forehead, and his skull was split open, the blood welling out as he fell. Baptiste, having recovered from his tumble, severed the Blackfoot's neck from behind with a hand axe.

A riddle of rifle fire, and the other two lay flopping.

"They're pulling back!" shouted Provost. "Campbell, look over there! Ain't that a sight for sore eyes now? Don't that just *shine?*"

The main body of the trappers, perhaps three hundred of them, were riding in at full tilt. And the Blackfeet were moving away, leaving their dead lying on the open ground. The trappers rushed out of the willow thickets and began taking the scalps of the Blackfeet. They took up as well the mutilated, scalped body of old François Bolliere.

When they returned to the main camp that night, a scalp dance was performed by the half-breeds and the women. The trappers watched in grim fascination.

"All in a day's work, hey Beckwourth?" Bridger pounded him on the back, eyes glittering with excitement. "Well, let's hope there ain't too many days like this one. But I'll tell ye something. I'm thinking that Bugs' Boys ain't done with us yet. They ain't going to take this lying down—we're going to have to keep our hands on our hair for awhile. They going to be back, sure as bear shit."

"You don't suppose we could just pay them to stay away, do you Gabe? It'd be a whole lot less draining on a man, I give you my word on it."

"Only wages them bloody bastards will take has to be paid out in trappers' scalps. But they won't try to fight the whole company. They'll be tryin' to get us two or three at a time. Siksikas are patient, that's sure now."

"Why do you figure they hate us so?"

"Some say they're paid by the British—Hudson's Bay. Some just think they don't want any of us into their lands."

"What do you think, Gabe?"

"Me? Why I think you cain't trust 'em for the same reason you cain't trust a damn white bear. Just the way they are, is all."

Once things had calmed down, Black Harris drifted over to share a campfire with his friends—Le Blueux, Cahuna Smith, La Jeunesse, and Beckwourth. They cooked hump rib and roasted some boudins over the coals, boiled up a big pot of coffee.

"Come on, Mose, we got some time now. So tell us what happened on the trip with Sublette. Some of us weren't sure we'd ever see you again," Beckwourth said.

"It is time to tell the story to your companyeros. *Moi,* I am ready to listen *de toute la nuit,*" Le Blueux laughed.

"It's a fair night for a tale," Harris agreed. "Stick me a chunk of that buffler meat so's I can eat while I gab."

"Comment préférez-vous le bifteck?" La Jeunesse asked.

"Come on, Little Frenchy. Speak at least a snatch of American so's this poor nigger can understand ye. Sometimes I figger coyotes talk better'n you pork-eatin' Froggies."

Baptiste made a pretence of going for his knife.

"Wants to know if you like your meat well done or half-raw," Beckwourth said.

"Aw hell, I've been eatin' her raw so long I probably couldn't digest her if she was genuine cooked. Spear me that one over there."

Cahuna Smith grabbed the chunk of meat bare-handed, juggled it momentarily, and deposited it on Harris' tin plate.

Harris cut off a piece, stuck it, brought the knife to his mouth, chewed, nodded.

"Well," he said, "that damn fool Sublette wanted to walk on over to St. Louis—said we had to get there by March. You remember we took us some pack dogs and some snowshoes, and off we went. Got back just a few days ago."

"Aw buffler shit," Cahuna said. "We know all that, dammit. What happened out there?"

Harris laughed, then continued.

"Snowshoes worked good enough," Harris said, "but we run into some Blackfeet. Should have been off to the north, but they wasn't. Instead of goin' up the Sandy to South Pass, we crossed the mountains and come up to the pass from the high plains. Then we moved down along the Platte, and the weather went bad, Goddamn wind that liked to blow a man over backward. An' cold, God it was cold. Sometimes we holed up, dug down into the snow for places to sleep. Then we walked nights and slept during the day when it was warmer. You should of seen us—ice all over our beards and eyebrows. Better, of course, when the snow was comin' down. When it cleared out it got dreadful cold. You'd spit and it'd freeze in the air, an' I ain't lying, either."

"Wagh!" Cahuna Smith said. "Any chance to take game?"

"For a long while we didn't. Then we got Pawnee sign, and Billy Sublette wanted to visit 'em. That's when I reminded him how them Pawnees had taken old Jim Clyman's gun and possibles the time he was trampin' across the plains. You was down at Fort Akinson when Clyman crawled in, wasn't you, Pierre?"

"*Oui*. He was in very bad shape, that one. Good man, Clyman."

"Well, Sublette must of starved with Clyman once. Anyhow, I figgered them Injuns had eatin's, all right, but I also figgered we might be makin' the meat, so we just kept on goin'. Later we picked up a trail of some Omahas, and we knew we had to do somethin'. Billy, he was hallucinatin', and I was stumblin' and lungin' as I walked. We found the Injuns, Big Elk's village, and they took us in and fed us. Nothin' extra to take along, though. Them Omahas was about ready to starve too. Then, down by Grand Island, we shot us a raven and ate that—didn't even take time to cook 'er. And just an ocean of whiteness ahead. Them plains is wide enough during the summer, but in winter they grow, I tell you. When we was still about two hundred miles from a settlement, one of our dogs come up bad lame and wandered into camp an hour or so late. Well now, I made a little fire and thought things over. This nigger just couldn't see starvin' to death with a perfectly good lame dog around. So I says, 'Bill, let's eat that dog.' And he says, 'Ain't eatin' no damned dog.' Hell, we've all ate dog. Remember when you brought in that wolf, Jimmy? It was a goodun. Dogs taste real good, an' that's a fact. It ain't no wonder the Injuns grab a fat dog when they've got company. 'It's hungry times, man,' I says, and I even reminded him how Old Glass ate worms and maggots and a rattlesnake before he found him a dog to kill. Anyhow, we sure weren't that bad off. Then Billy says, 'Mose, you talk dumb. Ain't no rattlesnakes in the middle of the damn winter.' And I says, 'We don't need no snake. We got us a dog that's on his last legs anyhow.' But Sublette was feelin' sorry for the dog, after he carried our pack for us clear across the mountains. Also, he wasn't thinkin' too clear. 'No choice,' I says. 'Either we eat summat or we starve to death, an' this coon wants a better place to go under.' Finally old Sublette was too exhausted to argue any more, an' he shrugged and give in."

"Sounds like you could have starved to death just while you were talking it over," Beckwourth said.

"Well," Harris said, "I picked up my hand axe and went to get the dog. It knew somethin' was goin' on—started whimpering dreadful. I hit him on the head but didn't kill him. He got up. I lunged again and damned if I didn't miss. So weak from not eatin' my reflexes was gone. Then I swung again, and the head flew off of my axe, and the old dog limped off into the night."

"So what the hell'd you do?" Cahuna Smith asked.

"Well, the idee was soundin' better to Billy all the while. So we went to find that dog. We found him, curled up in the snow, bleedin' some. We grabbed him, and I used my knife on him. We carried him back and laid him on the flames to singe him off so we wouldn't have to skin him. That damned dog still wasn't dead, and he managed to kick himself back out of the fire. An' that's when Sublette grabbed an axe and crushed old Bowser's skull."

"I hope it didn't take this long when you were doing it," Beckwourth laughed.

"Longer," Harris said. "Lots longer. I'm givin' you the short version here. So we ate our dog and went to sleep. Next morning I tried to get Billy to admit the dog tasted good, but he just refused to talk to me for an hour or so. Then about two days later we shot us four turkeys and cooked 'em up good. They tasted even better'n the dog. Next we followed some Kaws, and when we caught up, they give us food. Sublette traded 'em his pistol for one of their horses, an' we both got on, an' by God we got into St. Louis on the fourth day of March."

"*Monsieur* Harris," Pierre said, "how do we know this is *la vérité?*"

"How's that again?"

"The truth," Beckwourth said. "For instance, how do we know you ate the dog?"

"Didn't see us bringin' that dog back, did ye? You just go ask Sublette—he'll tell you the same damned story."

"He might give us the long version," Beckwourth said. "I think we might be better off just letting her lie."

"Some niggers won't believe nothin'," Harris said, rising, spearing another chunk of meat from the fire.

Other parties were arriving now. General Ashley and Bill Sublette, and in their wake some three hundred pack mules, loaded heavily with all the goods necessary for the Rendezvous and the Indian trade. More parties, one after another.

And the Rendezvous was begun. Dancing, shouting, fist fights, a knife fight in which two French trappers killed each other, jumping contests, shooting contests, stick games, gambling.

Snake warriors sold their women sexually for powder and lead, for long knives, for trinkets and mirrors and scarlet cloth and beaver traps. Buffalo robes for pistols. Packs of beaver plew for rifles.

Medicine water. Arwerdenty. Whiskey. Ashley's Special. Rotgut.

The trappers were informed by Black Harris—his words later verified by the General himself—that Ashley had sold his entire interests in the mountains to Davy Jackson, Bill Sublette, and Jed Smith, presuming that the latter would make it back from his venture to the Pacific Coast. The General had decided, Harris told them, to return to St. Louis to enjoy the fortune he had amassed through his own efforts and through the efforts of his loyal trappers.

The General had decided to live the life of a gentleman.

Previous to the Rendezvous, Beckwourth had taken Light in the Trees for his squaw. She was the widow of one of the men who had been killed when a bank slid down as they were excavating bunkers for caching packs of beaver plew.

Light in the Trees was a small girl, a Snake, and still quite young—with a light complexion for an Indian, intelligent, trim, and quick of movement. She seemed considerably pleased with her new mate, for Wright, her erstwhile husband, was known to have been extremely brutal with her. And she made no pretense of mourning for him. She was fearful of love-making at first, but gradually Jim had been able to bring her around. He tried to get her to tell him what happened with Wright, but she would only say, "I do not wish to speak of those times. They are gone now."

Bridger kidded Beckwourth: "Nice little papoose you've got there, Jimmy. Is she a good one in bed?"

"She was a virgin," Beckwourth replied, not smiling.

"That so? All the noises we heard from Wright's tent, a man wouldn't think so."

"I mean she was a virgin once I got past the little bit that Wright used."

Bridger laughed.

"Seriously," he said, "I think you got a good one. They ain't all."

"Wright needed killing," Beckwourth responded. "It's enough to make a coon believe in justice. He did things to that little girl, Gabe. She won't talk about it, but I know. A man can always tell."

"Guess you're right on both points," Bridger nodded.

Light in the Trees.

Now Beckwourth took her and rode along the shoreline of Bear Lake for perhaps five miles and set up his tipi. The drunkenness and violent good-humor of the Rendezvous had never greatly appealed to him, and since he had undertaken his mountain marriage, the go-ings-on at the great encampment were less attractive than ever.

In part, the remove down the lake was designed for the protection of Light in the Trees, for at the Rendezvous, all the women tended to become a kind of free-floating community property. Even squaws who had taken trappers for their husbands might well end up being raped, either by the Whites or by the Indians. The preceding year Beckwourth, along with a group of others, had witnessed two braves and one trapper, all sotted with Ashley's Special, chase after an Indian girl of perhaps twelve years of age, catch her, pull her down. They held her legs apart and took turns raping her. Finally the two braves fell into an argument, and within moments they had plunged knives into each other, and both lay dead in a heap beside the still-sobbing girl. The trapper had removed the knives, wiped them on his leggings, and walked off whistling. The spectators applauded. Beckwourth had gone over to help the girl up, and she had spit at him.

But Jim had another reason for wishing to be alone with Light in the Trees. If, following Wright's death, he had taken the girl into his lodge primarily to protect her, it was also true that he had been attracted to her for some while. At first she had seemed like a small, wounded bird, so he had tried to ease her fears by being very gentle with her. After a time she had responded to him, and what began simply as an arrangement of convenience rapidly became more than that. He had begun thinking of Light in the Trees as his permanent escort and had even considered, should he ever choose to leave the mountains, that he would take her with him. It was good to be with her, it was good to have her to talk to, it was good to have her beside him, the two of them dressing out the beaver plew.

Now they were alone together really for the first time. They roasted chunks of antelope thigh over the orange-red coals, and Jim brewed some coffee in a tin pan. A half-moon hung out over the lake, and a second moon floated in the still water at the end of a long silver band of light. Somewhere back in the low ridges above them, a pair of wolves howled, and a soft breeze wafted in over the lake. From the little point of land where they were camped, they could see the reflected lights of the fires at the Rendezvous, off to the north. Even at a distance of five miles, occasional muted fragments of human voices could be heard, and once the report of a rifle.

"Wonder who's gone under?" Jim mused.

"It might not be that," Light in the Trees answered.

"No, it might not. One can hope for the best."

"Do you like the taste of the coffee?" she asked. "It does not taste good to me."

"Put more sugar in it, little lady. Make it sweet. Then you'll like it."

"I have tried that. It still does not taste good . . . Jim."

"Wonder what the wolves are yelling about?" Beckwourth said, rising to get more wood for the fire. "Sounds like just two of 'em. Jim Beckwourth and Light in the Trees, up on the hillside, yelling their heads off."

Light in the Trees laughed softly and looked away, out across the moonglittering lake.

"Got a hell of an idea," Jim said. "Let's go swimming and then come back and make love. . . ."

"I would like that. Yes, that would be good."

Jim built up the fire, and then he and Light in the Trees stripped naked and walked down to the water, moving slowly through the trees and brush and moonlight. They held hands as they walked, and Jim felt large and awkward and even foolish. He also felt like a boy again. He remembered holding hands with Eliza, holding hands before either of them had done more than to imagine what other things they might do. It all seemed distant now, something that had happened to another person, in another lifetime.

"Light in the Trees," he thought. "Tonight she is her name. . . ."

He imagined what they looked like, walking together, naked in the moonlight, holding hands. He smiled. A great sensation of warmth came over him, and he squeezed her hand, felt her hand tighten against his.

"Such a small hand," he mused. "Such a small, gentle, wild creature. It's better now, all of it. It's better, having her in my lodge."

They dived into the water and swam out toward the moon, stroking smoothly through the strangely placid water, cold water, tingling the skin, gliding around them.

"Do the beaver swim at night, in the moonlight?" she asked,

turning in the water, lying on her back, the dark nipples of her breasts just touching the surface, her long black hair fanning out on the water around her head.

"How do you think the beavers make love?" he said, splashing water at her.

"Speak the truth. Do the beavers do that?"

"I don't know. But that's what they should do. They should swim and make love in the moonlight."

"The Long Knives have strange thoughts," Light in the Trees said. Then she slipped beneath the surface, and Jim had to look around to see where she had gone. She emerged further out in the lake and called back to him:

"We must swim out to where the moon is."

"It runs from us," he called back. "We can never catch it. Let's go back and make love instead. Perhaps we can catch it that way."

Then she swam toward him, and they did not speak again until they had reached the shore, slithering up through the shallow water and onto the sand. Beckwourth put his hand behind her head and rolled over against her, kissed her. She returned his embrace, drawing herself close to him. He rose to one knee, lifted her in his arms, and stood up.

"I will carry you back to the fire."

"My husband is a very strong man."

It took a few moments for the word to register upon him. What had she said? *Husband.* He could not remember that she had ever called him *husband* before. But it was true, and he saw it now, clearly. He had found his mate, had taken her as a squaw without ever realizing what had driven him to do it.

The slim wet body in his arms.

"Light in the Trees," he thought as he carried her back up through the moonlight, "my woman, the trapper and his Indian bride. Perhaps one day I will take her with me to St. Louis, perhaps we will have children. . . ."

He could feel the excitement in his loins, an awkward sensation as he strode along, up the incline to where the campfire continued to blaze. Then Light in the Trees touched him, grasped hold of him, and said, "This is where a wife should always put her hand." She laughed and sang some words in her own language, words that he didn't understand.

SMITH, JACKSON,
AND SUBLETTE

Castor canadensis, an industrious rodent, glossy tan-to-dark-brown underfur with a natural tendency to mat or "felt." The oily undercoat is waterproof, for the beaver lives among lakes and streams and dines on aspen, alder, willow, and various water plants. When frightened, the beaver slaps the water with its flat, scaly tail, making a sound like that of a rifle being discharged, when heard at a distance. The animal uses this tail to propel itself through the water, though it has webbed hind feet as well. Its amazing lung capacity allows the beaver to remain underwater for as long as ten minutes. It lives in low, dome-shaped aquatic lodges constructed of interlaced branches and mud, thus providing a nest for the offspring. Largely monogamous. Breeds in winter. Dams streams with stones, mud, and trees. Long incisors and dextrous forepaws. Can cut down five-inch-thick aspens in three minutes. Works faster on willows. Furs used for the making of hats in Eastern America and in Europe. Skins commonly referred to by the mountain men as plew.

Light in the Trees saw them coming, and she called to her husband.

Four men were approaching on horseback, an Indian and three half-starved Whites. Beckwourth hailed them, and they rode into the camp. It was Jed Smith, Robert Evans, and Silas Gobel.

"I'll be damned!" Jim said. "It's the Reverend himself. Jed—you look like you've gone under and come back. . . ."

Smith leaned forward on his horse and said quietly, "Lazarus has returned. We smelled your cook fire and couldn't resist 'er."

"Evans and Gobel too—climb down off your horses and sit a

spell. We've got an antelope shank just about done and a pot of blackberries. I'll brew up some coffee, if you're interested."

"Son of a bitch!" Gobel laughed. "Coffee! When's the last time we had coffee, Bob?"

"Nothin' satisfies this coon," Evans said. "Couple weeks back we was drinking mud, an' I told him to pretend it was coffee. It's all a matter of how a man thinks about things, but Silas an' Jed, they just won't listen to me."

Jed Smith frowned at his companions and then said to Beckwourth, "We'd be pleased to share food with you, Jim."

As they ate, Beckwourth noted that Evans, Gobel, and the Indian guide all kept glancing at Light in the Trees. Only Smith made a point of not looking at her.

"A damn strange duck," Jim thought.

But the man had made it to California, and now he was on his way back to the Rendezvous, even though he'd had to leave most of his men behind. The little Bible-toter wasn't much for talking, but he gave Beckwourth a brief account of what happened. After encountering all manner of difficulties, Jed and Evans and Gobel had crossed the snow-choked Sierra—Mt. Joseph, he called it—had lost their animals, and had wandered through the deserts on foot, ate the last of the dried meat from their remaining mule, then nearly starved to death or died of thirst several times. But hell, they'd made it back to Rendezvous, and only a few days late.

Evans and Gobel, Jim knew, would spend most of what remained of the Rendezvous telling the whole story in great detail, telling it over and over. And each time they told it, the story would change some. After awhile they'd be picturing themselves loading their pistols with pieces of baby lightning that grew out of the rocks and of shooting Indians who were twenty feet tall and had two heads. They would claim to have been nearly drowned by a river mirage that was so real it was made out of genuine water, but water a man couldn't see, even if it could drown him. Beckwourth studied the two men: he could see it in their faces.

Jim stood up, grinned, and said, "If you boys can relax for an hour, give us time to pack up our things, we'll ride on back to the Rendezvous with you—it's only five, six miles on up the lake. I came down here so Light in the Trees and I could be by ourselves for a spell."

"Sounds like good company to this child," Gobel responded. "We'll even give ye a hand in gettin' things together."

They reached the Rendezvous, and Smith went directly to see Jackson and Sublette. Gobel and Evans proceeded to get drunk and, in high spirits, began their tale-telling.

They found an enthusiastic audience.

Two days later the Blackfeet actually attacked the Rendezvous, and in their advance they surprised three men and two women belonging to the Snakes. The five had ventured some distance from the camp and were gathering roots.

The Blackfeet killed all five and scalped them.

The old prophet, O-mo-gua, backed by a group of his Snake warriors, addressed Bill Sublette:

"Cut Face, three of my warriors and two women have just been killed by the Siksika. You say that your trappers are fighters, that they are great braves. Now I wish to see them fight, so that I will know your words are true."

Sublette said, "You will see them fight, O-mo-gua. None of my men are cowards. You will see that they are ready to die for their Snake friends."

Sublette addressed the company of trappers. "Let all cowards remain in camp!" he said. "We're going out to whip them Blackfoot bastards and whip them good! We ride in ten minutes. Get your guns and powder and shot and head for the horses. We're going on the warpath!"

More than three hundred trappers were mounted within minutes, certain, under the influence not only of their earlier victory over the *Pieds Noirs* but also of an indeterminate quantity of ingested medicine water, that they were more than a match for the Blackfeet and all the grizzly bears in the mountains as well. Out of the camp they poured, with Bill Sublette at their head. And the warriors of the Snakes were with them.

The Blackfeet, soon alerted, fell back before the combined charge of the trappers and the Snakes. It was a running battle for five miles, until they came to the mouth of Weber Canyon, where the Blackfeet took refuge in a natural stronghold. From this fortress, the *Pieds Noirs* made repeated sallies, enjoying a great advantage over the zealous trappers and Snakes.

A Blackfoot warrior, in proving his bravery, issued out alone, either confident in the strength of his medicine or tempting death. Bill Sublette calmly aimed and fired, breaking the backbone and rendering his victim helpless, the lower body paralyzed as he bled internally, the arms waving about.

"Beckwourth, you come with me," Sublette said. "Let's drag that murdering son of a bitch in and get his scalp before the Blackfeet pull him back."

Sublette and Beckwourth, crouching low, ran forward to where the stricken Indian lay, each grabbing a leg, and began to drag him back to the trees—the Blackfoot all the while attempting to grasp at weeds to prevent his being hauled away. At this moment an Indian sprang over the breastwork and used the back of his gun to deliver a heavy blow to Jim's head. Beckwourth dropped his pepperbox, staggered about, picked up the handgun, and finally ran for the trees, while Sublette fired at the assailant, missed, then knocked him down with his fists and smashed in his face with the pistol butt.

"Damn you, Beckwourth, get your ass out here and help me drag this son of a bitch in! Now we've got two of them!"

Jim shook his head, trying to clear the dizziness, picked up his rifle, and scrambled back out to Sublette.

"What the hell you mean, running? Grab this son of a bitch, I'll get the other one."

They dragged their men to the cover of the trees, one dead and one still alive.

The drunken battle raged on, but after a few hours of fighting, the Ashley medicine water had fairly well worn off, and the men began to get hungry. At this point Sublette requested his Snake allies to destroy all their Blackfeet enemies while the trappers went back to get something to eat. But when the trappers left, the Snakes left too, and the entire group arrived back at the Rendezvous together. The allies ate quickly, got more whiskey to take with them, and returned to the field of battle, only to find that the Blackfeet had unaccountably left.

"Damn strange," Cahuna Smith said. "The bloody bastards have left their dead lying all over the place."

"Ain't that a peculiar thing?" Greenwood said.

"There are many scalps here to be taken," Chief Gray Owl said.

A hundred and seventy-three scalps. Numerous quivers of arrows. War clubs. Battle-axes. Lances. Dead horses.

Eight trappers wounded, but none gone under.

Eleven Snake Indians killed, in addition to the five slain earlier. But none killed in battle was scalped.

The trappers tilted back their cans of mountain whiskey and drank.

General Ashley was leaving for St. Louis. Before going, he addressed the mountain men:

"Mountaineers! My friends! When I first came to the mountains, I came as a poor man. You men, through your efforts, have provided me with an independent fortune. If I can manage ordinary good judgment, I will never want for anything. For this, I am indebted to you, all of you. Many of you have served with me personally, as my companions. We have sat around many fires together. For your faithful and devoted services, I wish you to accept my deepest thanks. I will forever remember you and the times we have spent together. My friends, my companions, I am now about to leave you, to take up a different type of life at my home in St. Louis. When any of you come to St. Louis, you must come to visit me, and we will talk over the dangers we have endured together. I will most willingly share my hospitality with you. But now I must say goodbye to the toils and the hardships of the Rocky Mountains. Farewell, mountaineers and friends! May God bless each of you. I wish shining times for you. And it is my profound hope that each of you is able to hang on to his hair. Goodbye."

Jim Beckwourth walked over to where General Ashley was standing and stepped up to him to shake hands.

"Jim," said Ashley. "I meant to tell you—Major Biddle's bear was alive and well when I left St. Louis. He's had a big cage built for it, and the animal is quite the curiosity of the town."

"Goodbye, General Ashley. The mountains won't be the same without you."

"The mountains are the mountains," Ashley said. "They don't need any particular man. They just need men—men like you. I like brave men, Jim, and you know that. But I want you to think about this. You take more chances than you need to. Sometimes such men lose their hair, and I'd like to think of you living to a ripe old age—at least to forty. Be careful of yourself, and pay attention to your health. And above all, learn caution. When you come to St. Louis, you must come to see me. I'll help you in any way that I can. Goodbye, James Beckwourth."

"Goodbye, General," Jim said. He wanted to say more, but suddenly his mind was blank.

As the General left camp, the air was filled with cheers from the entire crowd. A few then watched as Ashley's party rode away, but most of the men returned to the entertainments of Rendezvous.

Now it was Smith, Jackson, and Sublette. And rumor had it that Jed Smith intended to return to California. To walk back to California, if that was what was required.

He had to pick up his men.

Davy Jackson and Bill Sublette split their forces, with Sublette's men marching up country to the land of the Flat Heads, on the Snake River, where they discovered that peace had been declared between the Flat Heads and the Blackfeet. The trappers were delighted with the news, for now more time could be devoted to trapping and less to fighting, and the take of plew would be great.

The trappers spent the remainder of the summer at their leisure, hunting, gambling, lying, making love to their Indian women, and trading. The cold weather of autumn would soon be upon them, and the harvest of beaver would begin.

"Jim," Le Blueux said, "if you think you can stand being out of the bed with Light in the Trees long enough, I show you the biggest teets a child ever sucked on, such *tetons. Mon Dieu,* I tell you they are beautiful ones."

Beckwourth looked up. He was relacing his possibles sack.

"What's on your mind, Pierre? I can tell that something's up."

"Ah Jim, me I think the problem is to get something *down.* You go into the tipi so early these nights, you have no time to speak with your friends."

Baptiste stood behind Pierre, smiling broadly.

Le Blueux continued: "Now perhaps if you would share with your friends *un peu,* we would not so much be thinking of going up into *les montagnes* where the *grossecorne* sport and the mountain goats dance and where the wildflowers they bloom even now."

"Big tits? The Teton Range, over by Jackson's Hole?"

"C'est ça, that is the very place. You *et moi et Baptiste."*

"I tell you what. Baptiste can stay here. Someone will have to service Light in the Trees while we're gone. What do you say?" He raised an eyebrow and turned to La Jeunesse.

"Me, I wish to go to the mountains also. I wish to be a squaw man only for an hour at a time, for otherwise I would die of having no sleep, *alors!"*

"All right," Jim said. "Sounds perfect to me. I guess I'd better tend to Light in the Trees *good* tonight, so it will last while I'm gone. You know how insatiable these women are."

"Insatiable?" Pierre laughed. "They are not the ones with the stiff pizzle, *mon frère.* They are not the ones."

"Best you listen to the voice of experience, old friend. I tell you they're insatiable."

They rode.

They crossed the mountains rather than following the Snake River upstream around them, dropped down into Jackson's Hole, then upriver to the lake which lay crystalline in the sunlight, little waves lapping at the pebbles along the shore, and the blue sky burning down, the great, pointed mountains rising massive and sheer on the other side.

"*Les tetons,*" Le Blueux gestured. "*Le Dieu de la terre* could suck his fill from these, *c'est vrai!* And He made many of them and did not worry about the other parts of the body. They are beautiful, *non?*"

It was late afternoon, and the huge peaks were partially mirrored in the water. Long shadows drifted across the stillness, and the lower ridges were black with only a hint of blue-green. The great jagged mountains thrust upward, upward, the snows of winter still heavy upon them in places. And the highest spires gleamed a pale red, so thin and yet so intense that Beckwourth imagined he could actually taste the color.

"What's that word the Pawnees use? Saynday. Old Man Coyote. He's the God of this country. Maybe of all the mountains, He created this place last and left it just like it was."

"*Non,*" Baptiste said. "The God, He created this place first and did not have enough energy left for all the other places in the world."

"It do *shine,*" Jim agreed.

"Me, I think we should swim. What do you say, friend of me? Let us swim out and drink from the mountains that dream in the water."

"Better we swim two at a time," Baptiste said. "We have seen no sign of the *Pieds Noirs,* but we must not forget them. I will stay with the horses and rifles as you two swim. Then I will swim also. In any case, it is better."

Beckwourth and Le Blueux stripped off their clothes and dived into the water, laughed as they emerged once more to the surface, and splashed about like young bears, dousing each other with spray, floating on their backs. Baptiste stood by the horses and watched. He laughed as Le Blueux and Beckwourth wrestled in the shallow water.

It was darker now, still light but the shadows were heavier. The points of the Tetons glowed red-silver.

"Pierre!" he shouted. "It is my turn now. You come stand by the horses and let Baptiste swim. *Attendez ici,* I swim clear across the lake!"

Later, in the pale light of a full moon, the three men rode north to the head of the lake and made camp. Soon their small fire was burning brightly, and strips of venison killed that morning were sizzling on spits over the open flame. Somewhere back in the canyons a wolf was howling.

"Ah Jim!" Le Blueux said. "Look what Pierre has found in his saddlebag—*la bouteille!* It is a night to drink, not so? Here, my friends, you will each drink first, for it is your first time to see these mountains of God."

The bottle was passed.

Le Blueux's mind seemed to drift away after he had sipped from the bottle of Ashley's Special. A long silence followed.

"You hear something?" Jim asked.

Le Blueux looked up, started to smile, and then didn't. "It is nothing," he said.

"Come on, old hoss, what is it?"

"Is that I am thinking of time. I am thinking of Ashley. And I am thinking I will have to leave the mountains in a few more years. You see my beard, Jim? It is *gris*. And it is only the mountains, they say, that live forever. The men, they grow old. The mountains stay always young. *Ciel!* I go swimming, and I breathe like an old buffalo."

"*Mon Pierre,*" Baptiste said. "It was told to me that you were born with a beard of gray."

"Perhaps is so," Le Blueux said, brightening now. "In any case,

Le Blueux, he will probably die here in these mountains, *je crois que oui*, for is no other place in the world that will have him."

"Ain't no other place in the world a child would ever want to be, if he was thinking right," Beckwourth said.

"Not too many years and the settlers come. Just like always before. Once there were no Whitemen in all of America—no cities, no roads, just the animals and the Indian people. But we come and we move always to the west. There be cities here in the Rocky Mountains, I tell you that. And it will not be good, *zut!*"

They had been gone for two weeks. When they returned, Beckwourth found his tipi empty.

"Saw ye ride in," Black Harris said. "Don't know how to say this, but I guess I'm the one to say it. A bunch of the squaws went out to pick berries and got took by a party of *Pieds Noirs*. I'm sorry, Jimmy, dammit I am. No way I can make it easier. Cahuna wanted me to do the tellin' since he has trouble talkin' about things."

Beckwourth steeled himself, anticipated what it was.

"They captured Light in the Trees?"

"Not that easy," Harris said. "Here's the whole thing, straight out. The Injuns raped 'em I guess and then killed 'em and cut off their heads. Cahuna and me, we thought we heard screams way up the canyon, so we rode up there. The *Pieds Noirs* heard us coming, and they lit out quick. We just got a glimpse of the murderin' bastards. Then we rode over and found the bodies. We brought 'em in and buried 'em just outside the camp. Cahuna carved a wood cross and put her name on it."

Cahuna Smith, standing behind Black Harris, stared fixedly at the ground.

Beckwourth picked up an axe and drove it into the trunk of a young tree.

"My God, no. . . ."

"I'm sorry, Jim," Cahuna said softly. "This child is. I knowed you was real fond of that little squaw. Such a pretty one, too."

Beckwourth sat down, tossed off his beaver cap, and ran his fingers through his hair.

"Christ, I shouldn't have gone off," he said, his face contorted with grief and anger, the big shoulders shuddering, the fingers wrung tightly together. "Oh my God . . ." he said, shaking his head back and forth, something deep inside him still attempting to deny the thing that could not be denied.

Emptiness inside. No—fists in his guts, fists pounding out from his insides, claws tearing at him.

"If you'd been here," Harris said, "wouldn't have been no different. Things just happen, that's all. Always will, as long as there's Blackfeet."

"As long as there's Injuns and Whitemen and Niggers like us, you mean."

Harris nodded twice.

"Guess that's so, Jimmy. But things just happen, and we ain't never ready for 'em when they do."

"That's so, Jim," Cahuna said. "It's so, just like Moses says."

Black Harris tried to think of some words that would help, but his mind went blank for a long moment. It didn't seem like there were any words, but finally he said, "They's lots of Injun gals, if you want to get you another. . . ."

Beckwourth looked into Harris' eyes, then at Smith, who was still staring at the ground. Was it possible that they simply did not understand? Or maybe they understood too well. Maybe they'd been in the mountains so long that individual deaths no longer mattered to them. Or maybe it was because they realized that regret accomplished nothing. One had to worry about the living, just that, in order to stay alive. Just the way things were. And the mountains didn't care.

He yanked the axe from the tree and then gave the slim trunk a stunning blow, the axe leaping from his hand at the point of impact, spinning through the air, and striking the rocks off to one side.

"We got some coffee on, Jim," Cahuna Smith said after a moment. "You go on over with Moses. I'll get Pierre and Baptiste."

And so Jim Beckwourth's one-man war against the Blackfeet was begun. The anger seethed through him, and he knew that he wanted to kill. He would probably never find the Indians who raped, murdered, and mutilated Light in the Trees, and he knew it. But he could take his revenge against the entire Nation, one at a time, whenever the opportunity presented itself. He held a small advantage, he realized, for the Blackfeet didn't know that he, personally, was at war with them.

"They'll learn about it though, sooner or later. In the long run, my hair will end up hanging from a lodge-pole, but not until I've sent a few hundred of the bastards off to the Spirit World."

It was an insane idea, but the longer he thought about it, the more compelling the idea was: a clearly-defined enemy, an object for his rage, a focus for the violence within him. What was this thing within human nature that could so casually destroy the innocent beauty of a Light in the Trees? Was it crouched there, in his own blood as well? If so, he would use it against itself, even if it meant his own death. Whatever it was, it was human. It was called *Pieds Noirs*. A grizzly mauled a man like Hugh Glass and left him for dead, but that was different. Only the human willfully inflicted humiliation and pain and death—some deformed thing inside the human brain.

Call it *Pieds Noirs*.

The Indians believed in medicine. What was his own medicine? Was it powerful enough to accomplish the task he had set for himself? He had ridden through the lines of the Blackfeet and had emerged all but unscathed. He had done it not once but several times. Already he had numerous scalps to his credit. Perhaps he simply *couldn't* be killed by them. If that were true, then perhaps his driving urge was not completely insane. He would become an avenging angel.

Small groups of Blackfeet came into camp, were interested in trading. He was friendly with them, quickly picked up the rudiments of their language—got so he could converse with them fairly well. And when Bill Sublette began to consider opening a post among the Blackfeet, Beckwourth suggested that he should be the one to run it.

"You think they don't remember about the day in the willows? Christ, Beckwourth, they'd have your hair dangling from a lodge pole in no time. They don't forget. I need someone who's on good terms with them. A hell of a lot can depend on this, if we can get their trust."

"With the Blackfeet," Jim said, "or with any of the Injuns for that matter, the greater the brave, the more respect they've got. If I'm the one they figure has been best at fighting with them, then I'm the one that would have the best chance of making this thing succeed."

Sublette fiddled with the ring on his finger, then got up to get some rum.

"You drinking, Jim?"

"Never turn down a free one, as my daddy said."

"Maybe you've got a point. Let me think this thing over. They don't know it was your squaw they killed, do they?"

"No way they could know."

"You think you can keep your hair on up there?"

Beckwourth took Cahuna Smith and Baptiste La Jeunesse with him.

Le Blueux said, "Remember, if you do not come back, Old Pierre, he has no friends left in the world."

"Just an old, gray-bearded French coon with no friends?"

"It is true, c'est vrai."

"In that case, we'll make her back. Hell, we ain't going to be up there but a month."

"We make the company rich, us!" Baptiste laughed.

Cahuna said nothing, pulled on his moustache.

They rode north. The Blackfeet, having asked for the post and having been told of their coming, greeted them with great enthusiasm. Within some minutes, however, Beckwourth knew they had recognized him.

"If there's trouble," he thought, "it'll come now. Better for it to come now than later."

As-as-to, the head chief of the Blackfeet, approached him.

"You are Beck-wourth?" he said.

"You are As-as-to, the great chief of the Siksikas."

"I am As-as-to. You have killed some of my warriors, maybe."

"I am the one who rode through your lines on the day of the willows."

"There were two of you that day. Where is the other?"

"He is not here. I came alone. You have asked for a trading post, and Sublette has sent me to give you one."

As-as-to stared at Beckwourth. Finally the chief of the Siksikas spoke: "It is good. You are safe as long as you trade with us. No harm will come to you. That is my word."

"As-as-to is a great chief."

"The other one's name is Jarvey," As-as-to said. "Also Calhoun." Then he turned and walked away.

Baptiste and Cahuna had stood silent as Beckwourth and As-as-to spoke. Now Cahuna mumbled to Beckwourth, "That son of a bitch knows too much. We're goin' to be walking on eggs around here."

WIFE WITH NO EARS

The Antelope People are very wise. They know where to find water, even though they sometimes live where a man might die of thirst. These antelopes love the high, dry prairies, great barren ridges, near-deserts, even badlands. Some Whitemen believe that the antelope live without drinking, but this is foolishness, for all animals must drink in order to live. Wherever antelope are found, they are always in splendid condition. However parched the land may be, the antelope find water, for their noses are keen. Antelope find hidden springs or pools of rainwater that are caught in stone. If a man is in such country and cannot find water, he should watch to see where the antelope go. He should do nothing to frighten the Antelope People: they will show him where to drink.

The trading post thrived. Notwithstanding a few difficult moments, the three trappers were soon accepted fixtures within the community of the Blackfeet. The fur trade proceeded briskly, as the Indians exchanged their plew and buffalo robes for the usual run of foofuraw and vermilion, assorted trinkets and baubles, knives and needles, powder and shot, medicine water, and scarlet and yellow cloth.

After about a week As-as-to came to Beckwourth. Behind him stood an attractive girl who was clothed in the white leather of the mountain sheep, the front of her dress decorated in design work of porcupine quills and red glass beads.

"Beck-wourth needs a wife," As-as-to said. "This is my daughter, Young Owl. I named her that because even as a young child she had great wide eyes. She is your wife, Beck-wourth." With this short speech, and not waiting for Jim's consent to the arrangement, As-as-to motioned for Young Owl to enter the trapper's lodge.

Beckwourth was taken quite by surprise. What did the gesture mean? The daughter of the chief to be his squaw? But he maintained his composure, his face betraying no emotion, and he spoke as though he had been waiting all along for As-as-to to bring Young Owl to him.

"I give thanks to Heavy Shield," he said, rendering the chief's name into English.

"She will be a good wife," As-as-to said. "The warrior Beckwourth needs such a wife."

After the chief had departed, Jim spoke to Cahuna Smith: "What in hell do I do now? That girl's in the tipi, waiting."

"Guess you better bed her," Cahuna said.

"Me, I wonder why he has done this thing." Baptiste was looking back at the tipi, his brow furrowed.

"You think he knows about that, too?" Jim asked.

Cahuna frowned. "Light in the Trees? Damned if I know. Makes sense though, don't it? Means he's paying you back."

Baptiste squatted down and idly stabbed at the dirt with his knife. "Me, I think this Heavy Shield is a very smart Indian. *Enfant de garce,* he finds out many things. Be glad when we can leave, *mon frère.*"

A few days later a party of Blackfeet warriors returned, bringing with them the scalps of three Whitemen. Beckwourth's blood boiled with suppressed anger.

"It may be they were our friends," Baptiste said. *"Mais non,* one of them is not gray and thin in the middle."

"Murdering bastards. Best we just ignore the whole thing, hard as it is."

"Yes," said Cahuna. "Hold onto our tempers if we want to hang onto our hair."

A scalp dance was held that night, and there was great rejoicing.

Young Owl came to Beckwourth with the information that her people were glad with the dance and that she, too, wished to dance.

"Those scalps belonged to my people. If you are my wife, you must not dance."

Young Owl turned and went out through the lodge entrance.

Jim stayed in the tipi, but Baptiste and Cahuna walked over to observe the dancing. When they returned, Beckwourth criticized them: "You had no business out there, either of you. Them's our own people!"

"Run cool, Hoss," Cahuna replied. "Our job here's to fit in so's we can trade for furs. Couldn't do no harm to look."

"Jim," Baptiste said. "Young Owl, she is out there dancing. She is very good dancer."

A flood of anger washed over Beckwourth. Without thinking, he grabbed his battle axe, strode to the ring of dancers, and shouldered his way through. He saw Young Owl and came up from behind the gyrating girl. He grabbed her by the hair and jerked her backward, then struck her a blow with the battle axe. The flat of the blade bounced off the girl's head, bounced hard, and Young Owl dropped immediately to the ground, as if dead. Beckwourth proceeded to drag his wife through the crowd of stunned Blackfeet and Flat Heads, deposited her in a heap by a clump of willow bushes.

The drums ceased, and the Indians were quiet, as if not comprehending, for the moment, what had happened. Then a ripple of angry voices. Jim did not look back at them but rather walked slowly and deliberately to his lodge.

"It'll come now," he thought.

He could hear the whisper of an axe as it arced from the firelit circle and into the shadowed area where he walked. He waited for the impact between his shoulderblades.

So, his temper had gotten the better of him at last. His anger cooled quickly, was replaced by a dull fear. Just a few more steps to the tipi. He could hear the increasingly angry voices behind him. Would they fall upon him now? Overpower him and throw him into the spiraling flames of the big fire? Somewhere down deep, a voice was saying, "It wasn't her fault. She's not the one. She wasn't the one. She didn't kill Light in the Trees. The men did it, the same men who are going to burn you alive."

The axe did not strike, was never hurled.

Baptiste had been watching from the lodge entrance. He reached out now and pulled Jim inside.

"*Sacré Dieu!* What have you done? These *Pieds Noirs,* they will cut us to pieces!"

"Had no right to lose my temper that way," Beckwourth blurted out. "This child's a damned fool. I've got you boys into it, good. Son of a bitch! Grab the Hawkens—cut through the back of the lodge. Maybe we can get out to the horses before the *Pieds Noirs* have had time to realize what's happened."

"Ain't no use," Cahuna said. "A dozen of 'em went that way as soon as you kilt your squaw. Best we can do now is take a few red devils with us, then light the powder keg and go up with 'em."

"*Oui,*" Baptiste said. "It is better than the torture, *c'est vrai.*"

As the three trappers grabbed for their weapons, they heard the shouts from the milling throng by the fire:

"Kill them! Kill them! Kill them!"

But then As-as-to's voice:

"Stop! Hold, warriors, and listen to your chief!"

The noise subsided.

"Young Owl was my daughter. I have lost a daughter, and her brothers have lost a sister. But you have lost nothing. She was the trader's wife—for I gave her to him. When your wives disobey your commands, you kill them, for that is your right. It has always been this way among the Blackfeet. Young Owl disobeyed her husband, for she told me that Beck-wourth had forbidden her to dance. She disobeyed. She had no ears. He did as you all would have done, and we must not harm him or kill him, for I promised the chief of the trappers that if he would send me a trader, I would protect that man and return him unharmed. He must not be harmed while he is here. Later, if you should meet him in battle, then you may kill him. We must trade with these Whitemen. They sell us powder, and we must have powder to fight the Absarokas, for they have guns and powder. They trade with the Whitemen. If we kill this Beck-wourth, when I have given my word to the chief of the trappers that I would protect him, he will not send us any more traders. They have eaten our meat and drunk of our water. They have smoked the tobacco with us. When they have sold their goods, we will let them return in peace. These are my words."

Among the numerous Flat Heads present at this time was their well-known warrior, Bad Arm, who now spoke loudly to As-as-to: "Chief of the Blackfeet! You are yourself again, and you have spoken well. The Flat Heads and the Blackfeet are at peace. If you had killed these traders, my people would have fought with the Black-feet once more. We would have raised the battle axes again, for these are our Whites, and the Flat Heads would have avenged their deaths!"

Cahuna Smith, rifle in hand, turned to Beckwourth.

"Jim, can ye make out what the devils are sayin'? I understood the Flat Head—what did the other'n say?"

"I think they've decided not to kill us," Beckwourth answered.

"*Mon Dieu!* Maybe we live to see the sun rise again. Jim, you must not kill any more Blackfeet women, even if they are your wives!"

As-as-to then made another long harangue, after which the camp became quiet. Then the scalp dance was continued, and the laughing and shouting once more drifted on the night air.

About an hour later, As-as-to came to Beckwourth's tipi.

"You did right," he said. "Young Owl had no sense. She had no ears. She did not listen to what her husband told her. You had a right to kill her. I say this even though she was my own daughter. But I have another daughter, who is younger than she was. I give her to you in place of the bad one, for then you will know that I wish to trade honestly."

He presented Small Nose and left without further words.

Cahuna Smith and Baptiste La Jeunesse entered the lodge as soon as Heavy Shield had left—were astonished to find another Blackfoot girl standing there, her eyes downcast.

"What in hell you got here?"

"Another wife," Beckwourth answered, "to replace the bad one. Heavy Shield has just given me his other daughter."

"*Belle-mère de Dieu!*" Baptiste sputtered. "Jim Beckwourth, you lead the charmed life. I do not believe this!"

"Don't rub on that charm too hard," Cahuna said. "Gold paint'll come right off."

"Well," Jim thought when the others had left, "let's see what kind of a package I've got here. She's a damned sight prettier, anyhow."

He gently drew the girl down upon his bedroll and touched her face with his hands.

"I will not hurt you," he said in the language of the Blackfeet. "I will make love to you, but I will not hurt you."

Small Nose did not resist.

During the night, as Jim and Small Nose were sleeping, a noise in the dark tipi. Jim was awake immediately, but he did not move—except to reach over slowly for his pistol. It was, he imagined, one of the sons of As-as-to, intending to take his revenge despite the words of his father. Jim pointed the pistol at the figure crawling through the tipi entrance, snapped back the hammer, and said in an even voice, "Stop where you are or I'll kill you."

What he heard next was a sobbing, mumbled, incoherent voice— a woman's voice.

"Who are you?" Jim asked.

"Me. Young Owl. I want to sleep with my husband."

Beckwourth's mind raced: she wasn't dead! Stunned, but not dead.

"Go away!" he said. "I have a new wife now. Your sister is my wife, and she has ears. I do not want you any more."

He could hear her choked sobs in the darkness. He wondered if she might not begin howling at any moment.

Small Nose was awake.

"Let her come to bed with us, my husband. She will be good now, and you will have two wives. She is my sister. Please let her come to bed with us. If you do not wish to have two wives, then I will go away, for she was your wife before I was."

"Young Owl, are your ears open?"

"Yes. I will listen now, I promise I will listen. My husband's heart was crying because of the scalps of his people, and I should have heard his words. I will do what you wish."

Small Nose had crawled across Beckwourth's body in order to reach her sister, whom she then held in her arms as a child.

"Come to bed, my sister, and we will both make our husband glad. He is a strong man and needs two of us."

"I used to have a way with the ladies before old Jim here whipped me in that fist fight. Think he musta took my medicine. I'm asking for a rematch soon's we get back with Billy Sublette." Cahuna Smith grinned broadly, pulling at his moustache.

"I never take rematches," Jim said. "I was lucky once, and I know it. But I'd be happy to trade you two Blackfoot wives for a plug and a half of tobacco. Lord, they exhaust a man."

Baptiste was stabbing the earth with his knife again.

"Le Jeunesse, what you doing there?" Smith asked. "You always said you weren't no squaw man."

"Me, I'm not. But *alors,* two wives, I don't know if it's right."

"When among the Blackfeet, do as the Blackfeet do," Jim said. "For otherwise, a child's subject to lose his hair."

Baptiste put the knife away. "Maybe I'll talk to that little one, *la jeune fille* who is always asking the questions. Is because I do not think like an Indian, *peut-être.*"

Because of all that had happened, the three trappers found it necessary to proceed with great care for the next few days. They were more generous than usual in their trading, and the Blackfeet seemed to sense this immediate advantage, with the result that trade was more brisk than usual. The trappers bought a few horses they did not actually need, and a first-rate beaver skin brought as much as four butcher knives and a plug of tobacco.

The days went on, and the supply of trade goods diminished. At last Beckwourth informed Heavy Shield that it was time for them to return to Sublette's camp.

"Will you take your wives with you?" As-as-to asked.

Beckwourth had been worried as to how this might turn out, but before he could answer, As-as-to continued:

"It is better that they should stay here, for sometimes bad things happen to Indian women who marry trappers. When they are lonely because their men are away, they do not have their own people to turn to. I would not wish anything to happen to my daughters. It is better if you give them presents when you leave and then send other presents later. Is this what you will do?"

"I think Heavy Shield speaks wisely."

"Good. Beck-wourth is a brave man. I know that you have killed many of my braves. I could have let my warriors kill you when you struck Young Owl with your battle axe."

"Heavy Shield is very generous. I will make him a present of the beautiful black horse with the white nose."

"I do not wish to own the black horse, for that is Beck-wourth's horse. It may have bad habits, for a Whiteman does not ride like a Siksika. I want the Nez Perce horse."

"I will give him to you. He's a very fine horse. I bought him from the Snake Indians."

"Yes. It is the same horse they stole from me in the time of the new grass. It will be good to have him again."

"Then I must give you another horse also. You can pick any one you want from my string."

As-as-to laughed and mumbled something that Beckwourth could not catch. Then he continued: "You have been my son-in-law. Now I must tell you something. If we should meet in battle, I will try to kill you, but not now. I have given my word to Sub-lette. I will tell you something. Some of my braves will try to kill you after you have left our village. You should ride fast, for that way you will be able to tell Sub-lette that the Blackfeet are pleased with the trading. Tell him As-as-to wishes to have a trading post for the Siksikas again when a year has passed. I will keep Beck-wourth's wives for him one year. If you return to trade with us, your wives will warm your tipi. If you do not return, I will tell them that you are dead, and they will each find another husband. These are my words."

Beckwourth told Smith and La Jeunesse of Heavy Shield's advice, and the three men followed it most carefully, setting out on a forced march which, in good fashion, put distance between themselves and the Blackfeet. On the second day, they fell in with a group of Flat Heads who had been at the village of the Blackfeet and who had apparently been following a parallel course.

"We did not think it would be good to join you until today," they said. No other explanation was needed. And so they continued, escorted now by the friendly Flat Heads, no longer feeling it necessary to hurry, and arrived at Sublette's camp two days later.

The trading venture had, all things considered, been a huge success and the crisp autumn air of the mountain country sang in the trees, while at night the coyotes wailed at the moon. Just after dawn the year's first frost shone a dazzling white on the tall yellow grasses along the stream.

"You were a damn, pig-headed fool!" Sublette shouted. "Procedure, man, you've got to learn procedure! That little temper fit might have gotten all three of you killed."

"Calm down, Bill. Everything turned out all right, didn't it? And I sure don't like folks shouting at me."

Sublette looked down at Beckwourth's hand. Jim's thumb was stuck under his belt, right next to the knife. Bill Sublette looked up quickly and turned casually to the chest where he kept his supply of whiskey.

"All right. I admit it. You men did a good job up there. We've made a fine profit, and it looks like the trade avenue with the Blackfeet is open now. But damn it, Jim, you've got to use your head.

Sometimes one thing is more important than another. Anyhow, they weren't our people. Britishers, maybe, who knows? Sorry I shouted. Guess I need to keep hold of my own temper as much as you do. Here—have a drink with me?"

Pierre Le Blueux was overjoyed that his friends were back safely, their hair intact.

"This coon wasn't sure we was goin' to make it there for a spell," Cahuna Smith laughed. "But we did 'er, though."

"That story, it is *incroyable!* You amaze me. *Enfant de Dieu!* My beard, it gets white just listening."

Later Le Blueux spoke to Beckwourth alone.

"Friend of me, why did you wish to go to the villages of the Siksika? Pierre, he would like to know this."

"Well," said Beckwourth, "before you can hunt down a bad bear, you've got to know what its habits are."

"*C'est ça,* it is as I thought. *Mais non,* did you learn who it was that killed Light in the Trees?"

"It doesn't matter," Jim said. "The Blackfeet killed her."

Bridger was fishing. He'd had no luck yet this morning, but if a man didn't have patience, he didn't have anything. The fish were patient, but the trouble with fish was that they weren't very smart. Occasionally there'd be a big old trout that would elude a man's best efforts, and probably that sort of fish was smarter than the others, for otherwise he'd never have lived so long. But mostly fish weren't very smart. What it came down to was—either they were hungry or they weren't. If the fish were biting, and if a man knew what he was doing, then he'd catch fish. It was a simple matter, mostly, like all things in the mountains. It took a man awhile to learn what the rules were and to learn that it was the nature of the rules to change every now and then—or that there was more than one set. After that it was just a matter of following them and every once in awhile changing the rules to suit oneself. Fish always followed the same rules. An Injun did too, mostly. Whitemen, sometimes they didn't.

More than one child's bones were bleaching out on the prairie because they hadn't figured out when to follow the rules and when not to.

The autumn sunlight was warm and good, and Bridger stared into the clear, gliding water of the stream, uncoiling itself out through the meadow here, just before emptying into the river. The aspens were beginning to turn toward gold, and the beaver had been good. The buffalo had been running in little groups, thick as pear seeds, and so there was plenty of meat to be had. A man couldn't expect things to keep going this way forever, of course, because that was one of the rules. . . .

Something bothering the horses.

Bridger reached automatically for the Hawken, wedged his willow pole between some exposed roots, and moved deftly up the bank.

"Damn this coon's soul, would you look at that!"

Blackfeet. They were approaching the small herd of horses, and in broad daylight. He made a quick count—about forty of them, all on foot. They'd have left their own horses up over the ridge, naturally enough.

"Bold as brass, in the middle of the day. Them boys ain't following the rules. Hell, a man can see our camp from here."

Bridger took careful aim at the closest of the Blackfeet and fired. The rifle smoke drifted up through the aspens, and he began to reload immediately.

An Indian lay kicking in the dry grass. The Blackfeet were on a dead run now, driving the horses before them. A couple had managed to get mounted, but the horses were rearing up.

Bridger walked over to where his own horse was tethered, and as he did so, looked back at his fish line. A small disturbance in the water. A fish had taken bait.

"Don't pull my line loose, now," Gabe cautioned as he turned his horse about and clapped his heels to the animal's side.

A number of trappers were riding hard from the camp. He shouted to them, and the chase was on. Beckwourth was at the head of the group, on that big black horse of his, the one with the white blaze mark.

"Old Jim and that horse," Bridger thought, "they just sort of reverse each other's colors."

The main body of horses went one way and the Blackfeet another, into some dry brush up against a rocky bluff. The Indians who were mounted made their escape. The others took cover and began to return the trappers' rifle fire. A few arrows flashed out from the brush but fell short of where the trappers had pulled up.

"What have you got here, Gabe?"

Beckwourth was grinning.

"They was trying to make off with our horses in broad daylight. Stupid Injuns, I'm thinking."

"Blackfeet? Yeah, I can see that they are. I think maybe they've gotten themselves into a bit of trouble."

Pierre Le Blueux dismounted and moved off quietly to the right, crouching low and moving from one bit of cover to the next. The other men began to move up, firing as they did so.

First they saw the smoke.

Le Blueux had ignited the dry grass, and the wind was driving the flames in a broadening circle ahead and into the thick brush where the Blackfeet had taken cover.

"Me, I think they come out soon," Le Pointe said.

"Going to get warm over there real quick," Bridger agreed. He had taken cover behind a slab of rock and was reloading his rifle. "You know, Old Le Blueux's about the smoothest fella I've ever run into. He just sees a problem and right away solves it is all. He don't only think like an Injun, he's more Injun than they are."

As expected, the Blackfeet charged out, only to be met by a burst of rifle fire. Beckwourth sighted down, fired, and laughed—reloaded quickly.

"That's one," he said.

The Siksikas drew back, leaving six of their fellows either dead or dying. The pattern was repeated several times, and twice more Beckwourth's shots did their work. Finally the dry brush had become a swirling inferno, and no further arrows or rifle shots came from the area at the base of the bluff.

But Sublette, who had now arrived, was not pleased.

"Damn it, Beckwourth, did you light that fire? You men weren't using your heads, none of you. Bridger, why didn't you stop the thing? All you had to do was shoot a couple and save the horses. They'd have gotten the idea. Now there's what? Forty some dead Blackfeet? As-as-to can't ignore it now. Maybe you've lit a bigger bonfire than we can put out. It's taken years to get on the right side of these *Pieds Noirs,* and this may just have queered the whole damn thing."

"Beckwourth, he did not light the fire," Le Blueux said. "Old Pierre, he did it."

"Calm down, Billy," Bridger said. "In two weeks we wouldn't have had nary a horse if we hadn't stopped 'em, you know that as well as me. You don't just saunter in and run off a man's horses that way."

Sublette's temper had begun to cool.

"Did you have to kill 'em all?" he asked.

"It's like with a mule," Bridger answered. "First you have to get the brute's attention. Well, we got their attention now. Besides, three, four got away. That's how many managed to steal a horse. Looked to me like all four of them was your horses, Bill."

Bridger scratched his forehead and spat at a little pine tree. He missed and thought about spitting again.

Then he remembered the fish.

RUN FROM
THE BIG BELLIES

Accursed Mad River, the Snake, it rises below the Tetons in Jackson's Hole and runs south, rounds the range, swings north, then south again and west, turns slowly to the north once more and cuts through the Big Canyon, Hell's Canyon, Seven Devils Range on one side, the Wallowas on the other, is joined by the River of No Return, the Salmon, then runs westward, completes its thousand mile course, and mingles with the River of the Nez Perce, the Great River of the West, the Columbia. In the Big Canyon one finds rocks covered with petroglyphs, very old, for the place has been sacred for a long while. The lower slopes of this canyon are mostly grass-covered, interspersed with sheer walls of stone. Far up the trees begin, the walls rise high to the mountains, and the river rushes madly through the unending rapids. In springtime, mists blow through the gorge, and in lush pockets beside the water, many wildflowers, ferns, and ponderosa pines grow, protected and hidden away from the savage winds of the lateral mountains.

The trappers found a large group of buffalo and, by effecting a surround, managed to bring down a good supply of meat. It would keep them busy for awhile, skinning and butchering and curing the flesh.

As the men were so occupied, six horses turned up missing—two of Beckwourth's string and four belonging to the Swiss, Aleck Alexander. There was no sign of Indians about, so the horses must simply have strayed off.

"We must not allow *die pferde* to run away," Alexander said. "They will run clear to St. Louis. *Es ist kein gut.*"

"Two of them are mine and four are yours. So I'll chase them the first third of the way, Aleck, and you can chase them the last two thirds. That seems fair to me."

"*Mein Herr Beckwourth,* we must both go."

The two men agreed to rejoin the company at the Buttes, and so saying, they moved off in search of their horses. The weather was cold now, though there had been as yet no snow—just frost that melted each day by noon. The men took along a few traps, so as not to lose their time completely. Once they had regained the horses, they would trap their way back.

They followed the tracks. Then there were other hoof marks. Jim drew up on his reins.

"Look at that, Aleck. I'm thinking our horses went out and stole themselves some Indians."

"*Versteh nicht*—was you mean?"

"Our strays got rounded up."

"*Ja,* Jim, I see."

They continued to follow where the tracks led but did not say much now. They kept their eyes open, their hearing attuned to the slightest of noises. What had begun as a minor problem of a few runaway horses had taken on considerably greater dimensions. More tracks came in from the east.

"How many you think they are? *Ich denke an mich, nicht gut. Sollte geh' wieder?*"

"Speak English, damn it. How long you lived with Whitemen, anyhow?"

"I have lived my whole *leben mit* Whitemen. You think *die Schweizer* come from *ein* foreign country. This here *ist das* foreign land. *Vereinigten Staaten mensch*—they have never *gelernt zu sprechen* civilized language."

"You've probably got a point there. Let's hole up here for the night—think about this thing for awhile. It could be the Blackfeet, drawing their parties together for some reason or another. No way of telling. What do you figure, Aleck? About thirty of them ahead of us?"

"*Ja,* about thirty. *Dreissig oder so.* I think we should forget about *die pferde.*"

"Maybe you're right. This child sure don't want to get tangled up with the *Pieds Noirs* just now—not with just two of us. How many Blackfeet have you killed, *mein freund?*"

"I have killed two—one the *andere* day at the *feuer* and one *letzte jahr.*"

"Well, let's take cover. Wait until it gets dark—then we build a *small* fire back over behind those rocks, and we'll cook up a chunk of mountain cow."

They waited for full darkness and then half-cooked their meat over the flames of twigs that were fed, a handful at a time, into the fire. A cold wind was spilling down from the mountains, but they buried the fire with sand and took turns sleeping.

It was a long night.

First a thin grayness until the eastward peaks began to glint with a soft rose color. Bluejays began to call and then were silent for a few moments before breaking once again into their raucous cries. Jim had been dozing, but now he was fully awake. His fist tightened around the barrel of his rifle. He listened. Heard nothing.

Alexander was still sleeping. Jim rose, stepped around the boulders, and relieved himself.

"Jesus, God, and all the Saints!" he whispered. "Would you look at that?"

Between two and three hundred Indians. They were moving on horseback, at a good pace, across the meadow below. Beckwourth crouched down—these were not Blackfeet. *Gros Ventre.* Big Bellies.

Aleck Alexander was awake now, rifle in hand.

"*Was tun wir nun?*"

"Lay low. And pray to God they don't see us. And hold onto our hair."

The convoy of *Gros Ventres* had nearly passed by when one of the

127

trappers' horses whinnied. Four Indians at the tail of the group pulled about and rode slowly in the direction of the boulders. Then they spread out.

"We ride for it," Jim said. "We ride like hell."

The two men mounted and charged from behind the rocks, passing easily through the four Indians, and rode madly in the direction from which they had come the day before. The Big Bellies howled and gave pursuit.

Over his shoulder Jim could see that more of the Big Bellies had joined the chase.

"*Ach,* they gain on us!"

"Keep riding, Aleck, and pray for rain!"

"*Was für,* rain? *Du bist* Goddamn fool! *Regnete,* shit!"

"That's more like it!" Jim shouted back. "You people got any gods in Switzerland?"

Alexander, head low to his horse's neck, ignored the remark.

"If you do, then just pray to one of them mountain demons that we don't meet up with a whole troupe of *Gros Ventres,* heading this way."

Rifle fire behind them. Out of range. The two men held low in the saddle and continued to urge their mounts forward.

Beckwourth's black stallion was beginning to lather.

"Keep going, fella, this ain't quitting time yet!"

Gros Ventres ahead, perhaps twenty or so.

Jim swung his horse up a side canyon and Alexander followed. The hooves clattered over bare rock as the horses splashed through a big creek, then through the soft grass beyond. The Big Bellies momentarily gained on them, and shots whizzed past. Then the Indians were also fording the stream, and the distance between them lengthened once more.

"Going to dead end," Alexander shouted. "*Wenig—tot!*"

"We don't have much choice of roads! Keep low!"

Within a mile the meadow along the stream narrowed down, then vanished into a cover of yellow pine.

"Up the hill! If the horses can make it, we got to get up that ridge!"

The Indians were closing rapidly now. The trappers cursed their horses, urged them upward. The summit was close—another drainage beyond—a chance to make distance—move northward. But no time to think. Time to act on instinct alone. Flight. Desperate.

A ball struck Alexander's horse in the shoulder, and the animal collapsed, hurling its rider forward, rifle still in hand. Alexander leaped to his feet, grasped Beckwourth's arm, and was hoisted onto the horse. But with a double weight, the animal stumbled heavily, straining toward the summit of the ridge.

Made it.

Over the crest and down, the horse leaping logs and bursting through the underbrush. Reckless descent.

"Don't bust a leg!" Jim shouted into the horse's ear. "Don't bust a Goddamn leg!"

Where the hillside benched out into a small clearing, Beckwourth pulled the black stallion to a halt. The animal's eyes were wide, its nostrils flared, and its muzzle and chest lathered badly.

"Aleck, head for the creek. I'll send the horse on down the hill, and I'll go the other way. They'll follow the horse.

"I cannot run well. Take *das pferd und* save yourself."

"No use, Goddamn it! Do what I say—get down to the creek and hide. Hide good. Stay until they've gone."

Beckwourth struck the horse with the flat of his knife, and the big black plunged off, down the mountainside and through the trees.

"Get moving, Aleck! We can still save our hair!"

He was running now. Not too fast. Saving his strength.

He followed a deer trail along the mountainside, not down, not up—just running, making as little noise as possible.

Had the Big Bellies left their horses and come over the ridge on foot? Had they stayed with the horses—perhaps there was another way around? He would have heard the crashing of brush if the horses had come over the ridge, the way he had come. They were either on foot, or they knew some low spot in the mountain and would come up the next creek canyon—in any case, they would pick up the trail of the black.

If his stallion had run away from the Big Bellies, his chances of escape were much better. He would have a good lead on the Indians before they overtook the riderless animal. Then they would double back. But if the horse had run toward them, they would know quickly. They'd be coming up the mountain from the drainage below him. It could be one thing, it could be the other.

It made no difference.

Had Aleck found a hiding place down in some rocks? An opening large enough for a man to crawl into, an opening under a fractured-off slab of basalt? Did Aleck have the patience to wait it out? Jim had heard no rifle fire.

Meaningless to think about it.

Why keep running? He might be running directly toward them. He might be running away from them.

Beckwourth stopped, leaned on his rifle, waited for his breathing to slow. He listened intently. There were no crashing sounds in the brush. No voices. He stared down at the meadows below but could see nothing, nothing that mattered. Three deer browsing in the grass near the stream. The water glittering in the early morning sunlight. No one had passed that way or the deer would have been gone.

Where was his horse? It would have gone to the water, stopped. But he could not see it. Had it fallen, broken a leg after all, broken its neck in its mad plunge down the mountainside?

He saw it then, partially hidden among the willows beside the stream. Its nose was in the water.

"Drink easy, fella," Jim whispered. "Don't drink too fast. It's all right. You'll be an Indian pony now for awhile."

Walk. Stay under cover. Listen. Every sense aware. Feel.

He came around the head of a sharp ravine and angled across the other side, moved out toward a point of rock which overlooked the valley. He would be able to see them from here.

He caught two forms moving across the rim just above him. Big Bellies. Close. Looking for him.

They stood on the point, gazed out over the valley. They must have crossed the ridge to the south. Beckwourth scanned the upper slope for some sign of the horses. He could see nothing.

On foot, then.

He could pick off one of them, easily. But the report would be heard. Even if he could get the second one, nothing would be gained. He pulled back into a small hollow in the rocks and waited.

Loose pebbles trickling over the edge of the rim. They were coming his way. They were climbing down and would pass just below him. He readied the pistol. If they saw him, two quick shots and then he would run. Around the rim, keep heading south. He would have to encircle the entire drainage or most of it, swing to the east, and then move north once more.

The two braves passed below him. Then one stopped and motioned to the other. Had Beckwourth dropped something in the loose rocks, and they had seen it? What were they saying? He could not hear the whispered voices.

He fired the pepperbox twice and heard the reports whip out among the trees and wing their way over the valley and echo.

He was running again.

The brush lashed at his face. Something sent him hurtling down a dry ravine, and he lay momentarily stunned, was unable to find his rifle. Then he had it once more, crawled up the far bank, and moved onward, found a good deer trail and lengthened his stride.

But the trail vanished.

He moved through rocks and dense brush until the land opened before him. He paused and crouched to rest, his breath coming in spasms, the air searing his lungs, the blood pounding in his eyes.

"Calm," he thought. "Calm, calm, calm."

Four *Gros Ventres* riding toward him, gesturing to each other, speaking excitedly. They hadn't seen him. He drew back. Waited. Watched.

The four Indians split up. Two rode upslope. A third proceeded a few feet further and then also disappeared into the trees. The fourth rode along at the edge of the trees, studying the hillside above. He was coming directly toward Beckwourth.

The others were out of sight.

Knife.

The Indian passed within a few feet of where Beckwourth crouched. He could smell the sweat of the horse. The horse sensed him, jerked its head. Jim leaped upon the Gros Ventre and plunged his knife into the Indian's back as they fell. Two more slashes and his enemy lay inert upon the ground.

"Calm. Stay calm. Get your Hawken. It's more important even than the horse."

But the pinto moved only a few paces and stood, as if waiting. In a moment he was mounted again, drummed his heels into the horse's sides, and set out at a gallop across the open ground, angling eastward. He hung low to the animal's back.

Where were the others? Was it conceivable that just a few had followed him over the mountain? Not unless something of far greater importance had lain ahead of them. Where was the main body of Big Bellies going? Toward Crow country? Toward Davy Jackson's camp?

Then they were riding parallel to him, coming across now, closing the distance that lay between them. He pulled his horse to the east, toward the cover of forest.

He sighted on a low spot in the ridge and rode toward that.

His mount was not a fast one. An Indian on a Nez Perce horse was gaining ground rapidly, far out ahead of the others. Jim heard the snap of the rifle. Even before the sound registered upon him, a bloody streak had appeared along his horse's neck. The animal plunged away from the pain despite all that Beckwourth could do to retain control. Turned upslope.

The Big Belly was attempting to reload. Jim fired over the crook of his arm. A bad shot. The Nez Perce horse reared, hurling its rider backward, and collapsed to its knees. Jim watched the Indian bounce like a tumbleweed in the wind.

Then he too was flung free of his mount. He landed on some low brush. The horse slid on its side, the neck bent back. The rifle was gone. No time to find it.

Run.

He moved up the hillside, heading now for a ragged rim where the horses could not follow. He drove himself onward, hurtled his body upward, gasping, until he had reached the top. He lunged over and sucked for breath. His vision was blurred. He pressed at his eyeballs with the tips of his fingers. He shook his head, peered back over the rim. Four shots left in the pistol, but he couldn't take time to reload. He tore off his coat and leggings. He was going to have to run. He couldn't be encumbered by clothing. He cinched the belt, the knife and the pistol on it, around his middle. Then he sucked for air again.

They had left their mounts. They were climbing toward him. He slid down, scrambled along the ridge for perhaps fifty feet, drew up again behind some matted brush. They were close to the summit now and within range. He fired carefully, four times. Three clean hits. A fourth was shot in the arm and scrambled for cover. There were three more. And far below, crossing the open spaces, a cluster of mounted *Gros Ventres.*

"Like fleas on an old dog, Goddamn them!"

He turned and ran, making great leaps down the mountainside.

How much time had passed? The sun was still low in the morning sky. Two hours, no more. Two hours ago he and Aleck had been sleeping.

He needed water. He had to have water.

But the wild sensation of leaping down the mountain brought with it a terrific feeling of strength. He knew it was partly illusion. It made no difference. The nature of the game was coming clear. *All he had to do was to outrun thirty Big Bellies, whether they had horses or not.*

He was strong. He could do it. He was Jim Beckwourth. None of the Blackfeet—no, and none of their ragged cousins the *Gros Ventres* neither—could kill him. Had he not once ridden right through them, as though they were children playing games? Had he not struck the daughter of As-as-to in front of the warriors of an entire village and left her for dead? He was Jim Beckwourth, by God!

133

"Iggerant dunghead! Cain't you tell blind luck from what's real?"

He didn't know whose voice it was. The voice was inside his head.

He leaped a fallen log and plunged downward, oblivious to everything except the motion of his body. The clear, free motion of his body.

"Hooraw, coon! Yuh made that 'un."

The Big Bellies were on foot now. They'd stay on foot. They would rise to his challenge. They'd try to run him down, but he'd exhaust them—he'd lie back, if he had to, and ambush them.

"Goes against nature, coon. It's a pride thing with them Injuns. They kin outrun any child in the mountains."

They hadn't outrun John Colter. Beckwourth had heard the story many times. Colter, barefoot and bareass naked, had outrun them, had gotten away. And they weren't going to outrun Jim Beckwourth, either.

"Them's doin's, right enough. That nigger could run. Yup, that's *some* now."

Keep the mind clear. Don't listen to voices. Run. Keep alert. Absorb every sight, every sound. Outrun them. Out think them.

He threw himself down beside the stream and drank, forced himself to drink slowly. Grabbed a handful of chokecherries, spat out the seeds. Drank again. Breathed deeply. Listened.

Noises up the mountainside? How many of them? Just two? Couldn't be more than two.

He moved out, purposely running downstream, and was glad when the canyon opened out into wide meadows. He was breathing easily now, he was stretching out, his body was rising to the challenge. He stayed to the open ground, but near enough to the trees so that he could veer and take to the cover of the forest again at any moment if he had to. And he deliberately did not look back for what seemed a long while.

He slowed for a moment, not stopping, and looked behind him. He could see them, two of them. They were still coming. But he had opened up a lead, a big lead. Perhaps as much as half a mile.

They were expecting him to run himself out. They were loping, just keeping him in sight. *They knew he couldn't last.*

They were wrong.

He could outrun any Indian on earth.

"Wagh! They goin' to catch you and stake you out on an anthill. Mebbe they skin you alive first."

He fell into a rhythm. He counted two hundred strides and looked back. Two hundred and then look back. Two hundred.

They had stopped!

He stopped. He stood there and watched them. He had done it, would they give up? He breathed in deeply, his chest heaving. The sweat was pouring over his face. His arms glistened with sweat. A little cloud of gnats swarmed about his mouth.

The two Indians were moving once more.

"Iggerant dunghead, yuh shouldn't have stopped. Just encouraged 'em."

He ran.

Eased up somewhat, but the dance continued. Two hundred strides, look back. Two hundred strides, look back.

The muscles in his legs were loose and easy, but his feet were nearly numb. They didn't hurt, they were just numb. Two hundred and look back, two hundred. . . .

For the first time he consciously wondered how far it was to Sublette's camp. The land was familiar now. He had ridden over these same hills, across these same meadows. The streams all flowed down into Blackfoot River. The camp was on the bend, where the river turned westward for forty miles before joining the Snake. Another ten miles and he was subject to meet a party of trappers. Twenty miles to the big bend, to the camp.

How far had he come?

The sun was now straight overhead, behind him.

He was running in the noontime of the world. Four ducks broke from the still water of a beaver pond, and a bunch of prairie hens scattered before him. The sunlight was hot on his shoulders, and a hawk or an eagle sailed against the cobalt sky to the north. Two hundred strides and look back, two hundred. . . .

He could no longer see his pursuers. Were they hiding among the tall clumps of dry grass? Were they face down in the stream, drinking? He stopped, stared back to the south. Tried to detect even the slightest hint of motion in the grass. But he could see no one. He scanned the low ridge, noted the narrow saddle. He tried to envision the entire lay of the land—did the stream make a bend just ahead? Had his pursuers cut across to the next drainage, thinking to ambush him downstream, past the point where the two creeks joined?

He moved on, loping now, two hundred strides, look back, two hundred strides.

Wolves.

They had brought down an antelope. Beckwourth ran directly toward them, waved his arms, shouted at the big gray dogs. They snarled, bared their teeth, and then grudgingly backed off. Jim slashed open the belly of the antelope with his knife, cut out the liver, chewed off a mouthful, carried the remainder with him, and ran onward. Two hundred strides, look back. . . .

The wolves had returned to their kill.

He moved up into the trees to the east of the long valley, slowed to a walk, and climbed on toward the crest of the ridge. If he had estimated the time properly, the Indians would have been through the low westward saddle before he had begun his move in the other direction. They could not have seen him. He was safe, at least for a while.

He dropped down over the crest and slanted along the ridgeside. His thirst was tremendous, but he wanted to remain on the high ground. His mouth was filled with dried saliva, and it was difficult to breathe. He remembered the trick of sucking on a smooth stone, but there were no smooth stones—only jagged fragments of basalt. He tore off a cluster of pine needles and chewed on them. It helped.

Beckwourth found a hole in the rocks and climbed into it,

sat with his back against the stone. The sweat was dripping down
his face. His eyes stung. Only then he realized the ammunition for
the pistol had been in his abandoned possibles sack.

A huge white bear loomed up before him. Its eyes were red, and
blood dripped from its jaws. Then it faded and was replaced by the
image of himself and Pierre Le Blueux swimming in a lake at the
foot of great, towering mountains. Then this, too, faded.

He needed water. He needed it bad. But he had to rest first. He
had to get some of his strength back.

How long had he slept? He scrambled out of the hole in the
rocks. He looked about: the sun was dropping westward. An hour,
then, or longer?

"Iggerant dunghead! You want them savages to be eatin' your
brains, do ye?"

"They had time to come back looking for me," he thought.
"Goddamn it, Goddamn it!"

The sensation of thirst was dull fire in his throat. He felt dry and
old, and his muscles had stiffened. At first he could hardly move.
He would walk slowly for awhile and then begin to lengthen out.
No point in running. No point in running when a man doesn't
know whether he's running away from trouble or toward it. No
point at all.

He noted the clumps of red willow halfway down the mountain—
willows and aspens in a shallow draw. He moved toward them.

No running water, but the earth was wet amidst clumbs of sweet
grass. He dug with his knife until finally a small puddle, with ago-
nizing slowness, began to form. He sucked up a mouthful of the
muddy water and swallowed. Waited for the puddle to form once
more. Drank again. Drank and waited and drank and waited. And
then he ate the remainder of the antelope's liver, the meat caked
with grit and dried almost black. He could chew the meat, could
swallow again. And then he drank once more.

He walked northward.

He stayed away from the forks of the stream, keeping to the high ground, and continued several miles in this fashion before crossing back over to the open land along the stream. The sun was now low to the horizon, and the clouds to the west were beginning to glow with a faint redness. A wind was flowing from the south, a strangely warm wind for this time of year, a wind that promised rain within the next couple of days. And the sun went down in a halo of blood.

He was almost to Sublette's camp. He looked forward to the campfires and sizzling strips of meat. His hunger was great, and he thought back to the teal duck, a long time back now, and the little fire he had built there on the wind-swept, freezing prairies of the Platte River. His strength seemed to increase as he approached.

Had Aleck made it? They would ride out early to find him.

But there was no odor of smoke in the air—or only a very faint trace of an odor. And the horses were gone. The camp was empty! Gone.

No. A single fire on the far side of the giant cottonwoods. Perhaps Baptiste had waited for him?

"Butthead coon! Ain't no Whiteman in his right mind stays behind by hisself in a deserted camp. You forget about Injuns? Dumbass, you never learn. Them Big Bellies is still goin' to stretch your hide to a tree."

Beckwourth moved downwind to the smoke, came up through the aspens and the willow brush.

Just one tipi. A single Indian squatting by the fire. Two dogs lying on the ground next to him.

A wave of relief but also of disappointment passed over him. This was not one of his pursuers. The dogs. Another Indian in the tipi perhaps? Only one horse, tied short to a cottonwood branch.

The odor of cooking meat came to him. He was maddened with the smell. A Flat Head? Blackfoot? *Gros Ventre?* In the darkness he could not discern any telltale markings on the tipi. An outcast, some Poordevil just wandering about? A squaw inside? That would account for the lodge. Were other horses tethered somewhere near?

One of the dogs barked, then growled softly, and lay still. The

Indian was suddenly alert, strode over to his horse, passed out of Beckwourth's vision.

Sublette and the men must have moved on, perhaps downriver to the confluence with the Snake.

"Another forty fucking miles," Jim thought with some degree of despair. Every bone and tendon in his body seemed to hum with an aching numbness. He did not have the strength to go on.

"Hooraw, coon. I knew you'd give out. See what I mean about them Injuns?"

"I can make it."

"Naw, you cain't. This'n is coming 'round behind you right now. Goin' to put a knife in your back and lift your ha'r slicker'n buffalo shit."

Jim slipped across, still downwind, in the direction of the horse. He needed that horse.

One of the dogs stretched, got up, ambled over to the tipi, and lifted its leg. Then it stared in the direction the Indian had gone, wagged its tail, and walked back to the fire to investigate the cooking meat. It sniffed at the roasting strips of buffalo, wagged its tail once more, and with a sigh flopped down in the dirt. It slept. They were both sleeping.

He moved silently through the willows.

A form. No more than ten feet in front of him.

The knife spun through the short interval of space and inserted itself between the Indian's shoulders. He let out a fearful cry and collapsed where he stood.

The dogs were barking now, that high bark they use when the wolves are howling.

Beckwourth scalped his man, a Blackfoot, and moved cautiously to the tipi, having first taken the Indian's battle axe from the crumpled body. He cut through the rear of the tipi and looked inside. A squaw was huddled against one side. Even in the darkness, her eyes, perhaps catching some reflected firelight, glowed with fear.

"I will not hurt you," Jim said. "Where is the rifle?"

The woman did not speak.

He stepped into the tipi, knife ready, and looked about. Perhaps they didn't have a gun.

The woman cowered down, as if expecting to be killed. Beckwourth passed her by, through the entrance way, and walked to the fire. He grabbed for a strip of meat. It burned his hand. He skewered the meat with his knife and ran to the horse.

He still had forty miles to ride.

But what if Sublette had not moved on to the Snake River? What if they had gone south, looked for him and Alexander?

"Now that don't sound like Billy Sublette, do it? Wake up and piss, you dim-witted nigger."

Beckwourth rode toward the Snake River. He could make it by morning. He would sleep later.

He chewed a mouthful of buffalo meat and thought about Aleck Alexander. He'd started to like that square-shouldered little Swiss-German.

"Shame he don't talk better, though," Jim mused.

9

ALEXANDER'S WOMAN

To fill the meat bag: with a feast ready, the cook yelled out, "Hyar's the doins— freeze into it, boys!" Normal consumption for each man (when the hunting was good) was eight or nine pounds of meat per day. The buffalo intestines (boudins) were roasted and then gulped down without chewing. It was starve and feast, but when there was plenty, Lord how they ate. Like the Indians, they were content with buffalo meat alone, though a roast of beaver tail or elk or deer or antelope or a good fat dog or lynx gave variety. Some roots also, and wild plums and berries as the season provided. Coffee and flour and salt and molasses from the settlements, but buffalo was all they needed. If a man could always live on such didins, it was sure he would never die.

Three days later Aleck Alexander had made it, on foot, downriver to Sublette's camp. He still had his possibles sack, his shot pouch, his powderhorn, and his Hawken. He also had two dogs and a squaw, with whom Aleck attempted to converse in a dialect of German-Blackfoot. He was in high spirits and demanded to know where Herr Beckwourth was, inasmuch as Jim had not come out to greet him.

"He save *mein leben, sagte mir,* go hide *ins steinen. Wieder* he kills *den mann des meines* squaw. *Er ist* great *mann, verstehen sie? Er ist hierher, nicht wahr?"*

"Understand better if you talked Blackfoot," Sublette said. "How you ever expect anyone to know what you're saying, anyhow?"

"Beckwourth?" Alexander persisted. *"Ist* he here?"

"Yeah, he's here. Don't worry about that nigger. He's got more lives than a dozen wildcats. He's in his lodge, getting well."

Aleck Alexander walked quickly to Beckwourth's tipi, his Blackfoot woman following closely behind him, her eyes down, avoiding the stares of the assembled trappers.

Pierre Le Blueux nudged La Jeunesse as Alexander walked by.

"Me, I think sometimes things work out, *non?*"

"That's a good lookin' squaw," Red Beard Miller said. "Wonder if the little German can hang onto her?"

"There's plenty of squaws," Cahuna Smith snorted. "I like the looks of that one."

"Friend of me," Le Blueux said, "is because you think like a Whiteman. Better for you to leave her alone, that one."

"What's this, Frenchy? You figuring to guard the little German's bed for 'im?"

Le Blueux lit his pipe and gazed off thoughtfully before he spoke:

"Pierre, he has never killed a man except in self-defense—*à l'exception de un peu nombre, alors.*"

"You wanta tell me what that means, Le Blueux?"

"It means leave her alone, *c'est ça.*"

Beckwourth had arrived just after daybreak, told Bill Sublette what had happened, ate, and fell into an exhausted sleep. For the next two days he ran a fever and was often out of his head. Smith, La Jeunesse, Harris and Le Blueux took turns watching over him, applying cool cloths to his head, and waiting. He was still not well when Alexander came in, but the arrival of the Swiss brought his spirits up, and he talked with Aleck for a few minutes and also addressed the woman in her own language.

By noon he was up and about, limping badly, and quite obviously still in a great deal of discomfort.

"What I want to know," Bill Sublette said, "is why you two didn't turn the hell around when you realized the Indians had probably rounded up the horses. You're making a name for yourself, Jim, but you're doing it at the expense of the whole operation. If the Big

Bellies don't know you're one of my men, they'll damned soon fig-
ure it out. Some reason or other they don't like having their braves
killed by trappers, any more than the *Pieds Noirs* do."

"Bill, you've got to understand this. We absolutely didn't start
the thing. Christ, that would have been madness. Aleck and I would
have been more than happy just to let 'em ride on by. I'll tell you for
sure, I didn't much enjoy the whole business."

Sublette stared at Beckwourth and then grinned.

"Aw hell, Jim, I'm just glad you made it back more or less in one
piece. Let's go have a drink, what do you say?"

"Captain Bill, I'd like that just fine."

Sublette turned and yelled:

"Hey, Bridger! Gabe! Come on over to my lodge—I want to show
you something."

The trappers moved east along the Snake River to the falls. Here
they set up an early winter camp. They were in the heart of Black-
foot country, but with the good graces of As-as-to, the men were
able to go out in small groups to ply the streams of the mountains to
the south, streams which contained plentiful beaver.

Beckwourth prepared his traps early one morning, thinking to
break away from the group to which he was attached. He mounted
his horse and headed upstream toward the Caribou Mountains, inas-
much as this area had not yet been worked. Crossing two divides, he
came down into a delightful little meadow hemmed in by a dark
forest of fir and spruce. The air was cold, but midwinter sun had
melted out the light snow that had carpeted the area for the preced-
ing two weeks. All in all, it was one of those days when everything
seemed newly created and untouched. He rode easily down into the
meadow, whistling softly to himself.

Astoundingly enough, the Indian neither heard nor saw him, for
the Blackfoot had his robe spread out on the ground, apparently over
an anthill that was active in the warm sunlight, and was in the pro-
cess of freeing himself from lice. He pursued his business intently
and did not look up.

"Well now," Jim thought, "here's a rifle, a bow, a quiver full of arrows, a good robe, and a scalp."

He considered Sublette's words of caution, but he considered also that it was possible to hide the body so that the Blackfeet might never know what had happened to the man. He'd just disappear. And Beckwourth thought also of Light in the Trees and of his general distaste for Blackfoot warriors.

"No reason I should let this one live," he thought as he fired his rifle. The Blackfoot fell as though pole-axed. Beckwourth rode over to where the Indian lay and dismounted. He took not only the scalp but also the head, tying two locks of the long hair together, and hanging the head over the horn of his saddle. He thrust the body into a hollow log and continued his ride along the creek. Within a mile he had been able to shoot four beaver.

It was a good day.

The Blackfeet descended upon Sublette's camp—perhaps as many as two thousand warriors. The encampment lay in the bend of the river, a horseshoe, with the lodges pitched at the entrance, or across the neck of land, creating a barricade, but one that was highly susceptible to rifle fire and flaming arrows.

As-as-to did not call for a parley. He simply sent in small groups of warriors, charging furiously. The trappers held them off with rifle fire, and after the first advance, removed the women and children to the area behind the lodges.

Sublette was talking about a countercharge, but Bridger said, "Le Blueux thinks that's a bad idea, Bill, and so do I. We can hold them off, and they're takin' casualties, takin' them *bad*. Let's just swallow 'em as they come."

They came.

Twice they drove the brigade of trappers back from the line of tipis, yet they were unable to overrun the lodges themselves, so accurate and deadly was the rifle fire. And when the Blackfeet drew very near, Sublette's half-breeds employed their bows and arrows, for these men were as skillful as the Indians themselves.

Ultimately the charges of the Blackfeet began to slacken, and it appeared that they meant to set up a state of siege. They were settling in for the night, with the trappers cut off from escape.

"Beckwourth," Sublette said. "This one's yours. Take fifty men. When it's dark you can slip out on horseback, one at a time, close by the river on the far side. There's a narrow trail, a sandbar all along the water's edge. You know where I mean? Okay, I want you to slip out and reassemble in the stand of timber over there, to the southeast. When you see a flaming arrow go up, you come down on them from the rear. Make as much noise as possible. Shoot off your pistols. Yell like hell. The whole purpose is to get them going both ways, get them as confused as possible. When they start milling around, we'll come out in full force. The odds ain't good, but they could burn us out quick as hell if they took a notion to do it."

"They's some reason why they haven't done it already," Bridger said. "Maybe this whole thing's a fancy way of teaching us a lesson—just showing us that we're at As-as-to's mercy."

"Whatever it is," Sublette replied, "I'm not questioning it. I'm acting on it. The murdering bastards could as well be intending to starve us to death—or wait until we're starving, and then burn us. If we wait them out, the Flat Heads will start to thinking that they're at peace with the Blackfeet, and then we'll discover we've got three hundred hostiles in our own camp. They'd slit our throats while we was sleeping. Maybe that's what old As-as-to's thinking about. No sense losing too many of our own men if you can get some in-house Flat Heads to do the job for you. Either we drive 'em off, I'm thinking, or all of our hair is likely to end up hanging from lodge-poles."

"The main thing, Bill," Bridger said, "is not to get riled. We can handle this. A man's just got to use his head."

"That's what I *am* doing, Gabe. Now let's get this show on the road. Beckwourth, them Blackfeet think you've got medicine over 'em. If you don't believe that yourself, you'd best start right now. You've got to pull this thing off. Get you some men that'll stick with you and get to moving."

"I don't want Miller, I know that much," Jim thought. He

addressed the men and explained Sublette's plan. Bridger was standing beside him as he spoke.

Bridger looked out over the faces. He stared at one man in particular, then looked at Beckwourth. He walked over to Red Beard and whispered something to him. The two of them then walked to where Bill Sublette was standing.

"I got a little addition to the plan, Bill," he said. "I want a fire started in that dry brush just to the north. That'll give us two diversions. And I think this man's about the only one we could trust it to. He'll have to swim across to the far side—and he's a powerful swimmer."

"Sounds good," Sublette said. "All right, Red Beard, do what Bridger says. We got to act now or we'll all end up skinned and tanned and pressed into packs."

Le Blueux, La Jeunesse, Harris, Cahuna Smith, and Aleck Alexander rode with Beckwourth. There were forty-four men in all. Sublette had said fifty, but when Jim called for volunteers, forty-three stepped forward, and he chose not to press the matter. Forty-four: that was enough, that was plenty. And with more luck than skill, they all managed, one at a time, to slip out along the river.

They assembled in the woods to the south and waited. Waited for a flaming arrow to arch up into the night sky.

But Sublette and Bridger were waiting for another kind of fire. The minutes crawled on, like little snakes, early in the morning.

"Maybe he ain't made it, Gabe. Maybe they've gotten him. When he came out of the water on the far side maybe. You sure that guy's a good swimmer? Don't think I've ever seen him swim at all."

"Me neither," Bridger said. "But I figured if he wasn't, he'd tell us about it. Give him a few more minutes. I'll tell you what that coon is, though—he's a hell of a hand with a knife. You remember that big Frenchman he cut up at the Mandan villages, three, four years back?"

"I remember it. Real workmanlike. He'll handle himself just fine if he once gets out of the water. Took his scalp, too, didn't he? Without even thinking about 'er. Is that it over there?"

Fire. It was starting slowly. Even if it didn't get big, it would serve as a distraction. Then the flames went up in a white flare.

"Guess he managed to keep that powder dry," Bridger said. "Put our arrow way up there, Bill. I figure we're ready to do some fighting."

Suddenly the men were riding, and gunfire made little blue lines out into the darkness. The Blackfeet were instantly thrown into confusion, and the battle lasted only a few minutes. Tin cans of turpentine with flaming rag fuses were hurled into the midst of the milling Blackfeet, and tongues of fire ran on the ground or burst up into balls of flame. As-as-to's voice could be heard over the melee, and as rapidly as the Blackfeet could mount their horses, they streamed southward.

The dead and wounded were not scalped, under orders from Bill Sublette. The wounded were moved to one area, and the bodies of the dead to another. Those taken prisoner were released, to bear word to As-as-to that the heart of the Long Knife Sublette was good, and that Sublette did not bear any malice toward his Blackfeet brothers.

But more than a hundred and fifty Indians lay dead outside of Sublette's camp. And another fifty were seriously wounded and lay, untended through the night, close by their fallen kinsmen.

The trappers had lost sixteen men, many of them from the ranks of the half-breeds, who had plied the Blackfeet with arrows at close range. Le Jeunesse had taken an arrow through the bicep of his left arm, and Beckwourth had received a superficial wound in the leg, the result of a pistol fired inaccurately at close range. Even Bill Sublette was wearing a bandage, the tip of the small finger of his left hand had been taken off by a rifle ball.

Among the dead was Aleck Alexander.

The snows came. For days the sky seemed an exhaustless fountain of whiteness. Winds drove up the valley of the Snake River, and the snow drifted in against tree and lodge alike. It kept coming until the entrance ways to many of the tipis would have been buried except for the human traffic coming and going. The gathering of fuel alone became a major task each day until some of the lodges were simply abandoned. Trappers and Flat Heads alike crowded together, utilizing fewer of the lodges and thereby greatly reducing the necessity for wood-gathering ventures. Food supplies also diminished, despite the best efforts of the hunters to supply game. And still the snows continued.

When the skies finally cleared, they cleared over a world that had been transformed into a white desert—long, rolling waves of whiteness that reached back away from the camp toward the dazzling mountains beyond.

Then the winds descended from the northeast, and the drifts of snow were cut into fantastic sculptures of ice. The temperatures dropped, and a terrible cold hung over the river. Some of the horses froze to death where they stood and were butchered with axes. All of the smaller streams were frozen solid, and great sheets of ice formed along the Snake.

They found small birds dead on the icy snow, and these were eaten. Fish were found frozen solid in the little river, and these were chopped out. The men moved slowly, dressed heavily in furs, crossed the land on snowshoes. The moisture in their breath iced instantly on their beards. Several of the men lost fingers and toes from frostbite, and one morning Jarvey was found frozen to death in the woods close by the camp. He had gone out to gather fuel the afternoon previous and had not returned. No explanations as to what had happened were offered. His death was accepted, as were the cold and the hunger.

Bridger found a group of twenty deer, frozen in place where they had huddled together. The men fashioned a travois and went with axes to hew out this unexpected food supply. Eroquey's hand became stuck to the blade of his axe, so they had to build a fire and hold the bit of the axe against the flames until the trapper's hand came loose.

Jarvey's body had been interred in a snowbank near the Snake River. A week later it was discovered that the body had been removed. One assumed that the Flat Heads had dined on human flesh, but no questions were asked.

When the rains finally came, the snow grew sodden and gray. Great slabs of rotten ice broke off and slid down into the Snake. The snow was vanishing, and within a week the big river had become a foaming, raging monster of muddy, swirling brown water.

"We got to get out of here, " Sublette told Bridger. "Whether it's the curse of the *Pieds Noirs* or the curse of Smith, Jackson, and Sublette, I don't know. But if we ain't freezing to death, we're going to get washed away by that Goddamn Snake River. A Hudson's Bay trapper told me once he'd seen the Snake when it was twenty miles wide."

"Naw, I don't believe that, Bill. Ain't enough water in the whole mountains to cause a flood like that."

"Like hell there ain't."

"Bet he was talking about the Columbia, down where it runs into the Pacific. I've heard that it's that wide."

"Don't make any difference what he was talking about. We've got to get out of here as soon as we can move."

"Ain't arguing the point," Bridger said.

The winter broke, and the new grass was starting up all over the floors of the valleys. Sublette's camp moved south, toward Bear Lake. The Flat Heads accompanied them part of the way and then turned off to the west. Sublette's men continued, trapping as they went, and finally reached the big bend of the Bear River.

Jim Bridger stared into the rushing waters, high with the spring meltout, and remembered. He had wondered where the river went, had built himself a bullboat so he could find out. He'd taken to the river. He thought of the white water, himself alone in the boat, the stream thrashing onward, taking him into its groove, shooting him forward so that all he could do was hang on, hang on and even pray some. He could still feel the green energy of the water against the hide of the bullboat. That was a *shining* time, though he hadn't thought so at the moment. A man alone on a wild green river, being hurled downward, no way to control it, spinning through rapids, the river doing its best to hurl him out of his little craft. And then came the *real* white water, the river foaming madly, simply flinging itself down through one torrent after another until the bullboat was breaking apart and he was hanging on to the split branches of the frame and promising God that he'd do better in the future and then whooping with joy when he made it.

Where the river had calmed, he had poled in to the bank and set about repairing his craft. Far off he could see what looked like a bigass lake, a lake so big it might not be a lake at all. Wagh! It wasn't possible! It couldn't be—the Pacific Ocean? By first light he was back on the river again, easy going now, on down to the mouth. The water of the lake looked different, and it seemed like the bullboat was riding higher in it. He tasted the water. Salt. Salty as hell. So salty a man could no way swallow the stuff. He'd explored the shoreline for a bit, stared far across to the thin haze, low mountains that seemed to be floating there, miles and miles away, almost in another world. Then he headed back, on foot, to find his fellow trappers.

"I might of found the Pacific Ocean," he'd told them casually.

So he made a mistake. A man can get carried away if he's young and full of adventure, full of wanting to see *what's out there.*

"By God, it's still the biggest thing them coons ever saw. The Great Salt Lake. Bridger's Lake. Well, some call it Weaver's Lake. It don't matter none."

A long while back now. No, not really very long at all. Three or four years was all.

A man can change *some* in three or four years.

"Yep," he thought. "Just toss in a few grizzlies, a few pissed off Injuns, a few starvin' times, a few shinin' times, and a couple of hell-raisin' times at Rendezvous. . . ."

Aleck Alexander's woman had hacked off a finger and cut her stomach with a knife. She hadn't mourned the loss of her first man, hadn't had time to mourn. She had spent only one day in shock, trying to figure out what she was going to do, alone, and a long way from her people when Al-eck had come along, singing to himself in a language of the Long Knives that sounded different to her than any she had heard before. He had squatted down by the ashes of the campfire and waited, waited for her to come out to him. He had found the body of her man, and so he just waited. And finally she had come out. It didn't seem like he meant to rape her or scalp her, and she knew she was going to need protection, for a while at least. She walked out and stood near him, her eyes down upon the ground. It was her time to wait.

When he spoke, there was a good sound to his voice. He kept talking, just like he thought she understood everything he was saying. Then she looked up and, not knowing what else to do, crossed her wrists over her breast. It was the sign for love. And so he had stood up and walked close to her and put his arms about her in a very gentle way.

Now he was gone. And she lived in her tipi, with the two dogs. The big man, who didn't really look like a Long Knife—the one who had killed her first man—he had brought her into his lodge during the time of the terrible cold, but he had not wanted her to lie down with him. The other man, the one with the gray beard, he had also been gentle with her and had also not wanted her to lie with him. They had fed her and talked to her in the language of her own people. They had petted the dogs and had brought in enough meat so that they were not hungry too often.

Since the trappers had moved to the south, she was back in her own tipi once more. And the two men, the big man and the one with the gray beard, they continued to bring her meat to eat and continued to pet the dogs.

Didn't any of these Long Knives wish to lie with her?

When her people, the Siksikas, had attacked and Al-eck had been killed, she had been fearful that the Long Knives would kill her also. Instead they had brought her presents so that she would not mourn for so long.

Red Beard Miller had been thinking about Alexander's woman. She was a damned fine-looking squaw, even if she had taken off a finger and cut herself up over that little Swiss. It was to be expected. It was the way of Injun women.

"The coon and the Frenchy been taking care of her, but I figure that's all. Think maybe I'll take her some beads and stuff and see what the possibilities are." The thought appealed to him. It was still a while off until Rendezvous, and it would be good to have a squaw in his lodge, at least until then. He might even get to liking it.

"Might at that!" he said aloud.

He went to her and offered the beads and some red cloth, made the sign for lying down together. But she turned, went back into her lodge, and left him standing there by the entrance way, feeling the fool. Nevertheless, he left the gifts. The next day he returned with another assortment of baubles, and this time her eyes met his eyes. She said in English, "Yes, I would like to lift my dress with you." And Miller followed her into the tipi.

Baptiste La Jeunesse had observed the two days' drama, shrugged, and continued scraping his beaver hides. Later he heard the woman's wails and Miller's voice, cursing. He heard the hard, slapping sounds and the whimpers. And he felt anger, unaccountable anger. For there was nothing unusual in what was happening. Some men liked to whip on their women. He had heard of Whitewomen who actually liked it. Indian women too. But he put the hides away, took his rifle, and walked off alone toward a rounded-top mountain. Sometimes a man could think better when he was standing on the top of a mountain. A man couldn't see *humans* then. Or if he could, they were far away and very small, and it didn't matter.

10

RED BEARD'S EAR

"Ye think like an Injun" was a high compliment. And they learned to speak with a strong nasal twang, carefully stressed each syllable, as the Indians did. A man was "child," "hoss," "coon," "nigger." If a man was killed, he was "rubbed out" or "done gone under," and to take a scalp was to "lift ha'r." Reversion to savagery? Philosophy of the mountains was based on uncertainty of survival, for one could live on the plains, in the mountains, on the deserts, only by inuring himself completely to the whims of Isakawuate: men became callous to every danger, destroyed human or animal life without scruple, as freely as they exposed their own lives. Death was commonplace, danger was everywhere. Little mourning for those who went under, little or none. "That nigger's out of luck."

Miller had taken a can of arwerdenty to the tipi and forced Alexander's woman to drink also, not that she was particularly unwilling. But he wanted her drunk and completely without resistance of any sort. It was better that way. And when she did, in fact, resist his rough treatment of her, he backhanded her several times until she cowered away from him. Then he gulped at the whiskey, feeling little bursts of flame in his throat and stomach.

He pulled off her clothes, grabbed her by the hair, and took his pleasure—then lay back on the buffalo robe beside her and fell soundly asleep.

Pain.

The side of his head was on fire. He reached to his face and brought back a hand covered with blood.

His ear was gone.

The lodge was empty. The dogs were not sleeping outside. The red cloth was lying where he had left it. He grabbed it and held it to the side of his head.

"Going to cut off her tits and make 'er eat 'em," he mumbled and withdrew his knife. "Where is the slut?"

Had she fled to Beckwourth's lodge for protection? Well, they both needed killing. It was a good time to take care of matters.

Then he realized the horse was gone, the horse Beckwourth had ridden in on after that supposed run from the Big Bellies. And no dogs, not anywhere in sight.

Alexander's woman had left Sublette's encampment.

Red Beard stumbled over to the river, lay down at the edge, and immersed his head in the icy water.

The pain was sudden and terrific. He gritted his teeth and held his breath as long as he could.

Baptiste La Jeunesse was on his way back to the camp. As he came down through the scrub pines, he saw someone on horseback below him. He stopped, studied the figure. Then he recognized who it was. He set out, down the hillside, his possibles sack bouncing around his neck.

When he neared the woman on horseback, he slowed to a walk and made the gesture of friendship. At first the woman thumped her heels to the horse's sides and started out at a gallop. Then she drew the animal back, turned about, and approached Baptiste.

"What has happened?" Baptiste asked, noting the bruises on her face.

She explained that she had decided to leave. Had decided to return to the Siksikas, if she could find them.

"*Sacré Dieu,* it is a long way, this. In any case, how will you find things to eat?"

She made a gesture of indifference and looked back over her shoulder. There was fear in her eyes.

Baptiste noticed, now for the first time, the blood marks on her deerskin dress. The blood was fresh, he could see that. The woman did not seem to be cut. If it was not her blood, then. . . .

He decided not to ask any more questions. Whatever had happened, he knew that he would hear about it back at camp. There could be no secrets among a small group of trappers.

"Sing to the Coyote as you go," he said, "and take care, *ma soeur.*"

He handed her his rifle, powderhorn, and pouch full of shot.

Beckwourth, La Jeunesse, and Le Blueux together. A powerful sense of kinship among the three. In the mind of Pierre Le Blueux, these two were his sons. Had he not raised them to the life of the Rocky Mountains? And now they were accomplished mountain men, both of them, each having achieved excellence in his own way. Le Blueux pondered the two, the older brother and the younger brother. Quite different men. Baptiste who would never be a leader, for he was quiet by nature, an introspective soul, and strangely gentle for one who had chosen so fierce a life as this one. But loyal, and a fine trapper, excellent shot with a rifle, a man of genuine endurance and real capacity to take hardship. Beckwourth, on the other hand, might well be a leader one day—though he seemed to Pierre to lack the cool judgment of a leader. None could doubt the man's courage, and none could fail to admire him for his great physical strength. An excellent shot and well-skilled with a bow and arrow as well. A deft trapper also, though he seemed more interested in conflict than in taking plew.

Beckwourth's hatred for the Blackfeet, set in motion by the murder of Light in the Trees, had become a consuming one. And yet the Blackfeet were not much different than the other Indian peoples. Perhaps they had a greater sense of what rightly belonged to them. Perhaps it was simply that these *Pieds Noirs* did not really see the Whitemen as human beings. The trappers were, to them, like a plague of encroachment, a threat to their lands and their way of life. They showed no mercy, and they expected none. Seldom, as at the Snake River, would they attack in large groups against any sizable force of trappers. They preferred, as did all the Indian peoples, to incur as few casualties as possible—and so, if they could find a small group of enemies, they would gleefully kill them all. And it was certainly true that they were fond of mutilating and torturing their vic-tims—almost as if some terrible rage lay near their hearts.

The raping and butchering of Light in the Trees, for instance.

Perhaps the Siksikas could see their world ending, could see the buffalo vanished from their lands, could see the deer and the sheep and the antelope grown few. Perhaps they had heard enough of how the Whitemen treated the land, how they fenced it, how they sup-posed they *owned* it, how they built their cities. They sensed the na-ture of the great tide that would, within a few years, sweep over them and destroy them. They lashed out in a bitter and violent anger, attempting to destroy the inevitable force even as they themselves were being destroyed.

Le Blueux could see it coming. For twenty years he had been in the mountains. Oh, a few times he had been back to the settle-ments. But his life was in the mountains, in the wilderness, in the clear, clean beauty of things, of places and animals, of the great birds of the sky, of the infinity of rivers rushing down from the high places, of the canyons and the peaks and the forests where no Whitemen had ever before set foot.

Now he was growing old. How old was he? He would be forty-five this year. He had been Baptiste's age when he had first come to the Rocky Mountains. It was a long time ago. But it was not a long time ago.

Soon, he told himself, he would have to leave the mountains. But why should he leave? If he could not walk or run with the same tireless endurance he once enjoyed, he now possessed a certain wis-dom. He knew the habits of things. He knew the ways of the In-dians. He'd spent whole winters with the Cheyennes and the As-siniboines and the Flat Heads. He had taken several Indian wives and fathered their children. Among the Cheyennes he had a son who would now be, what? Fourteen years old, if he still lived. Perhaps the boy already had a gray beard?

The thought amused Le Blueux, and he laughed aloud.

And there was land to the west, land he had never seen. Jed Smith—already this young man had been to California and had crossed over the great mountains, had walked across a vast desert. How could he, Le Bleux, ever return to Quebec until he had seen these things? And to the north, a world of mountains lay to the north. He had seen some of them, but there were more, many more. He had heard of mountains that were much greater than even the Tetons. He had heard of whole rivers of ice flowing down from those mountains. He had heard of bears even larger than the grizzlies. The land stretched northward to the frozen ocean, a land of huge lakes and broad rivers and endless forests and frozen earth.

Why should he return until he had seen everything? It was natural for a man's beard and hair to become gray. But it was never natural for a man to give up being *who he was.*

"Mon Dieu! The *Pieds Noirs* and the Crows, they do not go away when their hair becomes gray. They live all of their lives here. It is *convenable, enfant de garce!"*

He thought about Long Hair and Rotten Belly, the great chiefs of the Crows. These men were older than he. And these men were very powerful. As-as-to and O-mo-gua, they were both older than he. Two Axe was as old as he.

"Mais oui," he thought "I will stay another twenty years, *peut-être."*

Then he remembered the settlements, the boats along the Big River, the growing cities, and the fenced lands.

He did not like to think of these things.

The river they followed flowed through a steep gorge, the walls studded with outcropped rock. The canyon faces and the stream bottom were thick with brush and young firs. The three men rode along, picking their way, and occasionally stopping to place a trap. They were not thinking of the Blackfeet, for they were well outside their lands: but suddenly the Blackfeet were there, a large group of them, coming up the canyon from below.

"Jim! Baptiste! *Sacré Dieu,* follow Pierre!"

They entered the brush, well aware that the Indians were advancing upon them.

"Looks like we're going to have to make a stand of it," Beckwourth said. "Maybe we better get up that ridge, up into those rocks. They'll play hell driving us out of there."

Le Blueux stared up the canyon wall to the spot Jim indicated. It was perhaps five hundred feet above them.

"We lose our horses," he said.

"Better we lose our horses than our hair. Baptiste, what do you think?"

"Me, I wish to know what Pierre thinks."

Le Blueux led his mount up through the brush tangle, and the others followed.

"Here, in the *buissons*," he said, "they cannot see us."

He had a small bell tied around his horse's neck. He now removed the bell and crept downslope to a large bush, to which he fastened the bell with his lariat and returned to Jim and Baptiste, the other end in his hand.

"*C'est ça,* we will fool them for a while, but I think we will lose our *chevaux* in any case."

The trick worked, for a slight motion of the rope caused the bell to ring. The Blackfeet fired shot after shot at the noise. When a warrior approached and was seen through the bushes, he was met by a rifle ball. Each time this happened, Pierre rang the bell.

"The gunsmoke, she does not rise in the right place!" La Jeunesse whispered.

"*Non,*" said Pierre. "But they are puzzled, I think."

The Blackfeet began to fire at random into the brush, but neither horse nor trapper was hit.

Beckwourth had been staring down into the tangled thicket, but then he glanced at Le Blueux. Pierre was filling his pipe, was lighting it. He seemed as easy and relaxed as if he were safe in camp.

"Pierre, what in hell are you doing?" Jim hissed at the older man.

"Me, I smoke my *tuyau.* A man should not die without smoking his pipe one last time, is it not so? Is a promise I make to my pipe."

"Baptiste, he's crazy! He's gone mountain loco!"

"Pierre," Baptiste pleaded, "this is *incroyable!* Me, I wish to get out of here!"

Two more Blackfeet made the ascent, climbing directly toward the spot where the little bell was ringing. Jim and Baptiste both fired, the Hawkens making nearly a single explosion, and the Blackfeet tumbled back down the canyonside, sliding in the loose shale.

"Pierre, what the hell's the matter with you?"

"Friend of me, is nothing wrong. We need only two shots. You and Baptiste, you shoot twice."

Jim Beckwourth stared at his friend, hardly believing what he heard. Then, in spite of himself, he burst out laughing—a laugh he felt obliged to stifle.

"*Enfant de garce, enfant de garce!*" Baptiste mumbled.

"You now do what Pierre does," Le Blueux said. He proceeded to bind his leggings and moccasins around his head. Beckwourth stifled another burst of laughter but followed suit. La Jeunesse shrugged and did likewise.

"Now we go," Le Blueux said. He moved noiselessly to the edge of the bluff, surveyed the stream bottom, and commenced to slide down the nearly perpendicular rock, the others following. They reached the stream, slid themselves into the water, moved close to the bank, and let the current carry them downstream for nearly a mile, passing, as they did so, directly beneath the large number of Blackfeet, who were still staring up the canyonside and occasionally firing at it.

The three men emerged from the water when they were well out of sight of the Blackfeet and ran across the wide meadow to the cover of forest beyond. They quickly climbed to the crest of the ridge and lay down, gasping for breath. They had lost their horses and guns, but the Blackfeet had lost six or eight warriors.

Le Blueux squinted one eye at his two companions.

"The *Pieds Noirs,* they not only lose some of their braves. *Sacré Dieu,* they also lose the scalps of two young trappers and one old man, *non?*"

Le Blueux untied his leggings. He picked out his pipe and held it up.

"Me, I did not even lose this."

A week following, Beckwourth, La Jeunesse, Cahuna Smith, and Le Blueux were all awakened by gunshots. The four of them had gone out to reconnoitre the various streams in the area and to search for beaver dams. The trip had been uneventful until this. Their hands were instantly upon their rifles, and they scrambled for cover.

But Cahuna Smith had been hit. A small hole had been torn in his coat, and bright red blood was pumping out. He flopped to the ground and rolled over on his back. Beckwourth crawled to his side.

"This coon's been fotched, Jim. Guess we ain't never goin' to have no rematch now. Pierre and Baptiste? They all right? Damn, I sure wanted to make Rendezvous this year. . . ."

He was dead.

It had all happened so quickly. Beckwourth tore open the sheepskin coat and tried to stanch the blood with his hands. But the blood had ceased to flow.

"*Mais non,* he is all right?" Le Blueux asked from behind the tree where he had taken cover.

Beckwourth replaced Cahuna's coat and pressed his eyes closed. Then Jim stood up, stepped into the open, and began firing his pistol at the Blackfeet. He did not so much see his enemies now as he felt them, felt the malign presence of these, the Blackfeet, rattlesnakes, fierce and cunning, the lurking, cruel presence that ran in the rivers and oozed from the sides of mountains, a death that grinned back from the shining peaks and the dark forests. He could not see them clearly, could not see them at all. *Could feel them.* The dark mouths of the beautiful land, the constant threat. And he knew his own fear as well, a fear turned to hatred, a fear turned to the on-going game of outwitting them, a fear translated into desperate rides, desperate runs, the faceless numbers, grizzlies, painted and swift and relentless. He walked forward, into the teeth of their hatred, the springs, the rivers of hatred flowing about him, his own hatred driving through the current. He saw his own body lying on the ground before him. The eyes were gouged out. The scalp was a red mat of torn flesh. An arrow had pierced his throat. And still the body moved, struggled to its feet, lunged onward toward the invisible foe.

The pepperbox was empty.

He screamed.

Waited.

He would feel the impact first. It would spin him about. His strength would go quickly. Then the noise, the snap, rifle-snap.

Cahuna's face before him. The mouth opening:

"Iggerant dunghead! Get your young ass back to them trees! Goin' to skin ye alive. . . ."

Beckwourth stared wildly about as though he had just awakened. The Siksika rifles were silent. They were drawing back!

Baptiste dashed out, grabbed Jim around the middle, and dragged him toward relative safety in the cover of the trees.

"They've killed Cahuna. . . ."

Then the great, strong arms of Pierre Le Blueux were about him, lifting him off his feet and wrestling him down.

Beckwourth breathed in deeply, covered his face with his hands, and went limp, collapsed to the ground, sobbing beyond control.

"*Mon Jim,*" Pierre snapped, "stop! We must get better cover. We cannot help him now. *Le regret de dolour,* it does no good."

The clear command of Le Blueux's voice brought Beckwourth back to his senses. He regained his composure quickly and, shaking loose from his friends, rose, walked over to the fallen Cahuna Smith, lifted the body, and looked up at Le Blueux. Pierre motioned, and the men withdrew to a stand of cottonwoods.

For an hour or more they attempted to exchange fire with the Indians. Finally the sounds of the rifles attracted a larger group of Sublette's men, and the Blackfeet disappeared. Beckwourth moved quickly about the area and, finding four dead Indians, took their scalps and fired his pistol into each of the faces.

That afternoon, with Sublette rendering a short service, they buried the trapper who was once, some said, a prizefighter.

"This child's goin' to miss 'im," Black Harris said. "He was a good coon for bein' a Whiteman."

The parties came in for the 1828 Rendezvous, followed by the Indians, including a large group of Snakes. Taken together, a small temporary city assembled itself at Bear Lake. A group of Mountain Crows appeared, as well as a few Blackfeet. The anger of some of the trappers and the long-standing enmity between Absaroka and Siksika notwithstanding, a remarkable degree of goodwill was displayed, with mutual avoidance replacing open hostility.

The year had been one of violence, and a number of the trappers had gone under: Wright, Jarvey, Alexander, and Cahuna Smith among them. Joseph Coty was gone. Pinckney Sublette, Bill's little brother, had been killed. Johnson, Godin, Logan, Bell, O'Hara. How many others?

The trappers had brought in more than seventy packs of beaver, over seven thousand pounds of furs. And otter skins, castoreum, muskrat, buffalo robes. This year they would be getting St. Louis prices.

Despite the numerous battles with the Blackfeet, prospects looked good. The venture with the trading post had, in the long run, paid off. As-as-to wanted another post this fall. It would be a gamble, of course. The partners were not about to forget either the pitched battles of winter or, for that matter, what had happened to the Ashley-Henry men on the upper Missouri back in 1882 and 1823. So relentless had the *Pieds Noirs* been in their continued massacres that even the Missouri Fur Company men had been forced to abandon the mountains and return to the river trade. But the lands of the Blackfeet were rich in beaver, and even if the truce was only temporary and highly conditional, the partners would take advantage of it.

One of the partners was not present. Jed Smith had not, as yet, returned from his second venture to California. They had heard some rumors, and it was possible that Jed had gone under. But it would be a mistake to bury Smith too quickly. Bears or Indians, Jed had a way of making it through.

Carnival time in the mountains. The watered-down and doctored-up whiskey was plentiful, and there were so many available squaws that competition actually pushed the prices down. The stick game thrived, and draw poker occupied more than a few of the trappers. There were shooting contests, jumping contests, foot races, and one or two knife fights.

Red Beard Miller, for instance, was in a particularly belligerent mood. More than one man taunted him about losing an ear to a squaw, and Red Beard didn't take kindly to such remarks.

One night a Spaniard named Gonsolves pushed him too far. Miller had lost some money at the rifle shoot, and despite the loss of a visible ear, he could still hear quite well.

"What you say, greaser?"

"I say, these Indian women, they are dangerous, *si? Malasuerte! Amigo,* you have made the *mal paso.* This is what I have said."

"Think maybe I'll cut me off one of your ears, then. Stick it in my horn to keep the powder dry."

Immediately a group of men surrounded them. Trapper and Indian alike encouraged the two, and it didn't take long for both knives to appear in the hands of their owners.

Beckwourth and Le Blueux saw the cluster of men and walked over to find out what was causing the excitement. They watched as the two participants circled each other, agile as cats, moving, feinting, slashing at the air. Then Gonsolves made his move, and Red Beard parried the Spaniard's strike and slashed the man's shoulder. The Spaniard swore and lunged. Miller's knife leaped to the other man's throat and deftly cut the windpipe. Gonsolves fell backward and Miller was upon him, pinning his opponent's knife hand and driving his own wide blade into the stomach. As Gonsolves writhed about in the dirt, still alive, Miller calmly lifted his hair. Then, almost as an afterthought, he plunged his knife into the Spaniard's heart.

Miller shouldered his way through the group of spectators, noticed Beckwourth standing there, and tossed the scalp in his direction.

"Little souvenir," Red Beard said. "Something to keep you thinkin' about me."

Then he strode quickly away.

"*Mon frère,*" Le Blueux said, "in any case, you pay no attention to this. *Alors,* it is time to find some women."

Red Beard went on a warpath.

First he and Eddie Sullivan purchased the services of a young Snake woman, brought her to Sullivan's lodge, and took turns screwing her. After two humps each, the squaw wished to leave, but Red Beard was having no part of it.

"Ain't done with ye yet, y'fuckin' slut!"

The woman tried to get away. Sullivan stood back, laughing as he drunkenly attempted to pull his pants back on. Then the squaw turned to Sullivan for help, but Red Beard grabbed her by the hair and hurled her across the tipi.

"Take 'er easy, Miller. Let's don't stir up no more trouble. This one's probably gettin' a mite sore."

The Snake woman began to scream. At that her husband entered the lodge, a pistol in his hand. Red Beard Miller, naked from the hips down and fairly well sotted with Rendezvous Medicine, threw himself headfirst toward the Indian brave, rammed him in the pit of the stomach as the pistol exploded, then fell forward, out through the lodge entrance, on top of the enraged husband. Miller grappled with the Indian, took his knife away from him, and stabbed him in the stomach several times. He had started to take his opponent's scalp when the woman threw herself upon him, clawing and biting. Miller stood up, the squaw clinging to his back, reached over his shoulders, grasped her by the head, and flung her down on the ground, knocking her unconscious.

Sully tried to calm Miller down, but Miller turned and dealt his friend a terrific blow to the side of the head, and the Irishman staggered backward, fell against one of the lodge-poles, and the entire lodge collapsed over the dead Snake, the unconscious squaw, the equally unconscious Irishman, and the cursing Red Beard Miller.

"Where's my fuckin' pants?" he roared.

He found them, then cut his way out through the side of the fallen tipi, and went to get some more arwerdenty.

As he staggered across the clearing, he came upon Beckwourth, La Jeunesse, and Le Blueux.

"Think I'll kill me two Frenchies and a Nigger!" he said, and then lapsed into a long string of incoherent profanities.

Le Blueux stepped in front of his two friends, confronted Miller.

"Redbeard *chien*," Pierre said in a quiet, deadly voice. "You come at Pierre with *le couteau*, and I will take away your toy, *enfant de garce*, and then I will break your back, *moi*."

Miller stared at Le Blueux. Were there two Le Blueuxs? He remembered Le Blueux all right. And what Sullivan had said about Le Blueux. The man didn't take prisoners. And now there was two of him.

"Aw buffler shit!" Miller said, turned, and staggered off in the opposite direction.

He had to vomit.

Bent forward, growling and snarling. Heaved. Shook his head. Heaved a second time.

"He has drunk too much Medicine, this one," Le Blueux said.

"Were you actually going to try to take his knife away from him?" Jim asked.

"Once, before you came into *les montagnes*, I have taken his knife away. He remembers this, Red Beard. He is afraid of me, *peut-être*. In any case, the old dog, he learns how to growl. *C'est fondamental*."

GOOD LUCK TO YE,
JIM BECKWOURTH

One who had lost his all would say simply, "Damn! There goes ha'r and beaver," and turn to solace of mountain rot-gut. Others danced with a "Hi-ya—Hi-ya—Hi-ya!" or expended their lusts with Indian women, indifferent or enthusiastic. The medicine water went round, and duels were fought with rifles at twenty paces. Drunken men carved each other with knives. One poured whiskey on the hair of a companion, passed out at the time, and lit him afire. When the kegs were empty and the goods traded, the mountain men rode off into the wilderness, and the grand hangover of Rendezvous wore off. Then the fall hunt commenced. They began high in the mountains and worked their way down until the lower streams were frozen. Next they scattered to winter camps. Some joined their wives' tribes, lived as they lived.

Bring out the tall tales.

Jim Bridger told one.

"I was up to Colter's Hell," he said, "and I saw an entire mountain that wasn't made out of nothing but glass, pure glass, as good as if it was blowed back in the settlements. Well, I couldn't see to the top of this mountain nor to the bottom neither, 'cause it was made out of glass. One day I went out huntin' and I spied a big old elk within shootin' range. I put my Hawken to my shoulder and took real good aim and fired—fired plumb center, and yet that old elk didn't fall down or nothing'. Hell, he didn't even run off. He just stood there, so I loaded up again and took me another shot. Just like before, not a damned thing. I fired a couple more times, and that elk still didn't move. I was beginning to think my shot was made out of that soft lead—you know the kind that just sort of evaporates in the air when you've got some critter dead in your sights and you fire and nothin' happens? Well, I got hopping mad then. I took my rifle and figured I'd club the damned thing to death, since my bullets wasn't doin' any good for me. I started runnin' towards that elk, and damned if somethin' didn't knock me flatter than a griddle cake. Then I realized what was wrong. You see, that entire mountain was made out of glass, and that glass was in fact a telescope that God had made and just sort of forgot and left there. That elk I was shootin' at was actually twenty-five miles away."

A silence lay heavy about the fire. The men tried to keep straight faces, and mostly they succeeded.

Then Provost said, "Hey, Jim Beckwourth. Why don't you tell us about how you outrun them Big Bellies up north. I don't know if that 'un's a story like Bridger's or not, but I'd be pleased to hear you tell 'er."

"Don't know what you heard," Beckwourth smiled, "but I do have a story I heard from old Pierre here, when he was up at Colter's Hell. I've never been there myself."

"If it don't take all night," Provost said, "let's hear 'er."

Le Blueux extended his arms in a gesture of resignation.

"I heard it like this," Beckwourth said. "Le Blueux was up at Colter's Hell about the time that Bridger was. In fact, he had been chased up a pine tree by a big old grizzly just a few minutes before Bridger got there and saw the elk, so Le Blueux got to watch the whole thing. He knew about the glass mountain, and he knew Gabe was never going to shoot the elk, so he just lit his pipe the way he does whenever there's nothing much happening, and he watched. Finally Bridger figured out about the glass mountain, only Pierre says he ran into the glass about six or seven times before he figured it out. And then he cussed a little and got onto his horse and rode away. Well, about this time Pierre was finished smoking his pipe, so he climbed back down from the tree. Then he walked up to the top of that glass mountain to take a good look around, but he slipped and slid clear to the bottom on the other side and landed right where the elk was eating sweet grass. The elk looked up and said, 'Good morning, Pierre. I've been wondering where you were. Actually, I came out here to wait for Jim Bridger, but I guess he's not going to show up.' With that the elk turned into a beautiful Indian girl with tits as pretty as the Grand Tetons, though smaller of course, and just about the size a man likes to put his hands on. 'My name is Pretty Elk,' she said, 'and I like to do everything in bed that a man ever dreamed of. Will you come to my lodge with me?' "

The men roared their appreciation of the good gibe at Bridger, and Provost said, "See what you done missed, Gabe? If you'd just of looked through that telescope a little closer, you'd of seen the tipi and you'd of known that elks don't have tipis, so it must have been an Injun squaw that was wantin' to get after your big old pecker."

Again the laughter.

Then Le Blueux spoke up:

"*Alors,* this story Jim tells, it is true. But there is one thing that he forgets. Me, I was at that time a Catholic monk, and so I could not go into the lodge with Pretty Elk. But when I go to find Bridger, he is gone back to trapping *le castor.* So Pretty Elk, she is still wandering around Colter's Hell, looking for him. *C'est vrai.*"

Many stories flew around the fires that Rendezvous, but one tale was told to a group of Crow warriors. The Absarokas had heard of Beckwourth's exploits against the Blackfeet, and they wished Caleb Greenwood, who had taken a Crow wife and who knew their language, to tell them who this man was. Greenwood pointed out Beckwourth to them, and they tried to talk with the man who had slain a number of their enemies. Jim, however, knew very little of the Absaroka tongue, and so the communications were mostly ineffectual. Gaining scant informaton from Beckwourth, the Crows appealed to Greenwood to tell them all he knew.

Since it was Rendezvous time, and since fiction is always somehow more attractive than truth, Caleb took a drink of arwerdenty, puffed on his pipe, and began.

"This man Beckwourth is indeed a great figher and has killed many Blackfeet and taken their scalps. I was puzzled about this too, when I first met the man, because I had always heard that the Crows were the only ones who had much success against the *Pieds Noirs,* the Siksikas. And that is because the Absarokas have been enemies with the Siksikas for so long, for more years than anyone knows, that they have learned all of the tricks of the Siksikas and know how to fight them. Now I don't know if this is true, but I guess it is. From what I hear, the Absarokas usually win when they fight the Siksikas, for the Sparrow Hawks are great warriors."

The Crows nodded gravely and admitted that it was so. They had drunk a little whiskey, something that A-ra-poo-ash and Long Hair had forbidden, and they were in a very congenial mood. No matter, the two great chiefs were not at the Rendezvous.

Greenwood puffed on his pipe once more and then continued.

"You know that twenty-five winters ago the Cheyennes attacked the Absaroka villages when most of the warriors were away, fighting the Siksikas. Some of you were alive then and remember this time. Some of you had not yet been born and so you do not remember. But you have heard the story from those who were alive at that time, for the Cheyennes gave the Sparrow Hawks a great defeat."

The long-haired Crow warriors narrowed their eyes and nodded. The memory of that terrible time was alive in the tongues of their story-tellers, and they were all familiar with it. Many times, since then, that story had driven them to victories over the treacherous Cheyennes.

"The Cheyennes had a great force, and they killed hundreds of Crows—the boys who were still too young to be warriors and the old men who stayed behind to protect the villages when the other warriors were away. And the Cheyennes overran the villages and carried away many of the Absaroka women and their children also. Most of these women returned when they were able to do so, and they brought back their children with them, for it is better to be a Sparrow Hawk than it is to be a Cheyenne."

"Yes," the men said, "that is true."

"Well, one of the children who was stolen was this Jim Beckwourth."

The men murmured in half-belief.

"He was a little boy at that time, and the Cheyennes sold him to the Long Knives, and that is why he never returned to the Sparrow Hawks. He grew up among the Whitemen and has become a great brave among them. He is especially good when fighting with the Blackfeet, for he was born a Sparrow Hawk and his blood is still Absaroka, even though he now lives with the Long Knives. That is why he has come here to the mountains, and that is why his skin is darker than mine and is like yours."

"That is true," said one of the Crows. "His skin is like ours."

"If he is one of us," another warrior said, "then the Long Knives must return him to us, for he was one of our *bar-car-ta*. The Long Knives must give him to us so that he can come to live with his people again."

Greenwood knocked the dead ashes out of his pipe. The matter had suddenly taken a turn that he was not totally comfortable with. He thought for a moment and then spoke again.

"No, he is one of us now. He is a great chief among the trappers, and he has told me that he wishes to remain with his friends. He will continue to fight the enemies of the Absarokas, but he wishes to live among the Whitemen who have adopted him. You have seen him beside the man with the gray beard. That man is his father now. Beckwourth wishes to stay with his father who adopted him."

The Crow warriors nodded and looked into the eyes of Caleb Greenwood. Some believed what the trapper had told them, and some were not sure.

The following day Greenwood related his tale to Beckwourth, La Jeunesse, and Le Blueux. They all laughed together at the story and at the naive belief of the Crows.

If they did believe.

"Now, old *Monsieur* Long Hair," Le Blueux laughed, "he would wish to investigate such a matter."

Beckwourth nodded wisely.

"Caleb, if I ever disappear," he said, "It'll be your job to come rescue me from the Crows. You remember that."

The great peaks of the Wind River Range shoulder the sky, and even in late summer, ice remains in the high couloirs. Bandings of snow linger along the north faces of the cliffs. At the foot of the mountains, a small river meanders through green meadows edged by spruce. If one understood about tongues of glacial ice, one would realize that not too long ago, perhaps just beyond the traditional tales of the Shoshones, torrents of ice moved down the mountains and ate slowly, slowly at the hard rock beneath.

At that time, whenever it was, the Blackfeet and the Crows had not yet come to this land.

But now a solitary moose shambles from the trees to the stream, ungainly, the face comic: the blunted nose and big mouth, the rough brown hide, the spindly legs, the flattened prongs of its rack tilting from side to side as the animal walks. The movements are purposive, intent, and utterly alone in the morning stillness, a stillness only occasionally punctuated by the cries of bluejays or the whistle of a marmot. The moose moves toward the stream.

By the water, even though it is late in the season, Indian paintbrush blossoms crimson-orange. Close by are the delicate red-violet clusters of the parry primrose.

The moose dips its nose into the water. Drinks.

And so the Rendezvous ended.

Beckwourth was attached to Robert Campbell's party, while La Jeunesse and Le Blueux were to return to Blackfoot country under the leadership of Davy Jackson. Sublette had decided that he didn't want Jim Beckwourth close enough to the Siksika to be able to exchange rifle fire with them. So, Jim, Pierre, and Baptiste embraced and talked about striking out as free trappers following the next year's Rendezvous.

"*Mon frère,*" Le Blueux said, "do not push at the one with the red beard, he is very good with the knife. A trapper with no hair, *alors,* he does not take many beaver."

"Miller's all right," Jim said. "We'll get along just famous. If not, I believe I can handle myself. Too bad Billy Sublette didn't send him up to trade with the *Pieds Noirs,* though. Sing to the Great Coyote, gentlemen. Pierre. Baptiste."

Campbell's party consisted of thirty-one men, all of them skillful trappers. Gabe Bridger was with them. And they began the long trek toward the Powder River—long by the standards of the civilized world, but the trappers had grown used to such marches.

The very size and scope and mass of the country diminished all distance, diminished the importance of time—so that days slipped into one another, and the seasons were as weeks. The wind soughed in prairie grass and through the pines over the high, barren plateaus, and the clouds drifted and vanished above them. The land into which they were going was called Absaroka, the home of the Sparrow Hawk people. But like all the land in the Shining Mountains, the Ammahabas, it belonged to the trappers too. Their land by right of their knowledge of it and their ability to survive in it. An island in time, but an island soon to grow smaller. Within fifty years the buffalo would be gone and the Indian peoples would be different peoples, no longer the wild hunters, and they would be forced to learn the nature of imposed limits. They would resist, of course, but the waves that had already begun to wash against the shores of their island would prove too great, and only the mountains would remain.

Beckwourth was sad to part from Le Blueux and La Jeunesse, men he thought of in some ways as father and younger brother. Sometimes Jim referred to Baptiste as his "boy," but he knew the appellation was not accurate, for Baptiste was not much younger than he was. And the Rocky Mountains, he knew, quickly tempered a man's blood and bone and mind, and a man became keen and strong. If not, his fate was death under the knife of Blackfoot or Arikara, and his scalp was taken.

Beckwourth did not know, when he left Rendezvous, how many of his friends he might have seen for the last time. How many of that large company, he wondered, would sleep in death within a season or two, no longer hearing the sounds of running streams or the savage yells of Cheyenne or Pawnee? Their white bones would crumble in the mountain wilderness or on the endless prairies, their cloven skulls trodden by the buffalo or gnawed by the wolf. For death was a simple fact. It came without warning. It was part of the bargain they all had made.

After a time Campbell's party arrived at the Powder River, arrived without accident, and began to trap. The sky was huge above them, and the beaver was good.

The most trivial incident may suffice to determine a man's fate. One of Beckwourth's traps disappeared, and he suspected that it had been stolen. Nonetheless, he and Bridger went out to make a thorough search, and they found the "stolen" trap two miles from the stream.

"You cotched a beaver, Jim," Gabe said. "He's still alive."

"How in hell did he get up here?"

Beckwourth killed the animal and began to skin it, cutting out the castoreum glands and removing the tail.

"Figger a buffalo was trying to steal your trap," Bridger said with a straight face. "The way I see it, that buffalo belonged to Pretty Elk. She'd sent him out to steal one of your traps so's you wouldn't be tellin' any more buffalo shit stories."

Beckwourth looked up, laughed.

"Buffalo crossing the creek, got the tie chain wrapped around one of its legs?"

"Yeah. Looks like something of the order."

Back at camp Beckwourth announced that his trap had been stolen by a buffalo.

"It's kind of an involved thing," he said. "But that buffalo belonged to Pretty Elk, the one that Pierre told me about—you remember that story I told over at Bear Lake? Well, Pretty Elk sent out the buffalo to find Bridger and bring him to her, and the buffalo was on its way to our camp when it crossed the creek where I had set my trap. . . ."

"Just got to keep waggin' that tongue, don't you?" Red Beard Miller said.

"You don't want to hear the story," Bridger responded, "why don't you just go find you a tree to piss up? Me, I want to find out what Pretty Elk's got on her mind."

"That Nigger's always shooting off his face," Miller said. "Some of us gets tired of it."

Beckwourth felt a rush of anger come over him. Without thinking, he grabbed hold of Red Beard and pulled him to his feet.

"I should have killed you a long while back," he said through gritted teeth.

Red Beard reached for his knife, but as he did so, Beckwourth hurled him back against a tree. Miller grunted, trying to catch his breath. The knife fell from his hand, slid a few feet on the packed earth. He lunged for the weapon, but Beckwourth grabbed him by the hair and flopped him over on his back, his own knife instantly at Miller's throat.

"Seems like a man would get the idea after a bit," he said, smiling pleasantly down at his pinned antagonist.

The other trappers, taken completely by surprise at the sudden confrontation, stood silently. Miller's eyes, unblinking, met Beckwourth's. Hatred. Pure hatred. He said nothing.

Campbell was there quickly.

"Either kill him or let him go, Beckwourth. If we got a burying to do, let's get on with it."

"Ain't worth killing," Beckwourth said, stepped back, and slid his knife into its sheath. "Miller, that's twice. Comes a third time, I'm going to put you under. Skin you and feed your hide to the coyotes."

Bridger and Beckwourth left camp for a few days to let tempers cool. They set out to lay some new traps on a drainage that hadn't been touched before.

"Don't exactly hit it off with old Red Beard, do you?"

"Can't say that I like him much."

"Well, he'll simmer down. It's best we don't be killing each other. They's enough hostile Injuns out there to keep us all busy. Best if we kind of stick together. If a bunch of coons like us cain't stick together, we got us some real troubles."

"Bad blood dies hard," Beckwourth answered.

Gabe and Jim trapped the creek to where it branched. Then they split up, intending to meet back at the forks later in the day.

It was a long parting.

Beckwourth had just set his fourth trap when he felt something. Like he was being watched. He was knee-deep in the water, and his rifle was out of reach, leaning against some dead willow brush on the bank. He turned slowly.

Indians. About twenty of them. Sparrow Hawks.

He was made a prisoner, taken back to their village.

Jim Bridger had set his traps quickly and had returned to the forks of the creek. Rather than wait for Beckwourth, he set off upstream to find him. He cut over a low ridge where the stream made an oxbow loop around it, but as he reached the crest, he drew down behind some rocks and observed the drama being played out below. He saw Beckwourth standing in the water. He saw the Crow braves. He saw the gestures and knew what they meant. He saw Jim's hands being bound behind him. He saw him placed on one of the riderless horses. He saw the Crows, and Beckwourth with them, disappear up the canyon.

There was nothing he could do.

The Absarokas were supposed to be peaceful, but a man could never tell when an Indian's mind was likely to take off in a new direction. Beckwourth's only chance was to break from the group and ride like hell. But a man could hardly do that with his hands tied.

"Good luck to ye, Jim Beckwourth. Wisht they was some way I could of helped."

Beckwourth rode quietly, a prisoner of the Crows. His one real chance lay in that story Greenwood had told at Rendezvous, and he knew it. It was a wild chance, but just maybe some of those Mountain Crows would be around before the rest of them lifted his hair. He didn't recognize the faces of any of his captors—but then he hadn't paid much attention at the time. Could it be that he was with some of the Crows from the Rendezvous?

Such was the case.

They had been watching him and Bridger from above. When the two men parted, the Indians came down for a closer look. It was the one: the killer of the Blackfeet. Their lost bar-car-ta. They would take him back to their village.

Now all the old women were summoned, those who had survived the attack of the Cheyennes and those who had been captured and who had returned. Beckwourth was stripped naked and made to stand while the old women looked him over.

Funny Deer, the wife of Big Bowl, spoke:

"If this man is my child, he has a mole over his left eye."

Hands were placed on his face, and his eyelid was pulled down.

"The mole is there," Funny Deer said. "This man is my son."

The Crows looked at one another and nodded.

"Greenwood spoke true," one said. Then a murmur of agreement. And after a moment, Big Bowl stepped forward, drew his knife, and cut his son's bonds.

BIG BOWL'S SON

Gods and demons.
Dawn, Protective Spirit, Power Above, Thunder, Mother Corn, Water Spirit, Sex God, Ghost, Sky People, Moving God, Sun, Evil Twin, First Man, Star People, Great Snapping Turtle, Flood Spirit, War Eagle, Evil Power, Turtle-Man-in-the-Moon, The Opposites, Sacred Eagle, Moon of Night, Buffalo Skull, White Bear, Disease-Bringer, Old Woman's Grandchild, Giant, Enchanted Owl, Gentle Manitou, Earth Spirit, Earth People, Wind God, Little Coyote, Spirit World, Two-Faced Being, Messenger of the Gods, Water Monster, Tree Spirits, Mountain-Where-the-Sun-Lives, Spider Woman, Volcano Woman, Thunderbird, Lightning Snake, Wolf Spirit, Whirlpool, Bear Mother, Dragon, Grandmother White Mouse, Raven, Bluejay: Ah-Badt-Dadt-Deah, Wakonda, Tirawa-Atius, Nesaru, Maho Peneta, Ketchimanetowa. Isakawuate. Isakakate.

Suddenly Jim Beckwourth discovered that he had an Absaroka family. Funny Deer was his mother and Big Bowl was his father. He had brothers and sisters as well—indeed, an entire clan to whom he was related in one way or another. Directly, he was ushered into Big Bowl's lodge, and his four unmarried sisters dressed him in new leggings and moccasins and then prepared him a bed.

Big Bowl knew a few dozen words of English, and Beckwourth knew even less of the language of the Crows. He was, however, passingly familiar with the universal sign language utilized by all the Indians of the mountains and the plains, and so his instruction in the tongue of the Absaroka was begun. Big Bowl questioned him about what he had heard of Greenwood's tale, and Jim indicated to his Indian father that the story was true—for, as he well realized, his life might depend upon his adherence to the tale. Big Bowl was a patient teacher, and when Jim signed that he did not understand a question or a word, the older man gestured carefully, using what sparse English he knew and repeating the Absaroka equivalents until his pupil comprehended the meanings.

Funny Deer brought food, and Jim ate. Finally Big Bowl gestured to the new bed which had been prepared for him in the lodge, and he lay down. Soon they had all retired, the lodge was quiet, and Jim feigned sleep. He heard Big Bowl and Funny Deer speaking softly to one another, but he could understand little of what was said. Then the voices ceased, and the lodge was completely quiet and dark.

Jim considered the wisdom of waiting for an hour or two and then slipping from the tipi, taking a horse, and attempting to make his escape, but ultimately he concluded it would be safer to play along with them for a few days and thereby gain their confidence. Their entire approach to him seemed to be friendly—even more than friendly. They were actually accepting a long-lost son back into their midst, or so they imagined. Apparently they *wanted* him to be one of them. There appeared to be no immediate danger, and he began to imagine that a trapper in the lands of the Crows, one who was believed to be a Crow, might well have an immense advantage over his fellow trappers. If he could lay his traps without the constant awareness of the danger of the Indians, he might even become a wealthy man.

He was mulling this idea when he fell asleep.

The following day Big Bowl spoke to him, the hint of a smile playing over the weathered features.

"Does my son wish to have a Crow woman for his wife?"

He then repeated the question, gesturing slowly as he did so. He spoke a third time in English: "Son want wife?"

Beckwourth recalled immediately As-as-to's similar offer, and he quickly considered the implications of the question. It was certain he was being accepted into the tribe. His position with these strange people would be considerably strengthened if he agreed.

"Yes," he said. "Your son wishes a wife."

But even as he spoke, he was still wondering how he might escape his new-found family and return to Campbell's camp. Nevertheless, something about this whole adventure fascinated him. He nodded again. Yes, he would take a wife.

Before long three girls were brought to Big Bowl's lodge, and Beckwourth was told their names: Still-water, Black-fish, and Three-roads. He looked carefully at each of the three girls, and at length he nodded to Still-water and then to her father.

Such was the courtship, and the marriage was joined. Big Bowl, Jim knew, would make presents to the girl's family. And his father explained to him, as well as he could, that Jim was not to speak with Still-water's mother thereafter, for such was their custom.

Within an hour Big Bowl's other sons—which included his nephews, as Jim gathered—presented themselves to him and gave him a string of twenty horses and also the weapons of an Absaroka warrior.

Beckwourth learned quickly that Still-water was not like the first of his Blackfoot wives. Still-water had ears. Obedient, gentle and affectionate, she was happy and honored to share the lodge of the Morning Star, as they had chosen to name him.

"I will teach my husband to speak the language of his people," Still-water said, gesturing at the same time, as his father had done. "I will be a good wife, and we will be happy in our lodge."

And so he had begun his life with the Sparrow Hawk People, thinking to trap their streams unmolested and return to the Whites when he was able. As the days flowed onward, Jim found that he was making great progress in learning his new language, a language said by some of the more experienced trappers, like Le Blueux, to be a difficult one. Still-water was especially pleased with the quickness with which the Morning Star learned.

"It is because you are one of us," she said.

Was it fate that had closed off his life behind him? Already

Beckwourth could see that there was much about the ways of the Absarokas that appealed to him, appealed immensely. And now, in the darkness of the lodge, Still-water slept in his arms. Sometimes she made little noises in her sleep, the contented whimperings, he imagined, of a wild animal that has been raised by human beings and so has become tame, yet knows it is wild.

The two bands of the Mountain Crows came together, and when the village was set up, A-ra-poo-ash, the head chief, called all of the warriors to an assembly, to which Beckwourth was conducted by Big Bowl. The gathering was large.

The chief, in full war dress, approached the two men.

"Big Bowl," he said, embracing Beckwourth's father, "it is good to be with you once more, my friend. Is this your lost bar-car-ta?"

"A-ra-poo-ash, it is good to see you. Yes, this is the one. Funny Deer recognized him, even after all these years. We call him Morning Star, the one who has lived with the Whites and has killed many Siksikas. Among the Long Knives he was called Beck-wourth."

A-ra-poo-ash placed his hands on Beckwourth's shoulders, looked up into his eyes.

"He is a big one. Perhaps he will soon go on a war-path, and we will be able to judge the strength of his medicine. Then he must have a new name, for he is still like a child among us. He has very strong arms, Big Bowl. Were our arms this strong when we were young men?"

"I do not think so. Mine were not, but Funny Deer's father had big arms like Morning Star's. My son is very strong, A-ra-poo-ash. He will be a brave warrior."

"You have killed the warriors of the Blackfeet, Morning Star?"

"Yes, A-ra-poo-ash, that is true."

"Now you must learn to fight like an Absaroka. Then we will be proud of you. Big Bowl, I must now speak to the warriors."

The head chief turned and walked away. Beckwourth and Big Bowl drew in among the other Sparrow Hawks.

"A-ra-poo-ash is a great warrior," Big Bowl said. "He has been our chief for a long while, many winters, and he has taken many coups. We were born in the same year, in the season of good grass. Now we have grown old. It may not be many winters before we must have a new head chief."

"Is he the one the Long Knives call Rotten Belly?"

"Yes. That is the meaning of the name A-ra-poo-ash. He was very sick once. That was many winters ago. And he had lain down to die. But when the Siksikas attacked our village, he rose from his death bed and charged out into the Siksikas alone, for he thought it was time to die. He struck coup several times, and the Siksikas became frightened and rode away. That is why he is called A-ra-poo-ash. Afterward he became well again. When the old chief staked himself out against the Assiniboines in the time of frozen grass, and was slain, A-ra-poo-ash protected the body, and the enemy could not take the scalp. I was with him when that happened. Then A-ra-poo-ash became the new head chief."

"Was Long Hair the chief of the River Crows at that time?"

"No. A-ra-poo-ash became chief before Long Hair. They are both great warriors and have led our people well. They are very close friends. It is good that we have these two chiefs."

"Sparrow Hawks! A-ra-poo-ash speaks to you. Now the leaves begin to fall from the cottonwoods, and soon there will be ice along the streams. This year has been good to us, and the deer and the antelope and the buffalo have been plentiful Our medicine has been good. There are many beaver in our streams, and we will set our traps and sell the skins of the beaver to the Long Knives, and we will be prosperous. Now a new thing has happened. I have just spoken with Big Bowl and have met his son, the bar-car-ta who was stolen from us many years ago when the Cheyennes attacked our villages and took our women and children. Ears of the Wolf has said that this is a good sign, our medicine is strong. We must teach this man the ways of his people, for he was only a child when he was stolen. He has lived with the Long Knives and knows their language. This will help us when we trade with them. The path ahead of us is a good one, and we will continue to be a powerful nation. I believe that Isakakate has caused Isakawuate, the Old Coyote Man, to return the one who was stolen from us.

"Absaroka is a good land. Isakakate has put it in exactly the right place, and the land has been good to us, and we pray that it will always be so. If we leave this land, it will be worse for us, no matter where we go. To the south are the great barren plains, and the water is bad. In the north the days are shorter during the time of frozen grass, and our horses starve, and the buffalo are few. Across the mountains there are great rivers and thick forests, but the people must go about in canoes and eat fish. These people wear out their teeth and are always taking fish bones out of their mouths, for fish is not as good to eat as the flesh of the buffalo. To the east are our friends the Hidatsa, who live in villages. These people are also Crows, and they live well, but they must drink the muddy water of the Big River. In winter the grass is gone, and there is no salt weed for the horses.

"Our land is in exactly the right place. There are high mountains, and the plains are covered with grass. There are many buffalo and antelope and elk. When it grows hot in the summer, we can go up into the mountains where the air is sweet and cool and there is grass for our horses. Clear streams come down from the snows of the mountains, and the water is good to drink. We hunt elk and deer and antelope when their skins are fit for dressing. The white bear people live in our lands and the mountain goats and the mountain sheep. In the time of the falling of leaves, our horses are fat and strong, and we can go down into the plains where the buffalo are, and there is salt weed in abundance. Absaroka is in exactly the right place. Isakakate caused Old Man Coyote to create this land for the Sparrow Hawks, and we are very grateful to both of them. We plant the sacred tobacco, and our medicine remains powerful. If we follow the will of Isakakate, things will remain as they have always been, and the Sparrow Hawks will continue to live well. Our war-paths will be good ones and our herds of horses will become very large. We are grateful to Isakakate and Isakawuate, for they have given us this land to be ours for as long as the rivers run and the snows fall and the grass grows. We thank the sun and the moon and the earth and the sky. We will listen to the voices of our grandfathers, and we will be happy when we hear the coyotes singing at night. Our fires will burn brightly if we continue to pay reverence to the earth and the animal people, and our enemies will flee from us. The scalps of the Siksika will darken our lodges. These are my words, Sparrow Hawks!"

War party

About forty men. They set out to steal horses, but the warriors desired to take scalps from the Blackfeet, their ancient enemies, and when they intercepted a band of eleven Blood Indians—a group of the Blackfeet—the chief ordered a charge. A madness came over Beckwourth, and he advanced on the line and struck one man with his war axe. The blade bit deep into the throat, and the blood sprayed into the air like the fine red mist of low fog drinking the sunrise. The Indian's voice failed, and he crumpled.

The Sparrow Hawks, curveting aside in Indian fashion, then came to Beckwourth's aid, and within minutes the last of the eleven was slain. Jim took his victim's lance, war-club, bow, quiver of arrows, and gun.

The head was twisted to one side, nearly severed.

The Morning Star had killed his first enemy, and the party hailed the achievement. The Sparrow Hawks painted their faces black in token of victory, and bearing the eleven scalps, returned to the village. Much singing and shouting.

Still-water met the Morning Star in front of their lodge, and he gave her the Blackfoot's rifle. His sisters came up next, and he gave them the other trophies. They laughed and were glad. The Morning Star's companion warriors were pleased to tell of his prowess, of the great strength of his arm—for he had not disgraced them. The eleven Blackfeet were dead, and no Sparrow Hawk had been seriously wounded. Many whom Beckwourth had not seen before now came to make his acquaintance, and the people grew wild with the victory as the ragged scalps were held high. Big Bowl gave gifts in accord with the Crow religion and called for a coat to be painted with the bright image of the sun, then to be hung with a scarlet blanket in the top of a tree as symbol and offering to Isakakate the Creator, so that He might continue to favor the family and make their lodges dark with their enemies' scalps.

Several bands, all at once, began the dances of victory. Beckwourth joined one of these, being careful to select the most active. At this the dancers shouted: "He is with us! His name is the Antelope, killer of the first man in battle—we name him the Antelope, and now he is one of us!"

The fires blazed in the darkness for some time, and then the flames drew down to the orange-red coals, and the dancers disbanded. Jim returned to his lodge and lay down with Still-water. She touched at his face with the tips of her fingers.

"My husband will be a great warrior," she said. "When he counts coup, each time he will be able to paint my face. I will show you how to do this. Then I will be very proud, and the other women will envy me."

The Antelope bit at his wife's neck and then held her in his arms.

"I should have painted your face? There are many things that I do not know about the ways of your people. You must teach me."

His mind was spinning with the events of the day. The other warriors had been pleased with his accomplishment in battle. They were willing to honor a man for his bravery. Among the trappers, little would have been said about such a thing. Except for Bill Sublette. Sublette would have said something. Something about taking chances. But that was a different world.

No sooner had Still-water drawn the buffalo robe over them than her hands were on his penis and her mouth was open to his own.

He became friends with Coyote Running, a tall, lean man, a solitary figure who kept lodge by himself—for his mother and father were dead, and he was without either brothers or sisters. The two men trapped together, exchanged knowledge of the craft. The Antelope was learning his new language rapidly and now had little difficulty in communicating. They enjoyed each other's company and caught many beavers and otters.

One day the Antelope's traps were empty, while Coyote Running had taken eight beaver. He offered half of these to his friend.

Beckwourth objected:

"No need for that, Coyote, your traps have been lucky. My luck returns tomorrow."

But Coyote insisted. Then he said that he wished the Antelope to sit and talk with him. Beckwourth sensed the urgency in his voice, and so they sat down to rest amid a clump of willows not far from the creek.

"Antelope, you know I am alone in the world, for my family has gone to live with Isakakate. And you are alone in a different way. You have lived many years with the Whites, though your blood is Sparrow Hawk. Perhaps this is why a bond has formed between us, two men who are alone."

"We are good friends, and what you say is true. We trap together and we think together."

"We must seal this bond," Coyote Running said, "and become brothers. We are both warriors, and we learn from each other. You have lived in the far-off villages of the Long Knives and have seen much. It is wonderful for me to hear you speak of these things, even when I do not understand. And I have told you many things about our people and our language, your people also, to whom you have returned. Will you be not only my friend but also my brother—and be as one man with me as long as the skies are above us?"

For a moment Beckwourth's thoughts raced over the whole course of his life, his mother and father, his proud and eccentric father and his dark-skinned mother, Jennings and Winey Beckwith, the two of them living their lives against all tradition, their mingled blood in him, himself heir to their wildness and in many ways outcast, rebel, a boy growing up on the edge of a wilderness, and a wilderness inside him. The Indians, fleeting shadows in a boy's mind, then the massacre that boy had discovered, the mutilated bodies, the blank horror and revulsion and fascination, then young manhood and an irresistible call from up the Big River, the expedition with Ashley, a new father in some ways, stern, begrudging of praise, the reproving eyes that did not altogether trust him. The Rockies, the Green River, and living with danger, embracing danger, Black Harris, Portuleuse, Cahuna Smith, little Aleck Alexander, his close friends Baptiste and Jim Bridger and the grand old fox of the mountains, Pierre Le Blueux, and that son of a bitch Miller, the mad run from the Big Bellies, the taking of Blackfoot scalps, trading with the Blackfeet, two Blackfoot wives, the mania of Rendezvous, Light in the Trees, Greenwood's humorous tale to the serious-faced Crow warriors—and a bolt shot back somewhere when a buffalo stole his trap, and his life, as if by design, was changed, and he was changed even without knowing it, and now he was as much the Antelope as he was Jim Beckwourth.

These thoughts and more flashed randomly in his skull as he looked across at Coyote Running, and he nodded.

"It will be good," said Coyote. "We must exchange our traps and our guns, our horses, all of our things. We will share our thoughts, hold nothing secret between us."

Coyote's blade nicked at their wrists, and their blood was intermingled.

They returned to Big Bowl's lodge. Funny Deer and Big Bowl were pleased to receive the Coyote Man as their son.

Big Bowl said to Coyote Running, "I have seen that you are without a family. This is good. My family will be your family, and now I have two grown sons, both of them warriors. Funny Deer and I are happy."

Coyote Running and the Antelope completed their exchange of property, but Beckwourth attempted to make the exchange equitable.

"Coyote Running has more than thirty horses, while I have only twenty. Let us exchange twenty for twenty. I would not be glad the other way."

"Horses come and go," Coyote said. "Tonight the Pawnees may

come and take all of the horses, and we will each have none. Then we must steal horses from someone else."

When it was explained in this fashion, the Antelope agreed to the exchange. He then laid his hands on Coyote's shoulders and said, "Does this mean we must share Still-water in bed?"

The serious-faced Coyote said, "No. Two brothers must not share one woman. It is not allowed."

Then he realized that the Antelope was joking.

The Indian looked down at his feet, scratched his arm, and then looked up.

"You have lived too many years with the Long Knives, I think. Why should I wish to have such a man for a brother? Maybe I will keep the extra horses after all."

A war party began to form, generated by whim and directed against no one in particular. Directed against the enemies, whatever tribe and wherever they might be found. Such parties came up like mushrooms after an autumn rain, large or small, volitional—no necessary score to settle except the call of adventure, the quest toward danger, the male groups, joking and fierce. Who went? A man consulted his medicine, thought of his dreams, remembered old grudges. But the risk itself was payment for the malicious, glad-hearted men.

"And horses," the Antelope thought. "It's not a matter of use, but something else, a strange, incurable fever, horse-madness. What happy thieves they are! They are totally crazy, I think. But the whim is contagious—it spreads like grass fire, and my feet are burning."

They had formed a large party, eighty or so, and he would be one of them, horse-thief Jim.

He asked if Coyote Running intended to go, but his brother declined.

"We are brothers," he said. "We should not leave our village together on these parties, for, should both of us be killed, then who would mourn?"

The Antelope smiled.

"Wouldn't Still-water mourn for her husband?"

"Yes," he said. "She is a good woman. But someone must kill the buffalo. Walk to those alders with me, Antelope. I must ask you something."

They moved to the edge of the village without speaking, sat down, and Coyote said, "You have been to war and have slain the first man with your axe, a very strong coup. That is why they call you the Antelope, for the antelope people run fast and gracefully and have tricky wisdom. They are handsome and quick. The time you went, did they tell you the war secret?"

"No," said the Antelope. "This is something I should know. Explain it to me."

"Antelope Jim, you are still like a child in our ways, though you learn quickly. You need not answer me, but you must answer the others. Have you fucked any of the women in the village?"

The Antelope burst out laughing. But Coyote Running was serious.

"No, I have touched no other than Still-water. Sometimes I am tempted, for our women seem lecherous. Their eyes are like the eyes of weasels."

Coyote's eyes gleamed, but his face was without expression. Already Beckwourth had learned that the Sparrow Hawks smiled more with their eyes than with their mouths.

"They will not believe you," Coyote Running said. "But tell them the truth, for this is important—this truth makes a man ready for battle. You will learn the war-path secret tomorrow when all must speak. I know your medicine is good."

The Sparrow Hawks rode out early, but shortly after midday they came upon a bull buffalo and two cows. They shot the bull, skinned and cut up the animal, and removed and cleansed the intestine in preparation for the ritual of the war-path secret.

It severs all bonds of alliance with the women. It purges all feminine weakness from those who go out on the war-path. Whatever the guilt, the men share it, and all the men know what each woman has done and with which men, each act of passion or lust, whether the woman moaned or laughed, how she had acted, what things were done to her, the times, whether during the day or at night. All would be told again when the party returned, then told to the medicine men. And the Antelope, the new warrior, was informed that he must never explain this war-path secret to any woman, or he called for instant death. It was explained that once a young brave had told his woman of the war-path secret. Immediately a great white bear had appeared and killed them both. Then the bear turned into a coyote and ran away laughing. Two of the older braves swore that they had seen the coyote running away. The others nodded.

So the Antelope swore by his gun, his pipe, his knife, and the earth and the sun and the moon and the sky, for these were the things most sacred to the Sparrow Hawks.

The group was large, and the afternoon waned. They had formed a circle, and each man held the intestine of the bull buffalo. As they had been joined in the hunt, so now they were joined by holding the intestine of the animal they had killed in preparation for war. Each man spoke, either to say that he had had no woman but his own or to tell those whom he had copulated with. A few men spoke of having had sex with the wives of other men in the group. Yet all of the faces remained impassive and without emotion. In terms of the war-path, all attachments to women were weakness, and in the knowledge of their common weaknesses, they were joined together and strengthened.

They ate of the roasted meat and then moved on until they came to the Big River, the Missouri.

They made bullboats, hide-tubs, and floated their guns and so forth across. It did not take long, and the journey was continued. Later the Wolves returned, reporting a village of Assiniboines on Milk River, some forty miles distant.

Broken Shoulder said, "They have too many horses. Their pastures are sparse. We must help these people."

The Sparrow Hawks reached the Assiniboine village, waited for darkness, tethered their own horses, and then glided like shadows down to the herd, its watchman sleeping. They went in among the horses and urged them away, half of their number, about three hundred horses. It all happened quickly, was expertly done. The rest of the herd was not disturbed, and the watchman continued to sleep. The Sparrow Hawks moved the horses quietly, slowly, very slowly at first, and then increased the tempo. They mounted their own horses and moved through the night, were not pursued, and came to the Big River the next morning.

In crossing, they lost many of the herd, for the animals mired in a sandbar and drowned.

The war party returned to the village, met no enemies. They had brought back no scalps, but the tribe rejoiced. No one had been either wounded or killed. The warriors had brought many horses, and the victory was sweet.

The Antelope was given seventeen horses when all were divided, more than his share. Of these, the Antelope gave five to Big Bowl, three to Coyote Running, and three to Still-water.

"These are fine horses," Coyote Running said. "Perhaps you should have kept this one, the war pony. He's worth ten of the others. I am sure that you will need such a horse soon."

"He is a gift to my brother," the Antelope said.

A few days later Beckwourth was summoned to Big Bowl's lodge. Black Panther, his brother-in-law, was already there.

Then Big Bowl spoke:

"My sons," he said, "your medicine is good—you will be chiefs one day. My other sons are young, and though they are eager to go into battle, they have no one to lead them. The eldest is eighteen, the youngest is ten. Funny Deer is now too old to bear children, and I do not wish to take younger wives, for some believe that a lodge is more peaceful when there is one wife only. I now wish you to take these boys and head a party. Some of my sons are adopted and two are my own. But all must become warriors. Our family needs horses, for I have been generous and have given away too many. Besides, the boys are foolish and otherwise will sneak out past our Wolves in small groups, at great danger to themselves. I think my sons are brave, but they lack wisdom, and they need the protection of strong medicine. Black Panther, Antelope, you are brave men, but warriors must not stay at home too long. Bring back horses and our people will listen to your voices. Do you hear my words and like what they say?"

Black Panther replied, "Some of your sons and nephews are young, and we may find great danger. What if some of them are killed or taken prisoners?"

Big Bowl turned away for a long moment and then turned once more to face Black Panther and the Antelope.

"If they are all killed, it is the will of Isakakate, and I will cheerfully submit to my old age without them, and I will die alone. But you are strong men and cunning. You will lead well."

ABSAROKA

Some residents of the grasslands burrow into the sod, as prairie dogs, kangaroo rats, ground squirrels, and pocket mice. They are hunted by snakes, coyotes, badgers, kit foxes, black-footed ferrets, and even grizzly bears. From above they are hunted by falcons, owls, hawks, and eagles. Other grassland dwellers escape their enemies by running—as, for instance, the pronghorn antelope, the fastest of all animals on the North American continent. Antelope have keen eyes and can see wolf or coyote at a great distance. Rump hairs bristle and rise, forming a large patch of white, signal to all other pronghorns. These, in turn, give signal to their fellows. The jackass rabbits are also very fast, their oversized hind legs enabling them to jump fifteen feet or more as they zig-zag away in wild flight. Buffalo are also powerful runners and seem to enjoy running. They are as fast as the jackass rabbits.

Leading their band of enthusiastic youths, Black Panther and the Antelope left the village, having decided to press on to the headwaters of the Arkansas River, directly to the Arapaho and Iatan villages.

The Antelope scouted ahead and brought back word of their location. When the Sparrow Hawks reached the first of the villages, they waited until the lodge fires had died down, then left their horses and moved silently over the ridge under a moonless sky, moved slowly, cautiously out into the big meadows where the herd was kept, perhaps half a mile to the north of the village. The Arapahos had no reason to suspect their presence, and the two guards were asleep. The Sparrow Hawks approached from the side away from the village, slithering among the horses and selecting out a good number.

The animals made no noise and moved along quietly until the horse-thieves had reached their own mounts. Black Panther, the Antelope, and the others mounted and departed hurriedly, riding all night and not resting until noon the next day.

The horses drank and grazed. After the men had eaten, they made their count: a hundred and eighteen fine horses. The boys were jubilant, but Black Panther and the Antelope cautioned them. The Arapahos could well be in pursuit.

They rode on, driving before them the herd of horses, stopping briefly just before sunset, then continuing through the night. The village of the Absarokas still lay some two hundred miles distant, and it was best to cover the larger portion of that distance as quickly as possible.

Black Panther had fallen back the preceding evening, but he caught up with the main group now and reported that the Arapahos had returned to their village. The two warriors congratulated each other and continued toward home.

But in the northernmost Green Valley, a Wolf came in with news: three Gros Ventres were coming toward them, driving a small band of horses.

"The Big Bellies owe me a horse," the Antelope said to Black Panther, "and maybe a scalp or two."

"I think they will give us both," Black Panther responded.

The Sparrow Hawks dropped back over the brow of a hill which lay directly in the route being taken by the Gros Ventres. When the Big Bellies had advanced to within ten paces, the Sparrow Hawks shouted the war cry and rushed upon the little group. The Antelope wounded one with a shot from his pistol—the Indian pitched sideways from his horse, and two of the older boys scalped him, one striking him with a coup stick, the other cutting his hair though he was not yet dead. The Antelope ended the Gros Ventre's agony with a shot to the heart.

Black Panther's arrow hit a second man as the horse wheeled about, and the shaft entered beneath the shoulder blade and emerged through the stomach. The boys pulled him down and made short work of him, just as they had the first one. The third Big Belly had been to the rear and, seeing the fate of his companions, galloped away, clinging low to his horse's back. Black Panther leaped onto his mount and gave pursuit, but the Gros Ventre's escape was successful.

As they rounded up the band of horses, which had scattered during the melee, the Antelope drew up on the reins of his mount and stared at a black horse with a white blaze mark on its forehead.

"Couldn't be," Beckwourth said to himself, then approached the horse slowly. The animal looked up, nickered, and then idly grazed on some sagebrush.

It was the black stallion he had lost the day he had run for his life. No mistake, it was the same horse.

Black Panther rode up beside him.

"This is my horse," the Antelope said. "The Gros Ventres stole him from me a year ago."

"He is yours, then. It is strange with horses. Sometimes they come back to us. Once I lost a horse to the Pawnees and got him back from the Snakes. Sometimes a horse is stolen many times."

Beckwourth dismounted and walked up to the black stallion. He reached out toward it, and the horse nibbled at his fingers.

"Where the hell have you been?" Jim said in English, as though the horse could understand. "Decided to come back, did you? That's your name, then, from now on."

"Does the horse know the language of the Long Knives?" Black Panther laughed.

Thus fate had returned the black stallion with the white blaze mark and had added thirteen more horses as well. Two of Big Bowl's sons had counted coup. Two scalps had been taken, two battle axes, one rifle, a lance, a bow, a quiver, and a small supply of powder and lead. The boys were elated and thought themselves the greatest of warriors. As the party covered the remaining distance to the Absaroka village, the talk was animated and continuous, in anticipation of the ovation and honor that awaited.

"Seven of these Gros Ventre horses were Crow horses," Black Panther said, "and one had been stolen from the Antelope when he was with the Long Knives. These eight are greater than all the others, for it is greater to recover a horse than it is to steal many new ones."

"Coyote Running tells me that Old Man Coyote has a strange sense of humor," the Antelope said.

"Isakawuate, he is a strange one," Black Panther nodded. "Perhaps that is why we are his people."

The band met no more enemies on the way home.

They entered the village with their faces painted the black of victory, and the entire village resounded with shouts.

Now the family of Big Bowl and Funny Deer was praised by the people: Black Panther and the Antelope were lauded and honored, their medicine known to be good. There was much talk about the recovery of the seven horses that had belonged to the Crows and about the recovery of the black horse that had belonged to the Antelope when he had lived with the Whites.

"He is truly one of us now," Coyote Running said so that all could hear. "Isakawuate has given him back his black horse."

"Great is the Panther, great is the Antelope, the lost son!" the chants went up. "Their medicine is strong!"

The Antelope embraced his father, his brother, and his wife. Then Still-water brought him food, and when he had eaten, the two of them went out to take part in the celebration.

Beckwourth considered how different the Sparrow Hawks were from the Whites. However little civilized men and women might wish to trade places and endure the harshness of Indian life, in numerous ways they would better themselves. Jim thought about envy, about the White practice of belittling the accomplishments of others. Such a thing was unknown to the Sparrow Hawks, for when a warrior had shown bravery, he was praised freely by all—his deeds remembered and spoken of with honor. His woman was honored as well, her position and status increased, and not grudgingly, but with generous goodwill. The Sparrow Hawks lived with a sense of wholeness, and the merit of any was espoused by everyone. Nor did the men and women who were married come to hate each other, and even affairs of passion were generally accepted and respected. If a man or a woman wished to part from the other, the process was amazingly simple.

"They see human nature as it is," he thought. "And the good of the individual is the good of the whole."

He knew it would be hard for the Whites to see great value in skillful horse thievery, but perhaps that was because the Whites didn't understand about horses. Even Jim Beckwourth had difficulty in seeing why it was better to strike an enemy with a stick than it was to kill him. He would probably never understand this, though he had already learned much.

Perhaps the Antelope would come to understand.

He also saw that the sometimes foolhardy bravery of his actions, sprung out of fears and a need to atone, somehow, for the fact of his birth and the mixed blood in his veins, his dark skin marking all action as suspect in a world of Whitemen, that this same rash bravery was accorded, among the Sparrow Hawks, the greatest honor.

Coyote Running embraced him once more, his hands on the Antelope's shoulders. He did not smile, Coyote, but looked straight at him and spoke only these words: "My brother."

Still-water clung to him, her moist breath in his ear.

"Come back to the lodge with me," she said. "I want you to fuck me from behind. I am the mare and you are the stallion."

The old head chief, A-ra-poo-ash, came to the lodge of the Antelope and Still-water.

"I wish to speak with the son of my friend Big Bowl," A-ra-poo-ash said, "for now I hear that you have recovered a horse you had once lost to the Gros Ventres. You and your horse have both come back."

"That is true," Antelope said.

"These are very strange things. Perhaps there is medicine in this. Tell me, Antelope, how do you know this horse is the same one?"

"Does a man ever forget a horse that has served him well?"

"No, a man does not forget. Even we who are old do not forget the important things that have happened to us. In the years that are past, I often went on the war-path. Sometimes I still go, but now the young men must protect me. It was not always this way."

"Big Bowl has told me of the many victories of A-ra-poo-ash," Antelope said.

"Did Big Bowl tell you how I got my name? Once, when I was the leader of the Lumpwoods, I was called Angry Bear. It is important to have the right name."

"Big Bowl said you were dying of the bad stomach. You got up and went out to strike coups against the Siksikas."

"Yes, that is what happened. The Siksikas were astonished that a single man would attack them in that way. They feared my medicine, and they all left. I think that Isakawuate made me sick so that I would attack the Siksikas the way I did. That is how I got my name, and some time after that I became the chief of our people. There were times when our enemies did not understand my name, but it was better that way. They did not know the Angry Bear was inside the Rotten Belly. . . ."

The old chief's voice trailed off, and for a long moment he said nothing. Then he continued:

"The years have been good to me. Antelope, your father and I have ridden together many times. Big Bowl has also counted coup many times. Perhaps we will ride the war-path again. It is not good for a man to stay away from the war-path too long. Remember this. It is good that you have joined the Dog Soldiers. You are a strong man. Your enemies will come to fear you, and you will take many coups."

Beckwourth trapped until late December. Some of the smaller streams were now frozen, and a light snow fell and stayed. Cold winds were dropping down from the north, and the leaves were gone from willow and aspen.

He tried to explain Christmas to Still-water, but she merely

looked puzzled and somewhat amused, as if hearing of some primi-
tive and outlandish custom.

"The days will grow longer again," she said patiently. "It has
always been this way. The sun will rise in the sky, and the time of
good grass will come."

So he walked out alone on the night he took to be Christmas Eve,
and he knelt in the snow and tried to pray, something he had not
done for quite a while. The air was sharp in the full moonlight, and
the horned owl cried as though he, too, were praying. But praying
to what? To the moonlit earth and the glittering, frozen snow? Or
was he just trying to get the mice to take fear and to scuttle from one
bunch of frozen grass to another, and the silent wings would drop
and cover their victim? Perhaps the owl was simply *preying*. And
perhaps this is the way it was with all things. The shadow of the
wings. The quiet drama of life and death. The immense beauty of
the mountains, white and gleaming, above the valleys, the immense
beauty that was its own cause and its own purpose and which was
complete in itself and needed nothing, not the hopes and fears of
human creatures, not the superstitions of the Long Knives, and not
anything but its own vast quiet magnificence. In the moonlit night
there were only the cry of the owl and the distant, wild laughter of
coyotes. And the shining outlines of the mountains.

The words of Two Axe, the Pawnee Chief, came back to him, and
he whispered them into the darkness:

"I will use you well, my brother. You died to save me, you
opened yourself to me so that I might shoot you and kill you and eat
of your flesh. May your spirit find its way into the other world."

The Antelope returned to his lodge where, as he discovered, Still-
water had also heard the laughter of the wild brothers in the night.
She urged him to lie down with her, and then she played on his flute
for a long while, until he begged her to finish. She bit him then and
told him that he must lie still, for he was a brave warrior and had
great endurance. Then, in her own good time, she finished what she
had begun.

The fire in his blood vanished, and he slept.

A few days later the Absarokas sent a trading party into the country of the Prairie Gros Ventres and the Mandans, where the Long Knives had established a trading post. The Antelope sent a full pack of plew, each of the skins marked with "JB."

The trader, a man named Kipp, inquired as to the identity of "JB," and Black Panther explained that the Antelope had once lived with the Whites and could make their signs. Kipp wrote out a note which he asked Black Panther to deliver: a request to the Antelope to visit the fort.

But while Black Panther and the others were away, the Crow village was attacked by Sioux and Arikara together. The assault was sudden, completely unexpected, and the Sparrow Hawks were momentarily thrown into confusion. But they gathered themselves at length and charged their enemies, driving through their ranks, until the attackers scattered and withdrew. The allies had made a mistake in supposing that all the warriors were gone, when only a small party was absent.

The Antelope dipped his battle axe into the brains of several. The blood ran down the haft and dripped from his wrist. Three horses were shot out from under him, and he was thankful he had not had time to get to Come Back. A rifle ball nibbled his shoulder, but left only a scratch.

The Sparrow Hawks took a large number of scalps, but there was neither dancing nor rejoicing, for all were busy attending to the wounded or mourning relatives slain in battle. Some of the women cut off fingers or scarred themselves with knives, and a dismal moaning and howling issued from a number of lodges.

The following day the dead were fastened in trees, where they would remain until the flesh had decayed and fallen from the bones. The skeletons would later be taken down and buried in caves. On this occasion no horses belonging to the slain warriors were killed, although, as Coyote Running said, such a thing was sometimes done.

No member of the Antelope's family had been killed, and he gave thanks to Isakakate.

Still-water wished to accompany the Antelope and Coyote Running as they tended to their traps. The three of them rode through the thin, late snow of the turning of the seasons until they came to the mouth of the long drainage that Antelope and Coyote had been working. They tethered their horses beneath some maples, where the snow was only an inch or two deep, and the dry grass, broken at the end of winter, projected through. From there they worked their way upstream, taking several beaver and resetting the traps.

At a bend in the stream, where the canyon opened out into a small meadow, Coyote Running signaled a stop—pointed. Perhaps fifty yards ahead was a bear, a big male black bear, newly emerged from hibernation, thin, apparently hungry, clawing half-heartedly at the base of a nearly dead pine.

"We're downwind," the Antelope said. "Let's move on up for a closer look at this fellow."

"Even black bears are bad-natured this time of the year," Coyote Running cautioned.

"If he gets ugly, we'll take home some bearmeat and a new robe. Come on, my friends. I want to watch him."

Coyote Running glanced at Still-water and gestured with his hands. The Antelope, he knew well enough, was given to unpredictable thoughts.

They moved forward, keeping to the cover of willow brush, and watched, Coyote Running and Still-water both uncertain as to why they were doing this thing. Antelope led until they were within a few yards, then motioned a halt.

The black bear hunched forward, straddling two pine logs taken down by the heavy winds of a few years past, the wood barkless now, the grain silver, weathered in the slow fire of wind and rain. The animal wobbled slightly and moved its massive head from side to side—the small fan-shaped ears, the heavy, dark fur, the snout lighter, almost cream-colored. The eyes were brown, only flecks of white showing, the unblinking eyes, intense, intelligent, metal-hot points of light reflected in them.

Staring, staring.

The nose twitched, the muscles tensed, all senses alert, sharp, puzzled and fearless.

Aware of something close by.

The animal rose to its hind legs, moved its head back and forth, looked for some motion. Then it dropped back to all four legs, its claws touched at the silver wood, and it shuffled slowly forward, still sniffing at the air, moved off up the hillside, away from them.

"Why didn't you shoot him, my brother?" Coyote asked.

"Just wanted to look was all. Hide's not much good right now anyway."

"Your husband likes danger, Still-water."

"He was a beautiful bear," Still-water said. "Only a white bear is larger. He was very big."

"Maybe he was a medicine bear," Coyote said. "Perhaps if we had shot him, we could have had a bear dance. Do you know about this thing?"

"Sometimes it is better to watch, Coyote. I think the bear-people have secrets that we should learn. But tell me about the bear dance."

"I will tell you," Still-water said. "We have the dance when someone has a bear dance vision. Perhaps if we had shot the medicine bear, one of us would have had a vision, I do not know. We would prepare the meat, make pemmican, and mix it with the marrow of buffalo bones. It is better in the fall when the chokecherries are ripe. Then we would make balls of the meat."

Antelope laughed.

"I thought you were going to tell me about a dance, not a dinner."

"Still-water is right," Coyote Running said. "This must come first."

"Then we would put red paint on the claws of the bearskin and tie the skin to a pole. Singers would carry their drums into the circle about the pole with the bearskin on it. Then they would hit their drums, and the bear songs would begin. One of the medicine men, maybe Ears of the Wolf, would then come out wearing a buffalo skin with the fur side out, and others would follow him, all dressed the same."

"Strange things happen at the bear dance," Coyote said and nodded.

"The dancers must fast before they dance," Still-water continued. "Then they are able to take things out of their mouths, for these are things that came into their stomachs during the dance, things like black dirt, white clay, elk chips, owl feathers, an eagle's tail, or parts of the bodies of bears or jackrabbits. Even horse tails or buffalo tails."

"This is all very strange," Antelope said. "How do they do these things?"

"It is the magic of the bear song dance," Coyote answered. "And sometimes other strange things happen too. Sometimes the young girls become crazy at the dance. When I was still a boy, I remember a girl who blew out clouds of red powder until she fell down in exhaustion. Her father then tried to help her dance, but she could not do it. So he burned some sweet grass, and she breathed the smoke from it, and then she was well again."

"In the season of dry grass, the bears dance in the mountains," Still-water said. "That is when the chokecherries and the wild plums are ripe. That is why we usually have the bear song dance in the autumn."

With the melting of the snow and the coming of the spring grass, the Sparrow Hawks sent out a war-party numbering about twenty, youths and more experienced warriors—but not one ever came back alive. Only the pack dogs returned.

Anger swept the village, and immediately another party was drawn together, including Coyote Running, his features hard with rage, and Black Panther. Fifty good warriors in all, and the Antelope was appointed their leader. Hatred for the Blackfeet pushed all caution aside, and the men mounted swiftly, silently, and moved out. The ride of a few miles brought them to the pitiful remains of the massacred party. The bodies, boys and men, were strewn about, butchered. The enemy's tracks were everywhere in the muddy earth, Blackfoot arrows in some of the bodies.

"They are not far, my brother," Coyote said. "We must move after them at once. They will not be expecting pursuit."

Black Panther knelt over the scalped form of one of Big Bowl's sons, a boy of twelve years, one who had taken coup against the Gros Ventres. The Antelope placed his hand on Black Panther's shoulder.

"Let us take revenge. They are not far away."

Black Panther nodded without speaking.

They left the bodies and rode onward, silently, and came within an hour to a village of nine lodges; already the Blackfeet were drunk, drunk at their victory dance, and the Crows came upon them at a full ride.

The dance was short.

The Crows killed every man except two, lookouts on the hill above, who made their escape. Forty-eight men fell to their weapons, and the scalp of each was taken. Not one of the Sparrow Hawks was killed, and only a few were wounded, none seriously.

The women and children were taken prisoner.

The Antelope scalped one of the men he had killed, took his weapons and clothing, and cut off his head with a hand axe.

There had been only a few women in the camp. The Antelope took prisoner a girl of about fourteen and a little boy about eight. These and the other prisoners would become Sparrow Hawks. The boys would grow to be warriors and would learn to kill Blackfeet. The Sparrow Hawks also took a drove of horses and many valuable furs—beaver, otter, and fox.

"When we take women prisoners," Coyote Running said, "no harder lot is imposed upon them than our own women endure. They are allowed to marry into the tribe, after which they are equals. Nor may the man who takes such a prisoner marry her. These women may mourn for a day or two, but they will soon come to see that they are better off than before they were captured. It is better to be an Absaroka than a Siksika."

The young girl the Antelope had taken would now become one of his sisters, and Big Bowl would find her a husband.

They burned the lodges of the Blackfeet and returned to their own village, stopping long enough to gather the bodies of their young men and warriors, where they lay, scattered about in the clearing that had witnessed their deaths. One old warrior had fallen face down in the fresh young grass, shot through the lungs, and in his death throes he had smeared the up-welling blood from his mouth all about him. Flies speckled the dried blood on the grass.

The Antelope lifted the old man in his arms and carried him to where Come Back was standing. The body, of course, had grown quite stiff.

But Black Panther said, "My brothers, our victory will make these burials less bitter, for our war axes have drunk their revenge. Our women will not grieve so loudly, but this is still a hateful task."

Coyote Running placed Big Bowl's son over his horse's back, and the Sparrow Hawks moved on toward their village, victorious and grim.

But then came a series of reverses for the Crows. Small parties of six or eight went out, came back mauled, many braves slain through the use of this tactic. The method made no sense to Beckwourth, and he would not go out with them.

The losses mounted.

The village became the scene of continuous mourning, the women mangling themselves in a shocking manner, fingers hacked off, lacerations on arms and breasts and faces. Many were bleeding, pulling their hair, moaning like beaten dogs. Fathers slain, brothers, lovers.

Jim Beckwourth found that he simply could not endure the pain of their cries. Where was Rotten Belly? The old chief had gone to visit Long Hair, and this was the result. The Sparrow Hawks were mindlessly destroying themselves. The young warriors would not listen to the Council.

Antelope and Broken Shoulder took some of the younger men and went out after horse thieves. They returned with four scalps and were engaged in performing the scalp dance when the last of the small parties came back, three men, all wounded, bearing six dead on their horses.

The dance was stopped, and Beckwourth went to his lodge.

When he awoke the next morning, Still-water was not there. But she returned soon, a mob of women with her.

"Antelope!" they cried. "Your medicine is strong. You must lead our men to victory!"

The Antelope did not answer. They repeated their words, but he did not come out. Then he could hear only the buzzing of their voices, and he wondered what they were up to. He learned quickly: together they lifted his lodge from over his head and moved it away from him, then threw leggings, moccasins, and other things at him—offerings made not without scorn.

"Enough!" he shouted and stood up. The women backed away.

"I will go with the warriors. Our revenge will be great. Tell your men I will lead them—all warriors—the old and the young stay home. My medicine has always been good and true. I do not come home without spoils. You know I speak the truth. Now we will put this medicine to the test. Tell Broken Shoulder to take some men and capture a silver-gray fox, bring it to me alive. I need it to complete my medicine. Then we shall seek a great victory. Now I have spoken. Go. I will wait and make my prayer."

He heard his own voice speaking, hardly believed what he heard. The words came suddenly. He could not control them. He truly did not know what he would do with the fox when it was brought to him—for he knew they would do as he said.

They left, and the Antelope sat back down, trembling, but not with fear. Still-water stood close, her eyes cast down.

Finally she said, "I'm sorry, my husband."

He stood up, drew her to him, and ran his fingers over her long, braided hair.

"It will be all right," he said. "My medicine is strong."

Again the words came without his willing them to come.

Two hours later the women brought the fox, which they had captured in a surround. The Antelope told Broken Shoulder and Black Panther to choke the little animal to death and then to flay it. They did this, and the skin was handed to him. He wrapped it around his medicine bow, closed his eyes, and told them the cunning of the fox had come into his head and that victory was assured.

"Go arm yourselves," he said. "Make your medicine and make your prayers. We will ride in the morning, with the first light."

The Wolves returned with news of the enemy. Thirty-seven Cheyenne lodges.

The Antelope told the Wolves to go back and to watch carefully.

"If anything happens, bring me word."

The Wolves appeared again the next day and said the enemy had moved their camp down Antelope Creek, not far from the Big River. The Antelope ordered the return of all the spies except ten.

"That is your creek," Broken Shoulder said. "What do you plan?"

"We will follow them through the canyon and attack at the mouth."

But as the Sparrow Hawks moved along, another Wolf returned.

"They have moved farther down and are encamped at the edge of the timber. They have set up their lodges."

"Then they will stay until we arrive."

The Crows approached the Cheyenne village with great caution, moving just a few miles each day. Finally they took a position on a hill overlooking their enemies and watched them carefully for a time. Then the Antelope divided his force into three groups, one to stay where they were, one to move to the opposite hill, and the third to follow him for direct attack and quick retreat, thus drawing the enemy into a crossfire. Broken Shoulder was to command one group, Scarred Face the second.

The Antelope spoke briefly to all the men:

"Sparrow Hawk brothers, you are brave warriors. Now we must work together, not as lone hunters. We must hold to our plan, for then victory will be ours. We will go down now. There will be time for Scarred Face's group to come around from the other side. Then my group will attack. When we lead them to you, fall on them quickly. We will regain our honor, and no one will think of the defeats we have suffered this spring. Remember that you are Sparrow Hawks. You are the people of A-ra-poo-ash and Long Hair. When we fight together, no one can defeat us."

When all was ready, the Antelope advanced. But suddenly they came upon two men, caught them by surprise, killed and scalped them. The Crows rode on until they came within full sight of the enemy. But the Cheyennes showed no intention of coming out of their camp. Only the dogs barked.

The Antelope had the two scalps brought to him and then rode forward alone, waving the clots of hair still slick with blood and slime. He shouted insults, but the Cheyennes would not move. The Antelope saw quickly enough that to charge with just his group, directly into their village, would have brought the Sparrow Hawks great loss of life, even if they were able to kill and scalp the last Cheyenne there. His instinct was to press the attack, but he thought of his people and their war customs.

He considered the matter: "We have taken two scalps, have lost no warrior, have taken no wounds. We have insulted them with their own bloody scalps, yet they do not respond. My medicine is still strong, and they respect it. They know their own fear, know they are marked as cowards. Two scalps with no loss is a greater victory than to kill them all, if some of our own warriors must die."

Once more he raised the scalps high and shouted at the enemy:

"Where are your warriors, Cheyennes? Have you only women and old men in your lodges? The Cheyennes have always been cowards! Your dogs are braver than you are! You are not worthy of fighting with. Even the Sioux know how to die more bravely!"

The men behind him shouted and screamed insults, but the Cheyennes did not move. The Antelope spit upon the earth, turned Come Back about, and rode slowly back to his men. The other groups poured down from the two hills, and they headed toward home.

The village received them with immense applause. No one wore mourning paint, and they performed the scalp dance in high spirits. The women of the village, those who had lifted his lodge above his head and taunted him, now hailed him:

"The Antelope's medicine is great! Our victory is sweet!"

The Antelope subsequently took several wives, for as a result of the heavy losses of spring, there were numerous women unattended. Still-water encouraged him in this, without jealousy, for it increased their power and station among the people.

In one case, however, he was not only courted but even bullied into marriage—for there was a young girl who followed him about, shyly at first, then more openly.

Her first words to him were these: "I wish to be your wife."

He laughed at her and stroked her cheek, telling her that she was too young.

Too young, perhaps, but not without determination.

"You are a great brave," she said. "You have the right to paint the faces of your wives, for you have killed the enemies of the Sparrow Hawks. I want you to paint my face when you return from the wars."

He answered her by saying, "You are very pretty, little one, but you are only a child. Your breasts have not grown yet. When you are older, then we will talk about it."

"No. I am old enough now. My mother died when I was young, and my father has been slain by the Piegans. I have my own lodge, my sister and I live together. She is a year older than I, and she must also marry. She has chosen her man. I will be proud to be one of your wives and to have you paint my face after a victory. You will give me many good things, fine clothes and scarlet cloth. And I can make you pretty things, leggings and moccasins. I can take care of your war horses and weapons."

He looked down at her, an expression on her face that both pled and demanded. In the world of the Whites, such a thing would be wrong. But in Absaroka, he wasn't sure which thing was wrong.

Then her eyes blazed definance or wounded pride, and she said, cupping her hands on her chest, "I will have breasts soon—see, they are beginning to grow. Then you will want to sleep with me."

The Antelope burst out laughing, something which startled the girl for a moment.

"We will move your lodge near to mine," he said, "and you will be one of my wives."

He took the girl, Nom-ne-dit-chee, to Still-water, telling her that the little girl was his wife. "You must dress her up finely," he said, "for she is one of us now. She will make a good wood carrier."

"This one is very young," Still-water said. "You must not lie with Nom-ne-dit-chee yet. You would split her open, and she would bleed to death. You will have to be patient, Antelope Jim, or we will all wear mourning paint."

The girl's eyes blazed again.

"I am old enough," she said. "I have never slept with a man, but I know what to do. I'll prove it to you! Your women can watch."

"No, little one," the Antelope said. "Little Wife, we must both be patient. That is your name now. Little Wife."

ENEMY OF HORSES

Far from home, the woman and her daughter had nothing to eat, and so they went to sleep on the big rock. In the night the woman woke up and called out for Helpers, but no one answered, and so she went to sleep again. It was almost dawn when the woman felt someone beside her. She reached out and touched a large, hairy leg: a white bear was sleeping beside her. When it was light, the bear stood up and said, "Here is meat for you and your young daughter. I will have to go now, and it will be best for you to follow me—go in the direction I do. When I reach the wide willows on Tongue River, I will wait there for you. Remember these words, my sister."

It was a good summer.

He considered making the trek over to Rendezvous, for he wanted very much to see Le Blueux, La Jeunesse, Bridger, and Black Harris—to assure them he was alive and well and happy with his new life. Further, he had three full packs of beaver, furs worth three thousand dollars at market value. But it was a long venture, and if he went, it seemed to him, he should go alone. At length he decided to deal with Kipp at the fort. The word, he knew well enough, would soon spread that Jim Beckwourth was alive.

So instead he spent most of his time hunting buffalo and trapping beaver in the high country, where the skins retained their prime condition much longer into the summer.

When midsummer came, he decided to hunt for mountain sheep, and Little Wife wished to accompany him. After being badgered for a time, he agreed, thinking she might be useful. As he had come to realize, she was particularly intelligent and curious, and as they rode upward into the mountains, she regaled him with any number of questions about his travels, the villages of the Whites, the great lodges—the city buildings—of which she had heard him speak.

Her breasts were indeed developing, and her body was now clearly that of a woman, or almost so. She was distinctly vain about her looks, something which amused him.

"Antelope," she said, "I want to know something."

"You always want to know something, Little Wife."

"Speak truth now. Are the White squaws as pretty as I am? You'd rather have White squaws, wouldn't you?"

"The Whites have only one squaw."

"Aren't the Whites wealthy? You told me. . . ."

"It's not that. They have different customs. It is their custom to have just one squaw."

"What if the squaw dies?"

"Then the Whiteman may take another squaw."

"And if the Long Knife dies?"

"Then the squaw may take another husband."

Little Wife was silent for a moment, then asked: "If you could have just one wife, would you choose me?"

"How can you ask that when the others have been so good to you? Don't you know that Still-water loves you?"

"Yes, I know that but . . . you'd choose her, wouldn't you?"

"I've never even fucked you, my girl. How do I know that I'd like you the best? I can't answer until I've tried you out," the Antelope said, trying not to smile.

"Will you do it tonight, then? When we make camp in the high mountains? The other women know I've never slept with a man. They make fun of me. They say I'm not really your wife. Will you do it to me tonight? I can do more than Still-water or any of them."

"I don't know," he answered, "you're still very young. I might hurt you."

"I am not afraid of being hurt. It is time for me to learn, and you must teach me. You are my husband. Otherwise I will have to meet one of the young men out in the willows. Shall I do that? Don't you want me?"

"Little Wife, don't you know how big my cock is? I would make you bleed and cry."

She smiled wickedly.

"Still-water told me that your cock is very small, and that is why you will not show it to me."

The Antelope burst out laughing, then whistled.

"All right, my girl, I'll make you my wife tonight, and tomorrow you will be sore and will not be able to ride your horse."

"But my horse will ride me tonight? I will bear you a child."

They camped in a small meadow below a cliff face, and Little Wife tethered Come Back and the other horses while the Antelope built a fire. He watched her upslope, her figure in the waning light, the cliffs above burning the blood color of the clouds. He could hear the sound of falling water.

"Isakawuate," he said. "This nigger gives you his thanks for all of it. You have created a beautiful world, even if you are careless about the details of things. I guess you must have been drunk with the beauty of the mountains, just like I am. You stay up there now, you hear?"

The Antelope and Little Wife ate their roasted buffalo meat and then got under their blankets. He still felt some hesitance about copulating with one so young, but her little minklike hands had found their way under his clothing, and the last of his qualms disappeared.

He was gentle with her, using his finger first, tickling, inserting, feeling her maidenhead. Her body stiffened, winced as he entered her, and she breathed in short little animal gasps. He could feel her hymen tearing.

"Relax now," he said. "Pretend you are bathing in the warm springs, and I will go slowly. The first time is always difficult."

Afterward she lay curled against his chest, her arms around him. He was just dozing into sleep when she spoke:

"My husband, I intend some time in my life to enter into the medicine lodge."

It took a moment for her voice to register upon him, but such an assertion, so strangely out of place, astonished him.

"It is dangerous," he said.

"Not if the woman is virtuous, then it is not dangerous."

The dedication of a woman in the service of Isakakate was highly unusual, the Antelope knew, for the woman must be virtuous, talented, and fit. She would have to claim fidelity to her husband, and should any man contradict her, she would not be admitted. If many men spoke against her, she might well be slain on the spot. However, if she succeeded, she would be greatly honored and accepted into the sacred service of Isakakate for the rest of her life.

"Is this your way of telling me that you will be faithful? You are my Little Wife, and I am honored to be the first with you."

"Yes, I will be faithful. You were gentle with me. The women say that most men are not gentle. But I wish to enter into the medicine lodge—then I will bring great honor to you, as you have honored me."

They killed several sheep during the next few days and then returned, the horses loaded with the skins and the meat, to the village. The Antelope went to the lodge of Coyote Running to present him with one of the hides. Coyote greeted him and introduced the Antelope to the young woman whom Coyote had married during his brother's absence. The Antelope was pleased with Coyote's good fortune and quite surprised to learn who his new squaw was—for he had known nothing of the matter.

"Sometimes these things happen quickly," he said.

The girl was none other than Grouse-feather, Little Wife's older sister.

"Why didn't you tell me that she had eyes for you, Coyote? We are supposed to share each other's thoughts."

"If I had known, I would have told you. She approached me on the day you left the village, was very shy toward me, said she would be my woman."

Big Bowl had offered to find a wife for Coyote, just as he had done for the Antelope. But Coyote Running had declined.

The Antelope remembered that Little Wife had told him months before that her sister had picked out her man. Apparently the girl was not so direct as her younger sister.

Coyote insisted that his friend should enter the lodge and take a meal with them, and he agreed. As it turned out, they had strips of buffalo tongue, something the Antelope had avoided eating before, inasmuch as the Crows did not even half cook it. Apparently Coyote had realized this and had communicated the information to Grouse-feather, for the meat was well-done, and the Antelope ate heartily. Afterward he praised the meat and asked naively what it was, though of course he knew. When Grouse-feather replied that it was tongue, Coyote Running grew suddenly fearful that in departing from his dietary rule, the Antelope might have infringed his medicine.

Coyote Running started up in horror, shouting, "Tongue! Tongue! You have harmed his medicine. If he falls in battle, they will blame both of us."

For a moment the Antelope did not know what to do, but he knew that he had to do something. So he bolted from the lodge, bellowing like a buffalo, sticking out his own tongue, and pawing the ground like a furious bear. Coyote and Grouse-feather rushed out after him, and he said, "This will remove the spell, let my medicine be strong once more."

They stared at him solemnly, while he could hardly control the laughter that roared inside. He hugged them both, told them again that everything was all right, and then held Coyote Running at arm's length and praised the beauty of his new wife.

In high spirits, the Antelope returned to his own lodge.

Little Wife and Still-water were giggling as he entered, and he could well imagine what they had been speaking of—for they grew quiet, while appearing more than a little bit smug about something.

"Now all of my wives will have the hide of a mountain sheep," he said, "while I alone shall be without one."

The strength of his medicine was accorded by all save a few. A minor incident, one which would have left him dead except for the luckiest circumstance, further enforced the belief that it was infallible. The Sparrow Hawks had made a surround, enclosing several hundred buffalo. On charging among the animals, the hunters discovered seven Blackfeet who, finding escape was cut off, quickly provided themselves with a sand barricade. In battle, the counting of coup had always seemed to Jim Beckwourth, if not to the Antelope, a foolish and dangerous gesture, more productive of casualties than victory. But finding himself now with a driver's staff of willow in his hands, he charged down on the Blackfeet from behind and struck one a powerful blow with the staff. Then, being without his pistol, he retired from the melee, declaring that he had wounded the first enemy and counted coup.

He watched as the others proceeded with the business of killing the Blackfeet. But a bullet struck him, hit the knife on his belt, and laid him out breathless on the ground. He arose bleeding from the mouth and, supposing the ball had penetrated his body, he imagined himself a dead man. He was carried back to the village, and the medicine man, Ears of the Wolf, hovered over him, searched for his wound. But there was only a bruise, no penetration. The ball was later found where he fell, flattened of course, by its impact against the steel of his knife.

His medicine was great! Bullets would not pierce him!

This was the conclusion of the Crows. And since it was somewhat better than the truth, he did not enlighten them.

A few still doubted, however, and among these was an ill-natured fellow named Bears Copulating—a large man, as large and perhaps as strong as the Antelope himself. One day this man proclaimed that Big Bowl had no bravery and was dishonest. Bears Copulating had not noticed the Antelope nearby, and a confrontation ensued.

"I think you have made a mistake," the Antelope said. "You must have been talking about someone else, not Big Bowl."

"You too, Antelope, you are no Sparrow Hawk. You come from the Whites. You pretend to be brave, but you are no brave."

The two men drew their battle axes and rushed at each other, but someone thrust a pipe between them, and they halted. To disobey this sign meant instant death.

Broken Shoulder spoke:

"Bears Copulating, you have said that Big Bowl and Antelope are not warriors. We all know better, for all of us have ridden in battle with either the father or the son. And the Antelope led us at the end of spring, when we regained our honor. But Bears Copulating is also a great brave. Who is the greater may be proven when we meet the enemy—then we may decide. Yet Antelope and Bears Copulating must never again attempt to take each other's life."

Thus an uneasy peace was established between the two, but soon the question of valor was brought to a test. On a small war party, with Bears Copulating and the Antelope both present, they came across an even smaller group of Cheyennes.

The Cheyennes knew they could not escape, and so they accepted battle.

"Come, Bears Copulating," the Antelope shouted. "You see their chief? Now we may decide who is the best man. You and I will charge him directly, riding side by side."

Bears Copulating agreed, though less than fullheartedly. The quarrel being well known, he could not do otherwise. They charged together. Antelope saw the Cheyenne chief open the pan of his gun and give it a slight tap with his hand, to make the discharge certain. As the two bore down upon him, he presented his piece and took deliberate aim. One death seemed certain—Bears Copulating or the Antelope would die in a moment, their quarrel thus ended.

Then they were upon the Cheyenne.

The Antelope grasped the muzzle of the gun at the very instant it exploded and cut the man down with the battle axe in his right hand. His left cheek was filled with powder from the discharge,

painful but otherwise harmless. Bears Copulating did not even
strike the chief, leaving the coup to his antagonist, and happy still
to be alive.

After the last Cheyenne had been dispatched, and in hearing of all
the warriors, Bears Copulating said, "Antelope, you are a great
brave. I was wrong to say what I did. We are now good friends."

The Sparrow Hawks returned to the village with three wounded
but none killed, and the Antelope elaborately painted the faces of his
wives. At the victory dance, Beckwourth was given an additional
name, Bull's Robe, conferred upon him by Big Bowl, his father.

Later his wives made much of the powder wound.

At times Beckwourth found it necessary to rehearse the details of
his former life in order to maintain at least the illusion of his other
identity. He had now been a Sparrow Hawk for so long that any dif-
ferent life seemed ever more a dream that he could recollect only in
fragments.

Perhaps the changing of names contributed to this: and now his
name was changed again, and he was Bull's Robe.

At the heart of it, though, was the wildness, the utter barbarian
simplicity of the Indian way—appealing to him, habituating. The
constant movement and the fluid passing of time always made the
present moment of vastly greater importance than any plans, any
thoughts of future years. While with Ashley and Sublette, he had
found himself doing things he had not conceived of, enduring hard-
ships he had not dreamed of. Brutal violence was the essential way of
things and was not to be wondered at. Then he became a part of that
violence, accepted it, joyed in it, the immediate risk and dare, his
life fated and protected by a medicine he did not understand and
sometimes did not believe in.

Why did he love the surge of battle? For he did. Only in retro-
spect was he horrified, unbelieving of the things he knew he had
done. Then to watch the women mutilate themselves in mourning,
the stoically self-inflicted pain, the wailing and sobbing. To witness
this was perhaps more difficult than anything else.

What force kept him there?

The great peaks, the running clouds, summer rainstorms, the first autumn snows silently falling? The cries of coyotes and wolves? Old Ephraim the white bear of the Indians? The Hawken cradled on his arm, the wind in the trees, the forests, rivers, mountains, plains without end? The great herds of buffalo, phantom-like deer gliding through the trees, antelope, moose, elk, mountain sheep, Brother Beaver in the streams?

Was it something more than this?

Quaking aspens burned their bright gold against the mountainsides, and smoke from the lodge fires hung to the ground. The streams ran low and quiet, and ice formed overnight where the water was shallow among the dark rocks of creek bottoms. Dry leaves began to whisper down through the still air, and the Sparrow Hawks huddled about the good warmth of the fire in the early morning. The breath of horses was little trickles of steam from nostril and mouth. Coyotes and wolves howled through the night, and pigeons made a clatter of wings among the trees. It was time for the journey to the trading post.

Beckwourth had decided to go with the party in order to attend to the sale of his own property. With furs worth three thousand dollars in St. Louis, he was eager to gain close to full value for them. The party rode to Fort Clark on the Missouri River, and there the trading began.

He chose to wait until his people had nearly completed their bartering, careful not to call attention to himself. He spoke only the language of the Crows, was dressed like a Crow, and his hair was now as long as a Crow's. But when one of the tribe inquired about the *be-has-i-pe-hish-a,* and the clerk could not understand and called for Kipp, Bull's Robe spoke in English:

"Gentlemen, this man wants scarlet cloth."

No doubt they were both astonished, and Kipp asked, "Where did you learn English?"

"With the Whiteman."

"You lived with the Whites?"

"Yes, for more than twenty years—in St. Louis."

Kipp scanned him from head to foot and then said, "You are not a Crow?"

"No, I am not."

"What's your name, then?"

"Bull's Robe," he said, "but in English it's Jim Beckwourth."

"Beckwourth! JB on those skins last year. You were reported dead by Captain Sublette. You've been living with the Crows?"

"Yes, I am one of them now."

The other Sparrow Hawks, of course, understood little or nothing of the conversation, but they were proud to see a Crow speak so fluently with the Long Knives.

Then Beckwourth said, "Mr. Kipp, you make a good profit on the Indians, but I think you should deal more fairly with me. I did not find these plew lying about in the meadows."

Kipp nodded and agreed that Beckwourth should set his own price, and so Bull's robe returned to his Sparrow Hawk brothers with a large bale of goods. His fellows rejoiced at his great fortune, and there was some talk that he had been given a high price as indemnity for his time of captivity with the Whites.

Upon his return to the village, Bull's Robe would be able to make various presents to all of his wives, some of whom he did not see for months together, and to his many other relatives. Further, he would be able to trade with his fellow warriors, for they now placed significant confidence in his integrity.

"We speak the same language," he thought.

On the trek from the trading post back to the Absaroka village, the group crossed paths with a party of perhaps two hundred and fifty Cheyenne warriors, while their own party numbered about two hundred and was encumbered by a still greater number of women. The Sparrow Hawks had surprised the Cheyennes, and the latter attacked immediately, in mid-afternoon, while they were still moving. Had the Cheyennes waited until the evening encampment, with the horses turned out, the Crows could not have escaped defeat. But as it was, every warrior had his war horse by his side, with lance and shield ready at hand.

The Cheyennes advanced. The Sparrow Hawks drove them back and then made their own attack. The enemy rallied and came at them with much screaming and shouting, but the Sparrow Hawks were united now and were able to repulse them, throwing them into confusion. The Cheyennes scattered into the forest where, wisely, the Sparrow Hawks did not wish to follow. Nine warriors had been killed and more than that number were wounded, including Bull's Robe, for an arrow had put a bad gash in his scalp. They had also lost one pack horse laden with goods from the post. Still nearly two hundred miles from their village, the Sparrow Hawks moved onward, subdued, carrying their dead with them.

Days later they reached home.

Big Bowl, who had not made the trek to Fork Clark, was highly agitated, for the Blackfeet had stolen a large number of horses from his herd. Indeed, the Siksika had depleted all of the herds.

"Bull's Robe, you will come with me. We must pursue these horse-thieves immediately. It is not right for the Blackfeet to steal the horses of the Crows. This is the opposite of the way things should be!"

At the end of a long journey, his hair matted with dried blood, the last thing Bull's Robe wanted was to set out once more. But he could see that his father would not be satisfied to wait. He thought a moment and then said, "Father, you have seen many winters. I am younger. Let me take Black Panther and some of the others, as many as are willing to go. We will bring back horses, but we must hurry, for though the snows have not yet fallen, they will come soon."

"My son believes his father to be an old man who cannot steal horses?"

"Someone must hunt for our women and protect them if the village is attacked."

"Why may Coyote Running not do this? Excellence in horse-thieving requires both the strength of the young and the wisdom of the old. By yourselves, maybe you and Black Panther would bring back only four or five horses. We have lost many more than that."

"You and Coyote together must stay to protect the village. We will return with many horses. My horse medicine is good."

Something in Big Bowl's eyes told Bull's Robe that his father was not convinced, yet the older man agreed to his son's plan.

The homecoming, then, was short. Two days later, with a large party, Bull's Robe and Black Panther moved toward the headwaters of the Arkansas, once again into Arapaho country. At length they arrived at a village of nearly a hundred lodges. But no sooner had they begun to lay plans for an attack than they discovered four Whitemen, whom they quickly surrounded. Bull's Robe rode forward in the hope that he might be able to overhear some bits of conversation.

"Wagh! No way out."

"What'll the bastards do?"

"If they take us alive, these coons'll burn us to death. Stick pine slivers into our hides and burn us like porkies."

"It's a war party—mebbe they got other fish to fry. Mebbe we're just a diversion."

"They be lookin' like Crows, Sonny. Mebbe they'll be lettin' us go."

Bull's Robe stepped forward and called to the trappers in English:

"Gentlemen. You're safe. My name is Jim Beckwourth. The warriors will do as I tell them. Come out—you'll have to stay in our camp until tomorrow."

"It's a fuckin' trap."

"Take my word, gentlemen. If we decided to kill you, you'd have no choice in the matter."

Bull's Robe welcomed the four Whites and listened to their story of misfortune—their horses stolen, their pelts taken. As it turned out, they had neither ammunition nor even a gun.

"Tomorrow we attack the Arapahos," Bull's Robe said. "If we succeed, I'll give you a rifle and twenty rounds. With luck, that should get you back to Santa Fe. You can tell people that Jim

Beckwourth's not only alive, but that he saved your lives. Maybe your luck returns."

The four trappers ate with the Sparrow Hawks but did not wait for morning—slipped off during the night, as Beckwourth had expected, for he had already given them the gun and ammunition. Under the circumstances, they were not likely to go walking into an Arapaho village, not if they valued their hair.

The attack was made. The Sparrow Hawks divided their force, with Bull's Robe's old enemy Bears Copulating heading one party and Black Panther and Bull's Robe the other. Bears Copulating had charge of driving off the Arapaho horses, which mission he performed with immense success.

Black Panther and Bull's Robe came down upon the village, and though the Crows deemed the Arapahos to be poor warriors, they defended themselves bravely. The Crows had hoped to take the Arapaho horses with as little fighting as possible, but as it turned out it was necessary to kill fourteen of their men. Four Crows were wounded, and these needlessly, since the men had stopped to scalp the fallen Arapahos.

In all they took nearly a thousand horses, a great capture, and everyone was in excellent spirits as they journeyed homeward. The skies darkened, and a light snow began to fall just as they came within sight of their own village.

The warriors were greeted warmly by their people, and the celebration began immediately. It was only then that Black Panther and Bull's Robe learned what had happened. Big Bowl, prideful old warrior that he was, had taken a party of his own on the day following the departure of his two sons. The two younger men were greatly worried about him, but they need not have been. On the next day after their arrival home, a party emerged from beneath the snow-hung trees. Big Bowl was at the head, and his warriors were driving an enormous herd of horses, perhaps three thousand in all.

The celebration was great.

Big Bowl was hailed by A-ra-poo-ash, who embraced him warmly.

"The next time my old friend rides out," Rotten Belly said, "I will ride with him. We will ride the war-path together, as we did many winters ago. If we die, then we will be able to travel to the Spirit World together. Where did you find all these horses, my brother?"

"They were grazing in the lands of the Siksikas. Some are the horses we just loaned them. I was afraid the Siksikas would not take good care of them, so I decided to bring them back."

Beckwourth was once again given a new name, Is-ko-chu-e-chu-re, Enemy of Horses, but the victory truly belonged to his father. None of Big Bowl's warriors had been lost, and none had been wounded.

"My sons," he said, "even though I am so old that I can hardly move, and all the strength has gone out of my arms, the medicine simply became too powerful, and I had to go."

"Your arms are still stronger than those of younger men, my father," the Enemy of Horses said.

Bitter cold now in the winter encampment, and the few inches of snow blew about wildly. Even the running stream was solidly frozen, and the Sparrow Hawks stayed in their lodges much of the time.

But during a midwinter respite, warm rain took away the snow.

It was then that a feud broke out, a grudge long-standing between the Foxes and the Dog Soldiers, of which Enemy of Horses was now the acknowledged leader. The Foxes were led by Red Eyes, and it was between this man and Yellow Belly, the younger brother of A-ra-poo-ash and a Dog Soldier, that the quarrel came to its head. Yellow Belly was a very brave man, but extremely disagreeable in his manners, insulting in his speech. Red Eyes was also renowned as a fighter, but his pride was reserved, and Yellow Belly's bragging offended him.

Pipe men were obliged to intervene to prevent open fighting.

It was proposed then that each man should take a number of warriors and go off to do battle against a common enemy. The question of bravery would be decided by the number of scalps brought back by each side.

Red Eyes quietly chose his men, but Yellow Belly declared, "I will win with fewer men. Red Eyes has nineteen men. I will take only sixteen and still bring back the greater number of scalps." He then approached Beckwourth and said, "Enemy of Horses, we must die together. Do not stay with these people, they are no longer brave. We will enter the Spirit World together, for there everyone is brave and the hunting is good."

"I have women to care for," Enemy of Horses said. "This is your own quarrel. I fight to destroy the enemies of the Sparrow Hawks and to protect my own life, for that is bravery and good sense together."

"You are a leader of the Dog Soldiers, and yet you will not go? I care nothing for my own life, and there are prettier women in the land of Isakakate. You must come with me, for perhaps your medicine will protect all of us."

"I do not wish Yellow Belly to think I am a coward," Enemy of Horses said, "and for this reason I will go. But you must cease your anger toward our brothers. Let the war party proceed as it will, and be ready to accept the result. Then you and Red Eyes may be friends again, and the Foxes and the Dog Soldiers will clasp hands."

"That is good," he said. "It will be as you say, Enemy of Horses."

Thus the parties were formed, and as the Sparrow Hawks moved along, Yellow Belly listened to the words of Enemy of Horses.

"You are a very brave man and the brother of our head chief, but you fight without regard to consequence. I, too, have often done this. Perhaps that is why we are both Dog Soldiers. But now we must be more careful. We do not wish to have any of our men slain. We must fight like the coyotes."

"We must use our heads then."

"Yes," Enemy of Horses said. "That is what we must do. Big Bowl has explained this to me many times."

After twenty days they broached a high ridge from which they could see far across the prairie. About thirty of the enemy were hunting buffalo.

"Cheyennes," Yellow Belly said. "Let us attack them in the open prairie."

"No," Enemy of Horses replied. "Their village is only three miles distant. We would soon be vastly outnumbered." He spoke to the other men and said, "Turn your robes the hair side out, and follow me. We'll lay an ambush."

The Cheyennes suspected nothing. They came toward the Crows, their horses laden with buffalo meat. At this point the Sparrow Hawks opened fire with their rifles, and a number of Cheyennes fell. The Sparrow Hawks emerged from their cover and scalped those who had fallen, took twenty scalps and some horses, and made for the timber, left the horses, and found refuge in a rocky place. The Cheyennes were brave, and they made repeated assaults, the bullets showering about the Sparrow Hawks without injury, while the Cheyennes were open targets. To scalp those who were killed, however, was out of the question.

One Cheyenne brave, Black Panther believed it was Leg-in-the-Water, of whom they had heard much, charged directly into their cover. He aimed his lance at one of the braves, a young man named Fish Beneath Ice, who shattered the spear with his battle axe and then dealt a stunning blow to the Cheyenne's shoulder with his second swing. Blood sprayed in the air, but Leg-in-the-Water escaped, leaving his horse behind him.

Only Yellow Belly had been wounded, his arm broken by a rifle ball. He made little of the injury, wielding his axe with his left hand as well as ever.

As soon as darkness came, they were able to leave their fortress. Moving down a rocky cliff to the ravine where they had left their horses, they rode at a forced march back to the Absaroka village, for the terrible cold had now returned, and to loiter would have been to freeze to death.

Enemy of Horses spoke of the bravery of young Fish Beneath Ice to Yellow Belly, whose arm he had set and splinted.

"Fish Beneath Ice saved us all from the great Leg-in-the-Water!" he laughed. "I think that Cheyenne is as crazy as a Dog Soldier."

"Leg-in-the-Water will someday be chief of the Cheyennes," Yellow Belly agreed. "He is a very great warrior. Three winters ago he fought against the River Crows and tried to kill Long Hair, but the Lumpwoods drove him off."

"So young Fish Beneath Ice has just acquired a big reputation. He has wounded Leg-in-the-Water in battle."

"He will be able to speak of this at the counting of coups," Yellow Belly said. "And he will be able to tell the story to his children and grandchildren when he is old."

"Your arm. Does it hurt badly?"

"I will tell you when we find out how many scalps Red Eyes has taken."

They arrived home twenty-eight days after their departure. The rival party under Red Eyes had returned a week earlier, with seventeen scalps at the cost of one man. Hence the party of Dog Soldiers was declared the victors, for they had taken a greater number of scalps with fewer men, and they had lost no one. Red Eyes acknowledged himself beaten and embraced Yellow Belly, whose splinted arm was badly swollen.

The party of Red Eyes could not join the scalp dance, for they had lost one man. Nor was Yellow Belly in any condition to dance, either. He sat to one side and meditated the sound of the antelope-skin drum and the odor of woodsmoke in the frozen air. He thought about Fish Beneath Ice's twin sister, Pine Leaf. He had been watching the girl for some time. She would make a good wife.

LITTLE WIFE'S FINGER

First the mature male buffalo will inspect a number of cows to determine which one is most completely in heat. This one he selects for courting. He stands next to her side or rump, always within a few feet of her, and will use head movements and momentary charges or even actual attacks to drive off rivals. He may even drive off the calf or yearling of his mate. The tending bull may be challenged and forced away by a more dominant bull—otherwise he will stay with the cow for about two days before he moves on to another mate. Even a strong bull will have trouble with his woman, and she remains in control. Often an amorous bull is rebuffed by a perverse cow, and she uses horns and hooves to discourage him. Once I saw a cow kick her lover in the nose, and he didn't blink. Then he licked the fur around her rump, and she became more agreeable. When the bull mounts the cow, he thrusts steadily for a few seconds and then releases his grip. I have watched the buffalos copulate many times. It is beautiful.

Snow in March, falling, melting, interspersed with rain—miserable weather, when grass started up from the earth and then ceased to grow. The buffalo disappeared, and it was necessary to move on in search of them.

The council met and decided to cross over the mountains, cross over Tongue River Mountain to the east side of the range, where the progress of spring would be more advanced, the grass more abundant, the buffalo grazing.

Big Bowl cautioned against this plan.

"There is still much snow on the mountain. A storm could come, and then many of us will starve or freeze to death. Even though I am growing old, it is not yet time for me to die. We should stay here for yet another moon."

Some agreed with him, but A-ra-poo-ash and the council concluded that the move was required, and so the preparations were begun.

It would be a hard journey.

While the Sparrow Hawks were preparing to cross the mountain, the Siksikas came in by night and made off with nearly a thousand horses. The Sparrow Hawks, with the difficult passage across Tongue River Mountain before them, chose not to pursue the horse-thieves. Three young braves, however, had actually ridden out after the Siksikas, acting on impulse, and as a consequence lost their lives. One of these was Fish Beneath Ice, who had wounded the great Leg-in-the-Water, the Cheyenne warrior chief.

Yellow Belly had been attempting to court Fish Beneath Ice's twin sister, but now the girl, Pine Leaf, cut off one of her fingers and went into mourning for her brother. Her grief was great, and she no longer had eyes for Yellow Belly. The chief's brother resigned himself and decided to pursue the matter at a future time.

The snows lay deep on the high ridges, deep from three days of late storm: and then the words of Big Bowl were remembered. The way through the mountain was almost impassable, and nearly a thousand of the remaining horses died in the snow, with many of the dead animals being slaughtered, the meat to provide a cushion against starvation. For the moment, even the dogs would have enough to eat.

Two scouts, sent ahead to discover the easiest route, did not come back, and the people knew the men were lost. At length, however, after serveral days of grim labor, the Sparrow Hawks managed the crossing and issued down onto the prairie to the east of the mountain barrier.

"The people should have listened to your words, father," Enemy of Horses said to Big Bowl.

"Young men are impetuous," he answered. "That is why there are more women in the world than men. That is why you have several wives that you must hunt for. Because their men did not think clearly. My friend A-ra-poo-ash should not have listened to his counselors."

"So many wives is not exactly a blessing to me," Enemy of Horses said.

Big Bowl was thoughtful for a moment before he spoke:

"A man should not have more than three wives, I think. I had a second wife once, but she was killed by a white bear. Funny Deer and I have been much happier since then."

Early in the afternoon they found a good site for the village, on Box Elder Creek, where the grass was lush. The buffalo could not be too far away. Scouts were sent out at once and returned shortly after dawn with news the Sparrow Hawks wanted to hear. A large herd of buffalo was close by, as well as the camp of the other half of the Crow Nation, under the great chief Long Hair. With these Sparrow Hawks, the scouts said, was a group of Whitemen.

Long Hair's group had apparently moved south, also following the buffalo.

The hunters joined forces and moved toward the buffalo immediately, for even the supply of horsemeat was dwindling. Already Enemy of Horses could smell the fresh buffalo and the cooking fires, wholly welcome after the hard time they had just come through. The men rode out in groups of fifty or more, their spirits high, the braves eager for the hunt. There was much talking and joking.

Enemy of Horses rode a pack horse rather than Come Back and took three of his wives with him—Still-water, Little Wife, and Cheyenne's Sister. Each of the women led a saddle horse, and the morning air was clear and fresh, chilly, but with the promise of a warm day, for the sky was immense and blue and cloudless. They managed to surround a group of buffalo, and the hunt began. The great animals fell more quickly and methodically than in less hungry times.

After a short while, however, they heard the cry of a war-whoop. Enemy of Horses turned to Coyote Running and said, "Perhaps these buffalo are Sioux in disguise."

Coyote laughed and said, "The young braves have gone mad with the hunt."

But the whoops were repeated, and Coyote and Enemy of Horses rode quickly to the top of a low, bare ridge where they were able to see a party of hunters making excited signals of distress. They turned their horses about and rode back to their wives, sending Stillwater and Grouse-feather to return to the village for their weapons. Then they signalled to the hunting party and together moved rapidly back up over the ridge and down to the group on the far side.

Red Eyes met them and said, "Siksikas. Up there. We surprised them. They've taken cover behind the big rocks and now they can't get out. But we will lose many men in order to kill them."

"How many?" Coyote Running asked.

"Perhaps a hundred or more. We've sent for help. These Siksikas have blundered into the midst of the whole Crow Nation, as they'll soon discover."

Enemy of Horses stared at the big rocks, a natural fortress, a wall of sheer granite—as though Isakawuate had designed it for no other purpose than for the battle that was to follow. Coyote Running looked at his brother—the face intense, fatal, all the good spirits of just a short while earlier now vanished. The hunt could not go on until the Sparrow Hawks had finished the bloody business before them.

It crossed Enemy of Horses' mind to signal the Blackfeet that he would give them passage to leave, for he did not believe they wished to fight any more than he did. But he knew that A-ra-poo-ash and Long Hair and the band of Whites would soon arrive—and because honor was at stake, the slaughter would begin.

"We will not rejoice tonight," Coyote Running said.

Within a short while, the two head chiefs and the braves of the River Crows had arrived, and with them the Whites, eager to watch

Indians killing Indians. Enemy of Horses felt a genuine sense of anticipation. What would Long Hair say and do? How would the living legend respond to the present situation? Enemy of Horses' mind leaped back nearly six years, to the time on the *Roche Jaune*, the Yellowstone, with Ashley, getting ready to bullboat their furs down the river. He remembered well.

Long Hair had not changed in either demeanor or general appearance—the same gaunt, dignified figure astride the war horse. It was probably even the same horse. The man carried about him an air of full authority.

Then another face, a face among the Whites. Was it possible? But there was no mistaking the man, the surly Kentuckian, Red Beard Miller—and riding with him a Crow woman. Had Miller then, like himself, taken to living with the Absarokas?

One or two things now began to make sense. A disconcerting story had been brought to Enemy of Horses some months earlier by one of the younger braves, a man who had spent considerable time with Long Hair's group. Apparently, at trading time, a Long Knife who lived with the Crows had displayed a good deal of fondness for whiskey, a fondness which Enemy of Horses devoutly hoped the Whiteman would never be able to cultivate among the Sparrow Hawks. The Crows generally abstained from drinking, and Enemy of Horses saw in this the key to their success in continuing to control their lands. Many of the Indian peoples became quickly addicted to the arwerdenty, and so long as the medicine water was in good supply, all other considerations vanished. But, so the story went, this Whiteman had drunkenly claimed to know Enemy of Horses and had said that he was not a Crow at all but a man of mixed blood. The statement could not have meant much to the Absarokas, Enemy of Horses thought, for his people valued a man strictly in accord with what he proved himself to be. And to this tale, accurate though it was, he had replied simply, "I am the son of Big Bowl, and all of you know me to be a Crow warrior."

"Black Panther," Enemy of Horses asked, "do you know who this Whiteman is, the one who has a Sparrow Hawk woman?"

"No. But I will find out for you. Is he one that you know?"

Black Panther talked with friends from Long Hair's group and then returned with what he had discovered.

"They call him Red Hair. He has lived with them for one year and is a good fighter, though he does not like to ride with the war parties. He is married to the woman."

In the rocks above, the Siksikas waited silently.

Enemy of Horses was not really worried by the matter, though he hoped that Miller's tongue was not often so lubricated. But now he moved toward the man and addressed him in English.

"Miller, it's me, Beckwourth. Looks like we're trapping together these days, and right now the stick's floating poorly. How do we roust out these damned Blackfeet? Maybe we should leave the matter to the Crows—that way our own bravery's not questioned. What do you say, coon, shall we stand back and watch the circus?"

"Well now, Big Jim. I've heard stories about your doin's. Sure you ain't going' to leave all the fun to them others. Figured a man like you could take 'em all by hisself. Think I'll join in too, though, just in case you might need some help. Be right behind you."

Had the man changed? Was the old hatred still there? Enemy of Horses wasn't certain.

"Suppose we don't really have any choice. I'll try to keep up with you, Red Beard, and maybe we'll both keep our skalps."

"Name's Red Hair," Miller said. "Anyhow, I was figuring to follow you, since I was sure you'd have a plan."

"Nothing in particular," Beckwourth said. "Maybe it's best we just stand back and see what the two chiefs cook up."

By now the braves from both groups had assembled, perhaps five to seven hundred in all. Occasionally an individual would make a run to the wall of rocks, taking shelter there. But several had already lost their lives in the process.

Enemy of Horses stripped off all his clothing down to the breech clout, and then he, too, made the run—and safely. Once below the rocks, he realized that the only alternatives were bombardment or simply storming the position. The first was impossible with light bore weapons, and the second was sheer madness. With a wild dash, and with perhaps more luck than daring, he made it back to the main group without so much as a shot being fired at him. A number of the Dog Soldiers milled about and praised his medicine.

But Coyote Running said, "Antelope Jim, Enemy of Horses, you truly act like one who wishes to die. That was not wise, my friend."

Enemy of Horses was about to agree with Coyote when Chief Long Hair stepped forward to address the braves:

"Warriors, listen! Our marrow-bones are broken—the enemy has chosen a strong fort. We cannot drive them from it without sacrificing too many men. Warriors, retreat! We must allow these Siksikas to return to their own lands, to their lodges and their women. It is not worthwhile to kill a few Siksikas who are this stupid. If we let them leave with their lives, they will remember next time and will not venture into the lands of the Absarokas again. These are my words, Sparrow Hawks!"

There was great wisdom in what Long Hair had said, and a part of Enemy of Horses' mind agreed totally. Was the old chief simply refusing to provide a spectacle for the Whites? Did he have some reason for wanting the Whites to suppose that he saw in this party of Blackfeet no real threat to the Sparrow Hawks? The Whites, as Enemy of Horses knew, would see only weakness in the actions of the Sparrow Hawks.

Now a sort of demonic urge possessed Enemy of Horses, for the blood had grown hot in his veins. With Miller and the other Whites in mind, he stepped forward.

"No! Dog Soldiers, those not afraid of death, listen! If the old men cannot fight, let them retire with the women and children. I tell you we can kill these Siksikas. If we attack and are killed, our friends here will mourn us, and those in the Spirit World will welcome us as brave men. Isakakate has put these Siksikas here for us to kill. If we retreat, He will be angry with us. He will not allow us to conquer our enemies again. The grass on the great prairies will wither, and the buffalo will vanish. Follow me, and these Whitemen will see how our Dog Soldiers fight their enemies!"

"Enemy of Horses!" the warriors shouted, not only his own men but the Foxes and Dog Soldiers and Lumpwoods from Long Hair's band as well, "Lead us and we will follow you to the Spirit Land."

Then Long Hair spoke again:

"Those who wish to follow the Enemy of Horses must do so. He speaks well, and his men are loyal to him. The Siksikas will die. Now these are my words. Do what the Enemy of Horses tells you."

"You are mad," Coyote whispered. "There are porcupine quills in your brain, but I will die with you. What do we do?"

"Red Eyes!" the Enemy of Horses shouted. "Are you with me?"

"I am with you!"

"Lead all the braves to the far side, where the rocks are lowest. Keep down and out of range until you see Coyote and me atop the high wall. Then pour over. For a moment, when they first see us, there will be confusion inside. Attack then, and try to save our lives."

Coyote stripped naked, and the two men took only their battle axes and knives, ran toward the fortress even as the others moved toward the low wall. The Blackfeet did not notice the two men, as Enemy of Horses had hoped would be the case, and they made it together without a single shot being fired at them.

"A seam in the rocks, up there," Enemy of Horses said to Coyote Running. "We can climb up."

"We go to die now, my brother," Coyote said. "I will follow you."

They made the climb easily and, once on top, the two of them shouted "Hoo-ki-hi!" and waved their arms as a signal to the others. Then they leaped down into the midst of the startled Blackfeet. Their axes bit deep, but both knew they were dead men if the others did not attack immediately.

Dog Soldiers, Foxes, and Lumpwoods poured over the low wall, and the attention of the Siksikas was diverted to this newer and more serious threat. For some minutes the carnage was fearful with the shouts and screams of the dying and wounded. The Blackfeet fought bravely, for they well knew their fate if captured. Some leaped down from the fortress wall and were skewered alive by the Crow warriors still below. The slaughter continued, and blood from the wounded formed pools in the hollows of the rock.

Blood everywhere.

The sickening, warm, vapor smell of blood, so much blood that it was difficult to keep one's footing—guts and brains and gore—the mingled blood of Absaroka and Siksika in the common pool of their insanity.

A short, heavyset Blackfoot came toward Enemy of Horses with upraised lance, but he slipped in the blood as he released his weapon, which would otherwise have pinned the leader of the Dog Soldiers to the earth. Enemy of Horses split open the Blackfoot's head with his battle axe, and the gray-pink brains spilled out. The man made a terrible sucking sound as he fell. Enemy of Horses looked around then and saw that Coyote Running had fallen. He flung his axe at Coyote's assailant, and the blade drove home just to one side of the spine. The Blackfoot crumpled on top of Coyote and was still breathing as Enemy of Horses pulled him back by the hair and used the man's own knife to scalp him. Coyote sprang up, a long gash in his shoulder.

"My other arm is still good," he laughed. "Are there more to kill?"

But then it was silent. A Blackfoot, half disembowelled, was trying to crawl away, slithering over his own intestines. Enemy of Horses walked carefully to where the Blackfoot squirmed through the gore and used his battle axe to sever the head from the body. He was required to strike three times.

A number of the Sparrow Hawk braves were dead, and many more were wounded. A group of Whitemen had also scaled the wall in the wake of the Sparrow Hawks, but only one of these was wounded. Red Beard Miller, now Red Hair, had also scaled the wall and had fought bravely but had broken a leg in attempting to leap down after an Indian.

"I'll live," Red Hair said when Enemy of Horses asked how he was, "and I'll probably live a lot longer than you will. This child ain't finished yet."

Coyote Running was standing by Enemy of Horses and so had witnessed this exchange. He did not understand the English words perfectly, but he guessed at their meaning. Later he said to his friend, "That man hates you. I think you will have to kill him."

"I hope you are wrong, my brother."

Coyote answered simply, "He is not a Crow."

But now it was time to care for the wounded and the dead. There would be no joy around the fires and the roasting spits of buffalo meat this night, for even though the victory had been great, the cost had also been great. Fingers would disappear from the hands of the women whose men were slain. And the few Blackfeet who had been captured would be turned over to the women, for torture. Their screams would be very loud, for the women of the Sparrow Hawks would be without mercy.

When Owl Bear, one of the old chiefs, passed under the wall at the conclusion of the battle, he noticed Little Wife among the women huddled there—and he addressed her:

"You are a wife of the Enemy of Horses?"

"Yes," she said. "Have you come from the fighting, Owl Bear? Is it over?"

"Poor little one," he said, "you have no husband now. The Enemy of Horses is gone—shot through the head as he leaped down into the midst of the Siksikas. You must go to his body and prepare the funeral rites."

Owl Bear told the story to Enemy of Horses just a few minutes after it had happened. "No sooner had I said this," he smiled, "and before I could put her mind at ease with the truth, than she grabbed a battle axe and cut off one of her fingers. I see now that it was no time for a jest, and I was instantly sorry for my false words. When she tried to stab herself in the forehead, I took the knife away—see, I have a cut on my wrist for my troubles. I'm sorry for what happened, Antelope Jim, but at least you know now that the little girl loves you better than any of your other wives. I calmed her down and helped to bind up her hand. You're a lucky man to have that one. If I weren't so old, I'd envy you."

Owl Bear clasped the shoulder of Enemy of Horses and then walked away toward the main group of Sparrow Hawks.

Enemy of Horses thought to find Little Wife immediately, but she found him instead.

"Whom do you mourn?" he asked. "your husband is still alive— it was not yet time to go hunting with Old Man Coyote."

"Owl Bear told me you were dead," she sobbed. "I thought you were gone."

"No, I will never die at the hands of the Siksikas. That is not my fate. No Blackfoot has power over me. Little Wife, you must learn not to believe all that you hear. Our men have a strange sense of humor, and it has cost you a finger. I will not leave you and pass away. Spread your robe now and carry the spoils of my first victim to the village. Then wash your hand carefully and bind it with herbs."

He took her hand and kissed the wrappings of rag.

"You love me well, Little Wife. Soon we will go together again to the mountains to hunt sheep, but you must promise me not to mutilate yourself further while I live."

Her eyes were moist as she kneeled and spread out her robe, into which Enemy of Horses placed the Blackfoot's rifle and other effects.

"My husband," she said. "I could not live if you were to die. I could not live alone without you."

Enemy of Horses stared down at Little Wife. Suddenly he felt very empty inside. The strength was gone from his limbs, and he wanted to fall upon the earth and cry as he had cried when he was a small boy. Despair and joy all at once had come over him, and he wanted to cry.

But he could not do this.

A-ra-poo-ash and Long Hair came to Big Bowl's lodge to congratulate the Enemy of Horses for having scaled the wall and having led the warriors to victory. Enemy of Horses had worried about how this matter might fall out, for he knew that he might well have affronted the great chiefs when he had publicly countered Long Hair's advice and urged the warriors to follow him into battle. But Big Bowl, A-ra-poo-ash, and Long Hair had been friends for years, and the victory resolved the issue, despite the casualties suffered.

"Your son is a brave man," Long Hair said. "Is he the one who was stolen as a child, the one the Cheyennes sold to the Long Knives?"

"That is what happened," Big Bowl said.

"One day he will be first war-chief of the Crow Nation. I say this now so that he will remember I said it." Then Long Hair turned to the Enemy of Horses. "Were you not with Ashley five winters ago on the Yellowstone River?"

Enemy of Horses was astounded at the Chief's powers of recollection. Or had Miller told him of this? But he retained his composure and nodded in the affirmative.

"I did not think Long Hair would remember me."

"You are a very striking man," Long Hair said. "I do not forget such men. And now you have come back to your people. You have led the Sparrow Hawks to many victories, and it is said that your medicine is very strong. I believe in your medicine, Enemy of Horses. Big Bowl is very fortunate to have such a son. I can see that his heart is proud. And A-ra-poo-ash is lucky to have such a warrior among his counselors."

"The words of Long Hair were much wiser," Enemy of Horses said. "Had I listened, no one would now be in mourning."

A-ra-poo-ash and Long Hair nodded. They said nothing.

Enemy of Horses continued:

"I have promised the mourners that in a few days I will avenge the loss of our braves or die myself and so pass away into the Spirit World, where there are no more enemies to fight."

"It will be good," A-ra-poo-ash said. "Yet as I grow older, I often wonder if there may not be another way. But that is not possible, is it? Siksikas and Absarokas have always fought each other. We have fought each other for a very long time. We will always fight—until the buffalo are no more. I do not know what will happen then. I have tried to look into the years to come, but my eyes are no longer keen enough."

When A-ra-poo-ash had spoken, Long Hair placed his hands on Big Bowl's shoulders, nodded, and the two head chiefs left the lodge.

"They are great men, my father," Enemy of Horses said.

It was as if Big Bowl had not heard his son's words. Then Funny Deer walked over to him and touched his arm. His mind seemed to return from some distant place, perhaps some buffalo hunt or war party of years past. He nodded and turned toward the rear of the lodge.

All who were present related the deeds they had performed, and as each spoke, the others listened with profound attention. Little Wife crawled up beside Enemy of Horses and whispered into his ear, "Husband, how many coups did you take?"

"None," he said, placing his fingers over her mouth, amused at the disappointment in her face.

But when the question was asked by Long Hair, he replied, "Eleven."

At this, Little Wife tapped eleven times on his back and whispered, "You have a crooked tongue, I knew you had counted coup. Why do wish to tell me what is not true?"

When Enemy of Horses had finished recounting his part in the battle, Little Wife bit him on the leg—bit him so hard that he could hardly avoid shouting out. He glared down at her and saw that her dark eyes shone innocently.

But his dreams betrayed him. He awoke, sweating, shouting. And Still-water said, "What is it, my husband?"

"A dream," he answered. "It is nothing."

But it was something: scenes of blood, moans of the dying, the maimed, himself mutilated, both arms hacked off, swarms of Blackfeet coming after him. He lay awake in the darkness of the lodge, the dream scenes refusing to die away, refusing to fade.

He had often resolved to leave this wildness and return to civilized life, but always the Enemy of Horses was sought out, the strength of his great medicine. Why had he survived when so many others had fallen beside him? Was this medicine not merely an illusion? Surely his luck would turn?

By now the word had spread, and many knew of his life. What must they think of the way he lived? Perhaps even in St. Louis?

Yet it was true that the Crows had never shed the blood of a White—or, if they had, it had been a matter of accident or the work of renegades. The Absarokas had guessed at something of the future—and they knew at some level that their world was destined to change. The Whites would come in ever greater numbers, and perhaps one day they would make strong allies and would value their Crow friends.

Self-interest also whispered to the Enemy of Horses, for as a Crow he could easily accumulate an immense stock of peltry, if only his Indian brothers could be persuaded to spend their time in trapping rather than stealing horses and fighting. In this, he supposed, lay the eventual key to the future path, with the Nation engaged in peaceful industry. A time would come, he knew, when the great herds of buffalo would be gone, and with them the nomad's way of life. Hadn't A-ra-poo-ash said the same thing in effect?

But if he questioned at all, Black Panther or Coyote might say, "The Blackfeet and Cheyennes steal our horses. We must fight to get them back or we must steal from others. How could we make our surrounds without horses? How could we protect our lives when our enemies attack our villages? The years you spent with the Long Knives make you think funny, and you do not speak like Enemy of Horses but like some other."

One thought of stealing horses from the Cheyennes or the Arapahos, and the traps were laid away in favor of the more important matter. But which was the more important matter?

Perhaps they would be forced to accept agriculture, then, and the trapping of furs, and even mining and leather work. How long would the fur trade last? Already the beavers were fewer. How many more years? For the present, though, the great changes of future years were not readily perceived, could not be predicted—were only felt by those who thought about them as a kind of omnipresent doom. He remembered the words of Pierre Le Blueux. He wanted very much to see Le Blueux again. And Baptiste. And Harris. And Cahuna Smith. Smith. Shot in the heart. The blood welling up. . . .

Something had grown inside of him which all but obliterated his past, a past now more like dreams than genuine memories. He was pregnant, he realized, pregnant and in labor, giving birth to himself.

While the tribes were still together, Enemy of Horses visited with Miller, who was healing.

"Beckwourth," he said, "this child is used to the Injun life, but I admit I miss them Kentucky hills, miss my family. Well, one day I guess I'll head back all right. But mebbe there's more back there for me, ehh? I expect you'll die out here, probably fucked to death by all them wives you've got. How many they be, anyhow?"

"Red Beard, I should have killed you years ago."

"Name's Red Hair."

"Whatever you want."

"Well, nigger, this leg'll be healed soon. Now me, I don't hold a grudge, but mebbe you got a point. Mebbe you should try it, that is. I don't figger any coon's luck holds out forever."

"Maybe I should. Well, we'll see how the stick floats when the time comes. But I think we'd be better off friends. We might get more plew that way, if you see what I mean."

Red Hair ran his hands down over the injured leg, looked up at Enemy of Horses, and squinted:

"Ain't you the logical one, now?"

BAR-CHEE-AM-PE
AND BOBTAIL HORSE

Milk River, Marias River, Teton River, Sun River, Smith River, Jefferson River, Gallatin River, Henry's Fork, Judith River, Musselshell River, Frenchman River, Poplar River, Redwater River, Clark's Fork, Bighorn River, Tongue River, Powder River, Yellowstone River: all these and a hundred more rise along the great arc of the continental divide or among the high lateral ranges, wave after wave of upthrust rock, peaks glittering in eternal snow, dark forests, high valleys, the waters gathering, gathering, pouring from the mountains, filling the broad channels, drawing together where Fort Union stands: the Missouri River, the Big River, the Big Muddy, great artery of the heartland, now curving south and east, drawing to itself the Little Missouri, the James, the Niobara, the Platte, the Republican—a running brown flood down to the Mississippi, out of the vast Western Wilderness, its willow-lined waters bearing the detritus of mountain and plain, Highway to the West, its length as great as the Mississippi itself.

The medicine men held council, and the decision was made to move the village. Isakakate was displeased with the spot and for this reason had allowed the Absaroka warriors to be killed. Revenge was needed: then the mourning paint would disappear.

The women took charge, and soon the group was on the march once more, removing to a spot some thirty miles southward.

As his wives reassembled the lodge of Enemy of Horses, Little Wife began acting in a frivolous manner. Still-water's words of reprimand had no effect in quelling her high spirits, and finally Enemy of Horses lost his temper and drove her away. She did not dare disobey him in this matter, and she stayed out of sight for two days. Then, in the evening, as Enemy of Horses was speaking to Black Panther and Coyote Running, she appeared in the entrance to the lodge, very much abashed.

"I know you are angry with me, but I want to sleep with you tonight. Then you will forgive me."

The husband was glad of his wife's return, but he kept his face straight:

"What will you do so that I will be willing to forgive? Have you learned some tricks while you were out in the willows?"

"I have been with no other," she said. "And I will obey hereafter."

Black Panther said, "She has no ears, but she is young. She will have ears when she is older. Let her lie with you."

Both Still-water and Little Wife made love to him that night, and afterward he fell into a very deep sleep. But sometime near morning he awoke, could hear the snorting of Come Back and the other horses tied near the lodge entrance.

He reached for his knife and crept out of the lodge.

In the thin gray light of false dawn, he caught sight of a stranger, one who was using a sharp pointed stick to move the leaves from his path. Enemy of Horses crouched, hidden, as the stranger continued his approach to the horses, to where the ropes were tied by the lodge entrance. Carefully, carefully.

When the man was close enough, Enemy of Horses jumped upon him, giving the war whoop as he did so. The Indian was strong, and his fear made him stronger yet—but Enemy of Horses managed to pin his arms so that he could not draw his knife, and within moments the two were surrounded by Sparrow Hawk warriors. Enemy of Horses leaped back from the stranger, and instantly the body was riddled with bullets.

The Siksika fell without a cry.

Enemy of Horses took the scalp.

And this single event was sufficient to remove the paint of mourning from every face in the village. All that day the people were in high spirits, though the scalp that had been taken did not heal the self-inflicted wounds or restore the dismembered fingers.

Shas-ka-o-hush-a, the Bobtail Horse. So damned many names that he had trouble keeping track of who he was. He thought. "My Absaroka brothers and sisters must be having the same problem, trying to get a fix on me."

"Coyote," he asked, "why do they keep changing my name?"

"A man's visions and deeds determine his name. It is a problem— you were not raised among our people, but you must not be concerned. The people have grown to love you, and your medicine is very powerful."

"I suppose it'll settle down eventually," he said, "but I think maybe I liked Antelope the best. Seems like I ought to have some say in the matter."

"Your mind is strange, Antelope Jim. You think about things too much. It's like asking why the snow falls in winter. Or why the white bear has a bad temper. Isakawuate has whims, Old Man Coyote, and that's why things are as they are."

"Just are? And that's why a man shouldn't think about them?"

"I don't know," Coyote Running said. "I think maybe that's it. Don't you like Bobtail Horse?"

Bar-chee-am-pe.

Pine Leaf. She was, Bobtail Horse realized, one of the bravest women who ever lived. She was tall, thin, and amazingly agile, quick strength lived in her tendons, so that she could move more quickly and run faster than many of the men. Her wit was adept, the mind strong, the will forceful and determined.

She was a beautiful woman, her body possessed great symmetry. Her breasts were small but well-formed, the legs finely proportioned, the hips graceful, and her whole being betokened a smoldering sexuality that did not intend to give itself to any man.

Her twin brother, Fish Beneath Ice, had been slain when the

Blackfeet stole the horses of the Sparrow Hawks just before the crossing of Tongue River Mountain. He had been a fine brave, even though he was still young. He would no doubt eventually have risen to great distinction. Now Pine Leaf vowed to avenge her brother's death, and she announced she would never marry until she had slain a hundred of the enemy with her own hand. She made the announcement with quiet dignity, in such a way that even Yellow Belly, who had sought her for a wife, was obliged to respect her words.

When a war-party started, Pine Leaf was the first to volunteer, and even though the old veterans winked at each other, the girl was accepted—for no one could fail to admire her ambition and her determination. When she chose the party of Bobtail Horse, he soon discovered that even in the fiercest struggles, Bar-chee-am-pe was promptly at his side, seemingly incapable of fear, able to fire a rifle without flinching and as skillful in the use of Indian weapons as the best of the warriors.

As spring turned to summer, and the war parties became more frequent, Pine Leaf and Bobtail Horse rode together often. His initial responses had been those of admiration, but as the summer wore on, he realized that his feelings had begun to change. He had begun to see her as an extremely desirable woman. He started to think of her in some ways as a female counterpart of himself. He was attracted to her intelligence and astonished both by her modesty and by her cunning and ferocity in battle.

Rendezvous time came and went, and though Bobtail Horse had again given thought to revisiting his former life, the presence of Pine Leaf kept him with the Sparrow Hawks.

One day in late summer, as they rode northward into the land of the Siksikas, Pine Leaf drew up beside him.

"Bobtail," she said softly, "why don't you give me your medicine bundle? You'd get another in no time anyway."

He reached across to pull at her long, braided hair, but she turned away quickly, so that he nearly fell from his horse.

"You are not fast enough. I guess I don't want your medicine anyway, maybe."

He laughed.

Her eyes were gleaming.

"Pine Leaf," he asked, "don't you wonder what it would be like to make love with a man?"

At first she looked down—then arched her eyebrow and wrinkled her nose.

"The old women have told me that men do not know how to make love. It's better to love a woman, maybe."

"I know how to make love to a woman," he said, holding a straight face.

They rode silently on for half a mile. Then he asked, "Will you marry me if we both return safely to the village?"

"You have too many wives already, Bobtail. Besides, do you think I could break my vow to Isakakate? It will take me years to kill a hundred of the enemy. I have only killed six. Six is not a hundred. Isakakate has heard my words—He would be angry with me, and my brother's death would not be avenged. I would get pregnant every year, and my children would suck all the milk out of my body, and my breasts would shrivel up. I do not think my breasts are large enough for me to nurse children. And you would probably want to nurse too, maybe."

"Damn it," Bobtail Horse said, "I speak from my heart. I want you to marry me."

"You have more wives than you can make love to."

"You respect my medicine, don't you? My medicine says I must marry you—for then I can never be beaten or killed in battle. I must have you as my wife in order to complete my medicine."

She laughed, seemingly delighted with this idea.

"Well," she said, "then I will marry you."

"When we return?"

"No, not when we return. I will marry you when the pine leaves turn yellow."

Bobtail Horse thought upon this statement for a few moments. It would soon be autumn. Was she speaking from the heart? Or was this another of her jests?

"You promise to marry me when the pine leaves turn yellow—this autumn, then?"

"Do the pine needles turn yellow in autumn?"

"No, the pine needles do not turn yellow. I think I will let the Siksikas kill you in battle. Speak seriously now. When will you marry me?"

She laughed again, pleased that she might have fooled Bobtail Horse for a moment.

"Do I understand that you will never marry me, Pine Leaf?"

"Great warrior," she said, "yes, yes I will marry you."

"When shall we be married?"

"Married? Oh, we shall be married after you find a red-headed Indian."

She burst into laughter once more, wheeled her horse about, and rode madly back toward the rest of the war-party.

A-ra-poo-ash had ridden with his warriors, and the Sparrow Hawks were in high spirits. Big Bowl had come, as well as Owl Bear and Red Bird, the old first counselor. Little Gray Bull and a number of his Lumpwoods. Red Eyes and the Foxes. Bears Copulating and Yellow Belly, the head chief's brother. Coyote Running had also ridden, with Black Panther remaining in the village, which was more than amply protected in any case by the presence of Long Hair and his many warriors.

"Our chief is thirsty for the blood of the Siksikas!" Coyote Running said. "We will score a victory, without question. Just think of the power of our medicine. Look at Pine Leaf, my brother—she's ecstatic."

"I just asked her to marry me," Bobtail Horse said.

"Did she agree?"

"Yes. When the pine leaves turn yellow. And when I find her a red-haired Indian."

Coyote Running laughed.

"She is also thirsty for the blood of our enemies, that one. Besides, how could one trust her in bed? If she didn't like what you did to her, she would scalp you. But I think perhaps she will marry you finally. I think she loves you already. Others have asked for her hand, but she always says no. Perhaps she will actually kill a

hundred first. Yellow Belly wanted Pine Leaf. He says he will wait
for her to take revenge for her brother."

Bobtail Horse looked doubtful, then said, "At her present rate, it
may not take all that long."

"Why are you riding a different war horse, Antelope Jim? He's a
good one, but why did you leave Come Back in the village?"

"My medicine said to ride the gray horse this time. He's a Black-
foot horse. I really don't know why."

"Medicine is strange," Coyote Running said. "Sometimes we
don't understand what it is trying to tell us."

The Wolves returned with word of a small band of Blackfeet a few
miles ahead—twenty warriors driving a large herd of horses before
them.

"Several are war horses of the Cheyennes," the Wolf told A-ra-
poo-ash. "The Siksikas are on their way home from stealing horses."

"These people grow tired," said A-ra-poo-ash. "We must shorten
their journey. We must show them the shortcut into the Spirit
World, but they can never get there with all those horses. Don't
they owe us some magic dogs?"

"They owe us many horses," Red Bird said. "Our warriors will
make them pay the debt."

"We who are the old warriors will make them pay the debt, too.
We have this new warrior with us, the girl Pine Leaf. Bobtail Horse
tells me she is very brave, and I would like to see for myself. Will
you count coup today, Pine Leaf?"

"Yes, Great Chief. I will count coup maybe."

"The young warriors will have to look to their honors today, for
the old men and the young girl fight together. Perhaps we will put
even Bobtail Horse and Bears Copulating to shame."

"We will also fight hard," Bears Copulating said.

"This is how we will do it," A-ra-poo-ash said. "Big Bowl, do
you remember when we took those horses from the Utes over on the
Seedskeedee? That was many winters ago, and we were strong men
then. That is how we will do it."

"We put them into a surround, like buffalo," Big Bowl said.

"Yes. We will put these Siksikas into a surround also. We have many chiefs with us today. Each will take a group of warriors, and we will encircle the Blackfeet and draw down on them all at once. The horses will mill about, and the Blackfeet will be thrown into confusion. Do you like this plan, Bobtail Horse?"

"The plan is a good one, A-ra-poo-ash."

The Blackfeet suspected nothing, for they were well into their own territory, having long since outdistanced their Cheyenne pursuers. As they came up through a narrow defile, the Sparrow Hawks fell upon them from all sides. Bobtail Horse drove straight toward the small group of Blackfeet, firing his pistol and lashing out with his battle axe. He had killed three of the Siksikas when a rifle ball tore through the gray horse's throat and the animal collapsed. Bobtail Horse was thrown over his mount's head and landed on his back among the Cheyenne horses. He rolled over and sucked for air but was momentarily unable to breathe. The battle axe had been wrenched from his grasp. A Blackfoot fired his pistol at Bobtail Horse, missing only because his own mount reared at the critical moment.

A lance took the Blackfoot in the back, and he also fell amidst the hooves of the milling horses.

Pine Leaf leaped from her horse and stood beside the fallen Bobtail, shouting the war cry, swinging the battle axe above her head.

Rotten Belly and Coyote Running charged in, followed by Big Bowl and Bears Copulating.

Bobtail Horse forced the air back into his lungs and got to his feet, grabbed his battle axe, and mounted the war pony of the Blackfoot Pine Leaf had slain.

"We must kill these Siksikas, all of them!" Pine Leaf sang above the tumult. "Look! Three are running away!"

A-ra-poo-ash rode after them, quickly overtook them, and struck one after the other with his coup stick. Then he drew back on his reins and brought his horse to a halt, gestured with his arms that the battle was over, and laughed as the three Blackfeet, still running at top speed, made for the cover of the forest.

In order to find sufficient grass for the large herd of horses and stay close to the buffalo herds, the Absarokas were obliged to move their village numerous times. When the leaves of the aspens flamed a deep yellow and fringes of ice formed at night on the grasses near the running streams, the Mountain Crows separated from the people of Long Hair and returned to the western side of the range, making their encampment on the Big Horn River, a branch of the Yellowstone.

The day after the village was set up, a scout returned with news.

"Cheyenne village. Twelve miles distant."

Incessant warfare began, and for twenty days the raids went back and forth. Horses were stolen. Hair was taken.

Bobtail Horse counseled the people to move their encampment to the south, for it seemed to him sheer madness for the two villages to remain so close together and to spend the entire winter, each attempting to annihilate the other. Many men would be lost, and no beaver would be taken.

Big Bowl and Coyote Running also spoke in favor of moving the encampment, but the words were not heard, and A-ra-poo-ash decided to stay.

The raids continued, and Bobtail Horse refused to participate.

Broken Shoulder said, "This is not like you, Bobtail. Why do you withhold your medicine when we are losing warriors?"

And Black Panther said, "I cannot believe my brother has decided to abandon the war-path in behalf of the younger braves. I cannot believe that his medicine is no longer strong."

Yellow Belly approached Bobtail Horse.

"I will ride against these Cheyennes. I will ride in the morning. Pine Leaf rides with me. It is my wish that Bobtail Horse should also come."

Bobtail Horse turned and walked toward his lodge, but he was intercepted by Pine Leaf herself, who frowned and said, "If you will not go, then give me your medicine bundle, and I will go to scalp the red-haired Indian myself."

He knew, then, that he had lost, and he gave in to the inevitable.

"Damn it," he said half under his breath. "All right. Tell the others that I will ride."

They did not wait for morning but went quietly through the darkness, Bobtail riding Come Back. By dawn light they looked down on the Cheyenne village, approached, and entered the sleeping encampment. Dogs barked, and a guard saw them, wheeling about on his horse in an attempt to escape. Pine Leaf shot an arrow into his back, and before he fell, Bobtail Horse cut the man down with his battle axe.

Pine Leaf, not wishing to lose the scalp, dismounted to take it—but her untethered horse followed the moving war-party and so left her afoot. Suddenly all the camp dogs were barking, and the Cheyenne warriors poured from their lodges and leaped upon their horses. Bobtail turned Come Back quickly and took Pine Leaf up behind him at a dead run. The Cheyennes, led by the great brave Leg-in-the-Water, were after them, but they made good their escape, as did Black Panther, Yellow Belly, and Broken Shoulder—who managed to drive before him a few Cheyenne horses in the process.

The party had suffered no wounds, while taking one scalp and seven horses. The victory was sufficient to cause the Absaroka to wash the mourning paint from their faces.

But now the Cheyennes were aroused, and Leg-in-the-Water attacked the Crow village with a large force. They should not have taken the Crows by surprise, but they did, and several men were lost, including Scarred Face and his younger brother, Long-tail Fox. Scarred Face had engaged Leg-in-the-Water in hand to hand fighting and was cut down by the Cheyenne's battle axe. Long-tail Fox attempted to protect his brother's body, and Leg-in-the-Water slew him as well. The scalped and mutilated bodies were later found where they had fallen.

In all, six Absaroka braves were slain.

The relatives of Scarred Face and Long-tail Fox appealed to Bobtail Horse to take vengeance, and he agreed. He selected a hundred and thirty warriors, including Pine Leaf, and they mounted and set out to waylay their enemies.

The Cheyenne force returned for a second onslaught against the Absaroka village, and from their cover the warriors under Bobtail Horse watched as the Cheyennes passed by, Leg-in-the-Water at their head. Coyote Running was present on this raid, and he said, "Why do we not come upon them from behind? We can harvest many scalps."

"And they would harvest many of ours, my brother. No—let us wait. Our village is large, and Little Gray Bull and the Lumpwoods are there with A-ra-poo-ash. We will take Leg-in-the-Water when he returns, for his men will be nursing their wounds, and our surprise will be doubly effective."

Yellow Belly and Black Panther listened as Bobtail Horse spoke, but they were not fully convinced of the wisdom in this plan.

It was then that old Owl Bear spoke:

"The Bobtail Horse is right, and his medicine has always been strong. Then the Cheyennes will move out of our lands. We must do as the Bobtail Horse says."

Pine Leaf said, "He led you at the place where the rocks were like a fortress, and all the Siksikas were slain. It was then that I knew I would avenge my brother's death and become a warrior. The Bobtail Horse has led us many times. He must lead us now against this Leg-in-the-Water."

All were convinced, and so the Sparrow Hawks waited.

But Bobtail Horse knew the danger. If the village were taken by surprise, many lives would be lost. He had chosen his force carefully and so had taken with him many of the best warriors—Dog Soldiers and Foxes.

The hours passed with maddening slowness, and indeed a longer time passed than should have been the case. Could something have gone wrong? A Cheyenne victory, the Sparrow Hawks decimated,

Still-water and Little Wife taken as captives, Big Bowl lying dead upon the earth, a battle axe between his shoulderblades? A-ra-poo-ash dead? Such thoughts as these tortured Bobtail Horse as the afternoon waned.

Then a Wolf came in on a heavy run, gasping for breath:

"They come. They are cut up badly. Our warriors fought well, and the village is safe!"

Bobtail Horse embraced the young man and turned to the others: "Make ready!"

An Absaroka force from the village was in pursuit, with A-ra-poo-ash leading, and the Cheyennes were moving quickly. Now the party of Bobtail Horse fell upon them, shouting wildly. The Cheyenne force was panic-struck, and they fled in all directions, each of the braves looking out for his own scalp. The Sparrow Hawks riddled them with bullets and arrows, and battle axe and lance did the rest.

Leg-in-the-Water fought a delaying action against several of the Crows. Bobtail Horse saw what was happening and, fearing that the Cheyennes might rally behind their great warrior, he urged Come Back forward and rode directly at the Cheyenne. Leg-in-the-Water turned to meet the charge and, as the two horses came together, swung his axe at Bobtail Horse's head. But the leader of the Dog Soldiers turned aside at the last moment and struck Leg-in-the-Water a stinging slap with his coup stick. The Sparrow Hawks let up a great cheer and surged after Bobtail Horse. At this point Leg-in-the-Water turned his horse and rode for the cover of the forest.

Sixteen scalps and the horses and weapons of the fallen warriors. Pine Leaf alone had killed three men with her lance.

As quickly as the victory was complete, Bobtail Horse motioned to his warriors, and they rode to the Cheyenne village, where the Sparrow Hawks took captive a dozen women and children who were unable to flee to the surrounding woods. Then they burned the lodges.

As the Absarokas moved back toward their own village, Coyote Running said, "I think maybe these people will now understand

253

they are not welcome in the lands of the Crows. I do not think they will return for a while. But when we next meet them in battle, my brother, Leg-in-the-Water will try to kill you. You struck coup and let him go. He will not be able to forgive the insult."

"I do not fear this Cheyenne," Bobtail Horse said. "His medicine is not stronger than mine. If he is angry, then it will be easier for me to kill him."

Pine Leaf rode up beside Bobtail Horse and Coyote Running. She held up her three bloody scalps in a gesture of victory and laughed.

"You should have killed that Cheyenne, maybe," she said.

"My medicine said not to," Bobtail Horse replied. "There will be another day, my sister."

The Absarokas moved on to the Clark's Fork of the Yellowstone, where they found many buffalo and good grass for their immense herd of horses. As the winter was all but upon them, Bobtail Horse secretly wished that a raiding party might sneak in one night and, if it could be accomplished without any Sparrow Hawk casualties, relieve them of at least half the horses, for the animals would be a great burden in the cold weather ahead.

"At least," he thought, "such an idea proves that I have not become completely Indian."

While at the new encampment, the Crows were visited by a small party of Whites, among them a man named Winters, who delivered a letter to Bobtail Horse from Kenneth McKenzie of the American Fur Company. McKenzie wished to engage the services of Jim Beckwourth in establishing a trading venture with the Crows. McKenzie promised a good salary and was known to be among the most able of the fur traders. To accept such an offer, the Bobtail Horse realized, would in numerous small ways effect a change in his position among his adopted people. The world was changing around him, around the traditional, violent life of the Absarokas. More trappers each year. Fewer beaver. Even the great herds of buffalo were smaller than in years past. If a man could just remember. If he could just hold in his mind exactly how things had been, he would be more aware of how they were now. Only the mountains remained the same, the great peaks of the Bear Tooth Range, the Wind River Range, the Tetons.

Even as Bobtail Horse was lost in thought, Jim Beckwourth realized that he could not fail to pursue the matter with McKenzie.

He told Big Bowl and Funny Deer that he intended to journey to the fort.

"I will take Still-water and Little Wife with me, and I will return in eighteen suns, if Isakawuate allows me to prosper."

Big Bowl seemed worried, but said only, "Your medicine is strong, my son. You must move silently through the forest, like the wolf. We will await your return."

Bobtail Horse and his two wives rode out in the morning and proceeded toward the imposing wall of the Bear Tooth Range, for though the nights were growing intensely cold, there was as yet no snow. To cross these mountains late in the season, two women and a man, could well have proven fatal—if a blizzard had struck. But the ascent was not difficult through the low pass, and their journey would be perhaps a hundred miles shorter. The snow did come, but they were alrady down to the Big Horn, and the storm passed quickly, leaving the rolling lands about them a stunning white desert, the snow blowing and spiraling on tricks of the bitter cold wind, throwing off whole sheets of white fire under a rich blue morning.

Except for drifts, the snow was not deep, and the horses were able to move along easily enough.

Bobtail Horse shot an old bull elk, apparent outcast from the herd, and there was good eating by the campfire under the cold stars as Bobtail Horse and his two wives listened to the mournful wailing of coyotes all about them, eyes gleaming at the shadowed edges of the firelight.

They slept huddled together under their heavy buffalo robes, alone in the moon-washed silence.

The little party arrived at the fort in safety, and Jim Beckwourth closed his business with Kenneth McKenzie, taking with him ten pack horses laden with goods for trade with the Indians. Other goods were to follow, as weather permitted, by boat up the Yellowstone. McKenzie and Beckwourth shook hands, and the trader presented his new employee with a good deal of crimson cloth, beads, and various sorts of foofuraw for his wives, as well as a good store of powder and lead and a dozen new rifles. Little Wife in particular was greatly pleased, and though Still-water was more restrained, her husband knew that she too was delighted.

Vast prairies. Huge mountains. Great rivers singing down from the snowfields.

The buffalo moving, millions of them, antelope, deer, bighorn sheep, mountain goats, eagles and hawks and vultures, fish in the streams, muskrats, beaver.

Wildcats, lynxes and lions, prairie dogs, jackrabbits.

And over all a vastness of sky, immense and blue and boundless, the sun and the moon, and at night the burst of starlight, white fire of the heavens, almost touchable.

Isakakate created it all. He thought it. He formed it entire in His mind, and made it perfect, without flaw or blemish.

And He held the exquisite vision in His mind, looked at it all, and then decided to create the people as well, for He wished to present His vast dream to someone, that they should know joy, that they should live together, the men and the women and the children and the old people. Dream the dream that He had created and held in His mind, see it perfect as He saw it.

So Isakakate the Creator called Old Man Coyote to Him, and He said: "Isakawuate, this is My dream—I place it in your mind also so that you can make it for Me, form it out of the earth and the air and the fire and the water."

And then Isakakate slept and began to dream once more.

Old Man Coyote looked at the dream, and he thought to himself, "This is a very big dream. It will take me a long while to build it. I may get tired sometimes. And I know I will be very hungry from so much work—I may have to leave off whatever I'm doing to catch a prairie dog or two. Well, if He dreamed it, He should have built it Himself—if I make some mistakes, it's not my fault. Incidentally, He forgot to dream about mosquitoes and rattlesnakes—I'll put those in, and a few other things. All these animals and birds will have to eat—I'll have them eat each other. Ha ha. And so no one gets bored, I'll have the tribes fight constantly. When the warriors bring home their dead, the women will wail and mourn and cut off their fingers. Isakakate's sleeping—He won't notice. *Isakawuate, make Me this dream.* Now, that's a big job. I'll start on it tomorrow, or the next day. Damn, I'm hungry."

And so that's what happened. Our Creator dreamed the world as a perfect thing, and Old Man Coyote put it all together.

It's possible that he made a few mistakes. He's careless, that Isakawuate, and he has a very strange sense of humor: but we pay him reverence too, for the part of the dream that he built is very beautiful, and we know he never meant us harm. He's very much like we are, and many times he has helped us.

Part of his spirit lives in Cirape, the little coyote of the plains and basins and mountains. We often hear his songs at night when he calls to his woman and his woman calls back. Cirape has a mind like ours, and his songs are wonderful to hear. We also give thanks to him, for he is always near us, he is always watching.

When we hear his music, we can look into our campfires and remember how Isakakate dreamed the world and how Old Man Coyote formed it out of the elements.

Listen.

Cirape knows we are talking about him.

Listen.

When Bobtail Horse returned with the string of pack horses laden with goods, there were great demonstrations of joy, particularly among the women, who were most eager to see what things had been brought. No whiskey was included among the goods, for the Absarokas as a people had chosen to avoid the medicine water long before the arrival of their long-lost son, and he saw no reason to encourage them otherwise. But the glad reunion was short, for Bobtail Horse immediately called a council and told his brothers that the Bloods were encamped no more than ten miles away—and that he had found the bodies of two of their young men, both scalped.

"We must avenge their deaths," he said. "We must drive the Bloods before us."

Yellow Belly agreed but believed that first a count should be made of the number of their lodges. Red Bird, the first counselor, and Rotten Belly both agreed, and a plan of action was devised.

"I will go with the Bobtail Horse," Pine Leaf said quickly when told what would happen. "We will return before it is light, maybe."

With his long journey to the fort and back just completed, there was nothing Bobtail Horse wanted less than a night-long foray into danger—but Pine Leaf looked straight into his eyes, and he knew that he had no choice. Certainly, for such a venture, he could think of no better companion.

The warriors set about preparing for a battle on the following day, and Pine Leaf and Bobtail Horse rode out of camp, through the heavy cold of forest and meadow, the streams frozen and glinting in the moonlight, the snow-encrusted clumps of grass like dark knives in the thin silver light.

They made their count, finding that the lodges of the Bloods outnumbered their own by just one: two hundred and thirty-three lodges.

"There are four, maybe six warriors to each lodge," Pine Leaf said. "They are many. Do you think they have seen our village?"

"No, no, I don't think so. If they have, some Blackfoot is probably counting tipis right now. But this village is quiet. They are sleeping. They do not know that we are close."

Pine Leaf and Bobtail Horse returned immediately, and the Wolves were sent out to keep watch on the band of Blackfeet—one to return at the first sign of movement. By midmorning one of these scouts rode in to report that the Bloods were in the process of relocating their village—they had packed up and had begun to move in the direction of the Sparrow Hawks.

In the clear, cold day, their great herd of horses trailing behind them, on they came—the men, the women, the children. The Bloods had no idea what the day was to bring them, for the Sparrow Hawks were ready and certain of victory over their hated enemies.

The Crows drew up to a high prairie, low cover, and their entire force lay concealed from view at no more distance from the route of passage than half a pistol shot. The Blackfoot chief led the large group, and with him rode five young squaws whose laughter could clearly be heard in the sharp air. One of these, Bobtail Horse noted, was a young woman of great beauty, dressed in deerskin decorated with bandings of scarlet cloth and strings of beads.

"Yellow Belly needs another wife," he thought. "If I can capture her, I will make him a present."

Pine Leaf saw where Bobtail Horse's attention was fixed.

"That one in the red rags," she said. "I will kill that one, maybe."

"A red-headed Indian," Bobtail said, "that's what we're looking for. Not a harmless squaw. But if you capture her, Pine Leaf, may I have her?"

"You have too many wives already," she said with a scowl.

Yellow Belly gave orders to charge, and the Crows descended upon their enemies. The Blackfoot chief, surrounded by his wives, saw his world collapse in a matter of moments, for Bobtail Horse rode directly at him, and though the Blackfoot attempted to turn his horse, the battle axe caught him where the neck joins the shoulder, and the blood pumped out in a fine red mist as he clung desperately to his mount. The horse reared in fright, and as the half-dead man fell, Pine Leaf pinned him to the earth with her lance. His screaming wives attempted to flee, and two of them were thrown from their horses. The girl with scarlet bandings, however, proved an adept rider, but Pine Leaf drew alongside her and, leaping from her horse, dragged the woman to the ground and claimed her as a prisoner.

The Bloods hardly had time to seize their weapons, so sudden was the charge—and further, they were encumbered with their women, children, and baggage. The battle was brief, and the victory belonged to the Crows. The Blackfeet fled, scattering as dust in a sudden wind. The rifles and pistols of the Absarokas snapped in the cold air, and their arrows and lances bit deeply. The narrow defile was quickly littered with the bodies of the dead and dying, slain horses. The air was alive with the screams of women and children. One old man, pitched from his horse, wandered about stunned, in circles, his hands pulling at his hair, until an arrow cut through his throat and he lurched backward and lay still. Complete devastation. Blood on the short, frozen grass—blood everywhere. All who were slain were scalped, and the Sparrow Hawk warriors laughed as they took their grim trophies.

The Absaroka lodges would indeed be dark with scalps.

A hundred and seventy scalps when all were counted. Nearly two hundred women and children. No Sparrow Hawk had been killed, but thirty had been wounded. As Bobtail Horse well knew, seldom in Indian warfare was such a toll taken. The Blackfeet had been dealt a stunning blow.

"These people have been our enemies since Isakawuate created us," A-ra-poo-ash said, "and though we hate them, we know that they are a people of great pride. We can expect a counterattack tomorrow."

It came on the same afternoon, but the Crows were not taken by surprise. The assault came even before the Crows had reached their own village. But the force of the Blackfeet had been broken, and they were easily repulsed—their attack was more a matter of pride in the face of disaster than anything else. In this second encounter, which was very brief, no one was wounded on either side.

The wind was cold and it blew steadily, even as dark clouds obscured the sun—and the Blackfeet fled in confusion. The Sparrow Hawks sent scouts to follow their enemies. Two days later the scouts returned with the news that the Bloods had passed out of the land of Absaroka.

THE WHIMS OF
ISAKAWUATE

The cougar or puma lives among many of the rough or broken parts of the plains and throughout the Rocky Mountains. The North American lion is actually a very shy creature, and will spend its days in thick cover, prowling at dusk and at night as often as not. Cougars have been seen high in the mountains, playing together and sliding down snowfields. Their senses are extremely acute, and sightings of the animal are quite rare, often only a blurred, moving form in twilight. Inexperienced hunters might well disbelieve the existence of such a creature, but the footprints, as large as a man's hand, indicate that they investigate the camps at night. They do not seem to have any hostility toward humans, as white bears sometimes do, and are not known to attack unless cornered. The cougar has powerful jaws and immensely strong forearms—this cat can kill a horse with a single blow to the neck. Sometimes they scream at night, high on the ridges, at which times they sound like women in pain or ecstasy.

As it grew dark, a soft snow began to fall. Three great fires were built, and the victory dance was performed. There was no wailing now, despite the wounded, and no Crow woman mutilated herself. The counting of coups took a long while, and the people were in a wild and joyous mood. Black Panther and Bobtail Horse stood together near one of the fires, and Pine Leaf approached them with her prisoner in tow.

"See what I have," she said. "A red-banded bird."

She turned to the woman and said, "Take off your clothes, Blackfoot. These men wish to see what you look like—they wish you to dance naked in the snow."

The Blackfoot did not understand at first, for she did not know the Absaroka language. Pine Leaf repeated her command, gesturing at the same time. Then, comprehending, the Blood woman did as she was bid—stood naked and yet with dignity in the firelight. A number of braves now clustered about, waiting to see what would happen.

Pine Leaf said, "Black Panther and Bobtail Horse, which of you wishes this woman to be his wife? Look, her breasts are much larger than mine—she is fit to bear you children. Who wants her?"

Pine Leaf looked straight at Bobtail Horse, her eyes full of challenge. Black Panther also turned to his brother, waiting to hear what Bobtail Horse would say. The other braves drew even closer, laughing quietly, voicing remarks of admiration.

"Black Panther wishes to take this woman as his wife," Bobtail Horse said. "Tell her to clothe herself once more, and she will go with him."

Black Panther nodded, spoke:

"Yes. I will take this woman as my wife. Her new name will be Stands Straight. She will come to my lodge, and my other wife will attend to her."

Later Pine Leaf approached Bobtail Horse once more and said, "You are generous to your brother. The woman was for you."

"I did not want that woman," he answered. "Pine Leaf is the woman I wish to marry, for she is a great warrior."

"I am not sure whether your words are true."

"I speak the truth. Besides, I do not like women who have large breasts. I like your little ones."

Coyote Running and Bobtail Horse trapped together through the winter and into the spring months. Their traps were lucky, and they accumulated a great number of plew. They were often away from the village for extended periods, something now possible with the Blackfeet gone from the lands of the Sparrow Hawks. And Bobtail

Horse had much time to think—of Pine Leaf far too often, for the girl had become an obsession with him. She wielded power, and she knew it.

"Our women are slaves," he said, "and yet they accept this. Our wives praise our superiority and do not question our wanderings. Among the Whites, this is not so."

Coyote placed more wood on the campfire and said, "It is not true, Antelope Jim, this thing you have said. The women are not slaves, unless we have taken them from the Cheyennes or the Siksikas, and they have not yet been married. That is what a slave is. Perhaps you do not see some things because you still look with the eyes of a Long Knife. Could this be true?"

"It is possible, my friend. Yet I have been in these mountains for a long while. Tell me what is in your mind."

"Grouse-feather married me and we built a lodge. But it is her lodge. Your lodge is Still-water's lodge, for she is your first wife. She runs things. The Absaroka women own the village—sometimes they move it and do not tell us, and then we have to look for it. And they are close with one another, perhaps even closer than the men. They have freedom to come and go as they choose. It is right that the men and the women live different lives. Isakakate wished it to be that way, and we do not question it."

"Yet Pine Leaf is not close with the other women. Against the Blackfeet she counted six coups, and few of us are her equal in wielding the battle axe and the lance."

"Yes, Bobtail. And she saved your life when your gray horse was killed. You are lucky to have her beside you in battle."

Bobtail Horse said, "Another time three of the weasel tails on my headress were severed by a bullet, and Pine Leaf laughed, 'These Siksikas shoot close, but Isakakate will not let them harm us.' Then she pitched forward into the battle once more."

"When she rides with us in battle," Coyote shrugged, "she is not a woman."

Bobtail Horse considered this remark. Simply stated, it solved the problem for Coyote.

Then Bobtail Horse said, "and yet we do not let her share the war-path secret."

"The war-path secret is not to be shared by women."

"But you said she is not a woman when she rides with us."

"If she is not a woman, my brother, then why is it that you wish to marry her?"

One day Coyote said, "We must return to the village now, for it is time to plant the holy tobacco, the op-pu-mite. It is well that we should be there. The summer will come soon."

As they rode along, Bobtail Horse said, "Why do we not smoke the op-pu-mite? We smoke only the op-ha-tskite, the tall tobacco."

"Short tobacco comes from the stars. That is why it is holy."

"But why do we plant it if we do not wish to smoke it?"

"We do not need to smoke the short tobacco because we can smoke the tall tobacco."

"Damn it, Coyote, you know that doesn't make sense."

"Makes sense. I will tell you the story."

"I know the story."

"I do not think you know the story," Coyote Running said, "for otherwise you would not ask such a question."

"All right, tell me the story then."

"Yes. It was when Isakawuate and his friends walked about on the new earth, and they saw one of the people. And he said, 'Look, there is a man, he is standing on the ground. We must look at him.' And so Isakawuate changed himself into the op-pu-mite, for no other plants were growing yet. And then Isakawuate said that the Absaroka should plant the op-pu-mite in the spring and dance with it, for it would be their means of living. The sowing of the seed is sacred, and one may only sow these seeds after being initiated into the Bacu-sua. And that is why we do not smoke it. Do you understand now?"

"No, and I don't think you do either."

Coyote Running was somewhat exasperated with his brother. He puzzled for a while and then said, "It has always been this way, Bobtail. It is not right to question things that have always been as they are. If we smoked the sacred tobacco, Isakawuate would not be pleased. Bad things then."

"Why would bad things happen if we smoked the op-pu-mite?"

Coyote Running shook his head. He could see that it was no use. It was worse than trying to explain something to a child.

With the coming of summer, Coyote Running and Bobtail Horse returned to their village and were reunited with their wives, who received them with enthusiasm. Their trapping had been hugely successful, and the wives knew well what this meant in terms of brightly colored cloth, beads, vermilion and the like, but they would have been glad to see their men even if nothing had been trapped at all.

Three of Bobtail's "accidental" wives had gone to live with the River Crows, so the harem was somewhat smaller than when the husband had left it. Still-water and Little Wife, of course, were there, for they were his favorites and they knew it and enjoyed their status as such. Also present were Cheyenne and Cheyenne's Sister, as he had named these two who had been taken prisoner and given to him, as well as Good-ears and Doesn't-run-fast, two Crow women who had lost their husbands to the Blackfeet.

The seven of them slept together the night of Bobtail Horse's return, and though he had been without a woman for a month and a half, he was able to copulate with only three of them, thereafter falling into one of the deepest sleeps he had ever known. Little Wife sucked on him and prepared him for Still-water, who held the senior proprietary rights. She, in turn, did not allow him to exhaust himself and finally said, "Now you must mount Little Wife and ride her, for she has missed you very much." This he did and was amazed at the astounding agility of the girl—she had always amazed him—and with Doesn't-run-fast chewing on his ear, he shuddered to climax. His wives, however, were not about to let him off so easily, and soon, with all of them nibbling at him, he grew excited once more and entered into the enthusiastic body of Doesn't-run-fast, pumped away like a devoted old stallion, climaxed, and fell immediately asleep, not to be awakened despite the women's continued efforts to rouse him.

Before dawn they were at him again, and martialing his somewhat renewed forces, he managed to complete his obligations to the satisfaction of Good-ears, Cheyenne, and Cheyenne's Sister.

"I want him again," Little Wife said, but Still-Water, in a moment of exquisite sense, said, "No, we must let him rest now. If he dies, we will have to mourn and then find other husbands."

Before Bobtail Horse fell back to sleep, he whispered, "Thank you, Still-water. You are truly my first wife."

That afternoon he went alone to the river to bathe. As he swam to the rocks at the head of the big pool, a tawny form arced down from above and sliced into the clear, cold water near him. It was Pine Leaf, who had followed him from the village to this deserted spot. She emerged from the water in a burst of bubbles and laughter.

"Pine Leaf. . . ."

"The great warrior has returned to his people? We heard that you had fallen in love with a white bear and were trying to father a new race of people, maybe."

She wore no clothes, but modestly kept concealed by the water. Bobtail Horse approached her, but she quickly submerged and angled away from him, emerging a few feet downstream.

"Bobtail Horse is slow. His white bear has exhausted his manhood."

"Come here, damn it."

"Have the pine needles turned yellow, maybe? I would never marry a man who could not catch me."

Then she was beneath the water once more, and he watched her long-legged body moving fishlike toward the shore. He swam after her, but it was no use. Now she was up on the rocks, her superb, lithe body wet and glistening in the afternoon sun, standing above him.

"Bobtail is old and slow! I will have to protect him from the hungry Blackfeet who wish to take his hair."

Then she was gone, gone so swiftly that he found himself half supposing he had imagined the entire interlude. He shook his head, dived beneath the water, and swam to the willow thicket where he had left his clothing.

Taking a string of horses, Bobtail Horse, Still-water, and Little Wife traveled to the south, across the Absaroka Range and down to the headwaters of the Wind River, from thence across to the Popo Agie, upstream to its headwaters in the Wind River Range. He wanted to see this land of huge peaks and high granite basins and lakes, and he had in mind to hunt for some bighorn sheep, strange creatures of the upland slopes and cliffs, they of the gracefully rounded horns and the mysterious, slotted amber eyes. Of all the animal-people, these were the most shy and the most nimble—these and the mountain goats—living their lives in a world of clouds and rocks and snows, high up where the spring flowers bloomed in midsummer.

Where the river came down from the mountains, they chanced upon three moose wading in the shallows. Bobtail Horse saw them from above, dismounted, and worked himself carefully downslope to within twenty yards of them. Lying in the tall grass, he aimed carefully—a point just below the ear—and fired. A young bull staggered, lurched, and fell against the bank, struggled to regain his feet. The others were gone. He reloaded and primed his weapon, approached the stricken animal, and fired again.

They skinned and butchered the moose, taking cuts from the thighs for their evening meal, stripping and cutting the remainder for drying, and pegging out the heavy hide.

That night, as they talked quietly around their fire beneath the pines, they heard a disturbance down by the stream: the yapping and baying of coyotes, and another voice, a strange, long scream that shot through the darkness. A moment of silence then, followed by the noise of coyotes once more.

"Cougar," Still-water said simply. "They are arguing over the meat you left them."

He awoke about midnight—could feel the storm presence in the air. Lightning over the mountains, and the roarings of thunder. He rose and strung a blanket between two trees. His wives were suddenly awake also. Working together, they quickly completed their task, and none too soon, for the lightning grew ever closer and the thunder was louder. Bobtail Horse lay chunks of pitchwood on the firecoals, and soon the flames were darting upward in the heavy darkness.

Then rain mixed with hail, great surges out of the sky, and forked lightning struck close, only a few hundred yards away, followed almost instantaneously by crushing waves of sound, as though the birth-throes of the world were being repeated.

"Isakawuate is playing," Little Wife said.

"Well, let's hope he doesn't get too playful and try to scalp all three of us."

"He will not harm us when we are with you. Your medicine will protect us."

Still-water laughed, "Perhaps Little Wife thinks Isakawuate is your friend."

"Got nothing against him, but I wish he'd take his playthings back up into the mountains. That was too close."

"Look!" Little Wife said, pointing. "Over there, a tree is burning."

"It won't burn long, not in this rain. I think he's trying to scare the squirrels down out of the tree."

"Isakawuate has whims," Still-water said.

"Isakawuate is the Old Man Who Did Everything," Still-water said. "I will tell the story of how Isakawuate created the people. Would you like me to tell this story?"

"Big Bowl told me part of it. Do you know the whole thing?"

"Yes. My grandfather told it when I was a girl. I remember it all. I will tell it to you and Little Wife. But maybe Little Wife knows a different story, for sometimes the words are different."

Little Wife nodded in anticipation, and Still-water began:

"Isakawuate was wandering around, but there was water everywhere. Then he heard voices that said, 'We are the only ones.' And Old Man Coyote looked until he saw four ducks, and two of them were small and had red eyes and two were large and had blue eyes. So he walked over to the ducks and said, 'I am here. You are not alone. Don't you think there may be others?'

A big duck said, 'Perhaps there is something way down in the water.'

'Yes,' said Isakawuate. 'Why don't you dive down and see what is there?'

The big duck dived down and was gone a long time, and finally the other big duck said, 'I think my brother has drowned, he has been down too long.'

'Do not be afraid,' said one of the red-eyed ducks. 'No, don't be afraid,' said the other red-eyed duck. 'Your brother is a very good diver.'

So Isakawuate and the three ducks waited. They sat and waited. Then the first duck came up from the water, and he was panting for lack of breath."

"Ducks don't pant," Little Wife said. "He was just breathing with his beak open. That is what the bird-people do."

"Yes," said Still-water. "That is what he did. And Isakawuate asked if he saw anything. But the first duck said, 'No, I went down very far but I saw nothing.' So the second big duck said, 'I will dive down and see if I can find anything,' and again the others waited and waited."

"I think I know why there are four ducks," Bobtail Horse said.

"Have you heard this story before, my husband?"

"No. I'll be patient and listen. Continue."

"So the first big duck said, 'I am afraid my brother may be

drowned, he has been gone so long.' But the first red-eyed duck said, 'Don't worry, he has not been gone long enough to reach the bottom.' "

"How does he know how far bottom is?" Little Wife asked.

"Yes," asked Bobtail Horse, "how does the red-eyed duck know this?"

"He just knows. So at last the second duck came back to the surface, and when Old Man Coyote asked if he had seen anything, he said, 'No. I went down very far, so far that I became very tired, but I saw nothing.' Then one of the little red-eyed ducks said. 'These big ducks cannot go down far enough. Let me try.'

So Isakawuate thought for a while, and then he agreed. But he said, 'You are small, so you must not go too far. I don't want any of you to die.' So the first red-eyed duck agreed, and then he dived down and down and down and was gone for a long time while the others waited."

Bobtail Horse said, "And then Old Man Coyote got hungry and ate the other three ducks."

Still-water laughed and said, "No, that is not what happened. Isakawuate did not eat any of the ducks. Perhaps later when there were more ducks he ate some of them."

"What happened then?" Little Wife asked. "Do not pay any attention to our husband. He's just trying to be funny. Did the red-eyed duck find anything?"

"At last the red-eyed duck broke up through the surface and laughed. Isakawuate said, 'Did you find anything?'

'Yes,' said the little red-eyed duck. 'I went down very far and I felt something, and I looked where I felt the thing, and I found this.'

He handed Old Man Coyote a piece of a plant. Then the Old Man Who Did Everything looked carefully at the piece of plant, and with his muzzle wrinkled in thought, he said, 'Where this came from, there must be earth. What your hearts have felt is true—there is something down deep in the water. So he turned to the second red-eyed duck and said, 'The other ducks are all too tired, so you must go down this time. If you feel something hard, don't touch it—keep going. Keep going until you feel something soft, but don't look at it. Take some of it in your bill and bring it up to me.'

'I will go,' the second red-eyed duck said, and he turned upside down and disappeared into the water the way ducks do. He swam down and down and finally he felt something soft. Then he closed his eyes and took some of the soft stuff into his bill and kicked hard against the bottom and shot up to the surface."

"I'll bet the soft stuff was the earth," Bobtail Horse said.

"Be patient," Still-water answered. "Stories take time. This one is almost finished now. 'Did you get something?' Isakawuate asked. The poor little duck was so tired he could hardly swim, but he came over to Isakawuate and spit out the mud into his hands and wiped his feet on the fur of Isakawuate's legs. 'Mud!' said Old Man Coyote. 'It is wet earth! From this we can make the world. Are the red-eyed and the blue-eyed ducks ready?' "

"And then he ate all four of them?"

"No, he did not do that. If he had done that, everything would still be under water. You can see that it is not under water. This is what happened next: then Isakawuate and the other ducks made the world. They divided the world by putting water here and there. And then they made the sky and the plants and the trees and the animals. They made the sun and moon and all the stars in the sky. And after a long while, Old Man Who Did Everything decided there were not enough animals, so he made the people."

"Why did he make the Blackfeet?" Bobtail Horse asked.

"He just did," said Little Wife, seemingly lost in thought.

Still-water said, "He made the people out of clay, just as he had made everything else. He made three groups of men and women and set them on the earth before him. Next he made some arrows out of clay also, and he put these in a row on the ground a long way in front of him. Then Isakawuate said, 'I do not know which of these groups is the bravest. But I want only brave people in this world, and so I will test you to find out. Run now. Run through the arrows, and the group that runs through them first will be my people.

These people will be the Sparrow Hawks, and they will learn many things and win many battles. So the first group started to run, but they came to the arrows and were frightened. They stopped and fell on the earth. Old Man Coyote said, 'Get up and go away, for you are not my people.' "

Little Wife said, "Those must have been the Sioux or the Cheyennes, for they grow frightened in battle."

"I do not know," said Still-water. "Then Isakawuate told the second group to run through the arrows, but they were also frightened and turned back. 'You must also leave me,' said Isakawuate, and they went away. Nobody knows anymore who those first two groups of Indians were. But now Isakawuate told the third group to run through the arrows, and they did. If they were frightened, they did not show it, and Old Man Coyote was pleased with this group. He said, 'You are a very brave people, and you will be my people. I will give you helpers to teach you, and I will let you live at the center of the world, between the mountains and the plains, where the Yellowstone River comes down out of the Shining Mountains and all the other rivers also, and there are great herds of buffalo and elk, and my little brother Cirape will sing to you at night.' And that is why we live here, and all the other tribes fear us and respect us, for we are the people who pleased Isakawuate."

"And then Old Man Coyote ate the four ducks?" Bobtail Horse asked.

Little Wife rubbed at her eyes and said, "I do not think our husband will ever learn how to tell the stories. He lived with the stupid people too long."

Great streams of water, hurling themselves down out of the Wind River Range, cascading down over sheer rock, fractured-off slabs of granite, leaping down cliffs and sending up spumes of mist that vanished in the air. High up in the mountains: crimson stalks of parry primrose, still blooming in midsummer.

A moose calf wallowed in the willows, where the flooding stream had overflowed its banks. It was almost perfectly hidden in the maze of reflecting water and green-tipped willow. It was very still. Motionless. Watching.

Cream-colored columbines nodding along the banks of the stream.

An alpine plateau, its flowery surface broken by lichen-spattered slabs of granite. Storm clouds hovering the high peaks. Gray light, and the storm gathered. Indian paintbrush, red, and clusters of wild carrot.

In clear, still waters, a cutthroat trout glided from one submerged boulder to another. A bullfrog crouched in the shallows, did not move. Bobtail Horse approached, and the frog leaped backward, darted away, was gone. The water rippled softly among the grasses and lily pads.

Broken granite, ice-scoured, pine and spruce, their resin heavy in the noon air. Dark heaps of cloud over the high peaks: Bobtail Horse could see where the rain slanted down. He could hear the voice of the thunder. Great masses of granite, jagged, their points touching at the billowing clouds.

On the cliff-face above them, watching the man and the two women: three bighorn sheep.

Bobtail Horse moved very slowly, very deliberately, and raised his Hawken. The sheep continued to watch. He squeezed the trigger. The rifle shouted and jolted his shoulder.

Two of the sheep were gone, little spurts of broken stone trailing down the cliff-face.

The third crumpled to its knees, died.

The summer waned, and they moved northward, to Jackson's Hole beneath the high peaks of the Tetons. Bobtail Horse intended to traverse the area called "Colter's Hell," where, according to the stories, huge gushers of boiling water spewed from the earth. He had not seen these before, and now he wished to do so.

They had been away from their people for more than two months, and Still-water and Little Wife urged their return. Bobtail Horse sensed something more than this, however, something called fear, for the land of the geysers was held to be inhabited by bad spirits. Some said that the land was an entry into the underworld. Stillwater and Little Wife had great faith in the medicine of the Bobtail Horse, yet they were somewhat doubtful as to whether the medicine was strong enough to protect them in such a place.

Bobtail Horse, on the other hand, was thinking about what seemed to him a far greater danger, for they were now well into the lands controlled by Bugs' Boys, the Siksikas.

As it turned out, Bobtail Horse would have to wait for another time to see the land of the geysers, for a solitary figure was riding down out of the pines above the valley. He wore buckskin and had a red band around his head. He carried his rifle ready, cradled in the crook of his arm. A single pack horse followed behind.

It was the old trapper, Pierre Le Blueux.

Bobtail Horse, recognizing his friend, waved his arms and shouted:

"Helloo Le Blueux! Jim Beckwourth here!"

As Bobtail Horse thumped his heels to Come Back's sides, he noted that Le Blueux's hands had involuntarily shifted slightly, were ready now to use the rifle if it were necessary. Bobtail grinned, waved again, shouted Pierre's name once more, and let out a war whoop.

"Trouble with Le Blueux," he thought, "is he don't trust nobody. . . ."

Then the two men were together, dismounted, were embracing one another. Bobtail Horse threw his arms about the bull-like French Canadian and lifted him off the ground. Le Blueux placed his hands on either side of Bobtail Horses's face, kissed him on the forehead, and then roared with laughter.

"*Mon éminent bison! Alors,* I have never given *le baiser* to a Crow warrior until this day! Put me down so that Pierre can breathe again, *peut-être.*"

"Pierre! Damn it's good to see you, old hoss! This child's missed you."

The two men talked rapidly, as if trying to draw the intervening years together all at once, to close up and bind together the edges of the gulf that had separated them. But after a few minutes they ceased speaking, held each other at arm's length, stared at each other, and then broke out laughing again.

Finally Bobtail Horse asked, "Where's Baptiste? How is he?"

Le Blueux shook his head, and his expression changed.

"Baptiste La Jeunesse, he is dead. It is very sad, Jim. *Mort. Alors, c'est ça.* The *Pieds Noirs,* friend of me. We who have come to the mountains, we have bargained this fate. Is because we have no other life. La Jeunesse and Beckwourth, they are my sons. *L'un est mort.* I must search for the other? *C'est la vie.* I am an old man now, *homme du bon vieux temps.*"

As overjoyed as Bobtail Horse was to come so unexpectedly upon his mentor, he was stunned by the news of Baptiste's death. It was like something was chewing at all of them, a bite here, a bite there. The hand of fate—their fate, as Pierre had said. In this moment he was Jim Beckwourth once more, and a fist of pain pounded at his stomach. And yet, that was the way a man died, and perhaps it was better for death to come soon than late—take him while his strength was still his own, not when he was broken and helpless with many years upon him. Better to die in the face of it. Better to die as Cahuna Smith had died. And Baptiste.

Still-water and Little Wife held back at a distance to witness this encounter of their husband and the Whiteman. They saw the two men embrace. They listened to the exchange of words in the language of the Long Knives, but they understood little of what was said. Still, they knew the words of the trapper had struck Bobtail Horse—they could see the sadness upon his features. After a time, they watched the two men embrace once more.

"Who is this man, Still-water? He is older than Bobtail Horse. Is this his White father?"

"I do not know, little one. I think it is maybe."

"Will Bobtail Horse leave us and go away now? He will go back to the lodges of the Whites?"

"He will not leave us. He will not leave Absaroka. I do not believe it. He is one of us in his blood."

"He must not leave us," Little Wife said.

Le Blueux had much to tell Bobtail Horse. With the death of La Jeunesse, Pierre was of a mind to quit the mountains: first a return to the settlements and then on to Quebec. What awaited him there? He wasn't sure. He'd spent twenty-five years in the mountains now and was nearly fifty years old. And what did he have to show for it? A little bank account down in St. Louis, but not much else. It wasn't that he was ready to quit it all, but time was catching up with him.

"*Alors,* it is a young man's life, this. But maybe I go up into the north country, *peut-être.* A good place to die, *mon frère.*"

It was all changing, and he hated the change. Two years back Sublette, Jackson, and Smith had sold their trapping interests to Jim Bridger, Tom Fitzpatrick, and Milton Sublette, Bill's younger brother—with Henry Fraeb and Jean Gervais in on the deal, too. It was the Rocky Mountain Fur Company now. Jed Smith had finally made it back from California after taking a big swing up through the Columbia River country and losing all his men and horses. Hudson's Bay Company had actually tried to help him out and had given him an escort back to the mountains. And now Smith was dead, killed by Comanches apparently, over on the Cimarron River. Nathaniel Wyeth and Benjamin Bonneville had both started their own fur companies, and, of course, there was the very real competition of Kenneth McKenzie and the American Fur Company.

"You work for them? *Mon Dieu,* Jim, they are the enemy."

"A couple more years," Bobtail Horse said, "and American Fur will have the whole thing to itself. Not sure how I feel about that, even if they are paying me a salary."

"*Enfant de garce,* Jim, that is the problem. There are too many men, there are not enough beaver. McKenzie's men, they follow Fitzpatrick all over the mountains last year—Fontenelle, Drips, and Vanderburgh. Last year Drips and Vanderburgh make winter camp right along with Bridger and Milton Sublette. *Incroyable!* Not enough beaver for everyone, *c'est ça.*"

Bobtail Horse was incredulous. "They *followed* Bridger and Milt?"

"Followed, *oui.* Trap the same streams. Friend of me, I tell you what. Your McKenzie he sends two caravans of goods to the Rendezvous, one from Fort Union and one from the East. If they get to Pierre's Hole first, all the free trappers maybe they sell to Astor. Fitzpatrick, he goes east to make sure Milton Sublette hurries. They are racing over the mountains. Rocky Mountain takes short cut and gets there first. *C'est vrai!* They win, but next year, who knows? In any case, is because there are too many trappers and not enough beavers. *Mon Dieu!*"

"Hide and seek in the mountains!" Bobtail Horse laughed. "Jesus, it's enough to make a coon happy he hasn't been part of it. Things are changing, but not here, not so much yet."

Le Blueux lifted his Hawken and sighted off at a big vulture that was riding the wind current over the ridge. He made a little clucking sound with his tongue and then put the rifle back down.

"Friend of me, is because you now think like Indian. Me, I am a Whiteman, stupid old French Canadian, *mangeur de lard.* The Indian, he does not look down the years the way the Whiteman does, *peut-être.* You are happy, *non?* You will stay a few more years, is so. Then the buffalo are gone. The people they will come across these mountains. *États Unis* will be in Oregon and California, I say it is so. Bonneville, he takes wagons to the west. It will come, Jim. I do not wish to be here then. The mountains, they will be spoiled. And we do it. Too many of us. *Alors,* I am very unhappy old man. When I first come to the mountains, they are new. It is time for me now to go."

The Bobtail Horse thought for a moment, then spoke:

"We can't stop the changes, Pierre. If we could look way down the future, it would probably scare the hell out of us. All of us. I know you're right, though. They're going to fill in all the blank spaces on the maps, and then they're going to run roads across. That's just what happened down around St. Louis when I was a boy.

And it's coming, sure as buffalo shit. But don't leave the mountains, Pierre. This is your place, and it's my place too. There's nothing back there for either one of us. And the only time we have to worry about is the time we have to live. It'll last that long, I tell you. They're a hell of a long way from taming the Rocky Mountains. A hell of a long way. They're not going to be building towns while those murderous Blackfeet are around. They're worth something in that way, anyhow. Absaroka, Cheyenne, Sioux, Blackfoot, Arapaho, Pawnee—sure as the Whites started moving in to take up farming, the Indians might just band together to drive them out."

"Lung disease, smallpox," Le Blueux said, "the Indians do not last long. I have seen this thing, it has happened in the East. Even the Crows could not fight against that. *Mon Dieu,* it is the way of the Whiteman and the Indians."

The Bobtail Horse stared off toward the mountains. For a moment his vision did not seem to want to draw into focus.

He knew his friend was right.

18

MEDICINE

The awu-sua, the dome-shaped sweat lodge, is put up only as a serious undertaking, for the Absarokas do not sweat except as a ceremony, when prompted by a dream or under the guidance of a shaman. The sweat is largely reserved for the old or those who have made a vow. A warrior might say to the Sun: "Uncle, if I win a victory, I will make a sweat lodge." In the center of the structure there is a pit for rocks, which are heated outside first and put in with a forked stick. Inside, they produce great heat. The votaries strip, and the shaman pours four quantities of water upon the rocks. Steam rises and becomes almost unbearable. When the buffalo robes are removed from the frame of the lodge, the bathers say, "Sun we are doing this for you. May we live until next winter." Then everyone says, "May we live until then!"

Le Blueux accompanied Bobtail Horse and his two wives back to the Absaroka encampment. Bobtail Horse put Doesn't-run-fast and Cheyenne's Sister at the disposal of his friend, a courtesy which Pierre resisted for a short time, until Bobtail said, "My friend, I am a powerful Absaroka warrior. I have many wives, and I am chief of the Dog Soldiers. What would my fellow braves think of me if I denied this hospitality to my adopted White father? You must copulate with my wives or they will feel they have failed me. They would believe that I was unwilling to share you with them. I can keep them in buffalo meat and foofuraw, but no man can service so many women. You must do this thing, Pierre. Have pity on your friend."

Once having accepted the nature of the arrangement, Pierre Le

Blueux suffered no further scruples and was able to pleasure both himself and the two Indian women quite successfully.

After a few days, however, Le Blueux and Bobtail Horse set out for Fort Cass. They had not traveled five miles when Bobtail Horse saw Coyote Running bearing down upon them, his horse at a full run.

"The Siksikas!" he said. "They are attacking the village—you must return!"

"Attack," Bobtail Horse said to Le Blueux. "You up to a little wrestling match with some Blackfeet?"

"*Oui,* monsieur, the gray-bearded one, he is ready."

The assault on the Crow village was in full progress when Bobtail Horse's group descended upon the Blackfeet from the rear. The Blackfeet were thrown into some state of confusion, and the tide of the battle was soon turned. Bobtail Horse had just entered into the conflict when Come Back stumbled and threw his rider to the ground. A Blackfoot warrior, taking good advantage of the situation, hurled his lance and, while missing Bobtail Horse, pinned him by the legging. As he struggled to free himself, Pine Leaf appeared from nowhere and drove her battle axe into the skull of the Blackfoot. Bobtail Horse sprang back onto his mount and, with the heroine at his side, once more entered the battle.

A moment later Pine Leaf's horse received a lance in its side and collapsed to its knees. Pine Leaf slid off easily and was immediately engaged in hand-to-hand struggle with a Blackfoot. Bobtail Horse swung about and rode upon the enemy from behind, knocking him senseless. Pine Leaf drove her lance through the man's chest and scalped him.

She shouted to Bobtail Horse, "I am all right now. I have him safe now, maybe."

The Siksikas, utterly disorganized, spontaneously began to flee the scene of the battle. Those who were not on foot were pursued by mounted Crow warriors and cut down.

Then it was over.

The battle had been disastrous for both sides. Thirty-one Sparrow

Hawks had been killed, while the Blackfeet had left more than ninety lying dead. But the first wave of Blackfeet had driven away a great number of the horses, perhaps as many as fifteen hundred.

There was to be no scalp dance, and the relatives of the slain went into mourning. Fingers disappeared. Knife slashes on face and breast. The Absaroka village was grim, and the silence was punctuated by the wails of the women.

"It is terrible, this," Le Blueux said. "I have not killed that many *Pieds Noirs* in a long while. Is a strange life here. *Sacré Dieu!* That girl who saves your life—she is worth ten warriors. Me, I could not believe my eyes! I thought it was a young man who looks like a woman. *C'est incroyable!*"

"She certainly is worth ten of the warriors, that one. Her name is Bar-chee-am-pe, Pine Leaf. She has taken a vow to kill a hundred of our enemies in order to take revenge for her brother's death. A twin brother. They were very close."

"*Très jolie,* that one. She does not marry, then?"

"No. She will not marry, she says, until her revenge is complete."

"*Enfant de garce!* The man who marries that one, he will wake up one day with no hair. She would destroy her man, *c'est vrai.*"

Bobtail Horse laughed.

"I have begged her to marry me," he said. "She tells me I must find her a red-haired Indian first."

"*Sacré!* You have already too many wives, I think."

"Pine Leaf keeps telling me that. Hell, Pierre, I've only got nine of them—and some of those I hardly ever see. They spend their time with the River Crows. After today, a number of men will take on extra wives—the wives of the dead. It is our way."

"*Beaucoup des femmes d'épouse.* More babies that way. More braves to fight the *Pieds Noirs?* You are lucky, *mon frère,* that you have made no babies yet. You would have to spend all your time hunting and no time to take the plew."

Bobtail Horse nodded.

"Sometimes I think it might be better that way. Maybe that's the only way to save the mountains? Start making hats out of something else—then no one would want the beaver, and the mountains might get lonely again. Not as many beaver right now as there used to be, nor as many buffalo either. Even the grizzlies are starting to get scarce, though I saw over twenty of them in just one day this summer, cantankerous bastards. We could stand a few less bears."

Le Blueux was looking cloudy in the eyes again, almost like an old dog, Bobtail Horse thought. Pierre had been worried about the end of the mountains as long as Bobtail Horse had known him, but it was worse now.

"Something has gone out of the man," he thought.

They rode to the fort.

Apparently the Blackfeet were up all over, lashing out at everyone and everything. Bobtail Horse had heard rumors that McKenzie's men upriver had come to some sort of agreement with the Blackfeet, but if it was so, the word hadn't made it down to Fort Cass.

The day after their arrival, a group of Blackfeet surrounded a small number of Frenchmen who had been sent out to cut logs, about a mile from the fort. The Siksikas shot and scalped one of the Whites, and all but one of the others made it safely back to the fort. Bobtail Horse mounted Come Back and rode directly toward the old buffalo wallow where a Frenchman was pinned down by a half dozen Indians. They fired at him as he came, the shots whizzing past. Bobtail Horse pulled up beside the Frenchman and motioned for him to jump, which he did. Then they rode for the fort. The Blackfeet were on foot, so the escape was easily made. They were within a few hundred yards of the fort, however, when five mounted Indians emerged from the trees and attempted to head them off. Bobtail Horse veered the black stallion toward the river, and the Blackfeet gave pursuit. They were gaining on him. He could see men standing along the top of the fort's battlements, watching. But nobody was doing anything. They were just watching.

"Iggerant dunghead," a voice said. "They don't care about yore hide—they just gonna stand there and watch yuh get yore h'ar lifted."

It had been a long while since he had heard that voice. Good to know it was still there, somewhere inside his skull.

He doubled back, the Blackfeet now in close pursuit.

"Make for the fort!" he yelled to the man behind him. "I'll try to hold them off—tell those sons of bitches to get out here and save my ass. This child don't want to get scalped with a whole damned brigade watching!"

Bobtail Horse leaped from the saddle, Hawken in hand, rolled in the grass as he landed, and immediately set out on a dead run for a pile of downed logs that hadn't been dragged in to the fort. He leaped over the logs and took cover. The Blackfeet curveted aside, certain now of their prey. They drew to a standstill and gestured at him, laughing and waving their arms.

"Shas-ka-o-hush-a!" they shouted. "The Shas-ka-o-hush-a is dead! We will cut out your heart and scalp you! Where are your friends the Absarokas now? We will cut off your manhood and push it into your mouth and scalp you while you gag!"

"Obviously," thought Bobtail Horse, "they know who I am."

He looked over his shoulder toward the fort. The men were still standing along the battlements, watching.

"Dumbass coon, now McKenzie ain't goin' to have to pay yore salary. He's prob'ly up there laughin' his civilized tail off."

"Could be you're right," Bobtail Horse said aloud. "Just shut your face and let a man think."

One of the Blackfeet was charging him on foot.

"Think you're going to take coup on the great Sparrow Hawk warrior, do you friend?" he thought. He waited until the Indian was nearly upon him and then fired his pistol into the Blackfoot's stomach. The Siksika fell forward with a deep grunt and collapsed against the logs. Now the other Blackfeet were screaming with rage. They spread out and charged all at once on horseback.

"Yur dead as a jackass rabbit," the voice said.

Suddenly one of the Blackfeet pitched off his horse. The snap of a rifle from one side, over by the river. There was no time to look: Bobtail Horse fired his Hawken and another Indian fell.

Two more. He had a chance now.

A rifle ball cut at his leg as he fired again.

He was wounded.

"Just a scratch, coon. Just gettin' started on ye."

Another rifle shot. A horse went over, carrying its rider with it.

Bobtail Horse leaped from behind the logs, the pain of the flesh wound searing through him as he did so. But he was up. He was moving. The Blackfoot was upon him, the rifle pointed. Bobtail Horse turned to one side as the shot exploded past him, and then he had hold of the Blackfoot's leg. He held on as the Indian attempted to shake him loose.

He fired the pistol and fell backward, the Blackfoot on top of him. He fired again. But the Indian was already dead.

He turned over, pistol still in hand, and gasped for breath.

Pierre Le Blueux was scalping the Blackfoot who had fallen beneath his horse.

"Friend of me!" Pierre shouted. "It is dangerous to fight these *Pieds Noirs* by yourself, *non?* I was not a very good teacher, *peut-être?* Sacré Dieu, I am old man and it is now hard to pull the scalps off. . . ."

The rifle ball had passed through the flesh of his leg, missing the bone, so the wound was not serious, however painful. After a single day of being flat on his back, Bobtail Horse was up and about, limping badly but moving.

Le Blueux said, "This McKenzie, he does not protect his men well. You work for the wrong people, *a vrai dire*. With such friends. . . ."

"Buffalo shit cowards," Bobtail Horse said. "Your countrymen, Pierre. They just stood there watching."

"They are the greenhorns, these. They are not *les hommes des montagnes*. They will learn, or one day they will grow suddenly bald and wear little red hats, very close *coupes des cheveux*. These men, they are hired in the East. They have never fought with the *Pieds Noirs* before. *Dieu,* they will learn. *Autrement, s'eteindre, se mourir.* You will be all right now, *mon frère?* Pierre, he must go by the boat down to St. Louis. Is possible I will be back next year, when I have spent all of my money on the ladies of the hotel, *les prostituées.* But I am a trapper *libre,* so I can go where I wish, *c'est ça.* We will be together once again, Jim Beckwourth. Is so, I feel it."

Bobtail Horse clapped his friend on the back and said, "Hell, Pierre, I don't figure you're ever very far away. Every time I set a trap in the water, I hear you right there behind me, telling me I still didn't do it quite right, and maybe ringing one of those little bells you keep on your horse."

"*Les clochettes,* they are very important, Jim."

"What are you going to do when you get tired of the ladies with the big tits? Indian women are a damned sight finer, I tell you."

"*Alors,* I do not know. *Mais l'homme,* he does not stay always young. Maybe it is a mistake, going back."

"That's just what it is. A mistake. But I guess when the hotel ladies call, a man's got to go. When you come back to God's country, though, I think you should come to live with the Crows. You and I will catch many beavers, we will take *le nombre monstrueux.*"

"You talk like the Frenchman with the bad tongue, Jim. It is from eating too much buffalo meat, this."

Two days after Le Blueux's departure for St. Louis, Bobtail Horse mounted Come Back and began his solitary ride upriver to the encampment of the Many Lodges and the Kicked-in-their-Bellies, who were gathered together—or at least they had been when he and Pierre had set out. Things would go far more smoothly, Bobtail mused, if the two groups could just manage to stay together, for in this way the Mountain Crows would remain a formidable force, easily capable of defending themselves against any enemy whatsoever. But the people were natural nomads, and sometimes even the two groups would split up into separate small villages. A-ra-poo-ash was old and seemingly lacked sufficient determination to hold the Sparrow Hawks together, even though he might wish it. All in all, the old head chief remained an enigma in the mind of Bobtail Horse. A good man, and one with a great reputation, but hard to understand. Perhaps it was simply that after enough years of continued battles and blood-lettings and deaths and mournings, the will to remain in control weakened, and it was easier to allow the people to follow their own whimsical natures.

The bad leg was bothersome—stiff and often quite painful.

Shortly after dark, Bobtail rode up a short way into a narrow side canyon, tethered Come Back, and hobbled about getting firewood. He built a small fire, formed wet clay from the streambank around a good chunk of elk meat, enough for morning as well, and placed it in the fire. He took the little tin pan out of his sack and set some coffee to brewing.

When he had eaten, Bobtail lay back against a small pine and gazed up through the interlaced boughs of the trees. The sky was perfectly clear, and the stars were cold, metallic white points. They appeared very close, as if hanging directly over the trees. There was chill in the air. Autumn soon—time to start trapping.

He pulled the buffalo robe about himself and slept.

Dreamed.

Saw a grizzly go after a coyote almost as large as itself. But the coyote stood on its hind legs and spoke to the bear.

"I am Isakawuate. I am Old Man Coyote, and you are a bear. I am the one who created your people, and that is why you must not attempt to bully me."

"Ha!" said the bear. "You are not the one who made me, for I am stronger than any other creature. My sister chewed up old Hugh Glass before the Long Knives came and shot her, even though she was probably already dying. Then I followed the trapper, and later I licked the maggots out of the wound in his back. Even the buffalo do not tell me what to do. You do not speak the truth, Coyote, for I made myself. No one else was strong enough to do it."

"White Bear," Isakawuate said, "If I take away your gifts, then you will know that I was the one who created you."

"I will break your back in my jaws," White Bear said.

So Isakawuate touched White Bear, and the bear dropped to all fours and was unable to speak any longer.

"Now you know," Isakawuate said. "Now you will always be an animal, and the Absarokas will shoot you and use your hide in their bear song dance."

When he had spoken, Isakawuate began to burn like fire, and then he was a fire, a twisting column of flame, and the white bear roared and ran off. Then the fire also disappeared, and darkness came. Strong winds were blowing, and the stars began to fall from the sky.

Bobtail Horse awoke, reached instinctively for the Hawken at his side, and sat up slowly.

Was something nearby?

He listened intently, rose, and stood with the rifle in his hands.

But there was nothing: only the singing of a solitary coyote, back up on the long opposite ridge. Come Back made no noise at all.

"Just a dream, I guess," Bobtail Horse said aloud. Strangely, he was startled by the sound of his own voice. The voice sounded discordant, like it didn't belong in this place. What belonged? The faint murmurings of the stream, the quavering bark and howl of the coyote. A soft, cold wind among the trees.

Bobtail Horse realized he was sweating. The rifle was slippery in his hands. His leg hurt. Torn muscles, the tissues mending now, invisibly reconnecting themselves within his leg, drawing strength from his blood, from the elk meat he had eaten, from the water he had drawn from the running stream to make his coffee.

He lay back down and pulled the buffalo robe about himself once more, but he was unable to sleep further. The voices of Isakawuate and White Bear kept repeating themselves in his mind, kept changing. Always the result was the same: the bear roared and ran off, the coyote became a column of fire, the winds blew, and the fire disappeared.

He drifted in and out of more visions. He was speaking with Le Blueux. And then he was speaking with La Jeunesse, who said, "I am dead, Jim. It is not bad here. It is quiet, and there are no more *Pieds Noirs* to fight. It is true, this, *c'est vrai*. You will like it here also when you come. It is the way of things."

"Have you spoken with Light in the Trees, Baptiste?"

"Non, *mon frère*. She is gone back to her people, that one. It is no good to think of her any more. She has gone *en bateau*. She would not stay with *l'homme des bois*."

"Does the sun ever rise, Baptiste?"

Wide awake now. The east was a thin gray blending almost to the color of silver, and the trees were dark shadows above him. The night was over.

He placed tinder on the dying bed of embers, and the flames were soon dancing upward. He stood beside them, enjoying the smoke that stung his eyes. He heated the remaining coffee, savored the bitter taste, and chewed on cold meat. Another day or two. It would be good to be home again.

His leg felt better, much better.

He would make good time this day.

Bobtail Horse limped to the stream, knelt slowly, carefully, and splashed cold water over his face. It would take only a few minutes now to get his stuff together, mount, and ride.

He hoped the old women had not convinced Big Rain to move the encampment another fifty miles off to the south.

"Why can't they just stay in one place, dammit?" he said as he swung up onto Come Back.

A graysquirrel flashed across the clearing before him, tail high, and went up a pine, quickly around to the far side, then began chattering at him, indignant at being disturbed.

"Let's move out, Come Back old mule. Let's go visit our heathen relatives. Our women folks miss us."

He whistled softly as he rode.

Two weeks later a war-party drifted over into the country of the Cheyennes, and Bobtail Horse was with them. The weather was good, and the Crow warriors were in high spirits, joking, looking for trouble.

They rode down to a plum-tree forest and discovered that it was full of bird song and the voices of Cheyenne women.

The plums were large, red, and completely ripe, very sweet and ready for eating. The women were busy picking fruit, filling their baskets. The jabber was incessant, like swarms of blackbirds. They didn't realize that the Crows were about to come into the plum forest to make a harvest of their own.

Bobtail Horse whistled: Dog Soldiers and Lumpwoods closed a circle about the women, who were taken completely by surprise and did not even attempt to run. The Crow warriors marched them to an open space where they were formed into a line so that the process of selection might take place. The old women, the matrons, and the unattractive were told to leave the line and to return to their village. These went away sullenly, their eyes burning hatred.

Fifty-nine females remained, all of them young and good-looking. But one in particular was stunningly beautiful—and she was the prisoner of Little Gray Bull, who already wished that a close friend of his had captured the girl, one who would make him a present of her.

"What is your name?" Little Gray Bull demanded.

"My name is Red Cherry," she said. She refused to look at her captor.

Bobtail Horse stared at the girl. He could feel the pressure of That-Which-Rises, so he turned Come Back and rode off, shaking his head.

It was time to move out quickly, for there had been three Cheyenne warriors amongst the women, and these men had slipped out when the surround was made. The village of Leg-in-the-Water was only about five miles distant, and Bobtail Horse knew that he and his Sparrow Hawks did not have much time if they wished to avoid a battle.

As the journey toward the Absaroka village proceeded, the Cheyenne women were gloomy for an hour or two, as was to be expected. After that, however, the captives brightened and amused the men with their smiles and conversation, for they had heard enough stories to know, or at least to anticipate, that their life with the Crows might be, in many respects, superior to that which they had among their own people.

"That one," Pine Leaf said, "she should be given to an old man who is unable to please her, maybe. Or are her breasts the right size for the Great Warrior?"

"Which one?" Bobtail Horse said without smiling.

"Is this possible? You did not notice her?"

After several days the Dog Soldiers and the Lumpwoods and the Cheyenne women reached the Absaroka village, and the group was applauded as it rode in.

Four of the women were adjudged to be the prizes of Bobtail Horse, and these, according to custom, would become his sisters and would live in the lodge of Big Bowl and Funny Deer, who would find husbands for them—thus adding significantly to the strength of the family.

Little Gray Bull, the captor of Red Cherry, gave her as a wife to Big Rain, the elected village chief.

Pine Leaf had captured two prisoners, and these she offered as wives to Coyote Running and Bobtail Horse. Coyote accepted the girl and said that he would call her Plum-picker. Neither the girl nor Grouse-feather, however, liked the name, so she retained her Cheyenne name of Morning Song. Coyote Running complained briefly about his lack of authority in his own lodge but soon decided that he liked his new wife's original name better than the one he had invented.

Bobtail Horse declined Pine Leaf's offer.

"You say that I already have too many wives. Why do you wish to give me another? It is Pine Leaf I wish to marry."

"This one has small breasts, like mine," Pine Leaf said. "I thought you would want her."

"You should give her to Yellow Belly. I saw him looking at her, and I think he would like to have another woman in his lodge."

"You do not want to have her then?"

"No. I wish to have you."

"Ah! You have found the red-headed Indian, maybe?" she said and laughed mockingly.

Bobtail Horse reflected that any mention of marriage was always so treated by Pine Leaf. Perhaps she was simply a woman who would never wish to marry? But the longer they rode together and the more he saw of the acts of heroism she was able to perform, the greater became his attachment to her. When Pine Leaf was away, or when he was away from her, he felt a stinging sense of emptiness. But when she was at his side in battle, his strength and courage were increased. Pine Leaf was perhaps the boldest of his warriors. To be sure, she was not so strong as a man, but she had the agility and quickness of a lynx and could kill an opponent while a lesser warrior was still preparing to attack. She asked no quarter and gave none. Already she was well-known among the enemies of the Sparrow Hawks, and more than one brave had sought her out in battle in the hope of taking her scalp, but always the issue had gone the other way. Her medicine was powerful, and it was feared.

In one thing, she believed, she was still not accepted among the Dog Soldiers, for she was not allowed to share the war-path secret. She had killed many in battle and would dare to follow wherever Bobtail Horse would lead—if indeed she needed to be led at all. None of the male warriors of her own age held so many coups or had taken so many scalps.

"Then why am I not allowed to share the secret?" she asked Bobtail Horse. "Why am I sent off with the women and children when the war-path secret is shared with those men who have had but one battle? This is not right. It is an insult to my medicine."

Bobtail Horse explained as much as he could.

"Pine Leaf is a great warrior, but she is still a woman. Tradition will not allow for the war-path secret to be shared with a woman, even if she is a brave warrior. Coyote Running and I have both proposed that you should be allowed to share the secret, but the others will not agree. 'We might have to speak of Pine Leaf herself,' they say. And I cannot answer this. 'When she is not with us, she is still a woman,' they say. 'If she told the other women, she would have to be killed, as well as all the women she told.' And they say,

'Isakawuate would be displeased, and we would all lose our medicine.' What answers should I give them when they say these things?"

"It is something about sex, then, isn't it?" Pine Leaf asked.

Bobtail Horse said nothing.

"Can you not tell me what it is? I would be happy then, maybe."

"If I told you, I would have to pay with my life."

"You speak foolish. No man among the Sparrow Hawks could ever defeat you in battle."

"I would have to submit to this death," Bobtail Horse answered.

Pine Leaf looked away, then returned her gaze to her friend.

"I would never speak of this thing to anyone if you told me what it is."

Bobtail Horse hesitated. The ice he walked upon was quite thin, and he knew it.

"Would you have me break my vow to Isakawuate?" he asked.

"Isakawuate has accepted me as a Dog Soldier. It is only the Dog Soldiers who do not accept me, maybe. My medicine could not be strong if Isakawuate did not wish me to be a warrior."

"That is true, Pine Leaf. What you say is true. If I tell you, both of our lives are in your hands. One slip of the tongue, and we are both dead."

"Bobtail Horse and Pine Leaf together could defeat all the others."

"Bobtail Horse and Pine Leaf would have to *submit* to the death," he answered.

She reached for his hand and held it.

"Then I must not ask you to tell me, my brother."

How could such a small thing be so important? If she knew, he thought, she would no doubt find the war-path secret a foolish game of boys, of men who were afraid that their dealings with women somehow weakened them and made them unfit for battle.

"Let me ask you a question," he said, "a question which you must answer with truth, even if you do not wish to tell me. Will you promise to answer such a question?"

"I have always spoken the truth to Bobtail Horse."

"That is true. I will ask the question then. Have you ever made love with any of the men?"

"Have I ever made love with you?"

"No. But that is not the question I asked."

"It is the same answer," she said. "Until I marry you, I will never make love to a man."

"Will you swear to this by the sun and the moon and the earth and the sky? For both of our lives will depend upon it."

"Does this mean I will not be able to have you take me into the willows before we are married if I swear to this thing?"

"Yes. That is what it means, Pine Leaf."

Suddenly she laughed.

"Let me think about this thing before I ask you any more questions, maybe."

Then she turned and was gone.

Coyote Running raised a war party and went in search of the Blackfeet. Bobtail Horse did not accompany his brother, but Pine Leaf did. The group returned in a few days, bringing with them the scalps of eight Blood Indians, a band of the Blackfeet. Coyote Running's party had lost two men, something which greatly annoyed Pine Leaf, for she was precluded from joining the dancing, even though she had counted two coups.

"I will go to war no more except with the Bobtail Horse," she declared. "Will you raise a party immediately? Let us go kill an enemy so that I can wash my face, maybe."

"I cannot do that until after I have been to the fort," Bobtail Horse said.

"It would not take us long. You and I will go together and steal horses from the Cheyennes. We could kill Leg-in-the-Water too."

"No, Pine Leaf. You won't have to wear that mourning paint long, but we must go to the fort before we do anything else. Many of our people have been busy with their traps these past two months, and they have many pelts. The people wish to trade and to buy things for their women."

Her eyes blazed up.

"You would go with me if I went down to the willows with you."

"Willows be damned," he said. "Sometimes we must be patient. You have said that I must be patient. You be patient."

"I never wanted to go to the willows anyway, maybe."

"I think maybe you did."

"The Bobtail Horse does not speak truth," she said and turned away from him.

The men watched from the battlements as the Crows rode in, the warriors proud on their war horses, the war bonnets trailing behind, the women in white deerskin with trappings of scarlet and yellow. Pine Leaf rode not with the women but with the Dog Soldiers, her position earned in battle, with white owl plumes trailing from her raised lance. By late afternoon some three hundred Sparrow Hawk lodges rose from the meadows surrounding the fort. The people were in a festive mood and ready to trade their furs for powder and lead and knives and steel hand-axes and needles and beads and bright colored cloth and vermilion and even such things as coffee, flour, and spices.

Kipp informed Bobtail Horse that Le Clerk, the hunter, had been killed.

"Goddamned Blackfeet," he said. "McKenzie's supposed to have a handle on 'em now, but it don't do a pinch of good. First rule them bastards have is *kill it*. It's goin' to require an act of God to make them people peaceful."

"I've got a grudge or two against those folks," Bobtail Horse said. "Like the last time I was here, and your men just stood there and watched."

Kipp nodded.

"At least that old Frechman didn't just sit and watch. He'd be a good man to have here at the post. I guess he went down to St. Louis, eh?"

"Pierre Le Blueux," Bobtail Horse said. "Maybe the best man in the mountains—been up here for twenty-five years and only down to St. Louis twice in all that while. He's kind of low on things right now—says it don't *shine* like it used to. But I figure he'll be back before too long."

"Sometimes they don't come back," Kipp said. "Sometimes they buy them a farm down in Missouri or Kentucky and get married, take to being dirt farmers. Could sure put him on right now, though, if he was here. I need another hunter."

"I don't think Pierre would care much for a life of dragging in meat. He likes to be setting his traps or just wandering around. Took me over to the Tetons the first time I was ever there. . . ."

Bobtail Horse's voice trailed off. He was thinking about the great mountains glittering in the late light. About swimming. About Baptiste La Jeunesse.

"Now you will go to war for the Long Knife who was killed?" asked Pine Leaf. "I will go with you so that I can wash my face."

"All right," said Bobtail Horse. "I will have Black Panther take my pack horses with him when the people return to the village, then you and I can go alone, together, and see what we can get into. Will this please you?"

"The Great Warrior has remembered his medicine," she said, smiling.

Bobtail Horse suggested to A-ra-poo-ash that the Absarokas proceed up the Yellowstone as far as Pompey's Tower and wait for him to join them there in four nights.

Yellow Belly looked perturbed.

"You and Bar-chee-am-pe?" he asked. "Will you go after Siksikas or some other thing, my brother?"

"We go on a war-path."

"I think he had better be after Siksika scalps," Coyote Running said, "or Bar-chee-am-pe will come back alone, with the Bobtail's scalp flying from her lance."

"We go on a war-path," Bobtail Horse said. "No other thing."

Pine Leaf and Bobtail Horse rode westward, hoping to surprise a Siksika or two and then to turn back into their own country. On the second day they heard a rifle shot and rode in the direction of the sound. They came to a crest of a ridge and looked down into the little valley beyond: four Blackfeet had just taken a buffalo cow and had turned it over on its back to skin and butcher it. They were busy with their work, not expecting an attack by two Sparrow Hawks riding alone into their lands.

The rifles of the Siksikas were stacked together, and the horses were tethered short perhaps fifty yards away.

"We can get them all, Great Warrior," Pine Leaf said. "Or I could get them by myself, maybe?"

Bobtail Horse pointed to a clump of pines on a rise that projected near to where the Blackfeet were working on their kill. The two Dog Soldiers led their horses behind the ridge crest and angled across to where the pines were growing. They were now within rifle range.

"We can get two of them," Bobtail Horse said. "But the other two will grab the rifles and use the carcass for a cover. By the time we get them, half the Blackfoot Nation may be on top of us. And we might not be able to take the scalps at all."

"I have a better idea," Pine Leaf said. "I will ride down to them, very slowly, and make signs of friendship. You come across from over there while they are watching me."

"You think they don't know who you are? They'll probably make a chief out of the man who brings in your scalp."

"They won't know who I am if I ride down to them slowly and make the sign for lying down together."

Bobtail Horse frowned.

"You think that's a fair tactic?" he asked.

"Against Siksikas, all tactics are fair, maybe."

Pine Leaf rode slowly toward the four Blackfeet. She was half way to them before they even noticed her. Then she stopped her horse and gestured, smiled, gestured some more. The Blackfeet were suspicious, but the repeated gestures finally began to work. One brave began walking toward her, grinning broadly. When he was close enough, Pine Leaf drove her lance into his midsection, then urged her horse forward, firing her pistol as she did so.

A second Blackfoot was hit.

The others leaped for their rifles, but now Bobtail Horse was charging at them from the opposite side, and the two remaining warriors went down under a hail of pistol fire.

Four scalps, four rifles, two bows and quivers of arrows, three battle axes, and eight horses. Even buffalo meat and a buffalo robe, but they could not take time for these. The gunfire might have been heard.

"We must ride!" Pine Leaf said. "When we come to the Yellowstone, I will wash my face. I do not want to wash my face with water from a Siksika stream."

19

THE BLOODY ARM

It is a great mystery why the Indian peoples are so constantly at war with one another, but fortunately for their own survival, it is almost universal that only the males are slain—otherwise the breeding population would soon diminish in dramatic fashion. If a victorious attack is made upon a village, the women and children are taken captives and commonly become accepted members of their new tribe. Hence, the bloodlines are crossed many times over, with a concomitant admixture of languages as well. One woman was said to have been captured three different times and so moved from one people to another in a few seasons, finally escaping and returning to the tribe of her birth after an interval of twelve years. In some cases such women are well-treated, while in other cases this is not so. Crow women often attempt to escape their captors, being generally loyal to their own kind.

The Cheyennes numbered about fifteen hundred, all warriors, and mounted. The small party of Crows, returning homeward, was surrounded and forced to take refuge, horses and all, in a deep gully. But the Cheyennes were hesitant to charge in directly, allowing instead the more daring among them to advance to the edge of the bank and hurl down their lances into the midst of the Crows, who responded with deadly rifle fire. Soon several Cheyenne warriors lay dead on the rim of the gully, and the Cheyennes became more cautious in their approach.

The head chief, old A-ra-poo-ash, was with the Crow scouting party on this venture, though he had seldom taken the war-path for several years, preferring to leave such matters to the younger warriors. As the Cheyennes continued to approach the top of the bank,

Rotten Belly appeared to lose heart, declaring that there was no hope and that the party would be infallibly wiped out. His son, a boy of sixteen, one who was just becoming a man, had accompanied his father, the chief.

A-ra-poo-ash now turned to the boy and spoke:

"My son, we shall all be killed here. The Cheyennes are very brave. They have surrounded us with a cloud of warriors. I do not wish it to be said that these Cheyennes killed my son. I must kill you myself before I die. Approach me, my son."

To Bobtail Horse's astonishment, the boy did as he was bid— stepped forward, dropped his hands, and closed his eyes. The Chief's knife flashed, and the boy crumpled to his father's feet. A-ra-poo-ash then rushed to the crest of the gully, exposing himself to the Cheyennes.

"Ho, Cheyennes! Leg-in-the-Water! Here I am, A-ra-poo-ash, the great chief of the Sparrow Hawks. I have just slain my son so that you could not touch him. Here I am! Come and kill me! I am ready to go to the Spirit World. Come kill me first, and then you can easily kill my warriors. I have slain many Cheyennes. Your scalps darken my lodge. Come, come and kill the old chief of the Sparrow Hawks. I will still take some of you with me into the Spirit World!"

The Crows were shocked at the suddenness of what had happened, but they were even more astounded at what was to follow. A-ra-poo-ash stood there, brandishing his battle axe, an easy mark for the bullets and arrows of the Cheyennes. Unaccountably, the Cheyennes withdrew, a little way at first, and then further. After a brief interval, they mounted their horses and departed.

One Cheyenne warrior remained, mounted on a Nez Perce war horse, facing Rotten Belly.

It was Leg-in-the-Water.

He held up his lance, gave it a jerk, and then turned and rode off after the others.

A-ra-poo-ash descended the bank, sat down, withdrew his pipe, and smoked in silence. Finally he spoke:

"Isakawuate has intervened and spared our lives. He has accepted the sacrifice of my son. But my trail grows short now. I will not live among you very much longer, and the Mountain Crows will have to have a new chief. Let us go back to the village and put on the paint of mourning."

Fourteen of the Cheyennes lay dead at the top of the bank, and their scalps and weapons were taken. Eight of the Sparrow Hawks were also dead, including the chief's son, and another ten were wounded.

Black Panther rode alongside Bobtail Horse and said quietly, "Leg-in-the Water has now repaid the debt—when you struck coup upon him instead of killing him. He has paid the debt to A-ra-poo-ash. Next time will be different. He will wish to take his revenge."

"It wasn't because the Cheyennes feared the medicine of A-ra-poo-ash?"

Black Panther thought of the parting gesture of Leg-in-the-Water. Then he shook his head, breathed out, and said, "Perhaps that was it, I do not know."

When the remnant of the scouting party returned to the village, the time of sorrow was begun.

A-ra-poo-ash mourned the death of his son for four days, neither eating nor drinking during this period. He retired to the point of a rocky hill, cut off one finger, and lay exposed to the sun by day and the frost by night. At times his voice could be heard in the village below, chanting and wailing. After the fourth night, he walked down to the village, entered his lodge, and slept.

That evening he emerged and called the warriors to him.

"I have been given a final medicine vision," he said. "I will not live much longer, but for now my medicine is strong—and I must take revenge upon the Cheyenne Nation. You are my warriors. You must now consult your own medicine. In the morning I will see who wishes to go with me."

Over two hundred warriors assembled before the lodge of Rotten

Belly the next morning, including Big Bowl, Black Panther, Coyote Running, Pine Leaf, and Bobtail Horse.

Big Bowl said, "My son, you must not go on this war-path, for if we were all to die, our family would also die. You must not come this time."

"Father, I have to go. My medicine is strong and may be needed."

"A-ra-poo-ash has said that his medicine is also strong. No, Bobtail Horse, this time you must not come."

And so the head chief departed in search of the Cheyennes.

Bobtail Horse sat outside his lodge, disconsolate. Still-water and Little Wife approached him.

"We have news for our husband," they said.

Bobtail Horse looked up.

"Is it good news that you have brought me?"

Still-water said, "Yes. This news is good news. Little Wife must be the one to tell you of it."

"What is it, Little Wife?"

The girl became suddenly shy, reaching back for Still-water's hand. Bobtail Horse stood up, looked into the eyes of each of the women.

Then Little Wife spoke to her husband:

"I have your baby in my stomach," she said, not meeting his eyes.

"My baby?"

It took a few moments for the words to register. Then he embraced both of his wives, lifting each off the ground with one arm.

That afternoon Bobtail Horse also raised a force of two hundred warriors, and within a few hours they had left camp, proceeding in a direction opposite to that taken by A-ra-poo-ash, toward Laramie Forks.

After four days of riding, they came into sight of a Cheyenne village. As they were surveying the encampment, a mile distant, eleven Cheyenne warriors approached, laden with meat, and made camp within a few hundred yards of where the Sparrow Hawk force was hidden. The Sparrow Hawks threw themselves flat upon the ground and lay there for over an hour, waiting for dark. It would not be necessary now to make a full assault on the village.

Slowly, too slowly for Bobtail Horse, the darkness came. Still the waiting continued—another hour, then two.

"They are asleep now," Little Gray Bull said. "Shall we kill them?"

"Yes. We will take them in a surround. Let us move."

Silently the Sparrow Hawks encircled the Cheyenne hunters and moved in close. A dozen shots in quick succession, and then the Sparrow Hawks rushed in with their battle axes to complete the slaughter. None escaped, and the scalps of all were taken.

Bobtail Horse's party was soon on the retreat, riding through the night, bearing away all the meat they needed, the eleven scalps, the weapons of the slain warriors, and nineteen horses. They returned to their own village and washed off the mourning paint. The entire village rejoiced, and Bobtail Horse was given the new name of Ar-ra-e-dish, the Bloody Arm.

A sense of gloom descended upon the village of the Sparrow Hawks, as many began to fear that A-ra-poo-ash had been lost, along with his entire party, since they had yet to return. Bloody Arm spoke to Little Gray Bull, suggesting that they should ride out to search for the missing band. They were joined in their deliberations by Red Eyes and Big Rain, the village chief.

"If A-ra-poo-ash has died," Little Gray Bull said, "then one of us will have to be the new chief, for I am the leader of the Lumpwoods, Red Eyes is the leader of the Foxes, and Bloody Arm commands the Dog Soldiers. If we should go out together and be killed, the Mountain Crows would be without leaders. No more than one of us should go."

"Big Rain must stay here to care for the village," Red Eyes said, "for his is a job which cannot be neglected."

Big Rain nodded his agreement.

Bloody Arm said, "The new chief would be either Red Eyes or Little Gray Bull. Yellow Belly might also be chief, but he is with A-ra-poo-ash. I am the leader of the Dog Soldiers, and yet I have not lived with my people long enough to be wise in all those things that are required of the head chief. My medicine is war medicine, and it is in battle that I am valuable to the people."

"The Bloody Arm is the one who assists us in trade with the Long Knives," said Little Gray Bull. "You know those at the fort, and you know how to tell us what we should get for the furs we have taken. This is also a powerful medicine, and no one else among us could do it. We would lose our trade with the Long Knives."

Red Eyes said, "This is true. I am the one who should go to find Rotten Belly."

"My medicine tells me that I must go," said Bloody Arm. "I am the least likely to be chosen as head chief if A-ra-poo-ash has gone to the Spirit World. And among his party are my brothers, Black Panther and Coyote Running, as well as the warrior, Pine Leaf. Yellow Belly is also with them. These are my Dog Soldiers. I will go. Those are my words."

After some further discussion, the others agreed, and Bloody Arm readied himself and mounted Come Back, riding out alone. For three days he wandered through the mountains, the specter of the possible deaths of his brothers and Pine Leaf going heavily with him. His thoughts drifted back over his life with the Sparrow Hawks, and scene after scene involving his father and his brothers and this girl who was somehow brother and sister and beloved all at once replayed themselves before his eyes. On the fourth day he found sign of their passing. They were heading back toward the Sparrow Hawk encampment! They were all right, then—or at least, a large portion of the group had survived.

Bloody Arm turned Come Back toward home and rode without sleeping until he had reached the Sparrow Hawk village.

The scalp dance was in progress.

A-ra-poo-ash had returned. The party had brought fourteen scalps of the Cheyennes, as well as weapons and more than a hundred horses. Astoundingly enough, a Crow warrior had once again struck coup upon the great Leg-in-the-Water.

Pine Leaf had done it. But her wrist had been broken as a consequence of the fact that her horse stumbled in the midst of the battle, and she was hurled from her mount. The wrist had been tied but not set, and the entire arm was badly swollen.

Few had been wounded. Yellow Belly had taken an arrow in the shoulder, the arrow having driven completely through the flesh without having struck a bone. Other injuries were minor.

Bloody Arm spoke to Pine Leaf:

"This is what happens when you go out without me. You must come to my lodge, and I will set the bone properly. I have no use for a crippled Dog Soldier."

"I struck coup after my wrist had been broken," she said. "And I killed two Cheyennes, though I could not take their scalps."

"I think Leg-in-the-Water will have to give up fighting the Absarokas. Each time he fights, he gets hit with a stick or an axe."

Still-water and Little Wife pinned Pine Leaf's arm so that she could not move, and Bloody Arm was able to set the bone, despite the swollen condition of the flesh. He cut two sections of cedar and bound the wrist with deerhide strips.

Pine Leaf closed her eyes but made no outcry.

Afterward she whispered to Still-water, "Is he this brutal when he makes love to you?"

"He is like a puppy when he makes love," Still-water replied just loud enough so that her husband could hear her words.

But Bloody Arm had stepped outside the lodge and stood in the night air, stood watching the scalp dance. He was trembling and did not wish the women to see.

When he came back in, he said, "Pine Leaf, I have a new name now. I am called Bloody Arm."

"You have too many . . . names," Pine Leaf said. She began to laugh, softly, and then forced herself to stop smiling.

At the conclusion of the victory celebration, Bloody Arm selected eight warriors, including Coyote Running, to accompany him on a trading expedition to the encampment of the Snake Indians—inasmuch as he had received an invitation from their chief to trade among them. When the Sparrow Hawks arrived at the Snake village, however, they discovered that a number of Utes were also encamped there.

"These Utes are our enemies," Coyote Running said. "We must keep close watch on our men, for otherwise we may never leave here alive."

As soon as Bloody Arm and Coyote Running were able to gather their seven warriors about them, they learned that the Sparrow Hawks had actually traded away all their guns for a band of Nez Perce horses. Since all the other goods had now been disposed of, Bloody Arm decided to leave the Snake encampment immediately.

Before they were able to reach the mountain, they were ambushed by a band of Utes who were well-armed with rifles and pistols. The Utes charged them, firing at close range upon the Crow warriors who were armed only with bow and lance and battle axe, while at the same time avoiding direct contact with Bloody Arm and Coyote Running. The Crows attempted to defend themselves, but when the Utes withdrew, five Sparrow Hawks lay dead.

The four who remained alive tied the bodies of their countrymen to the backs of the horses and continued the long journey to the Sparrow Hawk village.

A terrible mourning followed. Lopped fingers. Torn hair. Cuts on forehead and breast.

Bloody Arm called for a council. He cried out against the Utes and the Snakes as well, for they had invited the trading party and then allowed the Utes to make their attack as the Crows returned home.

"Sparrow Hawks! I call for five hundred warriors to follow me. We must wipe out this stain on our honor. We must chastise these

Snakes, for they pretended to be our friends when they were not. They lured us into a trap and then encouraged the Utes to take our lives."

Much debate followed as to whether the Utes or the Snakes should be attacked.

Finally A-ra-poo-ash rose and waited for the assembly to quiet.

"The Bloody Arm was there and knows best what happened. We must trust his wisdom and his medicine. Let him have all that he asks. This is my judgment."

The warriors gathered immediately, for everyone wished to go.

"We will ride together," Coyote Running said. "Black Panther must remain in the camp. I have a right to assist in punishing these Snakes."

Pine Leaf rode up, her lance in hand.

"The bone is not yet mended," Bloody Arm said. "I cannot let you go this time."

"I have a right to go."

"You must wait until another time."

"I am a warrior. Even with one arm, my medicine is strong. No one has to look out for me, but I must look out for you. You have said that I am a part of your medicine, and I will go."

She spoke her words as a demand, not a request. Bloody Arm looked into those proud, angry eyes, and he knew that it was useless to attempt to dissuade her.

"I am honored to ride with Pine Leaf," he said.

On the eighth day Bloody Arm's Wolves reported a large group of Snakes who were scattered into small bands, hunting buffalo. Bloody Arm divided his forces, with smaller groups to attack as they might and the main body of warriors to take the central camp. The tactic worked well, and the Sparrow Hawks harvested over a hundred scalps in addition to many guns and other weapons, as well as a herd of seven hundred horses. Owing to the element of surprise, no Sparrow Hawk was killed, an astounding thing for so large an attack, while sixteen were wounded, among them Bloody Arm, who had taken an arrow through the flesh just below his elbow.

Pine Leaf rode down on the hapless Snake who had fired the arrow and, as he turned to flee, thrust her lance between his shoulderblades. Dismounting quickly, she severed his head with her battle axe and rode back to Bloody Arm, the head cradled in her lap. She presented the head to the chief of the Dog Soldiers.

"Here is your enemy, maybe. Now your new name fits you, for the Bloody Arm has a bloody arm."

He had cut off the point of the arrow and had withdrawn the shaft from his forearm. The double wounds bled profusely.

"You will never make a good squaw," he said, gritting his teeth.

While the Wolves were reconnoitering, they saw two Indians sneak out of the camp of the Snakes and proceed down the canyon. This matter was reported to Bloody Arm, who told them to return and kill the two—Utes, as he supposed.

When the Wolves found the two Indians, they were huddling over a small fire and had their hoods pulled over their heads. The Sparrow Hawks fired twice, killing one of the men. As the second man leaped up out of his robe, the warriors realized he was a Whiteman. They took him prisoner and brought him back to Bloody Arm.

"We have accidentally killed a Whiteman," the Wolf said.

"How did it occur?"

"Ask this Whiteman. He will tell you."

Bloody Arm walked over to the prisoner, whose looks revealed that he expected to be slain at any moment, and addressed him in English:

"This is no place to be trapping beaver, my friend."

Surprise flashed over the man's face.

"You are safe now," Bloody Arm continued. "We are Sparrow Hawks, and we do not kill Whitemen. Your friend was killed by accident. My warriors could not see your faces. But you are lucky to be alive. We came to teach the Snakes a lesson. I regret that your friend was slain, but we had no way of knowing who you were."

"Crows!" the Whiteman said. "You must be Jim Beckwourth,

judgin' from your lingo. My name's Zeke James. That was old Blue Callahan your boys just put under. We was with Bonneville's outfit."

The two men shook hands.

"You tell Captain Bonneville that Jim Beckwourth saved your life—tell him that Callahan was killed accidentally. The Crows are innocent of any intention to kill a Whiteman. We'll give you horses and whatever else you need. Then you're free to go. Shall we bury Callahan, or do you want to take him with you?"

"What I could stand is a pull of whiskey—I've got a powerful dry. Guess I'll leave old Callahan with you. It's more than enough problem just lookin' out for live men. Dead ones ain't no good to nobody."

Bloody Arm stared down at the man but said nothing.

The Snakes sent forty warriors and a medicine chief to the Crows to negotiate a peace. All the blame lay at the feet of the Utes, they said—Utes who were in their camp against the will of the Snakes. They could not control them. They had attempted to convince the Utes to leave the camp before the arrival of the Sparrow Hawk traders, but to no avail.

"Did these Utes outnumber your own men?" A-ra-poo-ash asked.

"No. They were visitors in our camp."

"Were there ten Snakes for every Ute?"

"At least that many."

"Are your warriors so weak that you cannot control these enemies of the Sparrow Hawks? Do you think we shall send any more traders to your villages and let your friends, the Utes, murder them? Do the Utes send you traders? Are they your friends?"

"A-ra-poo-ash, we were wrong in what we did, and you have taken a heavy revenge upon our people. But now we wish to be friends again, for the Crows and the Snakes have been friends for a long time. Will you smoke the pipe with us?"

A-ra-poo-ash scanned over the delegation of Snakes as if to indicate that he could have them all killed on the spot. Then he looked away from them and toward his counselors—Red Bird, Bloody Arm, Little Gray Bull, Red Eyes, and the others.

"Yes," he said. "We will smoke the pipe of peace."

The conditions of peace were adjusted, presents were exchanged, and the troupe of Snakes rode out of camp.

"Truly I have grown old," A-ra-poo-ash said to Bloody Arm. "And yet, perhaps the way of peace is better, for they have been our friends. What would you have done if you were the head chief?"

"A-ra-poo-ash has great wisdom. I hope that I would have done as you have done."

"And I hope that I have done the right thing," the chief said.

Big Rain had four wives, one of whom was the Cheyenne girl recently captured in the plum forest. The girl was named Ba-chua-hish-a, Red Cherry, and was generally acknowledged to be the most beautiful squaw in the entire village. Bloody Arm had made special note of Red Cherry on the day of her capture, but he had said nothing—certainly not within hearing of Pine Leaf. But now, each time he saw the girl, he was more and more taken with her. She was not only extremely sensual, but also highly intelligent and aware of herself, as proud as Lucifer. She dressed in clothing that was uniquely ornate, the designs and colors blended in a way that was both Sparrow Hawk and Cheyenne—as though, in so designing her clothes, she was attempting to maintain something of the aura of her former identity.

Nearly all the other Cheyenne women disliked her, though she was much admired by the women of the Sparrow Hawks. And it was well known that numerous young braves were plotting ways to win her away from the village chief.

Big Rain realized there was little that he could do to control the urges of the braves. Indeed, he enjoyed the thought of possessing the one woman most desired by the others, for his stature as village chief was amplified. All the same, he mentioned to Red Cherry that the Cheyenne custom of cutting off the ends of the noses of adulterous women was not altogether unknown among the Crows. He pointed out to her two or three unfortunate squaws whose husbands had disciplined them in such a fashion, thereby rendering them less attractive to prospective lovers.

Red Cherry replied haughtily that she desired to sleep with no one other than Big Rain, and thereafter she insisted on sleeping by herself, in her own corner of the lodge. Big Rain was not completely pleased with this arrangement, but he had three other wives to content himself with, as well as the continued envy of the other braves in the village. Red Cherry was his property, and that was the way he intended to keep matters.

One evening Bloody Arm went to the lodge of Little Gray Bull, who had originally captured the Red Cherry.

"There is a woman in the village that I desire," said Bloody Arm, "and I must have her no matter what the consequences may be."

Little Gray Bull looked thoughtful.

"I will assist the Bloody Arm if it is possible to do so. Is this woman one of my relatives? Your medicine has brought us many victories, and for that reason it is right for your desires to be fulfilled. I think I know the woman of whom you speak?"

Little Gray Bull's expression was unnaturally serious.

"It is the woman you captured from the Cheyennes."

"Which one?" he said. "I captured three of them."

"My friend knows which one."

"Ah! The Red Cherry. Many of the warriors would like to take her to the willows to wrestle. It is a shame the weather is not better, for then there would probably be a permanent camp in the willows. I tell you, I would have kept that one if it had been allowed. But I am the only man in the village who must not think about nibbling at the nipples of her breasts."

"You're thinking about it right now," Bloody Arm laughed.

"Well, I will assist you then—and you can tell me what it is like."

"I'll try alone first. If I do not succeed, I will accept your offer."

Bloody Arm presented Little Gray Bull with a quantity of tobacco from the trading post, and then said, "I'd like you to call in all your neighbors this night. Encourage them to smoke as long as they like. Be certain you invite Big Rain, for he is the village chief and would be offended otherwise. Then bar the door of your tipi. Tell your guests the stories of your adventures on the war-path. Tell them of the day you captured Red Cherry and how you presented her to Big Rain. In the meanwhile, I will attempt to console myself for not having been invited."

"This is good tobacco," Little Gray Bull said. "I hope it smokes well."

Bloody Arm then went to the lodge of Coyote Running and called his blood brother outside to talk, so that neither Grouse-feather nor Morning Song could hear.

"I want you to act as a sentry for me. Stand outside the lodge of Little Gray Bull. There will be many inside smoking tobacco, Big Rain among them. . . ."

"My brother, do you intend to pay a visit to the village chief's lodge while he is away?"

"Something of that sort."

Coyote Running was delighted. He clapped Bloody Arm on the back and whistled softly.

"Would it not be better if you stood sentry while I made the visit to Big Rain's lodge?"

"Coyote Running must not think such thoughts," Bloody Arm said.

"Very well, I will do this thing for my brother. If you succeed, perhaps we should trade possessions once more."

"You wouldn't want Red Cherry to lose her nose, would you?"

"No," he said. "That one should keep her nose. When do we go out on this war-path?"

Bloody Arm went to Big Rain's lodge. He was dressed and painted in the extreme of fashion. As he entered, he saw Red Cherry half asleep upon her couch in the corner of the lodge—saw also the other three wives and the children asleep. He walked over to the couch of Red Cherry and laid his hand gently upon her forehead.

She moved slightly at first, then sat up.

"Who is it?" she said in the half darkness.

"Bloody Arm. I have come to visit you."

"Why have you come?"

"I have come to tell you that I love you. I wish to lie down with you."

"Don't you know that I am the wife of the village chief?"

"He does not love you as I do. Big Rain does not go on the warpath. He stays in the village, while I will be able to paint your face and give you many presents that I get in battle or from the fort. Big Rain will never be able to paint your face because he never takes coups."

"Big Rain will kill you."

"Speak softly, Red Cherry. We do not wish to awaken the others. But if Big Rain should kill me, think how the warriors will speak of you—they will say that the Bloody Arm was killed because he loved a beautiful woman who was the wife of another."

"Your father is Big Bowl. He would lose all his property and all his horses, and he would be poor in his old age. I respect Big Bowl, so I cannot do what you say, even if I should wish to."

"If my father loses his property and horses, I can win him more in battle. And he would be proud if his son could have Red Cherry as a wife. You could go to war with me, carry my shield. I would paint your face, and we could dance."

"Please go, Bloody Arm. If Big Rain returns and finds you here, he will be very angry. You must go."

"No," said Bloody Arm. "I will not go until you give me your pledge to be mine when it is possible for me to take you away."

"You are a very foolish man," Red Cherry said. "You would lose everything for a woman. There are many women in the village who are prettier than I am. And what about your own wives? How many wives do you need?"

But even as Red Cherry spoke, she slipped a ring off her finger and pressed it into Bloody Arm's palm.

"Go away now," she said, "and forget about Red Cherry. I am

only a woman who was captured from the Cheyennes, my real people."

Bloody Arm slipped out of Big Rain's lodge, the ring in his hand. Coyote Running stood amidst the shadows nearby the lodge of Little Gray Bull. He saw his brother approaching and whispered, "What luck?"

"My medicine is good in love as well as in war," Bloody Arm said, showing the ring to his blood brother.

"It is from her?"

"It is from the finger of Red Cherry herself."

Coyote Running grinned. "You have her then. But you must be very careful, my brother. Bad things could happen from this."

HOW ELSE COULD I EAT?

On the Clark's Fork side of Granite Peak, the great, sprawling mountain huge and white, a low pass between one drainage and another, vertical walls of dark black rock, rising, defining a high meadow rich with new grass, a cloud of monarch butterflies, a golden and black twisting whirlwind of them, floating, glinting in sunlight between the rock walls, a vague, soft, hovering charge of lightning beneath blue sky. In their midst appear three elk, a bull with half-formed, velvet-covered antlers and a shaggy beard down his chest. The two cows trail behind, and all three stop to graze at the fresh grass. More butterflies swirl up from the ground around the elk. A few of the fragile, winged insects alight on antlers and backs and on the large, yellow-white rump spots. The butterflies settle. Their wings pulse with delicate motion.

A great force of Blackfeet was moving toward the Sparrow Hawk village. The scouts had returned in high excitement, and the Absarokas made their preparations. Inasmuch as the Siksikas were moving in a course that lay somewhat to the east, it was unlikely that they had as yet discovered the location of the village, though the Wolves of the Blackfeet were no doubt searching and would discover the Sparrow Hawks directly.

A-ra-poo-ash placed Bloody Arm in charge of the Crow defense, with Little Gray Bull and Red Eyes as his subordinates. The warriors were assembled quickly, a great war party numbering perhaps two thousand five hundred—leaving just enough braves to fend off an attack against the encampment, should one come from some other quarter while the main body of the Sparrow Hawks was engaged with the Blackfeet.

As the Siksikas approached the Yellowstone River, they found themselves faced with the entire force of the Crows. The Blackfeet halted and then spread out their own warriors, until the two armies stood staring at one another from across the river.

After an hour of stand-off, a party of Blackfeet was discovered to have slipped down river, forded the stream, and moved up so as to create a diversionary attack. This party was quickly encircled by a much larger group of Sparrow Hawks, and the Blackfeet took cover in a tangle of driftwood on an exposed sandbar, where an earthslide from previous years had brought down an immense jumble of trees. The logs formed a perfect breastwork, at the top of which the Blackfeet were well-protected, no matter what the number of their enemy.

When the word of this reached Bloody Arm, he gestured to Red Eyes and Little Gray Bull to take command, mounted Come Back, and rode to where the Blackfeet were trapped. Black Panther and Pine Leaf were with him.

Beneath the pile of logs were two Crow warriors. Pine Leaf pointed them out to Bloody Arm.

"What in hell are they doing over there?"

Black Panther fired one barrel of his new over-under rifle at the fortress of logs.

"Perhaps they have decided to die?" he said as he reloaded. "Perhaps they have remembered the run you and Coyote made when we battled the Siksikas in the rocks. I think one of them is Crazy Eyes. I cannot tell who the other is."

"It is Bears Copulating," Pine Leaf said. "I can see his red headband from here. When they are together, those two compete in madness."

Bloody Arm dismounted from Come Back and handed the reins to Pine Leaf.

"Tether the horses and come around from the downriver side. I will take a few men and join our friends under the logs. You get above and shoot down into them. There is no way out for these Blackfeet. They are going to journey into the Spirit World. If they try to escape, we will be below to cut them short. Black Panther, take care of Pine Leaf. Her wrist is not yet well, but she will not admit it. Unless you are with her, she will try to kill these Blackfeet all by herself and end up breaking her other arm."

"We will take care, my brother. You do the same. Smell the air! There is a storm coming. It is a good day to die, I think."

"It's a better day not to die," Bloody Arm said, "like all other days."

Bloody Arm and four of his braves circled to one side of the log jam and then ran across the short intervening space to the protection beneath the logs. The run was made safely, with only two shots being fired from above.

"Bloody Arm!" said Crazy Eyes. "What are you doing here?"

"I thought we might wish to save your lives. This was a foolish place to come."

"We are old warriors," Bears Copulating said. "Look. The Siksikas are right above us. They know we're down here, but they can do nothing."

At that moment the muzzle of a gun was pushed down through the logs. The shot was right next to them, but no one was wounded.

"We will all be old warriors when we get out of here—old warriors or dead warriors."

"This is a good place to stay out of the rain," Crazy Eyes said. "It will probably rain before long. This is a good place."

As Bloody Arm looked up, he could see one of the Blackfeet standing above a narrow opening between the logs. He thrust his lance up, could feel it rip through flesh. There was a shriek from the Blackfoot, and Bloody Arm withdrew the lance, the shaft slimy with redness. The muzzle of a rifle appeared once more, and this time the rifle ball found a mark. One of the young warriors was hit in the throat. He collapsed as his lifeblood pumped rapidly out.

"Quick," Bloody Arm said. "Around and over the top! Our brothers attack from the other side."

The carnage was joined, and the Blackfeet fell in a rain of arrows and rifle fire, fighting back fiercely as their numbers diminished. Bloody Arm emptied his weapons and then jumped down among the remaining Blackfeet and slashed with his knife. Other Sparrow Hawk warriors leaped after him, and within moments the Siksikas were dead, except one who had been wounded in the stomach and lay against a log, gasping for breath.

A wail of lamentation issued from above. It was Pine Leaf.

At her feet lay the dead form of Black Panther, his eyes closed and his mouth set in a grimace.

Pine Leaf leaped down and stood between Bloody Arm and the wounded Blackfoot.

"This one is mine, maybe," she said. "All of you stand back. This one will pay for the death of Black Panther."

With her knife she cut out the eyes of the fallen Siksika and then plunged the blade into the man's groin, turning the knife as she did so. The knife fell again and again, until the blood was welling up from fifty knife wounds. A final thrust to the heart. She then scalped him and hewed off his arms and head. Bloody Arm and the others watched in stunned fascination as Pine Leaf completed her butchery.

The girl stood up, her wrist dripping blood and her clothing spattered with gore.

"Our brother is dead," she said simply.

They lashed the bodies of Black Panther and three others to their horses and rode hurriedly back up river to where the main battle was engaged. The Blackfeet had made several attempts to cross the water, and each time they had been driven back. Numerous bodies drifted downstream on the slack current. Finally the Crows attempted the same tactic, and the results were equally ineffectual. The main forces continued to fire rifle ball and arrow at one another from opposite sides of the Yellowstone, with minimal results.

Then the gunfire ceased on the Blackfoot side of the river, and a single figure stepped forward. The Sparrow Hawks put down their weapons—waited to see what would happen.

"I am As-as-to, Chief of the Blackfeet!" he called to the Sparrow Hawks in their own language. "Where is Rotten Belly? Years ago we fought in battle. Now I will fight him once more. Whoever wins, my warriors will return to our own lands. Where is A-ra-poo-ash? Does he fear to meet me?"

Bloody Arm strode forward, and after a moment Pine Leaf followed.

"A-ra-poo-ash is not with us this day. I am Bloody Arm, the Bobtail Horse! I have darkened my lodge with Siksika scalps. You see I can speak to you in your own language. My name is Jim Beckwourth. I married your daughters and left them. I will fight you!"

Before As-as-to could answer, Pine Leaf stepped in front of Bloody Arm.

"I am only a woman," she said. "But I will kill you in single battle. I have taken the lives of more than fifty of your warriors. The blood on my clothing is the blood of your people! I have just taken this scalp! Do you see it, Heavy Shield? Perhaps it belonged to one of your sons. I do not think you dare to fight me, and I am a woman! The great chief of the Siksikas is a coward. Those are my words."

"My God, Pine Leaf," Blood Arm whispered. "As-as-to is a famous warrior."

"Pine Leaf is also a famous warrior," she said quietly. "Do you doubt that I can kill him?"

As-as-to turned and walked slowly back to his men. Bloody Arm and Pine Leaf watched as the Blackfoot chief spoke with his counselors, then turned and walked back toward the river.

"Crows!" he shouted. "I will not kill either the one who married my daughters or the young girl. This is an insult you have thrown at me. Now we will cross the Yellowstone and destroy the Crows!"

At this point Bears Copulating let out a war whoop and charged his horse into the river. Within moments all of the Sparrow Hawks who were mounted followed, and suddenly the Blackfeet began to flee, leaping for their horses and galloping away. Rifle fire sputtered back and forth for a minute or two, and then the Blackfeet were in full retreat. The Sparrow Hawks did not pursue them.

Two Blackfeet were left afoot, and Bears Copulating rode them down, struck coup on them, pulled his horse to a stop, and roared with laughter as the Siksikas continued their mad run in the direction their fellows had taken.

"I do not wish the scalps of men who fear to fight a woman!" he shouted after them.

Bloody Arm drew up alongside Bears Copulating, and the two of them gazed after the Blackfeet as they disappeared into the trees.

"Would you fight such a woman as Pine Leaf?" Bloody Arm asked.

Bears Copulating turned his horse about.

"I do not drink firewater," he said.

The Absarokas gathered their dead and rode back to the encampment. Despite the great victory, Bloody Arm's Dog Soldiers were subdued—for Black Panther, one of their best, had been slain. Big Bowl said nothing when given the news of his son-in-law's death. He turned quickly and went to the lodge of Black Panther to tell the women. Within moments screams and wailing could be heard.

The family of Big Bowl put on the paint of mourning. The following day, the body of the Black Panther was dressed in the most costly manner, with trinkets, embroidered cloth, and other articles of value, to show the inhabitants of the Spirit World that this man was a great brave and had been much respected. The weapons of Black Panther were placed beside him, and the body was covered with the best of scarlet blankets. Big Bowl led his son-in-law's war horse close to where Black Panther lay and then fired his pistol into the animal's forehead. The horse collapsed on the spot.

When the burial was completed, Big Bowl said, "We will not speak his name again. Journey well into the Spirit World, my son. I am an old man, and I will join you before too many seasons. Isakakate, hear me! This man was one of our best."

The Sparrow Hawks would move the village. The bones of Black Panther and the others would be returned for later and placed in one of the sacred caves. Now the departed warriors had become a part of the medicine.

Still-water was astonished by her husband's plan.

"You cannot think to take Ba-chua-hish-a with you? Our family will have to forfeit all its property to Big Rain. Big Bowl will lose all his horses!"

"I have spoken with my father. He has already given away the horses to those who are close friends. We have taken precautions, Still-water."

"It will be as my husband says, then. Can you get us more horses so that we may have something to ride? Well, she's a pretty woman, and she will give you pleasure. She will make a good robe-dresser."

Still-water then hurried to the lodge of Big Rain and spoke with Red Cherry. Big Rain paid little attention to the speech of the two women, and soon Still-water left the lodge, carrying with her Red Cherry's moccasins.

The appointed time arrived, and though Bloody Arm had been concerned that Red Cherry might lose her nerve at the last moment, the girl was waiting for him. Bloody Arm and his new woman joined the party, thirty-four in all, and they proceeded into Black-foot country in their search for horses to steal.

Pine Leaf drew up beside Bloody Arm, looked coldly at Red Cherry, and said, "The Great Warrior has made a mistake in bring-ing this fat little girl with him. She does not know how to steal horses, and she is probably afraid when she sees fresh bearshit in the woods. I do not think I wish to ride at your side any more."

At nightfall of the sixth day, they arrived at the Mussell Shell River, near the headwaters of the Judith, and were in sight of an enemy village. A half moon hung in the cold air, and patches of un-melted snow were scattered here and there on the meadows. The fires had died down, and the Blackfeet were sleeping.

A large herd of horses clustered in small groups for perhaps a mile down the length of the meadows and, so far as the Sparrow Hawks could tell, there were no guards.

"They suspect nothing," Little Gray Bull said. "They may as well have brought these horses to our village. We will be able to take whatever we wish."

"We must still be careful. We are few, and the Blackfoot village is large. This is not a good night to rouse these people."

The Crows dismounted and slipped down the dry hillside to the horses. Coyotes screamed in the distance, and a horned owl moaned in the night. The horses of the Blackfeet moved along easily enough over the frosty grass and up through a draw to where the Sparrow Hawks had left their own horses. A quick count was made: a hundred and seventeen animals.

The Crows mounted and moved off as silently as they had come through the moonlit darkness. They rode on through the night, and after a few miles they were all in a festive mood.

"Even the grandfathers could not steal horses more perfectly than we have," Little Gray Bull laughed. "You see how smoothly things go when some of the Lumpwoods are with you? We have special skills at stealing horses."

"The Blackfeet will awaken and go out to check their ponies. They will think their horses have wandered off and been eaten by white bears or cougars, but they will not find any bodies."

"Lumpwoods are the finest horse thieves in the world," Little Gray Bull insisted. "We shall have to give some of our horses to the Bloody Arm, for Big Rain will take all that he has."

"I'm afraid so," Bloody Arm said.

"I do not think I wish to return to the village," Red Cherry said. "Big Rain will be very angry. What will he do to me?"

"He will do nothing," Bloody Arm said, "because he knows that if he does, I will kill him, regardless of the consequences."

"I do not wish to have my nose cut off. You would not want me then, and neither would any other brave."

"I promise that your nose will not be touched, pretty one."

"A squaw should think of these things in advance," Little Gray

Bull laughed. "Big Rain may be the village chief, but he knows that Bloody Arm is the leader of the Dog Soldiers. And he knows that Bloody Arm is friends with the leaders of the Foxes and the Lumpwoods. He will know that we all stand against him in this matter."

A long silence ensued.

Little Gray Bull spoke again: "Besides, Big Rain will get many horses and many goods from the family of Big Bowl. That will ease his anger."

When the party returned, the village rejoiced at their success.

Big Rain, however, did not rejoice. Instead he ordered his relatives to surround Bloody Arm and Red Cherry. Bloody Arm was seized by Big Rain and half a dozen of his sisters and was ordered to lie down on the ground, which he did without resistance. Armed with willow switches, Big Rain and his sisters administered a merciless whipping to the back of the Bloody Arm.

"Do not make this man bleed," Big Rain cautioned his sisters. "If we do, he then has the right to take revenge upon us. If he resists, then we can take his life. That is the law."

When the whipping was finished, Big Bowl was required to turn over his property, but Big Rain was disappointed to discover that Big Bowl's herd of horses had greatly diminished within the previous few days—as had his other holdings.

Red Cherry was returned to the lodge of Big Rain.

Big Bowl helped his son back to his feet, while at the same time squinting and clucking his tongue.

"My son, this is a very high price to pay for a pretty set of tits. Two wives or even three I can understand, as old as I am. But ten, my son? What good are ten wives to a man?"

"Thank you, father. I will bring you many horses and many goods from the fort. I will have a great number of beaver skins to trade very soon."

Bloody Arm danced in the horse dance that evening, though he owned only one. Come Back, his war horse, could not be taken from him. During the celebration he managed to convey a message to Red

Cherry to meet again the following night, at the same place. They would go again to steal horses.

After the dance Little Wife berated her husband.

"You are a fool to steal a married woman! How many wives do you need? I think you have done this thing because my belly is swollen up with your child and I am no longer attractive to you. I say you are a fool, and I hope the child is a girl—only maybe then when she grows up you would want her for a wife too."

Little Wife suddenly broke into tears. Bloody Arm attempted to take her in his arms, but she drew away from him. He approached her a second time, and then she allowed herself to be held.

"Can we go into the mountains again this time of dry grass? You and I and Still-water, like last time?"

"Yes, Little Wife, I promise that. You and Still-water are my best wives. I love you the most."

He held her for a long while and then asked:

"When will our . . . daughter . . . be born?"

"It will be very soon, I think."

Red Cherry was faithful to her promise, and again she was waiting when Bloody Arm appeared. They started out with only seventeen warriors this time, for the Lumpwoods had decided to stay at home. Pine Leaf also refused to accompany the venture.

On the morning of the second day, Red Cherry said, "I like to have you fuck me. I am your woman now, but you must paint my face as you said you would and buy me pretty clothes from the fort."

"I have given my word," said Bloody Arm. "We will have many years to lie together. And I will paint your face."

They met a small party of Arapahos—nine warriors, of whom six escaped immediately, and the other three ran for their lives, leaving their horses and rifles behind. Bloody Arm and Yellow Belly pursued them for a short distance and then returned.

"This is sufficient," said Bloody Arm. "We will go back now. I have to take another whipping."

When they arrived at the encampment, the ritual was repeated.

With the flogging over, Bloody Arm returned to his lodge. As he entered, Still-water approached him with a bundle in her arms.

"Here is something that will make your back feel better," she said. "Little Wife has given you a son. She thought perhaps you would wish him to be named Black Panther. Here, you must look at your child."

Bloody Arm held the bundle in his arms. It was small, so small, and the little eyes were tightly closed. Immediately as he took the child in his arms, it began to cry, its mouth pulling back and tears forming at the corners of its eyes.

"Black Panther has very good lungs," he said, feeling awkward and foolish. He realized that he didn't know how to hold a baby. He was afraid he might drop the child or injure it in some way.

You done got you a kid, Nigger Jim, a little bull calf. An' what the hell yuh been doin'? Runnin' around like an iggerant dunghead, chasin' after a squaw in heat—only she ain't in heat, you are. . . .

It was true. Was he out of his mind? The birth of his own child, and he'd been off with Red Cherry. Had he even thought about Little Wife? Had she even crossed his mind? Little Wife, herself not much more than a child, but one who loved him, one who honored him, one who was faithful to him. Indian women bore their children easily and often by themselves, sometimes out on the trail, dismounting, giving birth, then getting back on their horses, riding to catch up with the main group.

Still, he should have stayed close. If a man cared for his squaw, he did not ride on ahead. He found some reason to circle back, to be close, even if unseen.

Guilt swept over him, and he looked up from the face of his son, cast a questioning glance at Still-water.

"Little Wife is inside the lodge," his first wife said. "I think she wants to see you now."

"Is she all right? I. . . ."

"I was with her, Bloody Arm. Nom-ne-dit-chee is small, but we had no trouble. She is very happy now. Go in, my husband."

Again Red Cherry met him at the appointed place, and the two of them rode toward the mountains. The year was turning toward spring, and the red willows were beginning to bud out. Birds were singing, and a gentle rain began to fall as they rode along, the two pack horses following.

"Red Cherry, do you realize that these four horses make up exactly half of my string? This madness has cost me many horses, to say nothing of two whippings and what it has cost Big Bowl."

"I warned you this would happen, Bloody Arm."

"Yes, you did. I'll give you that much."

"Is the Red Cherry worth what she has cost you?"

"No one has ever set the price on madness."

"I do not understand you."

"The Bloody Arm does not understand himself. Look at the jackass rabbits over there—they're running circles. And smell the rain in the air! Grandmother earth is coming back to life. Can't you *feel* things beginning to move in the soil? I think I should have a book of poetry with me so that I could read it to you."

"I do not understand."

"Among the Whites," Bloody Arm explained, "some men are called poets. These are not like any Long Knives you have ever seen. These poets are like our story-tellers, but the Whites know how to write down their words the way we put sign language on the stretched hides of antelope and deer. But the Whites have a sign for every word, and they put these words down on paper and bind the leaves of paper together into books so that others may read the words and know what the poet wrote. Do you understand what I'm talking about?"

"I have seen a book. Is this the medicine of the Long Knifes?"

"Yes, I guess it is. The stories in the books tell many things. They tell of where the Long Knives came from, and they cover many years. They tell about lands far across the ocean. They tell about the great villages of the Whites, villages larger than anything you can imagine, and they tell about the lodges of the Whites, lodges that

325

are many times larger than the fort, lodges that are painted many colors, lodges that are built out of stones and are taller than the pines."

Red Cherry was caught with the wonder of what Bloody Arm told her. She tried to imagine what it was that he was describing.

"I have heard of the ocean," she said. "It is like a big lake whose waters cannot be drunk."

Bloody Arm nodded.

"The ocean is larger than any lake, many times larger. And there are many lands across the ocean. And many villages."

"Have you seen this ocean?"

"No, I have never seen it. I have read about it in books."

Red Cherry looked puzzled, but then she nodded.

"Is it always true, what the books say?"

"No, it isn't all true."

"How does the Bloody Arm know it is true about the ocean?"

"Some of the books were written by Whites who have seen the ocean and gone across it in boats—very large boats made out of wood from the trees. These boats have sails made of heavy cloth, and the cloth catches the wind and makes the boats go through the water. In this way it is possible to cross even the ocean."

"You have lived among the Whites they say. Is that true?"

"Yes, I lived for many years among the Whites. They taught me to understand books. They taught me their language, and that is why I am able to trade with the people at the fort. I am able to talk with them in their own language. That is why they trust me."

"Will you take me to see the villages of the Whites one day? I would like to see these lodges that are made of stones and are taller than the pines."

The Bloody Arm looked at the low cover of clouds and felt the warm spring rain on his face. He smelled the moist air and felt the good strength of Come Back beneath him. But he also saw himself returning to St. Louis, Jim Beckwourth with his lovely Indian bride. For a moment he could even see the two of them riding through the streets of the big Eastern cities he had only read about.

He could hear the admiration in the voices of the men and the women. Admiration and envy. And he could see slaves. He could see men and women working on farmlands that were not their own. He could hear voices saying that it was not right. He could see the faces of his mother and father. He could feel their blood mingled inside him. He could hear the voice of Red Beard Miller, and the voice was saying *Nigger* in a way that sounded completely different from the way Jim Bridger said it. He could smell the fresh hay in his father's stables. He could hear the voices of his brother and sisters. He could hear the baying of coon dogs far ahead at night in the woods. He could hear the crickets when the rain stopped. He could see himself and Eliza in the glade beneath the big oaks, the sunlight warm upon their naked flesh, the world young and brimming with promises.

The rain was still soft, but it was becoming colder now. A few flakes of wet snow had begun to fall. The wind was beginning to rise.

They camped along a creek that came down from the mountain. The stream roared through a series of cascades between canyon walls thick with pine. The air was heavy and rich with the odor of new sap, and their campfire burned brightly. Snow was falling, but here, beneath the trees, only an occasional fleck of white struck the earth, melting almost immediately. Buffalo meat sizzled on the spits, and Bloody Arm made coffee in a tin pan. A deer approached the edge of the firelight and moved its head back and forth as it watched them. Then it was gone, drifting into the shadows like a thing of mist. And somewhere on the ridge high above them a cougar screamed.

"That cat sounds like Red Cherry when she is making love," Bloody Arm laughed.

"She is much louder than I am. Would you wish me to scream like the cougar? I will do that if you want."

"Not necessary. Here, I think our meat's about cooked. I'll get it for you. There you are, my lady."

Red Cherry chewed off a mouthful of meat, getting grease on her face as she did so. It shone in the firelight as she ate. Bloody Arm tried to imagine her in a restaurant in St. Louis, candles burning, glasses of red wine on the table, perhaps someone playing a violin. The two images would not come together. He smiled, chewed on his own chunk of buffalo meat, and swallowed.

"Why in hell would you want to see the lodges of the Whites?"

"Because you promised that you would take me there one day."

"I think you would hate it."

"Would Bloody Arm be ashamed of me?"

"No," he said, rising to get more wood. "No, it's not that at all. I just think that you would not like it among the lodges of the Whites. For one thing, they wouldn't let you eat with your hands."

She frowned at him.

"How else could I eat?" she asked.

Bloody Arm stared up at the darkness between the trees, at the soft downfall of snow. He watched the darting motions of the snow-flakes as they sifted into the firelight and vanished. And he felt intensely alive.

"Maybe it's me that would hate it," he said.

RED CHERRY'S PRICE

They put the pleasures of the young women behind them and went out on a war party. After a while they stopped to sleep, and Cirape said, "I am the scout." The next day he saw the enemy camp. They put medicines upon themselves. Then Isakawuate came to Cirape and said, "Younger brother, look out for me. I am very sad now." Cirape said, "We will take revenge—see how my shield leaps up into the air?" Isakawuate nodded: "Your medicine will be strong now, little brother." Then even the Crane and the Vulture sang and made medicine, and Isakawuate said they did right. The warriors attacked the village, took scalps, and drove off many horses, even one picketed horse. When they reached home, Old Man Coyote was very proud, though before this he had been miserable. So he put black paint on his face and was proud of victory. That is why the Crows have done the same, ever since then—they imitate Old Man Coyote.

He was whipped for a third time.

At this point Little Gray Bull, Red Eyes, Owl Bear, and Yellow Belly went to the lodge of Rotten Belly, for, as they had concluded among themselves, the matter had gotten totally out of hand. The head chief listened and then said, "Why does the Bloody Arm need this wife? Is it not true that he already has nine women?"

"We were also young once," Owl Bear said.

A-ra-poo-ash laughed.

"I was never that young," he said.

"Perhaps the Bloody Arm has become crazy," Yellow Belly said. "But will he ever wish to fight the Siksikas again if he does not have this girl?"

"She is Big Rain's wife," A-ra-poo-ash said.

"Red Cherry will never stay with Big Rain," Little Gray Bull said. "Big Rain would have to cut off that one's nose, and even then he would have to tie her short, like a horse."

"Half the young braves in the village wish to sleep with Red Cherry," Red Eyes said. "I would like to lie with her myself."

"I have noticed this Red Cherry," A-ra-poo-ash said. "Perhaps we will do the Bloody Arm no favor if we help him? Already he has been whipped three times, and Big Bowl has become a poor man. I do not understand this thing very well."

"We have grown too old to understand such things," Owl Bear insisted.

"Perhaps it is as you say. Well, let us speak with Big Rain. He has already gained much profit from the Red Cherry. Perhaps he may be willing to set a price for her."

The head chief and his four companions walked to the lodge of Big Rain.

"Where is Red Cherry?" A-ra-poo-ash asked.

Big Rain was embarrassed by the question so bluntly put, but he answered, "This time she is not with the Dog Soldier. She is at the river with my other wives."

"I have come to speak to you of this matter. You have whipped the Bloody Arm three times, and you must not whip him again. I think that your wife Red Cherry loves this man and does not love you any more. For this reason she will always go with him. One cannot turn the Yellowstone and make it flow back up into the mountains where it is born."

"I wish to whip Bloody Arm yet one more time. If Red Cherry goes with him again, then I will cut off her nose so that she will no longer be attractive to any of the men. They all wish her to go off with them, but I will punish them all if they do. I will punish the Dog Soldier, and I will punish Red Cherry."

"If you did that," said A-ra-poo-ash, "Red Cherry would not be attractive to you either. You would have a wife with an ugly face, and you would not wish to look at her. Her cut-off nose would always remind you that she had wanted to lie with other men, and she would be no good to you."

"What else can I do?" Big Rain asked.

"I have thought of something," the head chief said. "I will tell you what it is. Little Gray Bull, Red Eyes, Owl Bear, and Yellow Belly will buy Red Cherry from you for the price of one war horse, ten guns, ten chiefs' coats, scarlet cloth for your other wives, ten pairs of new leggings, and ten pairs of new moccasins. I think this is the right price. When they have paid you this amount, then Red Cherry belongs to them, and they may do with her as they wish."

Bloody Arm's four friends gave each other sidelong glances.

Big Rain turned about and strode over to the lodge fire. Then he turned and said, "It will be as A-ra-poo-ash wishes. When the goods are brought to me, then Red Cherry will have to go with these men. After that I do not care what happens to her."

The four warriors went to the lodge of Bloody Arm and told him of the solution that Rotten Belly had found. Bloody Arm listened with much gravity. Then he spoke.

"My friends, you have to pay a high price for Red Cherry. Once you have her, what will you do with her?"

A long silence followed.

"We will give her to you," Owl Bear said. "Is that not what you wish?"

"My friends are generous to me. Red Cherry is a very expensive gift."

The four looked at each other and then back at Bloody Arm, who was seated by the fire.

"We do not have enough guns or coats," Little Gray Bull said.

Bloody Arm rose and embraced his friends, laughing as he did so.

"I think I know where I can get these things," he said. "I have already made my father a poor man. I must not impoverish my friends as well."

It was now nearly spring, and Bloody Arm started for the fort, taking Red Cherry with him. He continued in his passion for the girl's beauty—few Whitewomen, as he supposed, could boast such features. Her eyes were always bright, her mouth was sensuously formed, her breasts were large but not too large, her waist thin, her thighs exquisite, her legs long, and the rich olive color of her skin. But beyond all this, there was a special aura about her, some air or presence that fairly screamed for a man to go to bed with her. He could explain this no more than he could explain the insanity of the courtship he had paid her. He knew that many of his friends and relatives had thought he was mad. Perhaps it was so, but the madness had been delightful, was still delightful. His infatuation might well have cost him the friendship of Pine Leaf, however, and this he regretted immensely. It had certainly cost him the goodwill of Big Rain, who now regarded him with an evil eye or refused to look at him at all.

Big Rain—he had not loved Red Cherry. No, that wasn't it. He had loved her as children love the delicious fruit for which she was named. Or perhaps he merely loved the idea that Red Cherry belonged to him and that no one else could have her. Perhaps it was not even important to him whether she would lie with him or not. The evident desire in the looks of the other men could well have been satisfaction enough.

Now, as Bloody Arm was aware, Big Rain was attempting to pay his own secret courtship to Red Cherry, trying to get her to come back of her own free will. Well, one had to pay a price for such a woman.

"I know that Big Rain has asked you to return to him," Bloody Arm said. "I would not attempt to stop you, if this is what you wish. But you must know that he would certainly cut off your nose if you went back, for in that way he would be certain you would never leave him again."

"Why would I wish to go back?" Red Cherry asked. "I do not wish to be fucked by that man. I did not like it. I like it with you. I am your wife now. I want to stay with you."

"Well, little raccoon, I promise not to cut off your nose, no matter what you do. I will buy you many gifts when we get to the fort."

Late in the afternoon Bloody Arm shot a buffalo and, with Red Cherry's help, he proceeded to skin and butcher the animal. He knew what would happen next. It had happened before.

Red Cherry reached into the belly of the buffalo and drew out the intestines. She cut off about six feet of the small intestine, ran it between her fingers to clean it out, and then gave it a shake, as though it were a whip. Next she put one end into her mouth and began swallowing. She didn't even seem to chew. Slowly the entire thing disappeared.

Bloody Arm grinned as he watched Red Cherry.

God, how he loved it.

The Bloody Arm, Red Cherry, and two hundred warriors arrived at the fort. Again, Pine Leaf had declined to travel with her former friend. A number of women and children, however, had accompanied their men, and the mood was festive. The horses were turned out unguarded, since no possible danger was anticipated.

"Johnson Gardner's got most of the trade goods at his camp about eighteen miles downriver," Kipp said. "Word just came in—a little transportation problem. Mebbe the best thing's to ride down there in the morning. Take the tribe with ye. As good a place to do the tradin' as any."

But in the morning when Yellow Belly and a group of braves went out to bring in the horses, the animals were gone. The alarm was sounded, and the women and children were placed inside the fort. The war horses had been kept close by during the night, so the warriors mounted and rode out in pursuit of those who had taken the pack animals. The trail was plain.

They moved on throughout the day and then, crossing a low ridge, saw a fire below. Bloody Arm signaled a halt, and the Sparrow Hawks studied the camp. There were only about half a dozen horses. But angry voices drifted up on the cold spring air.

"Throw them in, damn them! Throw the murderin' bastards in!"

Bloody Arm shouted, "Halloo the camp! Don't shoot, boys, we're Crows! This is Jim Beckwourth! Gardner, is that you?"

"Come on down, but come slow!"

Bloody Arm and Coyote Running urged their mounts forward and descended the hill, the other braves following single file.

"It was Antoine Garreaux and the Arikaras," Gardner said. "They came down on us, and they was drivin' a big bunch of horses."

"Our horses," Bloody Arm answered. "We're trying to get them back."

"Well, the damned thieves got all my trade goods, too. They moved out of here fat, stupid, and happy—but we got two of 'em prisoners. Then Garreaux stood off at a short distance and demanded the prisoners back. I tried to swap 'em for the trade goods, them and our horses. Didn't do no good, though. They opened fire on us, and we exchanged the favor. They sorta forgot about their friends, then, and took off. But look what I got here—one of these two sonsabitches had it—this here is Old Glass's Hawken, sure as hell. Initials right there on the stock. Hugh was carryin' it just last month, and you know damn well he didn't trade it off. I'm guessin' him and Ed Rose are both lying dead around here somewhere, probably with no hair—though these two didn't have no scalps with 'em."

Bloody Arm looked at the big fire, obviously built up for some purpose, then at the two Arikaras bound in trap chains.

"Going to burn them?" Bloody Arm said, not asking.

"Just what we're goin' to do. If they took Rose and Glass under, they got it comin', and I guess they got it comin' anyhow. Think the fire's about good enough right now. That's just what we was about to do when you yelled down at us."

The Sparrow Hawks understood what was going to happen. Their eyes reflected the yellow torrent of flame.

"We must scalp them first," Bears Copulating said. "These are not good Indians."

"Naw," said Gardner, who knew the Crow lingo, "these boys is goin' to cook whole. You can get plenty of scalps when you catch up with the rest of them thieves. Just about twenty of 'em, I'd say."

The Arikara warriors did not utter a sound as they were lifted and thrown up into the open slot in the logs. Then they screamed and struggled wildly, but only for a moment. A blue column of flame towered high above the piled logs and brush, and Bloody Arm could hear odd popping and hissing sounds above the rush of the fire.

The Sparrow Hawks rode on.

By morning they had overtaken the Arikaras. As Bloody Arm looked down on the swale below, he could see a pitched battle in progress. The Indians had encircled a trade wagon, one that had apparently fallen behind Gardner's main group. At the moment when the Sparrow Hawks began to spill down from the rise, a terrific explosion went off, and the wagon scattered upward in pieces, a ball of fire and smoke at the center. The entire stock of gunpowder had gone off.

Bloody Arm signaled the charge, and the Sparrow Hawks came down off the rise all at once. The Arikaras had no time to recover from the blast, and the Crows' rifle fire and battle axes cut them up badly. There were far more than the twenty Indians Gardner had guessed at—perhaps they had joined a larger group of their fellows—and most of them fled, some on foot and some on horseback. In all, more than a hundred Arikaras lay dead, strewn about the area. The herd of horses had scattered after the explosion, but the animals were finally rounded up. The Arikara dead were scalped.

The blackened and dismembered remains of the traders were collected, bundled, and tied to horseback. The Arikaras had set fire to the dry grass around the wagon, hoping to drive the traders out of their cover so they could be picked off by rifle fire, but the traders had evidently elected to stay within the protection of the wagon. A number of badly-burned and blown-apart Indians lay nearby.

"It was not a good way to die," Coyote Running said.

"Maybe the better of the choices," Bloody Arm responded. "I think the boys must have blown themselves up on purpose, figuring it was better than letting the Rees do a job on them. Guess they figured they could take a few of the devils out with them."

Coyote Running nodded and then shook his head.

The Crows moved the horses, their own and Gardner's still loaded down with bundles of trade goods, back toward the fort. Gardner had followed in the direction the Sparrow Hawks had taken, and the two groups met about noon, then proceeded together to the outpost at the confluence of the Yellowstone and the Missouri. The Absarokas rode in with their lances held high, the Arikara scalps affixed to many of them.

The bodies of Edward Rose and Hugh Glass had been found, Rose with two others on a shelf of ice that was beginning to break up and move on down the Yellowstone, and Glass's body not too far from the fort. Old Hugh had fought to the last. His corpse was riddled with rifle balls and arrows, as though the Arikaras wanted to make certain, this time, that Hugh was dead. He had been scalped, of course, and one of his eyes was gouged out.

Bloody Arm stared down at the broken body.

"Hugh Glass," he said to Kipp. "The legend ends here. I've been hearing about him ever since I came to the mountains. Even the Indians know all about him. He was with Ashley in '23—got wounded in the Arikara attack. Look at those Goddamned scars— the man's half scars. The time he got chewed up by the bear, and left for dead, and crawled all that Goddamned way down to Fort Kiowa, still bleeding, more dead than alive, eating bugs and rattlesnakes and grass and bark, with just the thought of taking revenge on Bridger and Fitzgerald for leaving him out there to die, just that keeping him going, all busted up and still crawling and crawling and refusing to go under until he could get to the ones who had left him there to die. . . ."

"No man could have survived that," Kipp said.

"Hugh Glass survived."

"And finally caught up with Bridger and Fitzgerald both," Kipp said.

"And let 'em off the hook. . . ."

"And then fightin' the Rees over and over. . . ."

"And getting chewed on by other bears. . . ."

"And here he is, dead, Hugh Glass. You know, Jim, he don't look so big, lying there that way."

"Not until you look close," Bloody Arm answered, turned, and walked off.

But the image of Glass's body would not leave him. The terrible scars.

"How do you bury a man that isn't just a man but an idea?" Bloody Arm wondered. "How in hell can you bury an idea? In some ways he was all of us, and better than all of us. Bridger. Black Harris. Sublette. Le Blueux. La Jeunesse. Cahuna Smith. . . ."

It was as if he had seen all of their bodies lying there, the bodies not only of the mountain men but of the Indians also. Long Hair. Rotten Belly. Heavy Shield. Two Axe. Pine Leaf. Black Panther. It was as if Isakawuate, in some final act of creative enthusiasm, had brought the mountain men and the wild nomads together in order to witness their mutual destruction.

The body of Jim Beckwourth, lying there.

The two halves of the Crow Nation met at the Little Horn River and encamped there for the purpose of planting the sacred tobacco, the op-pu-mite. When the tobacco ceremonies had been concluded, A-ra-poo-ash and Long Hair called the two councils into meeting.

Red Bird, the first counselor of the Mountain Crows, rose to speak to the warriors.

"Sparrow Hawks! Red Bird has served you faithfully for many winters. I am now old, and I can be young no more. My body is weak from the many wounds I have taken while fighting our enemies. Once I was strong, but the war-path is for younger men. I will join the shamans, but I will always be ready to defend our village. In doing this, I will fight as well as I am able, for I have never done less. But my medicine for the war-path has grown weak, and I must let other warriors lead the parties. It is right for me, then, to give up my position as first counselor. There are others who are as brave as the she-bear and as swift as the antelope, and these men deserve to be promoted. I give up my position now. These are my words."

Long Hair then spoke:

"Red Bird, our hearts are sorry that you will no longer be first counselor to A-ra-poo-ash. You have served our people long and faithfully, and your counsel has always been good. All of the Sparrow Hawks have prospered. Your direction has been wise. I know that A-ra-poo-ash would rather that you remained as first counselor, but we must respect your wishes."

A-ra-poo-ash spoke:

"We know that Red Bird is not so strong as he once was, for then his enemies fled from before his gaze. Red Bird has received many wounds from the weapons of the enemies of the Sparrow Hawks, but he never turned his back to those enemies. Red Bird has long been my first counselor, and always I have listened to his wisdom, for his wisdom is great. Now old age comes upon him, as it comes upon me also. Soon I, too, will have to step aside, and the Mountain Crows will have a new head chief. But now we need another counselor. Will you name him for us, Red Bird?"

"No. I have never had any enemies among the warriors, and I do not wish to have them now. I would not know which man to choose, for all are brave."

"Call in one of the medicine men," said Long Hair. "In this way a new counselor will be chosen."

Ears of the Wolf came, and a blindfold was placed over his eyes. He then went among the gathered braves and laid his hands upon the shoulders of Little Gray Bull.

"This man is already one of my counselors," A-ra-poo-ash said. "You must select someone else."

The medicine man continued among the braves, placing his hands upon the shoulders of another.

"Long Bow is my new counselor," A-ra-poo-ash said.

The five counselors were now automatically elevated one position, with Broken Shoulder becoming number five, Yellow Belly number four, Little Gray Bull number three, Red Eyes number two, and Bloody Arm becoming first counselor.

Later A-ra-poo-ash drew Bloody Arm aside.

"Now that you hold the position that Red Bird held for so many years, I must call upon your wisdom as I formerly called upon his. So now I will ask you a question."

"What is this question, Rotten Belly?"

"Should a man exchange two buffalo robes for one buffalo robe?"

"Not unless the one is much finer than the two. Why do you ask this?"

"I have always had trouble deciding these things," A-ra-poo-ash said. "But now that I have heard your answer, it will be easier for me."

"I don't understand," Bloody Arm said.

A-ra-poo-ash placed his hands on Bloody Arm's shoulders and smiled.

"Tell your friends they paid too much for the Red Cherry," he said.

Then the Crow Nation split, the two great chiefs moving their people to separate encampments. The Mountain Crows crossed the Big Horn and proceeded to Sun River, a small tributary of the Yellowstone.

Bloody Arm gathered together a group of his Dog Soldiers, forty in all, and set out in search of Blackfeet and horses. After two days of riding, the Dog Soldiers were overtaken by A-ra-poo-ash, who commanded a group of one hundred and seventy-five warriors, including Pine Leaf. Bloody Arm did not wish the old chief to go to war, for he half expected that Rotten Belly would rush in and throw his life away—or that he would stake himself out and so go to his death with a number of others loyally about him. Bloody Arm considered the problem and decided there was but one solution.

"A-ra-poo-ash," he said, "I am your counselor. I believe now that my war-path medicine has grown weak. I would like to return to the village until I have dreamed a good dream and my medicine is strong once more. Will you come with me?"

"If this is true, Bloody Arm, then I will return with you."

The warriors rode back toward the village, but after one day, Bloody Arm stole away from the camp with seventy-five warriors and headed for the country of the Siksikas, trusting that A-ra-poo-ash would return to the village. But after another day, the old chief had overtaken Bloody Arm's group.

Rotten Belly was angry with his first counselor.

"Young man, you have given me bad advice, and then you stole out of our camp at night and took some of my warriors with you."

"It is not a good time for A-ra-poo-ash to go to war."

"It is a good time for A-ra-poo-ash to die. You are a great warrior, Bloody Arm. I was like you when I was younger. Now I am old. I do not wish to die in camp, as Red Bird will do. I want to die among my warriors. I shall never return to my village. I wish to die with you and Red Eyes by my side. And I wish to die with Pine Leaf fighting by my side, for no woman has ever been a greater warrior than she is. I was a great warrior once, and I will not disappoint my best warriors as I die. Often my people have been fools. I have given them good counsel, yet they have not listened to my words. I have fought for them for many years and have shed much blood for them. I tried to make them a great people, but often they have closed their ears. Now I wish to enter into the Spirit World, and I wish to do so with dignity. Bloody Arm, if you do not choose to go on this warpath with me, then you must go on another path. I will find the enemy alone and make my death."

As A-ra-poo-ash finished speaking, he dismounted. He placed the edge of his heavy shield on some buffalo chips and proceeded to address the warriors. Bloody Arm sat on his horse, stunned by the chief's words, hardly hearing what Rotten Belly now said.

"Warriors! A-ra-poo-ash speaks. You see my shield. You see my honors upon it. If my shield rises, then I will die before I return to our village. If my shield does not rise, then I will return."

The chief addressed both the sun and the moon for several minutes, gesturing with his lance after his words had ceased. Suddenly his shield shot up into the air as high as his head. No one saw him touch the shield—he could not have touched it.

Then the warriors believed the words of A-ra-poo-ash.

At this moment two of the Wolves ran in to tell the party that a group of fourteen Piegans was nearby, on foot. Immediate preparation ensued, and for the time being the miracle of the shield was forgotten. The Sparrow Hawks leaped astride their horses and rushed down on the hapless Blackfeet. The enemy, realizing that no escape was possible, took what cover they could.

A-ra-poo-ash was the first to charge upon the enemy. His war horse plunged in among them, and the arm that had wielded the battle axe for so many years now struck again. One Piegan fell, his skull crushed. A-ra-poo-ash wheeled about and drove home the axe once more. The other Sparrow Hawks, seeing their chief in such danger, bolted in after him and attempted to form a ring about him, but the old warrior was utterly determined. He jumped from his horse and with knife and axe assaulted the entire group of Blackfeet who, with one man attacking them in such fury, might well have turned to flee—but there was nowhere to go. Yet another Piegan fell to the knife of A-ra-poo-ash, the stomach slashed open and the intestines spilling out.

The Sparrow Hawks attempted to kill the last of the enemy before the chief was injured, but an arrow entered the body of A-ra-poo-ash just below the hip and passed clear through, the tip jutting out near the shoulder. A-ra-poo-ash fell, and the remaining Blackfeet were quickly hacked to pieces.

Rotten Belly lay upon the ground, the blood welling up from the two holes made by the arrow. Red Eyes, Long Bow, Pine Leaf, Yellow Belly, Little Gray Bull, and Bloody Arm formed a circle about him.

"Warriors!" the chief said. "I came here to die, and my wish has been granted. I will die with honor, for I have struck coup and have taken three of our enemies. This is the way a warrior should die. Now I will lead you no more, for my home will soon be in the Spirit World, in the land of Isakakate. Sometimes our people are foolish and do not listen to their chief, but I have loved my people and have led them as well as I could. Bloody Arm, come to me. You must take the place of A-ra-poo-ash. You are brave and wise. You defeat the enemy without losing your own men. You were stolen from us when you were a child, but Isakawuate has brought you back to us.

Your medicine is powerful. Warriors! Listen to your dying chief! You, Bloody Arm, are the only one who can keep the Sparrow Hawks together. When the people disobeyed my orders, I did not like to punish them for it. I loved my people too well. But the people fear the Bloody Arm and will do what he says. If they hear your words, they will increase and remain a powerful people. But if they do not listen, they will not be a people for two more winters. Our enemies surround our lands, and they are powerful. You must force the Sparrow Hawks to obey. My eyes grow dim. Bloody Arm, are you listening to me? I cannot see you."

"I am listening, great chief."

"I must speak quickly now, for I can see the Spirit Path opening before me, and I must go. Take this shield and this medal. They are yours. The medal was brought from the White Father many winters ago by the Red-Haired-Chief. When you die, Bloody Arm, it belongs to him who follows you. Listen. Tell Nam-i-ne-dishee, the wife that I have always loved, that if our unborn child is a son, to tell him who his father was. Bloody Arm, listen to me."

"I hear you, A-ra-poo-ash."

"Let my body be buried upon this spot. Let no one walk over this war-spot for one season. Then come and gather my bones, and I will have something good for you. Bloody Arm? I can hear the voice of Isakakate. The voice sounds like a mighty wind moving through the forest. He calls for A-ra-poo-ash to come to the Spirit World. Bloody Arm?"

"I am here."

"I must tell you one last thing. . . ."

Bloody Arm sent Pine Leaf and Yellow Belly, younger brother of the old chief, to inform the village of the death of A-ra-poo-ash. The body was buried in the way the chief had told them, and then the Sparrow Hawks rode slowly toward home. Bloody Arm cringed at the thought of what would follow—the self-mutilations, the tearing of hair, the raw wounds, the screaming and wailing.

Upon entering the village, Bloody Arm saw that all the lodges had been torn down. The entire scene was one of confused desolation. Unbelievable screaming and crying sounded everywhere. Men and women lay about in the dirt, blood running from their wounds. Some of the lodges had not only been torn down but burned. Bloody Arm felt weak, sickened at the sight. How could he lead these people? How could he stand up to this?

The mourning lasted until nightfall of the next day.

Bloody Arm ordered Big Rain to have the village moved to the Rose Bud, and the defeated people began the grim business of packing things up. The work proceeded in nearly total silence.

When the Sparrow Hawks reached the Rose Bud, Bloody Arm ordered that a council lodge be built. The counselors, the prophets, and the medicine men assembled in the building when it was completed. The records of the people were recited, and the final words of Rotten Belly were testified to by those who had been present. A lengthy ceremony followed, one which Bloody Arm but dimly understood. Owl Bear spoke first of the many victories of A-ra-poo-ash, and then he spoke of the many victories of Bloody Arm. When Owl Bear had finished, Big Bowl told the story of how Bloody Arm had been stolen as a child and how Isakawuate had caused the Cheyennes to sell him to the Whites and then how he had caused the lost child to be returned to the Sparrow Hawks as a grown man. Big Bowl recounted how it was that his wife, Funny Deer, had been able to recognize her son after so many years.

The medicine men and prophets listened carefully and then spoke among themselves. They spoke with the other counselors. And then Red Eyes rose to speak:

"Warriors!" he said. "A-ra-poo-ash has chosen Bloody Arm as the new head chief, and so it will be."

"Sparrow Hawks! A-ra-poo-ash was a great warrior, and he died as he had lived. In his last moments he struck coup six times and killed three Piegans in hand-to-hand battle. He has met his father in the Spirit World. As A-ra-poo-ash lay dying, the chief spoke of the

343

bravery of his people, and he spoke of their disobedience as well. A-ra-poo-ash and the council have now given me the job of leading his people, which I will do. A-ra-poo-ash intercedes for us in the Spirit World. Our buffalo and beaver will always abound if the people listen to the words of their chiefs. Now I am your great chief, and I will help the Sparrow Hawks to be a great and powerful nation. I have lived for many years with the Long Knives, and I know their medicine. I can speak to the Whites, and they understand all of my words, just as I understand all of theirs. If they cheat my people, I shall find out. Now my medicine is strong. I have the shield and the medal of A-ra-poo-ash, and these things will go to the chief who follows me. My medicine tells me that we must not make war on our enemies unless they have attacked us or stolen our horses. If these things happen, then we must attack with many warriors, for in that way we will win our battles, subdue our enemies, and keep our lands for our own. My medicine tells me that we must keep our people together, with no more than two villages at one time. These two must not be split into more, for this way we will always be strong, and our enemies will not dare to attack us. Long Hair is chief of the River Crows. He is a very great and wise chief. The Long Knives fear him and respect him, and that was true for many years before I returned to live with my people. Long Hair has great wisdom, and I will learn much from him. I have led the Dog Soldiers, and with them I have won many battles. But now my medicine tells me that we must lay aside our battle axes and lances for a season unless we should be attacked, for A-ra-poo-ash has told us to return for his bones after one season. When we do this, we will bury his bones in a sacred cave. Until then we must turn our attention to hunting and trapping, for our streams are full of beaver and our prairies thunder with the hooves of the buffalo. Our women excel all others in the dressing of furs and robes. By expending our efforts in such a way, we shall become more prosperous than any other people, and we will be able to buy everything we need. To do this, we must remain united—we must keep our villages together. If we are strong, we will be able to kill ten of our enemy for every loss of our own. The

Blackfeet and the Cheyennes will learn not to come into our lands, for they will suffer if they do. This is what my medicine tells me. But if you disobey me and break up into small villages, then I will leave you and return to my White friends. I do not wish to see our people become weak. I could not bear that. I could not stand to see our women and children carried away prisoner. I could not bear to see the deaths of our brave warriors. Obey me and assist me and give me your council, and I will lead you. Sparrow Hawks! These are my words."

When he had finished speaking, Bloody Arm turned and walked away from the assembly. The night was dark, and the stars were white-hot points of light in the sky. He walked to the edge of the river, lay down on a sand bar, and stared up at the stars. For a moment he seemed to hear the voice of A-ra-poo-ash, and, startled, he sat up. But there was only the soft, gliding sound of the water and the chirping of crickets in the distance. A shooting star flared across the heavens and then, an instant later, a second one. He watched the sky carefully, but there were no others.

He didn't hear her approach.

She sat down beside him on the sand, and they did not speak for what seemed like a long while. Finally she put her hand on his arm.

"The new chief spoke very well. He will be a great chief, maybe."

"Thank you, Pine Leaf. I have missed you."

345

THE GIFT OF A-RA-POO-ASH

Dances-Four-Times discovered the medicine dolls. This is the famous chief of long ago who was invulnerable in battle. Dances-Four-Times was fasting on a high peak when a sparrow spoke to him and told him to look westward toward I-as-ux-pec Mountain. There he saw seven men and in front of them a woman dressed in an elk-hide robe. She was holding a doll before her face. Her companions beat drums painted with skunk figures, and Dances-Four-Times could hear songs, and he learned what they said. Then only one woman was there: she was the Moon, and she held out the doll in its buckskin wrapper. After several songs, the doll came out and took the shape of a screech owl and perched on Moon Woman's head. Then the owl entered into the belly of Dances-Four-Times, and the chief dreamed of the Sun Dance Lodge. The doll is the Moon, and the lodge in the vision is the Sun's lodge.

The village of Long Hair arrived at the Rose Bud, and the people, together, entered into a period of general mourning. Long Hair cut off a large roll of his hair, and the Crows knew that the great chief had never done such a thing before. More fingers were lopped off, and many braves, after the example of Long Hair, also cut off portions of their hair. Some of the warriors cut twin gashes the length of their arms and then, having separated the skin from the flesh at one end, would grasp the hide with the other hand and rip it back to the shoulder. Some cut designs upon breast or shoulder and lifted the skin in a similar manner, thus producing, when the wounds healed, highly visible scars.

Coyote Running cut such wounds into his flesh, but Bloody Arm declined to do so.

"You are the chief," Coyote Running said. "You wear the paint of mourning, but you do not cut yourself."

"My brother, I do not believe Isakakate would wish the people to do these things. My medicine forbids me to do it. I grieve in my heart, for Rotten Belly was a great chief, and he loved his people. I owe him a large debt, for I never imagined that he would name me the new chief. But I cannot repay that debt by scarring myself. For those who wish to do so, it is right, but it is not right for me."

Coyote Running nodded, but he did not understand.

Long Hair spoke to the people.

"Sparrow Hawks, hear my words. I have lost him who was as a brother to me, for A-ra-poo-ash has gone to the Spirit World. Now the people mourn for their loss, but we must continue to live. It is not yet time for us to join A-ra-poo-ash. The chief knew this, and so he has named the Bloody Arm to lead the people of the mountains, and the council has confirmed this also. Now Bloody Arm is the new head chief, and I embrace him as my brother, even as A-ra-poo-ash embraced me as his brother when I first became chief of the River People. Together we are a strong nation, and all of our enemies fear us. We are friends with the Long Knives, and in the years to come they will value us as their friends and stand by us as our allies against the times of change which lie ahead. I am older than the Bloody Arm and may know more of the ways of our people, for he was stolen from us and raised to manhood by the Long Knives. But he is the greatest of our warriors, and he knows the medicine of the Whites. We two will work together to lead the Sparrow Hawks. Our warpaths will be good, and we shall live and prosper. Soon there will be more Whitemen living among us, and it will be different in our land. Our stories tell us of times that were different than this one— before we had horses or rifles. Our stories tell us of the time before we came to live in this land. Always the Absarokas have learned, and always we have remained a strong and proud people. It will be so now and in the times ahead of us. Bloody Arm and I will lead you, but we will need your counsel. These are the words of Long Hair."

Later, when the council met, it was once more necessary to choose a new counselor for the chief of the Mountain Crows.

Long Hair said, "Bloody Arm, you are a new chief. You should have counselors who are your friends. Who will you pick for your new counselor?"

"All of the warriors are brave men," said Bloody Arm. "I will follow the example of Red Bird and not select the new counselor myself. I wish Long Hair to decide."

Long Hair nodded and gazed about the council lodge. His eyes fixed on Coyote Running, and he walked over to him.

"Is this man your blood brother? I have been told it is so."

"Yes, he is."

"Is it true that you often share your thoughts with Coyote Running?"

"It is true. He has taught me the language and the ways of our people."

"Then Coyote Running shall be your new counselor. This is my choice."

The others nodded their agreement to the wisdom of Long Hair's decision.

"Bloody Arm, there is one other to whom you must listen, for there is a warrior among these people who is not present inside this lodge, and yet this warrior is as great as any of the Sparrow Hawks and is known and feared by our enemies. A-ra-poo-ash spoke to me of this warrior when I was last with him. We must learn how to live with the changes ahead of us. I wish you to bring the warrior-woman into the council lodge, for she must learn how the council works. She may soon be one of your counselors, for she has earned such a position. Yellow Belly, you are the younger brother of A-ra-poo-ash. Go find the warrior woman, Pine Leaf, and bring her to the council lodge. Long Hair has ordered it."

For a moment the warriors were stunned, hardly realizing what Long Hair had said. Then they cheered, and cheered again a few minutes later when Pine Leaf, uncomprehending, was ushered into the lodge.

"Bloody Arm," Long Hair said, "name your counselors."

"My first counselor is Red Eyes, the leader of the Foxes. Second is Little Gray Bull, leader of the Lumpwoods. Third is Yellow Belly, whom I now designate the new leader of the Dog Soldiers. Fourth is Broken Shoulder, a Lumpwood. Fifth is Long Bow, a member of the Foxes. And sixth is Coyote Running, a Dog Soldier."

"Warriors!" Long Hair said. "Look at this woman, Pine Leaf. Is there a warrior among you who is braver than she is? A-ra-poo-ash told me of how this woman asked to go to war so that she might avenge the death of her twin brother. She has counted coup many times and has slain many enemies of the Sparrow Hawks. She tried to save the life of A-ra-poo-ash when he was slain. He had asked this warrior to accompany him on his final war-path, for that is what I have been told. Is this thing true, Pine Leaf?"

Pine Leaf was unable to speak, but she nodded that it was true.

"Yellow Belly told me it was so. Sparrow Hawks, this woman must not be excluded from any of the councils."

"Will she be allowed to share the war-path secret?" Bloody Arm asked.

Long Hair tried to look thoughtful, but finally he began to laugh.

"A warrior must tell everything during the ritual of the war-path secret. Will you do this thing, Pine Leaf?"

"Yes, great chief," she answered.

"And you will submit to the oath of secrecy and tell the other women nothing of what you may learn?"

"Yes."

"Then that is how it will be. Do you agree with me, Bloody Arm?"

"Pine Leaf will share the war-path secret."

For a moment the lodge was filled with an uneasy mumbling, then laughing, then applause. The warriors closest to Pine Leaf turned to her and embraced her. Then everyone was embracing everyone else.

Long Hair's village departed, and with the time of mourning over, Bloody Arm selected seventy warriors from among all of the groups and set out on a war-path to ascertain his medicine as head chief, for such, he was advised, was the custom. Owl Bear and Red Bird, as former counselors, explained the necessity of this—for they had both accompanied Rotten Belly on a similar war-path many years earlier.

The Sparrow Hawks crossed the Missouri River and moved into the country of the Assiniboines. They fell upon a hunting expedition of perhaps thirty of the enemy engaged in skinning out and butchering a number of buffalo they had slain. Three of the Assiniboines, who were near to their horses at the moment of the Sparrow Hawk attack, rode madly away, apparently to get help from their village, fifteen miles off to the north, just as the Sparrow Hawk Wolves had reported.

The surrounded Assiniboines took cover behind the bodies of the buffalo, and those who had their rifles fired at any Crow who was bold enough to approach. The Crows circled their enemies and taunted them, and for half an hour no one was injured on either side.

"We will have visitors soon," Pine Leaf said. "We must charge these Assiniboines, maybe?"

Bloody Arm did not wish to take any casualties if it could be avoided, but he was forced to agree.

"Warriors! Move back into the circle. When I charge in, you must follow. Let none escape."

The circle was formed again, and once more the taunting began. A few shots were fired and a few arrows were let loose, but not many. Then Bloody Arm clamped his heels to the sides of the new war horse that Long Hair had given him and charged into the Assiniboines. The horse, not used to his rider, stumbled as Bloody Arm pulled him sharply to one side, and the chief was thrown to the earth. An Assiniboine lunged out at the fallen rider, battle axe held high.

Bloody Arm saw the blow coming and flipped over to one side so as to avoid the descending arc of the axe. He leaped to his feet and, knife in hand, awaited the next lunge of the enemy. Pine Leaf ran the man down with her horse, leaped off, and thrust her lance into him.

Bloody Arm heard the bark of a rifle. He watched Pine Leaf twist slowly about and fall.

The Sparrow Hawks charged in upon the Assiniboines with fury in their hearts and quickly killed the last one and took the scalps.

Bloody Arm kneeled above the fallen Pine Leaf. The rifle ball had entered her left breast and had emerged through her back, tearing away a small portion of the shoulderblade in its exit. The slivers of bone projected through the torn flesh.

But she was still alive.

"Am I hurt badly? I cannot feel anything."

The death scene of A-ra-poo-ash played itself over in Bloody Arm's mind. At that time Pine Leaf had kneeled beside the stricken chief. Now she lay on the ground, torn and bleeding. A terrible pain swept through Bloody Arm, and his instinct told him to hold and kiss the dying girl. But his voice said, "Lie still. Do not move. The bullet has missed your heart."

"I counted coup," she said and then passed into unconsciousness.

The new chief cut the blood-soaked deerskin from her shattered body, and Yellow Belly lay down a buffalo robe beside her. The two men lifted her carefully onto the robe and then attempted to stanch the flow of blood.

They rigged a travois and moved southward toward the Missouri, uneasy in the knowledge that the Assiniboines would be after them soon.

"We cannot move fast enough this way," Yellow Belly said. "Pine Leaf will die anyway, and the Assiniboines will catch us before we come to the river. Shall we take cover in the low hills and attempt to hold them off?"

Bloody Arm walked beside the travois. Pine Leaf was still breathing. He looked up at Yellow Belly, who said, "We will do whatever the chief wishes. His medicine is strong. It will take many Assiniboines to defeat us."

Bloody Arm knew that there would indeed be many Assiniboines. The enemy knew the size of their party and would bring two or three hundred braves, hoping to take the Sparrow Hawks as they attempted to cross the river. The only hope lay in a rapid retreat and a quick crossing of the Missouri.

"We cannot allow ourselves to be trapped," Bloody Arm said. "I will drag the travois on foot. I will head east, up river. Yellow Belly, you follow me for a short way and then cover the marks of the travois poles. I will send the others to the river as quickly as they can get there. I think we still have an hour head start. When you have covered the marks, follow our war-party and meet them at the river. Leave two horses for me at the mouth of Dog Creek. Take my war horse and the shield and medal of Rotten Belly. If I do not return, you must be the chief, for you are the brother of A-ra-poo-ash."

Yellow Belly nodded, but his eyes were not happy.

"Warriors!" Bloody Arm cried out, "ride to the Big River and cross it. These are my orders."

He fastened the poles to his shoulders and began walking. The first thing was to get up away from the plain, get up to the low red sandstone of the ridge. So long as Pine Leaf lived, he could not leave her. This bond was suddenly far more important to him than anything else. If they died together, that's the way it would be.

He remembered his flight from the Big Bellies.

He thought of the story of Hugh Glass. And he remembered Glass's body, the flesh torn to a sieve by bullet and arrow, the eye gouged out. The terrible network of scars on Glass's body.

He remembered Pierre Le Blueux and the trick with the bells. He wished Pierre were with him now. Le Blueux had made an art out of escaping from impossible situations.

"Goddamn it, Pierre, where the hell are you? Sitting on a canyonside, smoking your pipe? Blackfeet howling all round you?"

He made it to the sandstone and rested.

Was she still breathing?

Yes.

Rifle. Pistol. Knife. Powder and shot. Not much water. A strong body. He would not let her die. She was still breathing.

He saw the dustcloud from the hooves of their horses. A large group, hot in pursuit. He watched them as they crossed the plain. He gauged the point where he had left the Sparrow Hawks. Would the Assiniboines pass by? There was nothing to do but watch and wait.

They passed.

The Assiniboines would not be in time to prevent the Sparrow Hawks from crossing the river.

"So much for the strength of my medicine," he said aloud. "All we did was lose our new chief and our best Goddamned warrior— but maybe we haven't lost them yet."

He moved on, working his way slowly over the uneven ground, treacherous footing in places, the stone rotten beneath his feet.

Can't slip. Keep moving. Keep moving.

Creosote brush. Sometimes a shriveled cactus. Sagebrush where there was enough loose dirt for it to grow.

Keep moving.

Darkness. He rested.

He poured a few drops of water over her lips, and the lips moved. The bleeding had all but ceased. Was she bleeding inside? Was the lung slowly filling with blood, drowning her?

"Live, Goddamn it!" he said.

The lips moved again.

"Bobtail Horse," she said in a whisper that he could hardly hear. Then a pause as she fought to say what came next. "I don't like your new name."

Even in the failing light, he could tell that she was trying to smile.

He shouldered the travois and moved onward into the night.

"Moon rises late," he thought. "Go slow. Be careful."

His thirst was terrible, but he refused to drink. Necessary to save the water. She would have to drink soon. Lost so much blood.

The half moon crept up, and he was able to see where he was going. But it was still treacherous, it was still slow.

353

A movement in front of him.

Two owls. They hovered, moth-like, above a creosote thicket, the wings beating, the birds all but motionless in the air. Silver-white.

"After a jackass rabbit," he thought. "Good hunting, friends."

He approached, and the owls slid down the air, silently knifing away through the moonlight.

Birds singing. Meadowlarks. Along the vastness of the east a gray light was beginning. And then he heard bullfrogs.

Water.

He moved toward the sound, the happy, growling sounds of the frogs. A small, shallow pond in the bottom of an arroyo, a little stream that slipped down through a willow-edged channel to the river. A beaver dam, a tiny lake in the middle of grotesque stone forms.

He found a way down and came to the water. He lay the travois on the bank and fell into the pond, struggled for breath, and let the liquid pour back into his throat.

"Easy," he thought. "Not all at once." And he forced himself to wait. He could feel his stomach knot up and then relax. He drank again.

He pulled himself out of the water and twisted the moisture from his hair. Laughed. Laughed insanely.

Pine Leaf's voice, weak, a small, weak voice.

"Bobtail . . . am I going to die?"

"You're not going to die. We're going to make it. Our medicine is strong, this just tests it. We're going to make it, Pine Leaf."

She still did not open her eyes.

"You never took me to the willows. . . ."

They followed the little stream for two days and then came to the Big River. Sometimes she said nothing for hours at a time, and a terrific fear would come over him. He kept checking to see if she continued to breathe. It was impossible, but she was still alive.

Once he had slipped and fallen. She had screamed out. He began crying and petted her hair, but she did not regain consciousness. She kept breathing though, she was still breathing!

Now they were at the river. He knew what he would do next. He had been thinking about it for hours. Driftwood. Two big chunks of driftwood. He would cut strips from his leggings and lash the driftwood together, make a raft. Something heavy enough to stand the current but light enough so that he could swim behind it, push it through the water. He would lash the travois on.

If the current were too strong, the boat would tip and she would drown, but he wouldn't let it tip. He would move with the current. If a man once learned how to move with the current, he was all right. The current was not the enemy. It just was. And it could be used.

"Pine Leaf, can you hear me? Pine Leaf?"

The eyes opened.

"Bloody Arm?"

"We'll make it, girl. I have to find some driftwood. Make a raft so we can cross the river. I'll be back. Can you drink some water now?"

"Yes, water."

He held the flask to her lips. The water spilled over her mouth, but she was able to swallow some.

"Where are the warriors?"

"I sent them ahead."

"Where are we?"

"We're at the Missouri."

"The Assiniboines. . . ."

She passed into unconsciousness once more.

It took several hours to wedge loose two logs that were of suitable length and size and then float them downstream to the mouth of the creek, but finally he had managed to assemble the craft. He was just finishing his task, had sat down to rest, when a deer came silently to the water to drink. The large ears, the finely-shaped muzzle. A doe. It seemed to look directly at him but then lowered its head to drink.

Slowly he reached for his rifle, wondering as he did so if he could risk the noise of a shot. No reason to think the Assiniboines had come this way. He decided to risk it. The only food he had was some dried buffalo meat. Something fresh, perhaps he could get Pine Leaf to eat. The blood. What could he put it in? She could drink the blood. No time to solve the problem. The doe was lifting its head.

He fired at the deer's hindquarters.

The sound reverberated heavily in the narrow mouth of the arroyo, and the deer crumpled, lashed forward into the water. It was still alive as he grabbed it about the neck and middle and struggled back across the stream with the wounded animal, threw the creature down among the rocks. The rear legs were paralyzed. The shot had been perfect; he'd severed the spine. But the deer thrashed about with its front legs, attempted to rise. The wild, hopeless look in the eyes. He tore off his shirt, formed a pocket in the sand, and lay the leather garment over it. Then he grabbed the deer about the neck and held the animal above the little reservoir he had created. He slit the deer's throat with his knife, and blood spurted down to form a small red lake.

The shot had awakened Pine Leaf. Twice, as he wrestled with the deer, he had heard her voice.

"I've killed a deer, Pine Leaf. It's all right." Then, to the dead deer he whispered the words of Two Axe: "I will use you well my sister. You died to save . . . the warrior woman. You opened yourself to us so that we might shoot you and kill you and eat of your flesh. May your spirit find its way into the other world."

He emptied the flask and filled it with blood, took it to Pine Leaf.

"You must drink this. The blood of the deer. You must drink."

Pine Leaf opened her eyes.

"Bobtail?"

"Drink this. You must drink all of it. Deer's blood."

She drank. Slowly. Drank.

"It is good. Bobtail, it hurts when I breathe. It is hard to breathe."

356

He waited for darkness before crossing the river. He did not wait for the moon to rise. With the rifle, pistol, powderhorn, possibles sack, and medicine bundles lashed beside Pine Leaf, he pushed out into the black water of the river. For a long while there was no sensation of current at all, then, suddenly, it was there, heavy and powerful. He went with it. They were moving rapidly as he clung to one side of the little craft, tread his legs against the water, worked further out into the current.

Sandbar: snag ahead. He could hear the water rushing past it. Then the water pulled him and his hands lost their grip. Pine Leaf had gone one way, and he had been drawn the other! He tried to fight the current, but it pulled him under. He went limp and waited for the water to toss him up again.

He breathed air but could see nothing. Could hear nothing, only heavy noise of the river. He was carried. Quiet again: was that her voice? He swam toward it, could find nothing in the darkness. Had the little craft caught on the snag?

"Bobtail?"

Close.

He swam toward the voice, and his hand touched wood.

"I'm here. Hang on. We're going to make it, Pine Leaf."

He swallowed a mouthful of water and had to breathe out with a grunt in order to expel it from his throat.

"We're going to make it, damn it, we're going to make it!"

They broke loose of the current, through it, into slack water once more. When he felt sand underfoot, he pushed for the south shore. The line of willows. He could see them. He guided the craft in under the overhang of branches and struggled out of the water, breathed deeply.

He slept, awoke with a start. Coyotes yelling. Moonlight over the water, the Big River, shining black and inexorable, moving eastward through the wilderness.

He could hear Pine Leaf's breathing. She was having trouble breathing.

"Pine Leaf! Pine Leaf!"

She did not answer, but the breathing became less labored, more rhythmic. His heart was pounding in his throat, and he had to steady himself and wait for the spasm to pass.

He pushed out into the river once more, moved to the edges of the current, went with it. The river stretched before him in the moonlight like a huge, silver-black snake.

He thrust the log boat up onto the sandbar. A cloud of gnats shimmered in the early light, and it occurred to him that they, too, were beautiful—not as humans saw things, but in some other way. Even mosquitoes were probably beautiful if a man looked at them in the right way. But there were no mosquitoes along the river this morning, and he knew the season was getting ready to turn.

Was she still breathing?

Yes.

He beached his craft and loosened the wet thongs. He eased the girl up onto the dry sand and the tall grasses.

Smoke? Thin, a thin smell, the thin smell of a campfire.

"I'll be right back," he whispered to her, but she did not respond.

Bloody Arm grabbed his rifle, cleaned the old load out, and reloaded quickly. He moved off through the brush, away from the creek, and circled around from behind. Four horses, three of them war horses. Two Indians by the fire.

Crows!

He came up very quietly behind them. The horses did not whinny, and he was only a few steps from the fire when Yellow Belly turned around and saw him.

"It's a good day to live," Bloody Arm said.

Bears Copulating and Yellow Belly embraced their chief.

"We could not return to the village without you," Yellow Belly said. "The shield and the medal were too heavy for me to carry. Did the Pine Leaf die?"

"She's still alive. We came down the river on a raft. Bring the horses. I tell you, she's going to live."

They carried Pine Leaf back to the village. Her condition had not improved, and Bloody Arm took her directly to one of the medicine men before speaking with anyone. The girl had been unconscious for the past several hours, and she seemed to be growing worse.

"Is your magic strong enough to help her? I will give you whatever you want."

"I do not know, Bloody Arm. I think she will depart for the Spirit World before this night is over."

Ears of the Wolf placed his fingers on Pine Leaf's forehead.

"Her face is hot," Bloody Arm said.

"Yes. She burns my fingers. Do you have her medicine bundle, or was it lost in the battle?"

"Here it is."

"Good. If you wish the Pine Leaf to live, you must let me have your medicine bundle also. You must stay here this night, for I will need you to help me. But go now to your own lodge, Bloody Arm. Have you spoken with your father since you returned?"

"No, I came directly to you. Has something happened to my father?"

"Your father is well, but you will be given bad news. Let me have your medicine bundle, and I will begin."

Bloody Arm rode quickly to the lodge. Both Coyote Running and Big Bowl were there.

"Your wives are gone, my son, all except Little Wife, Nom-ne-dit-chee. She and your son are inside. The others have been stolen by the Cheyennes."

"They had gone out to pick the little red berries," Coyote Running added. "Grouse-feather was with them, but she ran away and hid in the rushes. Morning Song, my other wife, was also stolen. The Red Cherry is gone, and so is Still-water. Also Cheyenne and

359

Cheyenne's Sister, Doesn't-run-fast and Good-ears. The Cheyennes took them and rode away."

"Still-water gone! When did this happen?"

"The day after your war-party went out."

"Do we know which group these Cheyennes were?"

"There is no way of knowing."

"So Red Cherry has gone back to her people," Bloody Arm said. "But Still-water will come back to us if it is possible."

"We will take revenge upon these Cheyennes?" Coyote Running asked.

"I will also ride with my son," Big Bowl said.

"Pine Leaf may be dying. A bullet passed clear through her body. My medicine had grown weak. I am very tired. I will speak with Little Wife now."

Bloody Arm strode into his father's lodge. Little Wife and Funny Deer were sitting by the lodge fire, on a buffalo robe. Black Panther lay in a reed basket between them. Little Wife jumped to her feet and threw herself into her husband's arms.

"I knew you would return," she said. "Bad things have happened to us. I nearly went with them, but Black Panther was crying. He is too young yet to know better."

"Your husband is back, but he is stunned at this loss. And our friend Pine Leaf is dying from a bullet wound. She is with the medicine man, Ears of the Wolf. You must bring the little one, and we will go to where she is. Ears of the Wolf will do what he can."

The long night passed. The medicine man chanted and then unrolled the two medicine bundles and exchanged contents. He tied them together and hung them from a lodge-pole near the fire. Then he went into a trance and seemed to sleep, now and then speaking words, if they were words, in a language that neither Bloody Arm nor Little Wife had ever heard before.

"He is speaking to the spirits of the animal people," Little Wife said.

Shortly before dawn, Ears of the Wolf started up, his eyes wild.

He shouted more words from the strange language, turned about in circles four times, and then fell prostrate on the floor of the lodge, his breath coming in tortured gasps. Finally he quieted and seemed to fall into an extremely deep sleep.

"He has gone into the Spirit World," Little Wife said. "He is trying to bring Pine Leaf's spirit back to us."

Bloody Arm kneeled by Pine Leaf and saw that she, too, was now sleeping quietly and soundly. He placed his hand on Pine Leaf's forehead and nodded to Little Wife.

"The fever has broken. She is cooler now."

When the sun rose, Ears of the Wolf awoke. He stared about the lodge as though he thought he were still dreaming. Then he stood up.

"I have gone very far away," he said. "I walked through dense woods where many wildflowers were blooming. I had to climb all the way. At last there were no more trees but only grass and flowers. Above me were great cliffs of many different colors, and the sky above them was blue. I stopped and said, 'Where am I?' And then a large wolf came out of the rocks and stood up on two legs before me and said, 'The one you are searching for is not here. She started to climb up the mountain but then she changed her mind and went down the other side. I think she has made her camp by that little blue lake down there. Go that way if you wish to find her.' Then the wolf walked back inside the rocks, and I could not see him any more. I walked down to the lake, but she was not there, either. The campfire was still burning, but she had gone on. Then a bluejay spoke to me from the branch of a spruce. It said, 'She has returned to the village of your people. Go there if you wish to find her, Ears of the Wolf.' And then I awakened. I do not remember any more."

"Her face is no longer hot," Bloody Arm said.

Ears of the Wolf placed his fingers over Pine Leaf's eyes and chanted a prayer to the sun and the moon and the earth and the sky, his eyes closed and his face twitching as he spoke. Then he turned to Bloody Arm and said, "She will live. It was not yet time for her to go into the Spirit World."

Pine Leaf's eyes opened. She blinked a few times before she spoke. "Bloody Arm, where are we? Little Wife, is that you? Are the other warriors safe? I will have to sleep some more. I am very tired."

It was late in the season of yellow grass, and the time had come to gather the remains of A-ra-poo-ash. A more than usual number of shooting stars had been observed in the night sky, and the shamans had begun to take notice and to talk among themselves. Bloody Arm had wanted to mount an attack against the Cheyennes, but his counselors spoke against the idea.

"It would do no good," Red Eyes said. "We might take many scalps, but we would not get the women back. You still have Little Wife and your son, the Black Panther. And you have three other wives who have gone to live among the River Crows. You could call these three back if you wish to have more women in your lodge. The Red Cherry is beautiful, but we must not go to war for her."

"I am not worried about Red Cherry or about Cheyenne and Cheyenne's Sister. They are with their own people once more. The same is true of Coyote's wife, Morning Song. But the other three are Sparrow Hawks. It will not be good for them among the Cheyennes. And Still-water is my first wife. She taught me to speak our language. I wish to have her back. Damn it, Red Eyes, I owe it to her to do whatever I can to get her back."

Coyote Running said, "Our brother Red Eyes is right. I, too, wish to have my second wife back, but we do not even know which group of Cheyennes has taken our women."

Bloody Arm stared at his counselors. They were united against him. It was no use, and he knew it. And the time had come to go where Rotten Belly was buried.

"When we have come back and have placed the bones of A-ra-poo-ash in the sacred cave, then I will go alone to find Still-water. No one else must come who does not wish to."

"Sometimes Crow women return by themselves," Broken Shoulder said. "If such a woman wished to be with her people, she would try to come back."

Long Bow nodded agreement. "My father's second wife was stolen by the Arapahos," he said, "and she came back a year later. It took her that long."

In the morning of the next day, they moved the village, crossing the Yellowstone and continuing to the Mussel Shell River. Bloody Arm designated Yellow Belly to lead the march, while he and Little Wife, the child on her back, rode behind, alongside the travois which carried Pine Leaf. The warrior woman was gaining strength and seemed each day to be in better spirits, but she was not yet able to ride a horse.

"The head chief should be leading his people," she said. "He should not be at the rear with the women and children."

"Bloody Arm and Little Wife ride with their friend, Pine Leaf," he said.

"Pine Leaf is right, my husband."

"Yellow Belly is the brother of A-ra-poo-ash. It is good for him to lead the people. When we have set up the village once more, then I will lead our people to the death place of A-ra-poo-ash."

"It is good to have friends," Pine Leaf said. "Soon I will be able to ride again. I have not yet finished my war-path, maybe. I must kill another forty of the enemy. I have not yet kept the promises I made to the spirit of my brother, Fish Beneath Ice. After that maybe I will come to live in the lodge of my friends."

"I would like that," Little Wife said. "Our lodge is empty now. Still-water was also my friend. I liked the others too, but I did not like Red Cherry as much as my husband did."

"I think now that I feel sorry for Red Cherry," Pine Leaf said. "I do not know why, but I feel sorry maybe."

When the village was assembled, Bloody Arm led a large number of his people, both men and women, to the place where Rotten Belly had died. They moved slowly, for he insisted that Pine Leaf should go, inasmuch as she had been one of those present at the death of the old chief. All who had ridden that war-path were present, as well as several hundred others—relatives and friends of the old chief. Nearly all had wished to make the ride, but the village could not be left unprotected.

At the site of the grave, they discovered a fresh Indian trail passing almost directly over the spot, the tracks no more than a few hours old.

"Warriors! The Bloody Arm speaks to you. This trail is a Blackfoot trail. Our enemies have ridden upon the grave of A-ra-poo-ash! Two hundred men come with me. The remainder stay here to protect the women and children. Those who stay are to form a circle about the grave. The women and children are to remain inside that circle until we return!"

Bloody Arm then spoke to the girl on the travois.

"Pine Leaf, you cannot come with us. But give me your medicine bundle, for your medicine is strong, and we shall need it."

She handed him the bundle, which he placed beside his own.

"Sparrow Hawks! Now we will ride!"

After a march of only six miles, they came upon a Blackfoot village of twenty-seven lodges. The Absarokas fell upon the village with a terrible ferocity, for the death of A-ra-poo-ash was in the minds of all. The attack was unexpected, sudden, and devastating. Many of the Bloods ran before the onslaught. Those who did not were quickly killed, and the Crows did not even bother to take scalps until the battle was finished.

"Do not harm the women and children!" Bloody Arm shouted above the melee. "Lumpwoods! Foxes! Dog Soldiers! Leave the women and children alone! Bloody Arm speaks!"

But many had been killed already.

A number of young women and children were taken prisoner, and the others scattered out into the forest. Since the Bloods had recently returned from trading at the fort, many goods, weapons, ammunition, and bolts of scarlet cloth were taken, as well as a large number of horses, more than four hundred of them. The Sparrow Hawks, their thirst for vengeance sated, rode back to the grave of Rotten

Belly. None was killed, and only half a dozen had suffered minor wounds.

Those who had remained at the gravesite rushed forward at the return of the war party, and great joy prevailed. The electricity of victory, however, soon subsided, and the people became quiet as the body of the chief was taken up and wrapped in fresh buffalo robes. A specially decorated travois had been constructed to transport the remains, and the body of A-ra-poo-ash was placed upon it.

It was now late afternoon, and the thin cloud cover of morning had darkened. A light rain, a warm, light rain began to fall.

The Sparrow Hawks had just begun their journey back to the village when Little Gray Bull signaled a stop.

"Look!" he shouted. "What is that?"

A buffalo calf was standing in their path, its head slightly lowered, staring at them. Red ribbons were tied in clusters to its ears, and small bells hung about its neck. In the waning light of afternoon and the mist-like rain, the animal seemed almost to glow. The Sparrow Hawks gazed at the little buffalo, and an uneasy murmur went up. The animal backed up a few paces and then lowered its head once more. It shook its head from side to side, and the bells tinkled softly.

Then the animal turned about and was gone. The Sparrow Hawks continued to gaze at the spot where the buffalo calf had stood, and some believed they could still see it.

"It was a medicine calf," Ears of the Wolf said. "A-ra-poo-ash has given us a sign. Medicine Calf is now to be the name of our new chief, and he is to have no other."

THE VOICE OF
THE TRAPPER

The great meteor shower of late 1833 probably marks the true beginning of the for-
mally recorded history of the Indian peoples on the plains and in the mountains. It
was the year when the stars fell, and the rain of fire was visible over all of North
America. Night after night the strange, blue-green light of meteors streaked the skies
in a way that had never happened before and has never happened since. The Indian
peoples believed the heavens were falling and were terribly fearful they had offended
Isakakate the Creator, by whatever name they knew Him. But some felt the God
was warning the Long Knives to leave the Rocky Mountains. Then, abruptly, the
star-fall stopped. The skies returned to normal.

Nan-kup-bah-bah.
  Medicine Calf.
  Nan-kup-bah-bah.
  The little buffalo in the forest. Ribbons and bells. Glowing in the
misty rain of a late afternoon. The gift of A-ra-poo-ash. There were
several possible explanations for the animal's presence. Then it had
disappeared, and no one thought to follow or capture it. But perhaps
it had simply vanished, had returned into the Spirit World from
whence it had come. Or perhaps it had been an illusion.
  The bones of A-ra-poo-ash were taken to the sacred burial cave
and placed among the bones of many before him. The party had
been led by Yellow Belly, Bear's Tooth, and Ears of the Wolf, and
now they had returned to the village.

The Medicine Calf took Coyote Running, Little Wife, the Black Panther, and Grouse-feather with him to Fort Cass to speak with Samuel Tulleck, who was now in charge of the American Fur Company outpost. The Medicine Calf received his salary from the company and spent most of it on presents for his relatives, the many things that Little Wife wanted, hand mirrors, scarlet cloth and vermilion, and new rifles for Big Bowl, Pine Leaf, Coyote Running, and his other counselors. He talked with Tulleck about the fur trade, the prospects for the coming year, the competition from Rocky Mountain Fur Company, and the like.

The Medicine Calf listened to Tulleck, but he was thinking about the words of Pierre Le Blueux. It was all changing. Long Hair had spoken of the same thing, even without knowing what the change would be. A man could only guess, suppose, and imagine.

But the Medicine Calf knew that what was coming, however it came or however soon, meant an end. A great tide was washing up into the mountains and over them. It would spill into Utah and Oregon country and into California. He thought of the story of the beaver who had renewed the world. He thought of the story of Old Man Coyote and the four ducks, ducks that Coyote had no doubt eaten when it was all over. And Still-water, who had told the story and who was now a prisoner of the Cheyennes, perhaps already married to one of the warriors. He thought of Red Cherry and the others. And he thought of Pine Leaf, the warrior woman who was slowly regaining her strength and who fully intended to ride the war-path again. He thought of the little buffalo with the ribbons and bells. And Pierre Le Blueux: hard to suppose, but maybe the old graybeard had settled down. Maybe he was picking apples in his own orchard. . . .

A man could go crazy if he thought too much.

But the changes seemed real and present as he talked with Samuel Tulleck. It had been a year since the first steamboat had actually made it up the Yellowstone River to the fort. There would soon be more steamboats on the rivers. General Ashley was now a member of Congress. Bill Sublette had managed to smuggle a great quantity of liquor upcountry and was selling it to the Blackfeet and others. Pierre Chouteau, head of the United States Western Department, had been up the river the preceding year. An artist named Catlin was painting pictures of the Indians.

No one knew for sure where Jim Bridger was. Apparently Gabe had dropped out of sight for a while.

"A few more years," Medicine Calf thought, "and it'll all be gone, and none of us will know what happened to it. Only we'll know that things don't *shine* the way they used to. Maybe there'll be stories about it all, but the men who made the stories will be gone under. The beaver will be gone. It's hard to imagine: you see how things *are,* and that makes it so damned difficult to see how things are *going to be.*"

Samuel Tulleck nodded and lit his cigar. The little twist of smoke curled straight upward and dissipated into the heavy air inside the rough-hewn office.

Old Bullthrower was mounted on the wall: Glass's rifle. Almost like a trophy, or an antique.

"Yep," Tulleck was saying, "I figure the United States is about ready to make its big push to the Pacific. Just a matter of time now. . . ."

While Medicine Calf had been gone from the encampment, Little Gray Bull had slipped out with a number of the Lumpwoods. They had shared their plans with no one and had not been heard of since.

This information did not please the Medicine Calf.

Then a message came from Tom Fitzpatrick, who wished to have Jim Beckwourth visit him. Medicine Calf concluded that he should not leave the village at this time, and so Big Bowl and Coyote Running were sent to escort Fitzpatrick's company to the Sparrow Hawk encampment. When the party came in, there were thirty-five men and over two hundred horses. Fitzpatrick camped a short distance from the Crow village, and Medicine Calf went to visit his old friend and received a cordial welcome. Tom Fitzpatrick's hair had turned completely white, the result of a desperate escape from the Blackfeet.

"They call me White Head now," Fitz laughed.

With him was Sir William Drummond Stuart, a Scot who had visited Rendezvous that year. Also with Fitzpatrick were Dr. Benjamin Harrison, traveling in the West for his health, and Red Beard Miller, once again associated with Rocky Mountain Fur. There were others as well, all with various reasons for being along. Medicine Calf felt a sensation of disgust. This was no company of trappers.

Fitzpatrick wanted to open up trade with the Sparrow Hawks.

"Fitz," Medicine Calf said, "this is a strange bunch of men you've got with you. No offense intended. It's just that I wasn't expecting this sort of thing."

"Wasn't figuring to find you play-acting at being an Indian chief, either, Jim. The stick floats different, and we gotta act different."

Medicine Calf said quietly, "These are my people. I am no longer a Whiteman."

"Never was," said Miller. "You ain't no Injun, neither."

Medicine Calf stared across at Miller until Red Beard's eyes shifted to Stuart.

"Don't get riled," Miller said.

Medicine Calf stood up. He heard the click of a pistol. His eyes turned slowly to Stuart, who was holding a gun on him.

"Mr. Stuart, put the gun away unless you intend to use it. If you shoot me, my Sparrow Hawks will scalp and burn the last one of you. Fitz, you may trade for a week if you wish, but keep your dogs on their leashes. Goodnight, gentlemen."

The Medicine Calf turned and strode out.

As he walked to where Come Back was tied, he noticed that his warriors were inspecting the horses of the Long Knives. The men looked across at him with questioning eyes.

"We ride back to the village!" he shouted, leaped on Come Back, and moved away, his warriors trailing behind him.

He had just returned to his lodge when High Bull, the son of Little Gray Bull, came to him.

"It is a good night, High Bull. Do you wish to speak to me?"

"Yes." the young man said. "Did the chief notice the horses of the Long Knives?"

"I did not look at them closely. Are some of them horses that have been stolen from us?"

"One of them is."

"Perhaps the Long Knives traded for the horses."

"They have the war horse of Little Gray Bull, my father."

"Are you certain?"

"I am certain, Medicine Calf."

"I will find out about this thing. Go to Red Eyes and Yellow Belly. Tell them to gather their warriors. We will ride to Fitzpatrick's lodge."

"Yellow Belly has already gone to the Long Knife's lodge. The Dog Soldiers are with him."

"Why was I not told of this?"

"I came to tell the Medicine Calf."

Medicine Calf leaped onto Come Back and rode for the encampment of the Whites. He could hear the rifle fire and the yells of the Dog Soldiers. Had his medicine grown weak? Or perhaps his medicine was simply war medicine and not the medicine a chief must have. Little Gray Bull leaving in his absence. Yellow Belly attacking the Whites. His wives stolen. Pine Leaf injured.

"Goddamn them all!" he whistled through clenched teeth.

He urged Come Back to a full run until he drew up among the Crow warriors.

"Dog Soldiers of the Absaroka! Put down your weapons. This is the Medicine Calf who speaks to you! Put down your weapons immediately!"

He turned toward Yellow Belly, who tossed down his rifle in disgust.

"Sparrow Hawks! High Bull has just told me that the Whites have the horse of Little Gray Bull. Let us find out where they got this horse. If we kill these men, we shall never know what has happened. Why did you not tell me what you wished to do? Have I grown suddenly old and cannot accompany my warriors? I will talk with the Whites. If any one of you fires a shot or shoots an arrow until I order it, I will kill that man with my own hands. These are my words!"

The Dog Soldiers obeyed, though somewhat reluctantly. Their anger ran at fever pitch, and they wanted revenge.

"Fitzpatrick! Do you hear me? This is Jim Beckwourth. Hold your fire! I'm riding over to you!"

The night battle stilled to silence. The crickets began to sing once more. As Medicine Calf rode slowly across to where the Whites had taken cover, a long flash of pale green light flared through the heavens. Its trail seemed to glow long after the fire was gone. A single coyote screamed.

Medicine Calf knew that the guns of the Whites were trained upon him. He rode very slowly, then stopped. He dismounted and took a few steps forward.

"Tom Fitzpatrick! Come out here and talk to me. My warriors have not attacked without reason, though they did so without my permission."

Fitzpatrick emerged from the shadows beyond the fires. He walked out slowly, carefully. He held a pistol in his hand.

"Put down the gun or I will signal my warriors to attack."

"Where's your gun, Beckwourth?"

"It's under my belt. Put your weapons away and we will speak."

They stood facing each other in the flickering firelight, two men who had once worked together, lived together in the mountain camps, taken beaver together, fought together.

"Tom, the stick's not floatin' good tonight. One of your horses belongs to Little Gray Bull, the chief of my Lumpwoods. Where did you get this horse?"

"Shit, Jim, is that what this is all about? You had all of us holdin' on to our hair. If you want that damned horse, take it. I thought I could deal with you like a Whiteman."

"How did you get this horse? And how do you know which one I'm talking about?"

"The big red one, right? Jim, I was goin' to tell you—but then old Stuart got wound up and pulled the gun. We traded with some Cheyennes about a week back. Leg-in-the-Water told us they'd just put under an entire party of Crows. I bought that horse so's I could make a present of him. I sure as hell never expected to get damned near kilt for it."

"Where did these Cheyennes fight with the Sparrow Hawks?"

"Way up on the Big Horn, from what they said."

"You do not know?"

"Only what the boys said. I wasn't goin' to call 'em liars. We wanted to trade with 'em."

"You were not there at the time of the massacre?"

"Hell no. You think if I was, I'd come ridin' in here this way?"

"What's Miller doing with you?"

"Just signed on is all."

"Tell one of your men to bring me the red horse."

"That horse belongs to Miller," Fitzpatrick said. "You goin' to just steal him, or you fixin' to pay for him?"

"You said he was a present, and that means a present for the chief. It's my horse, then, and I will give him to the son of the man who owned him. If you don't bring me the horse, my warriors will kill all of you. Then we'll have a whole bunch of horses and some scalps besides. What's it going to be, Tom?"

Fitzpatrick's hand dropped to his pistol.

"For God's sake, Fitz, I'm trying to get your ass out of this. I don't want your blood on my hands. Bring me the red horse and let me use it to pacify my warriors. I'll wait here."

"You're holdin' the cards right now, I guess. I'll get the damned horse."

He turned and walked slowly back among the trees. After a few moments Medicine Calf heard an angry voice, and he knew whose it was. He stared up at the heavens—saw another meteor streak the night, then a third. It seemed like there were more each night.

Fitzpatrick returned with the big red horse and handed the reins to Medicine Calf.

"I'll withdraw my warriors now. I will need to talk with them. Hold your cover until after we have gone. In the morning I want you to break camp and keep riding. Don't camp again for at least three days. After that you'll be out of our lands, and you'll be safe. The warriors are not going to believe this story. They'll believe it only because I tell them it's the truth. If I should ever find out that you've lied to me, Tom, even though I trapped for you once, I'll find you and kill you myself. The Crows do not kill the Whites. But if the Whites have killed Crows, then the Crows will take their revenge. Do you understand me?"

"I hear what you're sayin', coon. But you ain't no Crow. I remember the days when you din't mind seein' a few Injuns go under."

"You're wrong, Tom. These are my people now. I fight only for them."

Medicine Calf turned then, led the big red horse to Come Back, mounted his own horse, and rode slowly back to where the Dog Soldiers waited.

"Iggerant jackass rabbit," the voice said. "Yuh got brains like buffler shit. Them boys was with the Cheyennes, and yuh know damn well they was."

"I know," the Medicine Calf thought.

"Dog Soldiers! I have led you in many battles. Hear what I say now! These Whitemen did not kill our brothers the Lumpwoods. The Cheyennes, always our enemies, killed Little Gray Bull and the others. The Bad Hand was told by the Cheyennes that all were dead. Leg-in-the-Water told him this. Their bodies lie far up on the Big Horn, and we must go to them and bring the bodies back, as hateful as that is. The Long Knives brought the big red horse to us as a gift to me. I will give the horse to High Bull, for it belonged to his father, the Little Gray Bull. Now we will ride back to our village and sleep. In the morning the Long Knives will ride away from our lands. If they stop to camp on either the first night or the second night, you may steal their horses and anything else that you want, but you must not kill them. One of these men has lived among our brothers, the Sparrow Hawks of the River, and he has a wife among Long Hair's people. The Bad Hand, who leads these men, was kind to me when I lived among the Whites. They did wrong in not telling us what happened to Little Gray Bull and the Lumpwoods. But they have given me the chief's horse. Now we must go back to our village. These are my words."

Medicine Calf slept fitfully, and his dreams were not good. He dreamed finally of a howling wind and snowstorm on the high plains. He held the teal duck in his hands, and its eyes were white hot. It beat him with its wings and flew away. He could hear the sound of laughter. Then his legs grew paralyzed, and he had to crawl forward through the thin, drifting snow that swirled about him like a dust devil. The rifle was frozen in his hands. Had he remembered to reload the weapon? He convinced himself that he had, and yet he was still not certain. He crawled forward, dragging his legs. Then he was near the stream, and once more he saw the deer among the willows. With great effort he managed to draw himself into a sitting position and lifted the rifle, took aim on the outline of the deer. He squeezed the trigger and heard the empty snap of the hammer. The form in the willows moved, but now it was not a deer. It was a trapper. The man walked slowly toward him, the rifle raised. In a moment would come the blast of the Hawken, but he would never hear it. The rifle ball would tear through his heart first, and he would be dead. "I must die with dignity," he thought. "I must die as Rotten Belly died." He attempted to sing a death song, but no words would form. He ceased in the attempt and stared at the face of the one who was within ten feet, the rifle aimed at his heart. He realized the man's face had no features: no eyes, no mouth, no nose. It was completely blank. But a voice said, "Iggerant dunghead nigger! Yuh forgot t' load yur rifle, didn't ye? *Sacré Dieu*, friend of me, is because you think like the Indian. Me, I am White. *Enfant de garce, c'est ça!*" Then the figure dematerialized before his eyes, the edges suddenly becoming blurred, the light beginning to show through the flesh. Then there was no flesh at all, only the invisible outline of a man. And then no outline. Even the landscape changed, and he realized that he was on the back of a huge beaver, and the beaver was moving.

It had been Pierre Le Blueux all along.

He heard the crying of Black Panther and sat up. Little Wife was pinching the child's nostrils together, and the crying stopped.

"Pine Leaf and High Bull are here," Little Wife said. "You must go on a war-path, my husband."

He was up immediately. The son of Little Gray Bull and the warrior woman stood before him. Pine Leaf held her lance beside her, the owl feathers hanging limply down the shaft.

"The Long Knives rode out in the middle of the night," she said, "and this morning the big red horse is gone, maybe. Will you call the warriors now? High Bull and I will ride with you."

"Are you well enough to do this thing?"

"I do not go out to die. My medicine is strong, and I will ride."

"High Bull, what happened?"

"The horse that the Medicine Calf gave to me was stolen. No other horses were taken. Your friends the Long Knives have taken him."

"These men are not my friends, and they are not friends to the Sparrow Hawks. We will go after them. High Bull, go to the lodges of Yellow Belly and Red Eyes. Tell them the Medicine Calf has said that we ride."

By late afternoon the Sparrow Hawks had overtaken Red Beard Miller. They found him watering the horses at a stream singing through the autumn sunlight, tall yellow cottonwoods from which the breeze licked down the leaves that fell in little spurts. Miller looked up and knew he was surrounded. There was no chance of escape.

"Warriors!" Miller shouted. "You know who I am. I am Red Hair, and I have lived four winters with the people of Long Hair. I have taken this horse because it is mine."

"The red horse belonged to Little Gray Bull, chief of the Lump-woods," Medicine Calf said. "You are now with the Long Knives. You are not one of the people. Give us this horse and you may go, but you are never again to return to the lands of the Sparrow Hawks."

"The fuckin' roan belongs to me, Beckwourth," Miller said, "You want this horse, you fight me for it."

Red Beard slowly drew his knife and held it out away from his body so that all could see the sunlight glinting from the blade. A rattle of disapproval went through the Sparrow Hawks.

"Warriors!" Miller shouted. "I will fight your chief. If I win, I will take the red horse and go. If I lose, the red horse belongs to Beck-wourth."

Medicine Calf saw Yellow Belly raise his rifle.

"Do not shoot this man! He is mine, Yellow Belly. I will fight him, and it will be as he says. Listen to my words. Warrior Woman will stay with me. She will hold her rifle as I fight Red Hair. If I am slain, then Yellow Belly is to be the new head chief. He is to have the shield and the medal that were given to me by Rotten Belly, his brother. Pine Leaf will give these things to him, along with my weapons and my war horse. Red Eyes and Yellow Belly! Do you hear me? These are my orders. Leave us and follow the Long Knives. You heard what I told Fitzgerald, the Bad Hand, last night. If the Long Knives encamp tonight or tomorrow night, then take their horses and their goods and return to our village. You are not to kill them. They have done nothing. It is this man, Red Hair, who has killed the Little Gray Bull. I did not see it, but this is what my medicine tells me, and that is why I will fight him. If Red Hair kills me, then Pine Leaf will allow him to take the war horse and leave our lands. If he should ever return, remember what Medicine Calf has told you. Then you must kill him. But he will not kill me. When you return from this ride, you will find his scalp hanging beneath the tail of the red horse. Now these are my words. Red Eyes and Yellow Belly, take the warriors with you and ride after the Long Knives. Obey your chief! Nan-kup-bah-bah has spoken."

Red Eyes and Yellow Belly looked at each other and nodded. They turned their horses and were gone. Pine Leaf dismounted and tethered her pinto. Then she held the rifle on the two men.

"Well, Nigger Jim, it's you and me, ain't it? Third time's a charm, as the sayin' goes."

Medicine Calf did not answer. He gave his weapons to Pine Leaf and tethered his horse beside hers. He unsheathed his knife.

The two men circled each other.

Medicine Calf heard the sound of the stream and the cry of a bluejay. He breathed deeply: the good smell of the air, the dry grass of autumn, the faint odor in the air when the leaves have begun to fall. He could feel the sunlight on his back, the grass beneath his feet, the texture of the dry grass even through his moccasins. Again the cry of the bluejay.

"It is a good day to die," thought Medicine Calf. "And it is a good day to live."

He was waiting for the voice of the faceless trapper, but it did not come.

Miller's blade leaped forward, and the steel ate at Medicine Calf's shoulder, nibbled at the flesh. He knew he was cut, but he felt no pain.

It would indeed be a good day to die—to go out at the top of it, to go out with his powers entirely his own. He had lived a world of lifetimes in these few years. A grand adventure. What more could possibly follow? What more was there for him to do? Baptiste was dead. Cahuna was dead. His brother-in-law, Black Panther, was dead. Still-water was gone. A-ra-poo-ash was dead. The mountains were beginning to crawl with Scot noblemen and painters. Soon missionaries would come to convert the Indians to Christ and whole armies of bluecoats to force them to their knees. It would be a good day to die, a good day to follow A-ra-poo-ash to wherever it was that he went—the sound of a great wind through the forest. . . .

The grinning, bearded face in front of him.

A sudden gust of wind, and a swirl of leaves in the air.

"Ugly fuckin' Nigger! I'm gonna cut your eyes out."

The voice was Miller's. Medicine Calf did not reply. He continued to circle his opponent, feinting, moving easily and rhythmically, as in a grotesque dance. Then the knife leaped toward him.

He moved under the arc of the blade and brought his own knife up from his knees. The steel drank flesh. Miller crumpled forward, falling on the knife, driving it in even further. One of his feet kicked twice at the grass, and then he did not move again.

Medicine Calf pushed the body over, withdrew the knife, and took Red Beard's scalp. Then he stood up and turned around, the bloody scalp in his hand.

Pine Leaf was sitting with her back against a sapling. The rifle lay in the grass an arm's length away. She held one hand to her chin.

"You will have to explain this knife fighting, maybe. It was good to watch. You explain it to me, and I will practice."

The Sparrow Hawks rode into the village with a new string of horses, a number of them loaded down with trade goods. Yellow Belly drew up his mount before the lodge of the head chief.

"Medicine Calf! Come out into the sunlight. We have something to show you!"

Medicine Calf emerged from the tipi and looked solemnly at the horses the warriors had brought.

"Did you have to kill the Long Knives?"

"No, we did not kill them. The Long Knives camped on the second night. We waited for their fires to burn down. Even their guards slept! These were very foolish men. We used the butts of our rifles to make the guards sleep more deeply. They were very tired, I think, and they needed to sleep. There was no need to awaken them. So we took all of the horses and rode away. The Bad Hand will have to walk back to Bear Lake now. Perhaps they will meet their friends, the Blackfeet, who will give them horses. I do not know."

Medicine Calf did not speak. He untied the big red horse, took it to High Bull, and handed him the reins.

"You must ride this horse well," he said then. "The scalp of the one who killed your father is where I said it would be."

He turned to Yellow Belly once more.

"Take the Dog Soldiers and ride up the Big Horn," he said quietly. He did not have to say anything else.

The autumn was long and pleasant, and at night the stars continued to fall. Ears of the Wolf observed four at one time, one low to the horizon and the other three directly overhead. The medicine man nodded and consulted his bundle of magic.

Medicine Calf led a war-path against the Cheyennes after the bodies of Little Gray Bull's party had been brought back. The mourning was in full progress as he left the village in the company of Red Eyes, Long Bow, and Pine Leaf.

"We must strike quickly," he said, "so that our people may wash their faces."

On the fourth day they reached the Badwater, crossed, and rode on toward the South Fork of the Powder. As they reached the divide between the two drainages, they found their way blocked by a single bull buffalo, an old fellow, one that had been driven out of the herd.

"This is a sign," Bears Copulating said. "We must shoot the buffalo so that we can perform the war-path ritual. That way we will be strong when we find the Cheyennes. One of our warriors has never shared this secret, Medicine Calf. Do you like my words?"

The head chief glanced at Pine Leaf, who looked at him questioningly.

"Didn't Long Hair forbid this thing?" he asked.

"You know that is not true, Medicine Calf," Pine Leaf protested. "I am permitted to take part in all the rituals. My medicine will be stronger, maybe."

"Bears, my friend," Medicine Calf laughed. "Let us shoot the buffalo. Pine Leaf wishes to be initiated."

The old bull, half blind, lifted its head, pawed at the earth. Bears Copulating and Medicine Calf approached the animal as closely as safety permitted, took aim, and fired. The buffalo grunted, wobbled, and fell on its side, the rear legs continuing to kick for perhaps a full minute. Red Eyes and Long Bow cut into the paunch, drew out the intestines, ran them through their closed fists to cleanse them, and nodded at Medicine Calf.

Bears Copulating cut out the liver, sprinkled a few drops of gall on it, and took several bites before passing the delicacy on to the others. A cooking fire was built close by the dead buffalo, and the tongue, brains, hump ribs, and thighs were prepared for cooking.

"This meat will be very tough," Pine Leaf said. "Why do we wish to eat it when we have better meat in our saddlebags?"

"We must eat the flesh of the tough bull because there is medicine in it," the head chief said. "You must not question what happens, Pine Leaf. Do exactly what the others before you will do. This is the war-path secret."

The Sparrow Hawks arranged themselves in a tight circle about the cooking fire and the remains of the old bull, and the intestine was stretched around so that all might hold a portion of it. Then Medicine Calf spoke the traditional words, specifying the purpose of the ritual, asserting that the warriors learned weakness from their women.

"A special kind of weakness comes from making love to a woman," he said, "and the weakness is greater if a man is not married to the woman. We must all speak of any women we have fucked, unless the women were our own wives. We must tell all that happened, and when, and where. If Isakawuate allows us to return from this war-path, we must repeat the story to one of the medicine men. We must speak even though the woman is the wife of another, for the bond among warriors must be stronger than the bond between a man and a woman. In this way Isakawuate will strengthen us for the battle ahead. The ritual is now begun, I have said so."

Pine Leaf listened to the tales of the various couplings, stole glances at those men whose wives were spoken of by other men, and stared at the dancing flames and the carcass of the old bull buffalo.

When it came to Pine Leaf's turn to speak, the Crow warriors were totally silent, but none wondered what the warrior woman would say more than Medicine Calf himself.

Pine Leaf raised the intestine before her and said, "My vow is well-known to all. I have sworn never to marry until I have had my full revenge against our enemies for the death of my brother. Fish Beneath Ice and I came out of our mother's womb together, on the same night. I am a virgin. I have never lain with any man. What I say is the truth."

The ritual continued, and all present were heavy with the knowledge that tradition had been changed. Never before had any woman shared in the war-path secret, and some still wondered if the war-medicine would be weakened by what had happened.

When the circle had been completed, the Sparrow Hawks ate the flesh of the slain buffalo, and the conversations were more than usually subdued. When all was finished in the way that was proper, Medicine Calf stood, gestured to the four sacred directions, and commanded that the war-path be continued.

As the Sparrow Hawks rode on, Pine Leaf said to Long Bow, "One day I will have something to speak of at the ritual of the war-path secret. But now my medicine is stronger. I can feel that it is stronger, maybe."

Long Bow glanced at Medicine Calf and then back at Pine Leaf. He nodded solemnly and gazed off toward a pair of vultures circling the blue sky to the east.

The following day the Wolves returned to report a group of thirty Cheyennes approaching. They were driving before them a large herd of horses, perhaps as many as five hundred. Medicine Calf split his party into three groups—one to engage the Cheyennes from the rear, the other two to descend from the adjoining ridges once the battle was in progress. Pine Leaf and Medicine Calf would come up from behind. Red Eyes and Long Bow would come down from either side.

The Cheyennes, supposing their own force as large as the one led by Medicine Calf and Pine Leaf, chose to fight. They wheeled and met the Sparrow Hawks head-on. Medicine Calf drew back and signaled for the other warriors to complete the surround, but as he did so, Pine Leaf charged forward, giving the war whoop, and engaged the entire force of the Cheyennes, who, startled at being assaulted by a single girl, turned and milled about. The lance of Pine Leaf sang through the air and struck the Cheyenne party chief in the shoulder. He clung to his horse, but the animal reared, and the chief was thrown off, falling backward against the lance, which shattered beneath him. Pine Leaf charged on, using her pistol to bring down two more warriors.

Medicine Calf sounded the attack, and within moments he had drawn abreast of the warrior woman.

"It is a good day to kill!" she shouted and then forced her horse to leap onward into the midst of the stunned Cheyennes.

"Damn little fool!" the Medicine Calf swore, following after her.

None of the Cheyennes escaped, and only three of the Sparrow Hawks were wounded, one with a pistol ball in his shoulder and two with arrows in their legs. Five Sparrow Hawk horses had been killed under their riders, but now there were many more horses. All the Cheyennes were scalped, and the Sparrow Hawks drove their newly-acquired herd before them as they rode toward home.

Pine Leaf had counted coup nine times in the fury of her assault, and she had taken five scalps.

"We should have let Warrior Woman fight these Cheyennes by herself!" Bears Copulating laughed. "She does not share the enemies with her fellow warriors! There was nothing for the rest of us to do. . . ."

"My medicine is still strong, maybe," she said thoughtfully. "I did not lose it all when that Assiniboine shot me."

"You have taken all of our medicine with you this day," Medicine Calf said. "You must give some of it back to us."

The faces of the Sparrow Hawks were washed, and Ears of the Wolf announced that a new medicine lodge should be built. It was a signal moment for the Absarokas, for tradition had been changed. Warrior Woman had shared in the war-path secret, and none could fail to admire the result.

Now the work on the new medicine lodge proceeded, and the

night sky was streaked with fire as the meteor shower gained in intensity. When the lodge was completed, Ears of the Wolf and the other medicine men and shamans called the most distinguished braves into the building for a rehearsal of their achievements and an enumeration of their coups. Pine Leaf, as the newest entrant into the lodge, spoke last, and Ears of the Wolf pronounced her statements true. Sham battles were then enacted to recount some of the more remarkable achievements, and Pine Leaf was called upon to enact her battle with the Cheyennes. She performed her part well and was applauded by the warriors.

Next the medicine men and shamans prepared the lodge for the ceremony of initiating a virtuous woman, should one come forward. The medicine men and shamans then entered upon their period of total abstinence from food and water. Only if one of the priests fainted from exhaustion would some slight nourishment be given him.

The skies were alive with moving fire at night, and on the fifth day the warriors were drawn up into two lines facing inward and waited for a female candidate to present herself at the lodge doorway.

"Nom-ne-dit-chee, the wife of Medicine Calf, offers herself for election to this lodge," the voice of Ears of the Wolf intoned.

Medicine Calf was astounded by the announcement and started forward to approach Little Wife. Then he stepped back into his place in the line. There was nothing he could do now. Who had dressed her for the ceremony? If she had come to him, as was the custom, he would have tried to prevent her from making the attempt. Had she been faithful? He believed so, but he could not be sure. So far as he knew, her name had never been spoken at the enactment of the war-path secret. But the women's lives were their own, and the men were often away. Medicine Calf stared across at Big Rain. This was a man who might speak falsely, and his reason would be that of revenge. Medicine Calf could think of no one else who would speak against Little Wife.

If anyone spoke, Little Wife would be beaten and disgraced. If many did, claiming sexual relations with her, Little Wife would be killed. And he, Medicine Calf, would have to assist in the killing. He continued to glare at Big Rain.

Nom-ne-dit-chee presented herself at the entrance to the lodge and then spoke:

"Warriors! Can it be said that there are no virtuous women among the Sparrow Hawks? Is it possible that our medicine men cannot make medicine and our shamans cannot prophecy and our dreamers cannot dream because so few of us are virtuous? It is shameful for women to be so faithless! If there are no virtuous women, the Sparrow Hawks will soon cease to be a great nation. Isakakate and Isakawuate will be angry and will bring defeat upon our warriors! Our lands will become wastelands, and the buffalo, elk, antelope, and beaver will all vanish. The animal people will go to the lands of a more virtuous people. Warriors! This day I have volunteered to carry the sand, the wood, and the elk-chips into the lodge. When I was a child, I saw the body of a woman who had been hacked to pieces because she had attempted to enter the medicine lodge falsely. Now I will enter. I will walk to the end of this line and pick up those things which I brought in earlier—the sand, the wood, and the dung of the elk. If any man besides Medicine Calf, my husband, has ever lain with me and has known my body, let that man speak. I am innocent, but I am ready to go into the Spirit World if there are those who would speak falsely against me."

Little Wife then walked forward between the two lines of warriors. She took the sacred bowl and placed the sand in it and then returned through the lines and emptied the bowl outside the lodge. She came back a second time for the wood and a third time for the elk-chips.

No one spoke against her, and when she reached the entrance way for the final time, the warriors applauded loudly. Pine Leaf stepped from her place in line and embraced Little Wife. Medicine Calf came quickly to his wife's side and embraced her also.

"I dressed Little Wife for the ceremony," Pine Leaf said. "She was afraid you would not allow this thing, maybe, so she asked me to do it."

Then Ears of the Wolf came to Little Wife and passed his hands over her head and shoulders. He extolled her virtues and proclaimed loudly that there was at least one virtuous woman among the Sparrow Hawks. Isakawuate, he said, would strengthen the medicine of the tribe.

"Medicine Calf," Ears of the Wolf said, "give your medicine shield to Nom-ne-dit-chee. She will preserve it and carry it for you. No one but you will have the authority to take it away from her."

It was mid-November, and still no snow had fallen. Each night the fire-play in the heavens was more intense, with long scratches of sudden flame bursting across the darkness. The people were uneasy, and many had begun to fear that the entire heavens would fall and that the world was about to end. Isakawuate would make a new world out of the destroyed remains of the old. The beaver were plentiful in the streams, but very few were trapped. The buffalo herds had vanished, but large numbers of elk and deer had moved down out of the mountains in anticipation of the change of seasons. The hunting was good and meat was plentiful. Even the camp dogs could sense the agitation of the people, however, and sometimes they barked and wailed through the nights.

Ears of the Wolf dreamed that the sky turned to fire. Then the fire ceased all at once, and the heavens remained as they had been before. He spoke to the people. The dream, he told them, signified that Isakawuate was telling the Long Knives to go down out of the mountains and not to return. Ears of the Wolf did not know whether the Long Knives would heed the omen, but he knew that soon the star-people would go back to being as they had always been.

Medicine Calf, for different reasons, agreed with the prediction of Ears of the Wolf. Such swarms of shooting stars, he knew, were not terribly uncommon, though this one had lasted longer and was more spectacular than any he had ever read about. Yet even he felt a certain uneasiness, as though something extraordinary were happening.

"I will ride into the mountains," Medicine Calf said, "and look for a sign. You are not to remove the village in my absence. Big

Rain, do you hear me? No matter what the old women say, the village must stay where it is until my return. Nom-ne-dit-chee and Bar-chee-am-pe will come with me. Already my medicine tells me that the Sparrow Hawks have nothing to fear. It may be exactly as Ears of the Wolf says, for the medicine man is very wise, and he knows how to explain the dreams that come to us from the Spirit World. We will return to this village before the new moon."

They rode along the South Fork of the Shoshone until they had come to the base of Needle Mountain and then turned toward the mountain itself. When they had worked their way to a high meadow ringed by the upward swellings of granite, they made camp. Above them the mountain glowed a thin crimson in the late light. A small stream splashed down through the meadow, sourced from a dwindling snowfield. The grass was good, and the horses were turned out to forage as they would.

Higher up the mountain was bare, rising to its summit. But here a few twisted spruces still grew, and Medicine Calf and Pine Leaf quickly fashioned a campsite while Little Wife nursed the Black Panther.

They built a fire and set to cooking some of the fresh deer meat they had brought up the mountain with them. They ate and sat about the fire. Pine Leaf asked to hold the child, and Little Wife handed Black Panther to her.

The waxing moon hung in the sky, just over the shoulder of the peak. Medicine Calf stood for a few minutes without speaking, and then the moon was gone. In the sky to the north, a flash of fire was faintly visible.

Once it was dark, they spoke little. Black Panther slept quietly beneath his blanket. The sky grew filled with strange, flashing lights. The three sat huddled closely together, and the vast display continued, quieted, burst into flame-streaks again, the lights coming as if in long pulsations.

An owl flew up into the firelight for a moment, hovered, and then vanished. Medicine Calf could hear the sound of falling water, high on the side of the mountain.

At last they slept, the three of them close together beneath the buffalo robes, the child with them.

Sometime before morning, Medicine Calf awoke. He had been dreaming, but he could not recall the dream. The sky above was now shrieking with silent bands of light, a dozen or more trails of fire at a time, some of the lights crisscrossing the others.

"How it all *shines,*" he thought. "Perhaps the world is ending. Maybe it is time."

At that moment a huge blue-green ball of fire flashed across the night. It made a sound almost like the cry of a coyote. Startled, he reached out with either hand and awakened Pine Leaf and Little Wife. They sat up quickly, instantly awake. The noise was gone, and so was the fireball, but a long luminous band of green-white light remained where it had been hurled across the sky.

"What was it, Medicine Calf? Did one of the stars come close, maybe?"

Medicine Calf did not answer. He continued to stare at the slowly-fading smear of light. But it was not the trail of a shooting star that he saw.

"My God!" he said. "Look!"

Pine Leaf and Little Wife stared into the night, but they saw only the vanishing stream of faintly visible luminescence.

A little buffalo. Red ribbons tied in clusters about the ears. Bells about the neck. The animal pulsed in the air, grew bright, and then faded away.

24

OUT OF THE BLIZZARD

The big mountains dream in the waters of their glacial lakes, long ridges cloaked in dark forests of fir and pine and spruce and tamarack, the highest peaks hewn out of granite or layered of metamorphosed sedimentaries, twenty million years since the uplift, and through that time erosion has carved out the range, cut back into the layered rock, cut down to the granite core: and the seasons run, the cruel lock of winter, the white world, the winds and the snows, springtime when the streams leap from the mountains, summer and the melt-out, high fields of wildflowers, the lakes clear and blue, autumn and the chill winds, aspen and cottonwood blazing with leafgold, long spumes of mist trailing from the peaks after the first rains and light snows, bush maples like crimson fires licking the ridges up to the twisted pines at timberline and the pure, naked glory of stone.

Pierre Le Blueux rode upriver from Fort Cass. He was coming home, and whether to die or to live made little difference to him. In the long run, perhaps it was all the same. If in some ways the mountains were different than they had been a quarter century earlier, they were still God's country—Isakawuate's country. There was still no other place he knew of where a man was free and knew he was free.

He had been down to New Orleans and had even thought about shipping out. Where to didn't make any difference. But then his nerve had begun to fail him, and he knew he had made a mistake. What a man was, he decided, depended upon where he was. When a man had climbed over a range of mountains or forded a river or swum in a lake, the man became a part of those mountains or that river or that lake.

And when he had thought about this, Pierre Le Blueux *knew* where he belonged. He would die where he had lived. He figured that just maybe he had a good bit more of living to do.

"Mon Dieu, it is not time yet to die! There are still plew to be taken. There are still lakes to swim in, *enfant de garce!"*

So now he rode up country from Fort Cass. He had figured to find Jim Beckwourth, if Jim had not gone under. But Jim was all right. Pierre had talked with Samuel Tulleck at the fort. His friend was still alive—or had been just a few months earlier—the new head chief of the Mountain Crows, according to Tulleck.

"Incroyable! And he is named the Medicine Calf, *le veau-médicine.* He is the head chief, *eh bien!"*

Tulleck had shown Le Blueux the rifle that once belonged to Hugh Glass—had told him the story of Glass's death.

Le Blueux shrugged his shoulders as he rode. He had known Glass. So would they find his own body one day, chewed up by a grizzly or the *Pieds Noirs.* But they had known the best of it, he and Hugh Glass. The mountains had been new then. Things *shone.* Light poured out of them. *Très éclatant.*

"Edward Rose. *Alors,* it is no loss, that one. Me, I think that he lived too long. He needed the Arikaras."

Now the skies were splitting open. *Les météores.* Each night there were more lights in the sky. And each night he camped, built a fire, ate, and watched the display in the heavens. He felt alive again. The last years would be good ones also. He was still strong, and he knew the mountains as well as any child alive, Long Knife or Indian. He could walk or ride all day without being tired. The forests and plains knew that he knew them, could survive among them, no matter what. Had they not called to him? Had they not told him to return?

He rode late the fourth night. Not enough moonlight really to see where he was going, but did it make any difference? So long as a man was in the mountains when he met his death, it was no great matter. To become a part of this earth, a part of this wildness, to be a part of it forever. . . .

Astounding lights in the sky. A rain of white fire, lacing the heavens. For the Indians, Pierre knew, this would have to be a time of powerful medicine. When the meteor shower was over, the configurations formed by the flashing lights in the sky would be discussed. Villages would be moved. Future war-paths would be planned. The meanings of dreams would be deliberated at great length.

His horse moved easily along through the darkness, and Pierre watched the sky, his Hawken loaded as always and cradled in the crook of his arm.

In a few more days he would find sign that would lead him to the Absaroka encampment. With luck, Jim would be there.

"I will stay on with the Absarokees *pour un peu*. That will be good, *peut-être*. I will put out some traps and catch *le castor*. *Alors*, it might be good to have a squaw *aussi*. Then I could beget a race of *petit Pierres*. They would all be born with gray beards, *aux cheveux gris*."

He rode all night and watched the sky. Such a time was too beautiful to spend sleeping. He could sleep later.

When the head chief returned to the Sparrow Hawk encampment, he immediately sensed a difference. Now that the stars had ceased to fall, conversations were animated, and the women sang as they worked, whether dressing out furs or bringing in cooking wood. Red Eyes and Coyote Running had led a brief hunting expedition and returned in good spirits, their pack horses laden with buffalo and antelope meat. Already the pots of tongues were simmering, and hind-quarters were roasting.

No more flame in the sky for two nights. The stars ceased to fall, and, as Ears of the Wolf predicted, the heavens became normal once more.

Medicine Calf went directly to Big Bowl's lodge and discovered that his father had a visitor. Big Bowl met him at the entrance to the tipi and said, "My son, one of the Long Knives has come to see you. I am glad you have returned, because I cannot understand this man very well. Perhaps you will understand him better. . . ."

Inside the lodge Pierre Le Blueux was just finishing his second helping of soup, and Funny Deer was ready to refill the bowl.

Medicine Calf embraced his mentor, and the two men alternately hugged one another and pounded each other on the back.

"Monsieur Calf, it is good to be with you again, it is good!"

The French Canadian with the gray beard was welcomed into the lodge of Medicine Calf and Little Wife, and before long he was sitting beside the fire, smelling the cooking spits of buffalo meat, and holding the Black Panther in his arms.

"Me, I am the *grand-père,* and this one, he is the *petit-fils. Monsieur Big Bowl,* is it all right for Pierre to be the grandfather also?"

"It is good for a boy to have two grandfathers," Big Bowl answered. "You can be his second grandfather."

"Oui," said Pierre. "That is good. Do you wish to smoke this pipe, Big Bowl? The tobacco is good. It is from Virginia. That is one of the places where the Whitemen grow their tobacco."

He filled the pipe and offered it to the father of the Medicine Calf.

"Don't drop Black Panther, Pierre," Little Wife cautioned.

"Non, non, I will not drop him. Here. It is better that he goes back to his *maman,* his mother."

"You will stay and trap with us?" Medicine Calf asked.

Le Blueux stared into the fire, then reached over, touched one of the strips of elk, and brought his finger back to his mouth. He considered his words carefully. It would be important that he speak in the language of Absaroka, better that he keep so many French words out of his speech. Among the trappers, it had never mattered. They understood him or they didn't, but usually they did. Here, however, it would be a matter of honor to speak the language of the Crows as purely as he could.

"I wish to live among the Absaroka," he said. "I would like to stay with the people of Big Bowl and Medicine Calf."

Medicine Calf broke out laughing.

Big Bowl looked oddly at his son. A strange response to such an assertion. From any other, such a reaction would be considered impolite. But, Big Bowl considered, the Medicine Calf had known this man, Pierre-le-Blueux, for a long time. Perhaps it was all right between them.

"You speak Sparrow Hawk better than you speak English, Pierre."

Le Blueux nodded.

"He will need a new name, won't he, father? What should such a man be named?"

Pine Leaf had been sitting quietly all this while, but now she smiled and spoke:

"Grayhair-on-his-Face, maybe?"

"I think that's an admirable name," said Medicine Calf.

"Grayhair-on-his-Face?" asked Le Blueux. *"Sacre Dieu!* That name, it is terrible!"

"Good. It's settled, then," Medicine Calf said, his expression suddenly quite serious. "Grayhair-on-his-Face it shall be."

A light snow, and then the weather turned warm once more. The time of autumn had seemingly returned, and the early morning frost melted each day by noon.

Coyote Running approached Medicine Calf.

"My brother, perhaps it is now time for us to search for our wives. I am told that the Cheyennes have made a great village on the north branch of the Platte River, at the foot of the mountains. If we took a small party, we might be able to spy on them without being noticed. Perhaps it is worth the chance."

"It is not much of a chance, Coyote Running. Do you miss Morning Song?"

"Yes, Grouse-feather and I both miss her."

"I would like to have Still-water back in my lodge. It is true."

"And not the Red Cherry?"

"If she came back, perhaps I would go crazy again. And Pine Leaf would not be my friend."

"I have already spoken with Warrior Woman," Coyote said. "She wishes to go squaw hunting also."

"I'll be damned!" Medicine Calf snorted. "Well, there's no way of knowing. Perhaps we might be able to capture Leg-in-the-Water and bring him home tied to a travois."

"It would be difficult to tie that one down."

"Even a white bear can be tied down, Coyote."

"What about Grayhair-on-his-Face? Would he wish to go too? He is a strong man. You fought together when you lived among the Long Knives?"

"Yes," answered Medicine Calf. "I'll see what Grayhair-on-his-Face thinks of the idea."

It had been some time since the death of Black Panther. The Dog Soldier's two wives, Autumn Flower and Stands Straight, had been living in the lodge of Big Bowl and had become his daughters. Autumn Flower, Big Bowl knew, had been meeting with young High Bull, and something was likely to work out there very soon. Each day Big Bowl anticipated that High Bull would come to him and ask for the hand of the girl. It would be good. Autumn Flower had come from the River Crows, and her parents were dead. High Bull would be his son-in-law. Perhaps he should encourage High Bull? Or perhaps Medicine Calf could do this thing.

On the whole, Big Bowl thought, it was good to have the head chief for a son. A word from the chief, and the entire matter might be resolved.

Stands Straight was another problem.

To many of the Crows, no doubt, the girl seemed haughty. She wasn't this way, of course, not once one got to know her. But she did not make friends easily with the other women, and she had had no suitors. Perhaps it was because she was a Blackfoot.

Then Big Bowl thought about Grayhair-on-his-Face.

This was a likely possibility. His son's friend was apparently serious in his intention to live with the Sparrow Hawks. Surely he would need a wife.

When they all ate together in the lodge, Stands Straight would not look at Grayhair-on-his-Face. But when the man was not look-ing at her, Big Bowl noted, Stands Straight sometimes stole glances at him.

"I think it is time for Stands Straight to be married again," Funny Deer said to her husband. "Why don't you offer her to our son's friend?"

"I never would have thought of it," Big Bowl said to his wife. "But since you have mentioned it, I think it is a good idea. I will do it tomorrow."

So Pierre Le Blueux and Stands Straight were married, and Little Wife, Funny Deer, and Grouse-feather helped them to fashion a lodge. Medicine Calf presented Grayhair-on-his-Face with twenty horses, a battle axe, two coats, and a quantity of tobacco. Out of his stores he gathered together for Stands Straight some scarlet cloth, vermilion, a hand mirror, needles, knives, and added to these things the beautifully-tanned hide of a bighorn sheep.

"I was going to ask you to accompany us on a hunting expedition, Pierre," the Medicine Calf said. "But now you will have other du-ties. Perhaps in the spring we can go."

"She is a pretty woman, this one," Grayhair-on-his-Face said. "*Très jolie, très gentille!* I am glad I have come back to *les montagnes.* When you return, my beard, it will no longer be *gris.*"

They had shared their plans with no one. They would go hunting, and that was all. Medicine Calf knew well enough how his counse-lors would respond, had he told them of his intentions.

The hunters would be gone a few days, perhaps a week or so, maybe longer.

Pine Leaf. Coyote Running. And Medicine Calf.

They rode out of the encampment with a string of pack horses behind them and moved up the Big Horn in the direction of South Pass and the Sweetwater River. From there they would descend to the North Platte and follow that river around the Laramie Mountains and onto the plains, where the Cheyenne winter encampment was reported to be.

On the sixth day, however, they came to the North Platte and turned south along the Medicine Bow, finally crossing up over the Laramie Mountains—to reduce the likelihood of being discovered, for they were now deep into the country of the Cheyennes. From the crest of the mountains they could see far to the east, the hills, plains, and bluffs of the North Platte country, the river having rounded the mountains to the north and now swinging out onto the great plains to the east. Below them, somewhere, was the encampment of the Cheyenne people.

The skies turned a heavy gray, with wind from the south, and the day was completely cheerless. About noon on the eighth day a light snow began to fall. After another hour it began to stick, blowing on the wind, clinging to the branches of the stunted pines and junipers.

By nightfall the winds had increased, and the snow was pouring out of the sky, driving almost horizontally to the ground. The horses were having difficulty, and finally the little party took refuge out of the wind, at the base of some castle rocks, where a great pine had become uprooted on the heights above and had crashed down the nearly vertical slope a year or two past. They would have a good supply of firewood, at least, and shelter from the howling wind and driving snow.

They built a fire in against the rocks and set to cooking portions of deer meat killed as they came up the mountains the preceding day. Medicine Calf tethered the horses near a tangle of chokecherry brush and kicked the snow away from some tall clumps of dead sweetgrass. The horses were not happy, but they grazed perfunctorily at the snowy grass, nickered, and stamped their feet.

"We have found a good place to die, maybe," Pine Leaf said.

Medicine Calf laughed.

"Not while we have firewood and something to eat," he said. "Let's wait until tomorrow before we talk about dying."

"This is a strange place we have come to," Coyote Running said.

"We have been hunting for days, and yet I have not seen a single squaw. Only the wind and snow."

"The Cheyennes are out there somewhere," Pine Leaf said. "They have tight lodges and are warm by their lodge fires. Why is it that we are not at home in our own lodges?"

Medicine Calf took a mouthful of meat, wiped at his face, and chewed, swallowed before speaking. He remembered another blizzard, nine years earlier, days of wind, snow, and rain, down on the South Platte.

"Where is *la bouteille?* That's what Grayhair-on-his-Face would ask if he were here. But likely he's not even thinking about us right now. My friends, if this storm keeps up for a day or so, we're in trouble. Even if it clears right away, it's subject to get colder than hell."

"Perhaps we should have gone to steal horses from the Siksikas," Coyote Running commented.

"Is our magic also good for snowstorms?" Pine Leaf wondered out loud.

"Well," said Medicine Calf, "if this were the last night of our lives, it wouldn't be so bad—we would die in the presence of Isaka-wuate. Listen to the wind coming through the rocks up above. It sounds like eagles screaming."

They continued to eat, the firelight flickering over their faces. The wind blew, and the snow fell. The horses stamped and whinnied, and the night went on. At last the three Crow warriors rolled close together under the heavy buffalo robes and slept.

The storm continued for another two days, drifts piling up around them, the rush of air turning to a sustained, intense wailing. Pine Leaf set about fashioning snowshoes from flexible wands of chokecherry and strips of green deerhide. Medicine Calf and Coyote Running dug through to the grass again and again, so that the horses would have something to eat, but each time the wind drifted the dry, stinging snow back over their little excavation. The horses continued to chew at the chokecherry and willow brush.

396

Still, there was plenty of firewood and enough meat for the time being. They talked little during the second day, all three now working on the snowshoes and finally finishing them. It might be necessary to leave the horses to their fate and set out on foot. But there was no point in doing anything until the storm had passed.

It was now the third night at the base of the castle rocks, and as they ate, huddled around the fire, a sandstone ledge far above them slipped loose and fell, shattering as it came, and raining hundred-pound boulders over the snow very close to them. The horses reared and thrashed about, and Medicine Calf slogged through the drifts to comfort Come Back and the others. With the animals finally quieted, he returned to the fire. The three Sparrow Hawks finished their meal in silence.

Again the three Crow warriors huddled beneath their buffalo robes, but sleep would not come to the Medicine Calf. He lay awake for a long while, his mind in a turmoil—lay still so as not to disturb his two friends. The storm continued, the snow continued, winds bursting and raging about them. At last he slipped from beneath the robes, got up, and put more wood on the fire—watched as the sucking wind drew off a long trail of sparks into the darkness of the swirling snowfall.

"It is a good place to die, a good time to die," he said aloud.

But his mind was on life, not death. The storm would break eventually, and they would continue their journey. Perhaps they would succeed and perhaps they would not. Maybe they would die under the knives of the Cheyennes, or, with astounding good luck, they might actually manage to rescue one or two of the women. Then they would return to the Absaroka encampment, and life would go on.

But what remained?

Their world would soon end. Medicine Calf could see this end, and it was much closer than any of his people could comprehend. There would be a short interval of years, a last bright flaring of a way of life. For himself, there remained an indeterminate succession of battles, of movements, of victories and defeats. There remained the constant necessity of demonstrating valor, of providing guidance for a difficult and unpredictable people. He had accepted the responsibility, and there was no way to put it down.

"I was not meant to be a leader," he thought. "I came to the mountains to find freedom, not the burden of leadership. When I have known a thing fully, it is my nature to seek elsewhere. But perhaps there's no such thing as freedom—maybe freedom itself is simply an illusion, a dream, the wailing of coyotes on summer nights. . . ."

He stirred at the fire and again watched the stream of sparks trail off into the night. He heard the stamping and nickering of the horses, uneasy as the storm raged on. He thought of the mountains and the lands still to the west—California, the valleys of California, where it was said the snow never fell. And he remembered Le Blueux's words about the lands to the north, mountains that contained vast rivers of ice. He thought about the country of the Oregon, where great solitary peaks rose above lush forests. And the canyonlands of the Southwest, beyond Flaming Gorge, canyons more immense than anything he had ever seen. And the sweep of the Pacific Ocean, pushing back against the continent, itself the ultimate limit to both the American West and the relentless push to occupy it.

"The human tide spills westward," he thought. "And my people stand in the way of what is going to happen, my people and the Blackfeet, the Cheyennes, the Pawnees, the Sioux, the Arapahos, the Apaches, the Navahos, and all the others. The great horsemen, the great warriors, the great hunters. All will vanish. My people. . . ."

They were his people.

They had chosen him to lead them, even though they did not know the path would lead to the Spirit World. The thing would come and it would come in its own time. The beaver would go and the buffalo would go, and the tribes of the plains and the mountains would be no more. The remnants would be herded onto reservations, but those people would not really be Absaroka, Blackfoot, Arikara, Cheyenne.

The world itself is a process of change, unending change. You cannot stop this thing, Medicine Calf. I have allowed you to be a part of what I have created, I have allowed you to live it and to watch it. You must stay in these mountains for a few more years, and then you must leave. Other adventures await you, adventures that you cannot now even imagine. You are my chosen warrior, the war chief of our people, even though you were not born among them. A warrior creates his own identity, and you have created yours. It has all been as I have planned it. When you leave, you will promise to return. It will be many years, however, before you keep your promise. You will return to our people to die. These are my words, Medicine Calf.

Pine Leaf was standing by his side. Now she spoke to him.

"Tonight you should take me into the willows, maybe. It will be cold, but we can do it while our friend sleeps. Later we may be starving and unable. Do you wish this thing, Medicine Calf?"

He turned to Warrior Woman, gathered her into his arms, and kissed her. They clung together, the snow swirling about them. They held each other for a long while, not speaking, perhaps not even thinking, not even noticing, at first, that the snow had ceased.

"I see stars in the east," Pine Leaf said. "Isakawuate has brought an ending to this storm."

"I could feel it ending," Medicine Calf said. "I knew it would end. The Old Trickster isn't finished with us yet. It is not our medicine to die in the snow. We will return to our people, and later we will go to the willows. . . ."

"My chief is thinking about that fat little Red Cherry. He is no longer interested in Pine Leaf. I think I will scalp her when we find her."

Pine Leaf tightened her embrace, and Medicine Calf could feel the amazing tensile strength of her grasp. He well understood why her lance could leap out with such force. He felt her clean strength and was glad.

She was laughing at him, laughing. And then he too began to laugh.

Morning came cold, deadly cold. But the storm was over, and the sky was clearing. They looked out on a sparkling, vast, white desert, the landscape rounded with snow and seemingly featureless.

"Down there!" Pine Leaf said. "It is an old bull buffalo. He flounders about, waiting for us to put on our snowshoes and come to kill him. He will give us enough meat for a long while."

"Isakawuate has sent us a big brown gift, to go along with his other gifts," the Medicine Calf said.

Far down below, in a flat near the rocky point of a low ridge, a buffalo was indeed attempting to plod along, thrashing his big horned head back and forth, occasionally bellowing in frustration.

"He's mired and helpless," Coyote Running said. "Let us take our rifles and go shoot him."

They moved across the whiteness, their feet sinking in the loose drifts despite the snowshoes, and finally they reached the buffalo. The animal ceased to struggle, and began to watch them, idly curious or perhaps not seeing them clearly at all. They had worked their way to within fifty feet of the old bull and aimed carefully. The three Hawkens made nearly one explosion. The buffalo, as if suddenly deciding to lie down, dropped slowly, little bubbles of blood frothing from mouth and nostril, splashing out flecks and ribbons of crimson on the snow, the head tilting over to one side, the tongue hanging out.

The hunters went to work with their knives, Coyote Running cutting out the liver and taking a mouthful.

They continued with the business of skinning and slaughtering. Medicine Calf cut out the hump and stood back, watched the other two proceed with their task.

Was that smoke?

He motioned to Coyote and Pine Leaf, pointed.

From here they could see around the low, rocky ridge that had previously blocked their view of the plateau beyond them, to the southeast.

Two or three miles out across the undulating plain that shone almost to a glare in the brilliant sunlight, they could see a large, dead cottonwood, the only irregularity in the gently rolling, molded surface. Its branches stood out against the snow-covered expanse of the plateau like the claws of an owl. Beside the tree rose a thin blue-white plume of smoke.

A campfire, certainly.

"Whoever's there," Coyote Running said, "they've heard our gunshots."

The three reloaded quickly, and Pine Leaf stood watch as the two men took as much meat as they could carry and wrapped it in half of the buffalo hide. Then they returned to their encampment at the base of the rocks.

The horses were uneasy, but they continued to chew at the brush.

When it was dark, Pine Leaf, Coyote Running, and Medicine Calf set out for the cottonwood, moving easily across the frozen snow, the half moon reflecting brightly on the white desert. Their breath went up in little filaments of steam from mouth and nose.

They approached with great care. The fire was still burning, and the shadow of the big cottonwood shimmered against the moon.

Two gray-white wolves slunk off, circled the three Crow warriors, and trotted away over the snow in the direction of the slain buffalo.

"Our brothers intend to share our kill, maybe," Pine Leaf whispered.

Medicine Calf nodded.

"Let's work our way around to the rise over there. Should be able to see what we've got."

They crouched low and moved through the moonlight, got down on their hands and knees, and came up behind the small outcropping of stone, their three rifles instantly in place and ready to fire.

Below them, in a hollowed-out area around the base of the gaunt snag, a makeshift shelter of buffalo robes had been strung up. Six hungry-looking pack horses were tethered to one side. The fire was large, and at the edge of it, a pot of meat was stewing. A group of about twenty women—Cheyennes from their clothing—huddled up close to the open flames.

Medicine Calf, Coyote Running, and Pine Leaf studied the little gathering for several minutes.

There were no men with the group. These were runaways.

Coyote Running looked from one woman to another. At last he nudged Medicine Calf and pointed excitedly.

"We have found your lost squaws, maybe," Pine Leaf said. "They have run away from the Cheyennes, and they have liberated a few others as well."

Medicine Calf nodded and studied the group of women. Still-water was there, and so were Red Cherry and Doesn't-run-fast, as well as Coyote's wife, Morning Song. Cheyenne and Cheyenne's Sister stood next to each other by the fire, along with several other women who had apparently decided to cast their fortunes with the Sparrow Hawks.

It seemed evident that Still-water was in charge.

"Well," Medicine Calf chuckled, "I suppose there's no way around it. We'll have to take them home with us."

"We could leave one as a sacrifice," Pine Leaf said. "I will pick one out and tie her to the tree. . . ."

Return to Absaroka.

Warm rains fell, and the drifted snow vanished about the dead cottonwood, the buffalo carcass, and the castle rocks. But the Sparrow Hawks and the Cheyenne women had already gone northward, around the mountains instead of across them, for the snows still lay heavy on the back of the range, and the high monolith of Laramie Peak remained white against the horizon. There had been slim time for the homeward journey before the next wave of cold, before the iron lock of winter took and held.

Then the earth froze, the sun was hidden, the air was fierce and laden with snowstorms, and winds howled across the prairies. Streams were transformed into long, winding sheets of ice.

Wolves and coyotes gnawed at the bones of the buffalo until the last shred of meat had been stripped away, and the ribs and skull and vertebra had begun their process of melting into the loose earth.

The river groaned and roared with the spring ice-breaking, and on the plateau beyond the castle rocks, a colony of prairie dogs worked at building their little hills, small crater-like forms in the sod. A sentinel barked at the approach of a coyote, and all the prairie dogs disappeared beneath the ground. Cirape waited, however, knowing the heads would pop up in a minute or so. And when one did, Song-dog would pounce and run off with his victim. The other prairie dogs would then reappear, undisturbed, a mother with her pups, a male crying the territorial call, two of the little gray-brown rodents giving each other a kiss of recognition, two more beginning to groom one another.

The leaves of the willows would come out, and soon the choke-cherries would be in blossom at the foot of the castle rocks. High above, the redtails, sparrow hawks, and golden eagles would drift on the air.

The man who had once been Jim Beckwourth would ride slowly down to the old cottonwood, whistle softly, and dismount. He would note the remains of an earlier fire, cluck his tongue, build his own fire, eat, and sleep under a sky blazing with stars. In the morning he would rise, rekindle the fire, make coffee, and gaze northwestward toward the still, white summit of Laramie Peak.

Around the upper end of the Laramie Range flows the North Platte, its source further west, high against the continental divide, while its branch, the Sweetwater, comes down from South Pass, a broad trench through the Shining Mountains. On the other side of the pass runs the Little Sandy, the Big Sandy, and the Seeks-keedee—in Rendezvous country. To the north of the pass rise the Wind River Range, the Grand Tetons, the Bear Tooth Range, Absaroka Range, Big Horn Mountains, the peaks white and glinting in sunlight, canyons dark and blue-green with spruce and pine, wide meadows and valleys lush with grass.

Our land is in exactly the right place.

Springtime, and the grizzlies awake, growling, ravenously hungry.

A mountain goat clings to a rim amidst dwindling snowbanks, eyes the empty space below, four thousand feet down to a glacial valley.

And somewhere, far to the west, the ghostly Buenaventura River continues to flow, waterless, crossing a vast desert, winding through sage-covered basin and range, a land crushed by the counterpointing of immense forces, bare, jagged peaks, wide grabens, shattered remnants of an ancient seafloor. Still the Buenaventura runs, crossing even the high spine of the Sierra Nevada, flowing down into California, a river of red wine whose course marks the path for another, human river to flow.

Brother Beaver, you are wise. Can you make this world again?

Masses of late storm cloud obscure the peaks of the Ruby Mountains, and lightning flashes in the dark, late afternoon. Westward the desert flushes to crimson, and a voice answers:

The world itself is a great beaver, and the beaver is moving.

THE LIFE OF
JIM BECKWOURTH
a chronology

1798 (1800?)	Born, the son of Sir Jennings Beckwith and his wife, a Mulatto woman whose maiden name had been Winey (?) Miskell.
1810	Jennings Beckwith moves his family to Portage des Sioux, near St. Louis.
1821	Jim Beckwourth goes up the Missouri to the lead mines; is a hunter for the party.
1823	Signs on with General Ashley; acts as hunter and scout.
1824	Legally emancipated by his father, Beckwourth, as a member of Ashley's group, crosses the Rocky Mountains and engages in the fur trade.
1825	Brief return to St. Louis, then back to the mountains.
1827	Runs trading post with the Blackfeet; has two Blackfoot wives.
1828	Captured by the Crows while on a trapping venture with Jim Bridger; adopted by Big Bowl as a lost son; first of several marriages to Crow women.

1829– 1832	Beckwourth distinguishes himself as a warrior; employed by Kenneth McKenzie of the American Fur Company; becomes leader of the Dog Soldiers and member of the council of Chief Rotten Belly (A-ra-poo-ash).
1833	Death of A-ra-poo-ash; Beckwourth is named head chief of the Mountain Crows; is given the name Medicine Calf; the year of the great meteor shower.
1836– 1837	Returns to St. Louis; senses estrangement from relatives and former friends; returns to the Crows; marries Pine Leaf; leaves Absaroka; is unable to negotiate a new contract with American Fur.
1837– 1838	Serves with the Missouri Volunteers in the war against the Seminoles; is a courier; becomes disenchanted with the military.
1838– 1842	Trades with the Cheyennes; may accompany Peg-leg Smith on a horse-stealing venture to California; Indian merchant in Taos.
1842	Marries Señorita Luisa Sandoval; builds El Pueblo (a trading post) on the Arkansas.
1844	Jim Beckwourth arrives in California.
1845	Fights against Micheltorena in the revolution of the Californians against Mexican control; war between the United States and Mexico; Beckwourth steals a large herd of horses and returns to New Mexico; finds Luisa Sandoval has remarried.
1846	Operates a hotel in Santa Fe; helps to quell the rebellion that was set off with the Taos massacre.
1847– 1848	Carries dispatches for the United States Army.
1848– 1849	Arrives in California; carries dispatches for the Commisariat at Monterey.

1849   Beckwourth opens a trading post in Sonora; Baptiste Charbonneau and Beckwourth keep an inn at Cold Springs; he removes to Greenwood.

1850   Prospects at Michigan Bluff; goes north to the Pit River; discovers Beckwourth Pass at the northern end of the Sierra Nevada on his return south.

1850–
1851   Probably goes back to Santa Fe.

1851   Opens the new immigrant road over Beckwourth Pass; leads the first wagon train across and down the Feather River to Marysville.

1852–
1858   Operates a trading post and way station in Sierra Valley to serve the immigrants coming in over Beckwourth Pass; publication of *The Life and Adventures of James P. Beckwourth* (Harper & Brothers: New York, 1856), manuscript written from Beckwourth's "own dictation" by T. D. Bonner.

1859   Goes to Kansas City, visits St. Louis, goes to Denver.

1860   Marries Elizabeth Lettbetter of Denver.

1861   Runs a store; manages a farm belonging to Louis Vasquez.

1861–
1862   Beckwourth and Jim Bridger are employed by Vasquez.

1862   Army guide, Colorado Second Infantry.

1864   Marriage with Elizabeth breaks up; Jim marries again, a young woman of the Crow nation, Sue; is acquitted of the charge of murdering "Nigger Bill" Payne; is forced to participate in Chivington's Sand Creek Massacre of the Cheyennes.

1865   Beckwourth testifies against Chivington at the Military
            Commission hearing; goes alone to offer himself to the
            Cheyennes; Leg-in-the-Water tells Beckwourth to return
            to "your White friends, but we are going to fight till
            death."

1865–   Leads an unsuccessful trapping expedition to Green
1866   River.

1866   A scout at Fort Laramie; later partners with Bridger,
            under Colonel Carrington; Bridger meets the Crows at
            Clark's Fork; reports the Crows are eager to see Beck-
            wourth; Lieutenant Thompson and Beckwourth ride out
            to visit the Crows; Beckwourth dies among the Crows,
            in his sleep, October (26?), 1866.

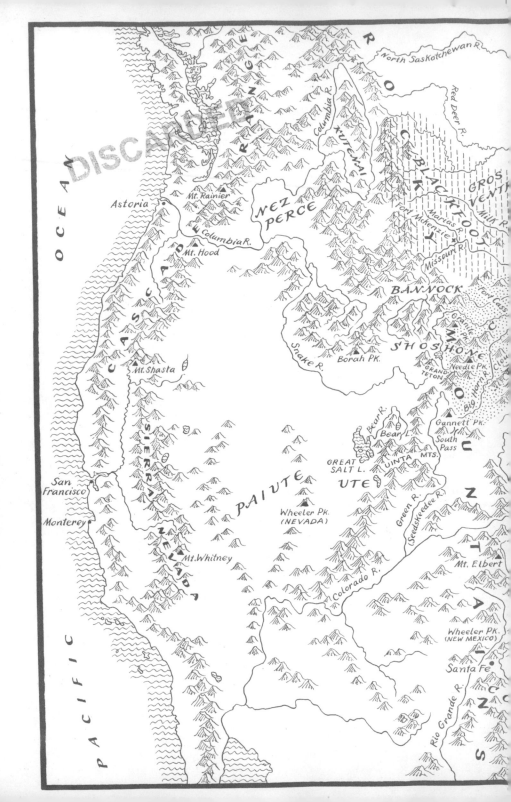